The

YANKEES
vs.
RED SOX

ReadeR

The YANKEES vs. RED SOX READER

Edited by Mike Robbins

CARROLL & GRAF PUBLISHERS

NEW YORK

THE YANKEES VS. RED SOX READER

Carroll & Graf Publishers
An Imprint of Avalon Publishing Group Inc.
245 West 17th Street, 11th Floor
New York, NY 10011

AVALON
publishing group incorporated

Compilation copyright © 2005 by Mike Robbins

First Carroll & Graf edition 2005

Library of Congress Cataloging-in-Publication Data is available.

ISBN: 0-7867-1445-X

Printed in the United States of America
Interior design by Maria E. Torres
Distributed by Publishers Group West

For Shondra,
even though she roots for the wrong team.

CONTENTS

ACKNOWLEDGMENTS

THE AUTHOR WOULD like to thank all those who assisted in the creation of this anthology, including Clint Willis, Carol Pickering, Taylor Smith, Will Balliett, Nate Knaebel, Claiborne Hancock, Mary and Stephen Robbins, Spencer Frazee, Rod Nelson, Wayne McElreavy, Bill Nowlin, Bobby Plapinger, Andy McCue, Steve Gietschier, Steve Steinberg, Tom Nahigian, Cecilia Tan, Zita Carno, Les Masterson, Martha Pardee-King, and Claudette Burke.

ACKNOWLEDGMENTS

INTRODUCTION

IT WAS A predictably cold early February day in Boston, but more than a million New Englanders gathered in and around City Hall Plaza to celebrate the region's greatest sporting triumph since the end of the Celtics dynasty of the 1980s. The New England Patriots had upset the St. Louis Rams in the Super Bowl. Patriots linebacker Larry Izzo seized the opportunity to lead the assembled throng in a celebratory chant of "Yankees suck."

That unfriendly refrain was once reserved for days when the Yankees were in town to hear it. Now it's used year round, and is emblazoned on tee shirts and bumper stickers across New England. Soon, no doubt, it will be incorporated into wedding vows and state mottos throughout the region. This chant, known simply as *"The* Chant" in Greater Boston, has even helped revive the subtle art of debate, as two hundred miles to the southwest, Yankees fans retort with equally well-reasoned rebuttals concerning the Red Sox.

The rivalry between the Yankees and the Red Sox stands unrivaled as the most celebrated matchup in American professional sports. It laps over the edges of the baseball season to slosh up in football celebrations—and political races. Democratic presidential hopeful Howard Dean tried to claim in late 2003 that he was a Red Sox fan, though in years past he'd pulled for the Yankees. "Of all the flip-flops," responded the camp of Dean's opponent John Kerry, "this is the most inexplicable and indefensible." Dean was soundly and rightly defeated in the crucial New Hampshire primary the following January. He soon gave up his bid for office.

The rivalry divides families. It divides the state of Connecticut. It leads some to question not just the quality of the opposing team's play, but the very nature of the opposing fans' being. There are Red Sox fans who insist that Yankee fans have no souls; otherwise, how could they root for baseball's forces of darkness? Yankee fans counter that it's Red Sox fans who must lack souls—if they had them, at least one Sox fan would have sold his to beat the Yankees before 2004. Then again, who's to say the Sox would have had the advantage even with Satan on their side? As Mickey

McDermott, who pitched for both clubs, quipped during an era of strong New York teams, "Everyone knows God's a Yankee fan."

Nor is this rivalry contested only among the boorish louts in the bleachers. It's equally intense among the boorish louts in the clubs' front offices. In late 2002, Red Sox president Larry Lucchino labeled the Yankees "the Evil Empire," after New York signed Cuban pitcher José Contreras. "That's how a sick person thinks," Yankees owner George Steinbrenner responded publicly. His private response is rumored to have been significantly more pointed.

And what of the players? We're often told that today's professional athletes feel no real animosity toward their opponents, who as often as not are former teammates. But for every Yankee who claims the Red Sox are just another club, there's a Don Mattingly to note that "It was natural to hate the Red Sox. It came easy." And for every Red Sox who professes nothing but admiration for New York's success, there's a Pedro Martinez to say, "I wish I'd never see them again. I wish they'd disappear from the league."

Even Yankee and Red Sox ballplayers whose blood doesn't boil when their rival comes to town acknowledge that the energy of the crowds gives these games a unique intensity. April games play out like October—and October games play out like history.

The team that would later be known as the Red Sox was founded in Boston in 1901; the club that's now the Yankees arrived in New York two years later. There is considerable debate over when their rivalry began. Some trace its origins to 1904, when the teams battled for the pennant on the last day of the season. Others maintain that Boston's 1920 sale of Babe Ruth to New York marked the beginning of the truly bad blood. Yankee Hall of Famer Yogi Berra once said it started in 1949, when his Yanks beat the Red Sox in the final two games of the season to snatch the pennant from Boston's grasp.

They're all right. The Yankee–Red Sox rivalry reinvents itself with each generation of fans. From 1903 to 1918, the rivalry was defined by the inability of the team from America's biggest city, New York, to topple the American League's greatest ball club, Boston. In the 1920s and 1930s,

Boston fans saw the Yanks race past their Red Sox in the standings—by fielding a team that included many former Red Sox players. Both teams were strong during the late '40s, and the rivalry played out in Septembers and early Octobers with pennants on the line. That happened again in the late 1970s, though by then the names had changed from Ted Williams and Joe DiMaggio to Carlton Fisk and Thurman Munson.

The rivalry gained intensity in the late '90s, thanks in part to the 1995 "wild card" rule, which gives teams that finish second in their division a chance to reach the postseason. The Yankees and Red Sox now not only battle to get to the postseason; they can battle *in* the postseason as well. The wild card rule gave us New York's dramatic comeback against Boston in game seven of the 2003 American League Championship Series, and it gave us Boston's dramatic comeback from down three games to none in the 2004 rematch. It remains only for some ambitious baseball executive to come up with a way for the Yankees and Red Sox to play each other in the World Series. Until then it will have to be enough that Yankee–Red Sox matchups tend to feel like World Series games, whatever time of year they're played.

There are pedants and killjoys who downplay the rivalry. They argue that dramatic comeback in the 2004 American League Championship Series or no, the results are too one-sided for the Yankees and Red Sox to be true rivals—after all, the Yankees have won 26 World Series since 1920; the Red Sox just one. Occasional exceptions aside, the Red Sox have a rivalry with the Yankees, they say, like a bug has a rivalry with a windshield.

What these critics fail to grasp is that the one-sidedness of the results is this rivalry's strength. The teams' strongly contrasting late-season success rates are what give them character. The Yankees have been defined by victory; the Red Sox by the continued loyalty of their fans through all the painful losses.

If the Yankees and Red Sox shared the glories and failures equally between them, they would be nothing more than two collections of highly paid athletes wearing different hats; their fans would be divided by little more than geography. Deciding which to root for would be like taking sides in an argument over which ZZ Top song is best, when in truth they all pretty much use the same three chords. (I'm a "Cheap Sunglasses" man myself, but I wouldn't pay $500 for a scalped ticket to see the issue settled.)

As matters stand, Yankee fans and Red Sox fans represent two entirely different ways of life, each with its own rewards and its own costs. Yankee fans can be confident that they'll experience the thrill of victory many times in their lives. But they pay a price for this success, for the thrill of victory diminishes when it becomes commonplace and expected. Yankee fans might never experience the level of baseball-related euphoria that long-suffering Red Sox fans felt in 2004 when Boston finally toppled New York and won a championship. Of course, Red Sox fans endured decades of suffering to earn this one celebration, so some might argue it wasn't worth the wait.

Truth is, the Yankees and the Red Sox need each other. Boston needs New York so the Red Sox bloated payroll will look less excessive by comparison. New York needs Boston because you can only get so excited about playing the Blue Jays and Orioles. Boston fans need the Yankees so there's someone to root for when the Sox have an off year—they can support whoever's playing New York. Yankees fans can say the same thing in reverse: who else but the Red Sox could have made so many Yankee fans pull for the Mets in 1986? Only the Yankees can make a May game in Fenway seem to matter, and—lately at least—only the Red Sox can make a September game in the Bronx *actually* matter, with the rest of the AL East so reliably eliminated by the end of August.

The Yankees and Red Sox need each other . . . but that doesn't mean they have to like each other. And that's what makes it so much fun.

—Mike Robbins

PRELUDE

It's a baseball cliché that all teams have hope in the spring. But Red Sox fans showed a particular resilience when they arrived full of hope for spring Training in 2004. Only months before, Yankee third baseman Aaron Boone's extra-inning homer in the seventh game of the 2003 American League Championship Series had won New York the pennant and crushed Boston's best chance at a championship in years. Yet the following March Red Sox fans were ready to believe in their team once again.

"IN BOSTON, THE YANKEES ALWAYS SUCK"

from *ESPN.com* (March 8, 2004)
by Jim Caple

FORT MYERS, Fla.—It is 10 o'clock on Saturday night, 15 hours before the Red Sox host a spring training game against the Yankees, and there are three Boston fans—Larry Scott, Dave Dybala and Patrick Whittle—spreading out gear on the sidewalk in front of the ticket window at City of Palms Park.

"They're putting more tickets on sale at 9 o'clock in the morning," Scott explains, "so we decided to get in line now instead of waking up early. That would be crazy."

Yes, rather than setting the alarm for 8 o'clock, it's much more practical to spend the night sleeping on the sidewalk outside the stadium.

Apparently, rooting for the Red Sox does things to a person, especially after a devastating playoff loss followed by an offseason trade of the league's best player to their hated rival. The game—which will be completed by players who will spend the summer riding buses in the minors—was sold out two months ago and a radio station sold a pair of tickets for $450.

Four hundred fifty dollars for a spring training game! And you thought Grady Little was the only moron in Red Sox Nation.

"This is the first meeting between the Red Sox and the Yankees since everything went down last fall," Scott says. "I think it will have the intensity of a playoff game. It's not your average spring training game."

I'm not sure what they're expecting. That Bob Sheppard will attack Pedro Martinez for throwing a beach ball too close to the dugout? That Tom Gordon and Travis Lee will assault a special ed teacher in the bullpen for playing a Jimmy Buffett tune too loud? That John Henry will challenge George Steinbrenner to a Texas cage match for buying up all the good sunscreen? It's a spring training game, for crying out loud. It will be shocking if the starting pitchers even scowl at each other while running wind sprints along the warning track in the fourth inning.

Camping out the night before a grapefruit league game? This is unprecedented. Lining up 15 hours before the first pitch of a game that doesn't count in the standings? That's certifiably insane. Sleeping on the sidewalk so you can see a few veterans put in their required four innings with less enthusiasm than Manny Ramirez? This is something no one else besides these three Red Sox fans would possibly do.

"You guys Red Sox fans?" say Eric Ferraz and Guy Sepielli as they stroll up at 10:30 with a half-case of beverage. "We've got the beer."

OK. There is beer now. So the wait will go a little faster and be a little more pleasant. But still. Down here in south Florida, roughly 1,000 miles from Fenway Park, these must be the only fans mad enough to endure a concrete mattress for a spring training game.

"You guys Red Sox fans?" a man yells from a car as it pulls up to the curb at 11 p.m. Sam King, a 55-year-old man in a Red Sox cap and jacket hops out of the car, grabs an armful of supplies, leans lightly on his cane and joins the five. "I knew there would be others here."

Has everyone in Red Sox Nation gone insane?

"I've got my wallet," King says, "just in case the guys with the butterfly nets come and take me away."

What sort of fans would spend the night on the sidewalk to get into a spring training game? The sort of fans who are convinced that Mia Hamm cost the Red Sox a trip to the World Series because she distracted Nomar with wedding plans—"What were they doing planning a wedding in November so close to the World Series, anyway?"—the sort of fans who are convinced Aaron Boone tore his ACL as karmic punishment for hitting the series-deciding home run off Tim Wakefield.

"I was watching the game at my brother's house. None of us even watched to see where Boone's home run would land because we knew it was gone," Scott says. "My brother just got up and turned off the TV and started walking away. I asked him whether he wanted us to lock up or what, and he said, 'No, I hope someone breaks in tonight and murders me.' He didn't come out of the house for two days."

This is what it's like to be a Red Sox fan. Yankees fans win so often that even losing a World Series barely registers—"You should be able to rip them for losing to the Marlins; but when you do, it doesn't faze them," Dybala complains—yet every loss for a Boston fan is permanently recorded for posterity and carried around like the tattoo of an ex-wife.

Root for the Yankees and you expect to win every year. Root for the Red Sox, and deep down, you always wait for that moment when Bucky Dent's home run sails over the Monster, the grounder bounces between Bill Buckner's legs and Grady Little places the bullpen phone on his own personal Do Not Call list.

Being a Yankees fan means buying World Series tickets in March. Being a Red Sox fan means every possible victory over your arch-rival is so precious that you're willing to sleep on the sidewalk to see a spring training game.

The Sox fans say they're glad the A-Rod trade fell through and they still have No-Mah at short. "I don't trust anyone who says he wants to be traded to the Red Sox and then goes and gets himself traded to the Yankees," Scott says. "There are just certain things you don't do in life."

Everyone is sure the bullpen will be so good that Pedro and Curt Schilling will only need to give the Sox six good innings each start. Ferraz boasts that Ellis Burks will hit .300 with 30 home runs. And Scott says he's actually glad that A-Rod is with the Yankees. "We want the Yankees to be as stacked as possible when they finally fall to us."

Near midnight, they are so optimistic about the upcoming season they are saying that reaching the World Series will seem cheapened if Boston doesn't beat the Yankees in the playoffs to get there.

Well, why not? It's spring training and last October's pain is almost five months away. It is a warm March evening in Fort Myers, yet this October seems close enough that these fans can almost see the World Series logo painted on Fenway's grass.

Or maybe that's just because it's still there from when the Red Sox foolishly painted it before Game 7 last fall.

"Hopefully, we'll all remember this night when we win the World Series this year," King says. "We'll look back and say, 'That's where it all began.'"

And with those words, this all-night vigil suddenly does not seem quite so insane. Perhaps this is where it all begins and where an 86-year wait ends. Perhaps this year really will be next year. If so, break out the beer and the camera—this is a night for celebration, a night that must be recorded for posterity.

The six gather for a photo; and as the photographer prepares to snap the picture, they smile and shout the rallying cry that defines our country's cradle of liberty, "Yankees Suck!"

The flash bulb doesn't go off.

Without missing a beat, someone moans: "Great. We're going to lose this year."

The rivalry between the Yankees and Red Sox is driven in part by the larger differences between New York and Boston. In the following piece, Con Chapman considers why these two great cities of the Northeast never seem to see eye to eye when it comes to baseball or virtually anything else.

"NEW YORK AND BOSTON"

from *The Year of the Gerbil* (1998)
by Con Chapman

IF BASEBALL HAD a Bible, the story of the rivalry between Boston and New York would appear in the Book of Genesis. Before the current version of baseball developed on the Elysian Fields of Hoboken, New Jersey, a picnic ground across the Hudson River from New York, there was "Boston Ball," also known as the "Massachusetts Game" or "town ball." That earlier variation of the game differed from the New York style of play in that runners were retired from the base paths by hitting them with a soft ball thrown at them, instead of touching them with the ball or placing it "in the hands of an adversary on the base." It is thus both literally and metaphorically true that as baseball moved southward from Boston to New York it was transformed from softball to hardball.

If baseball were drama, the Red Sox would be a little theater production of a classical tragedy that comes off as farce, while the Yankees would be a long-running Broadway hit that, while periodically staged by lesser casts, regularly repays its angels with box-office success. There is, of course, a Broadway play—*Damn Yankees*—about a Faustian bargain to beat the perennially-triumphant New Yorkers, based on the novel *The Year the Yankees Lost the Pennant* by Douglass Wallop. There is no *Damn Red Sox,* nor is one likely to be produced in the lifetime of any Boston fan living today. Being a fan of the Yankees has rarely involved the sort of sacrifice that other baseball fans must make from time to time, or for years on end, as in the case of the Red Sox. As a result, rooting for the Yankees has been compared by different sportswriters in different times to rooting for U.S. Steel or General Motors (when those corporations were the envy of the industrial world) or for the Nazis. The rest of America expects a certain minimal portion of abrasiveness and arrogance from every New Yorker, the way it expects cordiality from Southerners and shallow mysticism from Californians, but the Yankee fan is an enhanced version of this regional stereotype as a result of the team's history of success. In the 1938 MGM movie *Boys Town,* Mickey Rooney plays a cocky orphan from New York who boasts that he roots for the Yankees. Another orphan sums him up with two words: "You would."

This duality in America's national pastime replicates in the realm of sports a larger contrast between the two regions: New York is the Empire State and New York City is the Big Apple, the place where, as the song goes, if you can make it there you can make it anywhere. New York's Wall Street is the capitalist capital of America, while Boston's stock exchange is at best a regional affair. Will Rogers came up with a homely metaphor for New York's precedence in this regard: America's cow grazes all over the pasture, he said, but it gets milked in only one corner—New York. Boston, on the other hand, is a place where wealth has long been viewed as a consideration secondary to breeding, an attitude summed up by the Boston Brahmin in the John P. Marquand novel who, when asked how he made his money, replies "We don't make our money, we have it." While proper Bostonians once pretended to disdain newly-accumulated wealth, their contempt (to the extent that it persists to this day) is decidedly Pecksniffian. For example, an article in the *Boston Globe* in 1978, the year under consideration here, described the comparatively greater salaries an individual could expect to receive in various trades if he or she were to ply them in New York City rather than Boston. The idea of a New York newspaper reporting the cuts in pay a person would suffer by moving to Boston is improbable, since in this respect Boston is no worse to a New Yorker than anyplace else.

The typical New Englander is thus skeptical of wealth at the same time that he or she is envious of it. The skepticism springs from the knowledge that financial rewards entail financial risk, and the envy is the result of forces too obvious to require explanation. New England's aversion to financial risk is perhaps best exemplified by its distinction as the birthplace of the spendthrift trust, the instrument by which the region's mill owners and China traders kept their descendants from dissipating inherited fortunes in riotous living. Through these arrangements, the capital of New England was held by trustees who were loath to put the funds at risk for fear of violating the grave obligation imposed upon them as fiduciaries. As Elmer Davis put it in a 1928 article in *Harper's,* the trustees of New England "cannot take a chance. . . . And without taking a chance no region in a slump is likely to get itself out." *Fortune* magazine expressed the same view in an article on the business climate in New England five years later, noting that "A society may be embalmed in a can of trusts as a cod may find eternal youth in brine."

This indigenous fear of risk has been handed down through the generations in Massachusetts in the same way that low-number license plates make their way to cars currently on the road from old Yankee[*] ancestors who could afford automobiles before their neighbors. In 1980, when Apple Computer first issued stock to the public, residents of Massachusetts were prohibited from participating because the state's regulators decreed that the company's offering was too risky. The shares were sold on the New York Stock Exchange in one of the most successful public offerings

---

[*]The term "Yankee" has Dutch origins, although they are somewhat cloudy. It is derived from "Jan Kees," which means "John Cheese" in Dutch, and was probably first used by non-Dutch as a disparaging nickname for Hollanders. It was later applied by the colonial Dutch in New York to English settlers in Connecticut, and has since come to refer generally to a native of any northeastern state or, in the South, to any northerner.

ever to investors everywhere but Massachusetts, and purchasers of the stock profited handsomely.

The different seeds from which these regional strains have grown are exemplary of the later flowering they produced. New York was populated early on by Dutch settlers, descendants of a great trading nation capable, in moments of collective commercial frenzy, of such speculative excesses as the Tulipomania of the 1600s, in which the value of lovely but useless articles—tulip bulbs—was bid up to levels far exceeding their intrinsic worth by a population universally attuned to the prospect of selling them again at a profit. The Netherlands, a nation without natural resources, grew wealthy by hard work and by trading what little they had—mainly herring—for things of greater value. The fable handed down to us about the interaction between these people and the Indians who inhabited the land that became New York is that the Dutch were sharp enough to acquire Manhattan island for $24 worth of trinkets. The tale that we tell about the Pilgrims of the Massachusetts Bay Colony implies that, without the help of the agricultural skills of Squanto, a native of the Plymouth region, their community, with a socialist form of government they later abandoned, wouldn't have been around for the first Thanksgiving.

The Puritans preferred "honest gaine" through labor over the speculative pursuit of riches that caused the colonists in Virginia to succumb to gold fever and nearly perish as a result of their neglect of essential tasks, and they frowned upon excessive acquisitiveness. They fined Robert Keayne, the city's first import merchant, for price gouging, and compelled him to make a public confession of his "covetous and corrupt heart." Cotton Mather's "rules for trading" prohibited merchants from taking unfair advantage of their customers by selling above the "current price," meaning the price that a buyer who knows the value of a commodity would give for it. A seller who lived by this rule might find himself unprepared for the sharper attitudes of another clime when he went to buy something, which may explain why the Red Sox paid $400,000 in 1980 for Claude Edward "Skip" Lockwood, most recently of the New York Mets, a free agent relief pitcher in the fifteenth year of his career who produced only two saves and a 5.32 earned run average for the Sox before retiring.

Money is power, said a Boston preacher in the nineteenth century without a nod to Thomas Hobbes. He might have pilfered more profitably from Adam Smith, who pointed out that money's power is not intrinsic, but is unleashed only when one buys things. The regional contrast between Boston and New York in terms of financial acumen may be gleaned from the fact that when the Yankees bought Babe Ruth from the Red Sox in 1920, part of the consideration given by the Yankees was a loan, not an outright payment, and it was secured by a mortgage on Fenway Park. Thus, the Yankees not only obtained the best player in the game at the time and possibly ever, they got him in part with money they would get back later. They also could have foreclosed on the Red Sox' ball field itself if owner Harry Frazee had failed to make punctual payments on his promissory note.

The pinchpenny philosophy of the New Englander is so pervasive that tinctures of it can be found even in recent transplants from New York. Red Sox general manager Lou Gorman, formerly of the New York Mets, was asked why, in the thick of the 1990 pennant race with the Oakland A's, he passed up outfielder Willie McGee after the former star of the Cardinals' World Series teams of the 1980s became available for the waiver price. In response, Gorman asked a rhetorical question that has become a part of the Red Sox catechism of frustration: "What would we do with Willie McGee?" McGee, a former Most Valuable Player, two-time batting champion and three-time Golden Glove winner, went on to win the National League batting title that year. McGee was acquired by the Red Sox five years later during the pennant race of 1995 at a time when his skills had understandably declined; it was as if a WASP from Boston's North Shore had come home from a tag sale gloating to his wife about a great deal on a pair of used galoshes. The New Englander clasps his coin purse with both hands and turns away from potentially improvident expenditure while muttering the region's familiar homily: "Use it up, wear it out, make it do, do without."

New York is thus the place in America that serves as the hometown, usually adopted, of those who believe that money is life's report card. Boston, on the other hand, is often referred to as the Athens of America due to the large number of colleges and universities located there; it is, as a result, inhabited by more than a few people who believe that one's report card is, or ought to be, as good as money. Massachusetts in general and

Boston in particular are thus known to the rest of the world as places where the life of the mind can be preferred over an existence of superficial acquisitiveness without attracting critical attention; the *Dictionary of American Slang*'s definition of "Boston coffee" (tea) includes the explanation that the use of the term reflects the fact that "Boston is associated in the popular mind with an effete way of life."

The contemplative life and the attitudes associated with it are, of course, easier to maintain when one already has the cash that others so crassly strive for, and Massachusetts is also a state that might adopt as its motto "Don't touch the principal" on account of the inherited wealth that, meted out by trustees, sustains many of its inhabitants. This regional trait towards the intellectual is revealed by the tendency among those who write about the Sox to indulge in scholarly digression. A recent collection of essays about the Red Sox included fourteen footnotes; a similar collection of essays about the Yankees by the same publisher and of approximately the same length contained none. Robert Burton observed in his 1621 work *The Anatomy of Melancholy* that melancholy is a "common maul" of students, and results from "too vehement study." In choosing to cultivate his or her mind, a proper Bostonian who is also a Red Sox fan may accordingly have chosen a fertile field for the seeds of misery.

The "Athens of America" label has given rise to an analogy in which New York becomes baseball's Sparta, but the apparent parallelism disappears upon closer examination. The term "New York intellectual" is as much a part of the American vernacular as "New York deli." Athens was more populous and more densely populated than Sparta, as New York is by comparison to Boston. The Spartans are remembered for their austerity; New York is the American city that ranks second only to Hollywood, in popular imagination if not in truth, as a place where a life of unrestrained self-indulgence can be pursued. The golden age of Athens is remembered as a time of culture, sophistication and joyful living; Massachusetts is the puritanical state where sumptuary laws prohibited the working classes from wearing gold, silver, silk or hatbands for the better part of the seventeenth century. Sparta was a conservative oligarchy, New York is a liberal democracy, with five registered Democrats for every confessed Republican.

The only valid basis for the comparison would thus appear to be that the soldiers of Sparta were supposed to be invincible, as were the Yankees in their time. That, and the fact that Sparta won the Peloponnesian Wars, which is why there are today teams named the "Spartans," but none called the "Athenians." John Cheever compared the 1978 Red Sox to the Trojans and the Yankees to the Greeks, but this comparison is inapt as well. The incident that started the Trojan War was the theft of Helen by Paris, the son of the Trojan king; the Red Sox, as anyone who has been a fan of the team for very long knows, rarely steal anything. And it is the Red Sox who, like the Greek warrior Achilles, are always felled by the improbable blow to a weak spot—their pitching arms—in otherwise-sturdy bodies.

There are several reasons for the prevalence of impertinent classical allusions in writings by Bostonians on the Red Sox. The first is that the progress of a Red Sox season often follows the form of a tragedy, moving from early-season happiness to October misery. The team is thus likely to be examined in light of things Greek, although the resemblances that are detected by some observers are often no closer than Greek salad is to Boston baked beans. The second is that, since Boston must depend on its reputation as an academic center in a way that New York need not, pride in the intellect becomes a form of local boosterism among Bostonians, in much the same way that small towns across America celebrate local food-stuffs such as lima beans or pork ribs as the means by which they distinguish themselves. A Boston sportswriter's allusions to Greek history, literature or mythology in describing the Red Sox are thus likely to be as affected as the smile that the mayor of such a provincial community displays when he swallows the local delicacy at the annual harvest festival, and should be taken no more seriously.*

---

*Michael Gee of the *Boston Herald* seems to be the exception. In a recent column repeating the theme of Red Sox history as tragedy he referred to the "pity and terror" that Sox fans should feel when considering the possibility of meeting the Yankees, just as Aristotle would have. And in another, he noted that a particular loss by the New York Jets to the New England Patriots included all the elements of a tragedy except for a chorus and the fact that the Jets' coach didn't tear out his eyeballs at the end.

After the obligatory Athens-Sparta analogy, the invocation of Oscar Wilde's Dorian Gray to describe an aging veteran, a comparison that links a pitcher banished to the bull pen with Charlie on the MTA (the man in The Kingston Trio song who never returned from a ride on Boston's subway), and the opening lines of *A Tale of Two Cities*, the average sports-writer covering the Sox will usually have exhausted his store of literary allusions. While this deficiency should benefit those who read Boston's sports pages to find out what actually happened in the previous day's game, its potentially salutary effect is usually nullified by an overabundance of quotations from obscure rock 'n' roll songs (the most common being "Lawyers, Guns and Money" by Warren Zevon) popular with the current baby-boom crowd of Boston sports-writers. As this generation of journalists ages, and their favorite groups end up in the cut-out bins at local record stores, these allusions have become slightly less accessible to the average Red Sox fan than quotations from Shakespeare.

The dichotomy between Boston and New York, while exaggerated in general and subject to numerous exceptions in particular, is nonetheless real. Nineteenth-century Boston was, in the cartography of Dr. Oliver Wendell Holmes (the elder), the hub of the solar system. This boast was subsequently expanded by a sort of big bang of the communal ego so that Boston became a place so solipsistic (or provincial) that it was referred to, often by its inhabitants and frequently without irony, as the Hub of the Universe. "Hub Man Dies in NY A-Blast" proclaimed a parody of the *Boston Globe* several years back, putting into a headline's shorthand both the parochialism of which Bostonians are capable and their affected indifference to New York and all that it represents. More than a few news vendors had to refund money to patrons who hadn't heard the news, didn't realize it was fictional and saw nothing peculiar in the paper's angle on it. New York's view of itself in relation to the rest of America has perhaps been best expressed by the foreshortened maps of America produced by a number of artists showing Manhattan's streets looming larger in size and significance than the rest of the country from the Hudson westward.*

---

*The earliest was probably produced by industrial designer Daniel Wallingford, who moved from New York to Boston in 1935. The most widely-known of recent versions is undoubtedly that drawn by Saul Steinberg, which appeared as a cover of *The New Yorker* magazines.

Bostonians regard those who depart for New York with a mixture of contempt and affected puzzlement; the Boston Brahmin protagonist of John P. Marquand's *The Late George Apley* writes to his son, "Above all, I cannot imagine what you see in New York." In short, the New Yorker rolls his eyes northward towards Boston with condescension, and the Bostonian looks southward upon New York with disdain. The Yankee fan and the Red Sox fan do the same, in their smaller sphere of contest.

Boston may be the last stop on the road taken by shows bound for Broadway, but in terms of the arts, it might as well be the first since, to turn the chorus of "New York, New York" on its head, if you don't make it there, you don't make it anywhere. The distance between Boston's theater district and the popular stages of New York can't be measured in miles since the name "Broadway" is known around the world. By contrast, Boston's theater district has no popular name at all other than "Piano Row"—the now-unused nickname for the block of Boylston Street where the Colonial Theater is located, so-called because of the music stores that line its sidewalks—or the "Combat Zone," for the specially-zoned pornography area that surrounds it and which, at times when conscription has been in effect, appeared to have been invaded by servicemen. A discussion between two New York ladies in Henry James' *The Bostonians* is instructive on this point:

First lady: Well, you must be pretty desperate, when you have got to go to Boston for your entertainment.

Second lady: Well, there's a similar society there, and I never heard of their sending to New York.

First lady: Of course not, they think they have got everything. But doesn't it make your life a burden, thinking what you can possibly have.

And later, discussing a New York club that decides to give a lecture series, one of James's characters says, "It is New York trying to be like Boston."

Boston's reputation as a cultural stepsister to New York's child star originated with the asceticism of the Puritans, the congregation haunted by the fear, in the words of H. L. Mencken, "that someone, somewhere, was happy." In 1673, a citizen of Springfield, Massachusetts, named Samuel

Terry and eight others were fined by magistrate John Pynchon for putting on an "uncivill" play that was determined to be "Immodest and beastly." In 1876, the Puritanical school of literary criticism was institutionalized as the New England Watch and Ward Society, which was founded to stamp out books and plays considered to be offensive or dangerous to the public morals. Mencken had reason to know of the Puritanical morals that guided the Watch and Ward Society's aesthetic principles; he was arrested on the Boston Common and tried for selling pornography—an edition of his *American Mercury* magazine that contained an article on a small-town prostitute—in a case that tested the Society's system of informal censorship. In a contemporary world in which looser morals have triumphed, Bostonians bear the stigma of their history of civic righteousness like a transvaluation of Hester Prynne's scarlet letter; and like her, they wear their badge with a mixture of guilt and pride.

The Puritanical element of the New England temperament may help to explain why the Sox would trade a pitcher like Sparky Lyle to the Yankees when he was at the peak of his career. Lyle was a good reliever who averaged almost 14 saves a year in his five seasons with the Sox, but he began to produce at a quantum level higher immediately upon being traded to New York. In 1972, his first year with the Yankees, he saved 35 games, as many as he had in his last two years in Boston and more than any pitcher in the league. He saved 27 the next year and led the league again in 1976 with 23 saves. In 1977 he became the first relief pitcher to win the American League Cy Young Award, the award given annually since 1956 to the best pitcher in each league.

Notwithstanding his gaudy statistics, in his days with the Red Sox Lyle had represented the initial manifestation of a proletarian style of the radical will that reached its apotheosis several years later in Bill Lee's rebellions, and as a result he was viewed with a Puritanical disapproval by some members of management and Clif Keane, a local talk-show host who would later come to dislike Lee for the same reasons. Lyle rode a motorcycle and stayed out so late that he was the roommate of choice for players who wanted to take advantage of the amorous opportunities that fall so readily in the path of major league baseball players. He violated the principle of Puritan thrift by initiating a practice of sitting on birthday cakes given to teammates by

Red Sox fans, starting with one given to Rico Petrocelli. Petrocelli, a shortstop and third baseman with the Sox when Lyle broke in with the team in 1967, had received a cake from his fan club that he tried to hide from his teammates. Lyle, sensing the bourgeois individualism at work in the mind of Petrocelli, removed the cake from the locker where it had been hidden while the rest of the team was taking batting practice. When Petrocelli returned to the clubhouse after taking his swings, he saw Lyle standing naked with his back to a bench where the cake was sitting. "Look out for my cake," he yelled, but Lyle, feigning a deaf ear to his teammate's warning, squatted down. "Sorry about that," he said to the disheartened infielder. "Want a piece?"

Lyle's taste for night life violated the old Boston Brahmin's dictum (usually attributed to Rodman Weld, a forebear of William Weld, a governor of Massachusetts) that a Boston gentleman "never takes a drink before 3 o'clock or east of Park Street"—namely, before the stock market had closed or downtown among the unwashed and the madding crowd of business hustlers. After a night of drinking with Bill Lee in New York, Lyle is reported to have hailed a cab. When one stopped, Lyle asked the driver to take him to the Biltmore Hotel. The cabbie looked at Lyle and said simply, "You're leaning on it."

Part I

EARLY INNINGS
(1903–1950)

PART I
EARLY INNINGS
(1903–1950)

THE RIVALRY ESTABLISHED ITSELF, in fits and starts, during the first half of the twentieth century. The initial rumblings were felt in 1904, when New York and Boston staged a memorable pennant race in the American League's fourth year of operation. It was just New York's second year in the league, but already the club seemed to be on the verge of greatness.

It wasn't—the 1904 pennant race proved to be the exception. Aside from 1906, when New York came within three games of the pennant, neither New York nor Boston was very competitive again until 1912, when Boston won the World Championship. The New Englanders would win another three during the next six years, while New York remained out of contention. The rivalry during these years was a one-sided one, borne of jealousy, as New York's baseball fans (or "bugs" in the vernacular of the time) envied Boston's success. Boston fans had little reason to think about New York, since the team rarely posed much of a challenge.

This changed dramatically in the 1920s and early 1930s, when Boston sold or traded many of its best players—including the great Babe Ruth—to the Yankees. The influx of talent from Boston helped make New York the best team in baseball. The Red Sox fell to also-ran status. Now Boston fans had reason to dislike the Yanks—but New Yorkers wasted little time thinking about the uncompetitive Sox.

The pieces were finally in place for a full-fledged rivalry to begin in the early 1940s. At last, both clubs were strong at the same time. Boston finished second to New York in the American League in 1938, 1939, 1941,

3

and 1942. The Sox seemed poised to topple the Yanks—but that would have to wait until America was finished fighting World War II. Many Red Sox and Yankees players spent the 1943, 1944, and 1945 seasons in the military. In 1946 the war was finally over, and almost three decades of Yankee domination over the Red Sox came to an end as well. Boston claimed the American League pennant that year and returned to the World Series. Both Boston and New York would remain strong in the years leading up to the century's midpoint, and the rivalry was on its way.

Before Curt Schilling, before Bucky Dent, before even Babe Ruth and Harry Frazee, there was Happy Jack Chesbro. The date was October 10, 1904. Boston was baseball's defending World Champion, and New York was in just its second season in the league. Yet with one day left in the regular season, both teams had a shot at the pennant. It was then that Chesbro became the first man to permanently link his name to the Yankees–Red Sox rivalry— though back then the Red Sox weren't yet known as the Red Sox, and the Yankees weren't yet known as the Yankees. Chesbro was gunning for his forty-second win of the season. If he succeeded, New York would be well positioned to grab the American League pennant. If he failed, the pennant would go to Boston.

"DOWN TO THE WIRE IN 1904"

from *The Great Rivalry* (1991)
by **Ed Linn**

THE FIRST TIME THE rivalry went down to the last day of the season was back in old Hilltop Park in New York, with an overflow crowd spilling onto the field and upwards of a thousand Boston fans—complete with their own band, theme song, and assorted noisemakers—taking over the reserved section behind the Boston bench.

The year was 1904. The game, which marks the final shootout in the first great American League pennant race, was the first one to come down to us with a tag line attached to the score: "The pennant that was lost on Jack Chesbro's wild pitch."

It could just as easily, and perhaps even more aptly, have been "The pennant that was lost through the stupidity of the Yankee front office."

The opposing pitchers on that final day were Happy Jack Chesbro and Big Bill Dinneen, a most fortuitous pairing. Dinneen had defeated the

5

Yankees, 6–2, the first time the two teams met. That was on May 7, 1903, at the Huntington Avenue Grounds in Boston. A day later the Yankees came back behind Chesbro to beat Boston, 6–1.

Three weeks later, in the first game ever played between the Yankees and the Red Sox in New York, it was Dinneen who defeated Chesbro, 2–0, on two home runs by Buck Freeman, the Boston first baseman. Freeman was entitled. In 1899 (hardly a man is now alive) he had hit 25 home runs for the Washington club of the National League, the record that Babe Ruth would eventually break as a member of the Boston Red Sox. (If we want to carry these linkages further, it was Dinneen, who took to umpiring when he retired, who was behind the plate the day Ruth hit his sixtieth home run.)

By 1904 Bill Dinneen had already established a record that has been tied but never broken. In 1903, when the Red Sox defeated the Pittsburgh Pirates in the first World Series ever played, Bill Dinneen was the winning pitcher in three of those games. Not that Chesbro was any stranger to these crucial situations. In the two years before joining the Yankees, Happy Jack had been the leading pitcher in the National League for two successive pennant-winning teams.

Neither of them, however, had ever been involved in anything to approach the final week in 1904. After a dogfight of a pennant race, in which the lead changed hands five times in the final month, the Red Sox and Yankees (né Pilgrims and Highlanders) arrived in New York for a five-game series that was going to determine the American League championship. The fact that the Red Sox were half a game ahead meant nothing. Whichever team won three of those five games was going to win the pennant.

And that would seem to suggest that the Yankees, with their home-field advantage, were sitting pretty. Except that they weren't. In order to pick up a few extra bucks, the Yankee ownership had committed an error of such monumental proportions that two of those games—a Saturday double-header right in the middle of the series—had been shifted to Boston.

6

It is always written that the American League was "the brainchild of Ban Johnson." Johnson's vision was to take four teams from the old Western Association, of which he was president, and graft them onto four new franchises in the more populous eastern cities to create a second major league. In that respect he was the spiritual godfather of both the Yankees and the Red Sox. Ban Johnson founded the league, awarded the franchises, and very carefully stocked the teams in an attempt to build winners. The man was his own Rotisserie League a century or so early.

Boston and New York were the two cities where he felt it would be absolutely essential for the American League, if it were to have any credibility, to take on the National League.

They were also the most difficult cities. The problem in New York was that Johnson was stymied at every turn by the New York Giants' big-time connections at Tammany Hall. The problem in Boston was that he was unable to find any local ownership that was willing to buck the very popular Boston club in the National League—the Beaneaters they were called.

With time running out, he turned the franchise over to Charles Somers, a financier and lumber magnate who already had financial interests in three of the other new teams. Somers was the principal owner of the Cleveland franchise, and he had put up the money to back both Connie Mack in Philadelphia and Charles Comiskey in Chicago. Armed with Somers's money, Connie Mack hurried up to Boston and leased the Huntington Avenue Grounds. The stands were constructed in three weeks flat, just in time for the opening of the season.

To stock the teams, Johnson and his owners did what any new league does. They raided the older, established league. In this instance it could not have been easier. The National League had imposed a miserly salary cap of $2,400 that turned their players into sitting ducks. In 1901, the first year of operation for the American League, 111 of the 182 players on its rosters had been spirited away from the National League.

The Pilgrims (and for the sake of ease and clarity we are going to call them the Red Sox from now on) were able to acquire instant local identification by raiding the Beaneaters. Jimmy Collins, the premier third baseman in baseball, was lured away with an offer to become the manager and captain. They also grabbed Buck Freeman, the home run king, and Chick Stahl, a fleet, hard-hitting center fielder.

And then came the greatest coup of all. To that core of local heroes Ban Johnson was able to add the great Cy Young and his catcher, Lou Criger. Cy Young was not exactly coming fresh-faced off the farm. He was 34 years old when he arrived in Boston and he had already won 286 games.

As always seems to happen in these things, old Cy was clobbered in his first two starts and was just about to be written off as a has-been when he turned himself around. He finished the season with a league-leading record of 33–10. The next year the team found a worthy partner for him by stealing away the Beaneaters' star pitcher, Bill Dinneen.

To stop the hemorrhaging, the National League sued for peace. Which is to say they acceded to Ban Johnson's nonnegotiable demand to put a team in New York. To protect himself against Tammany Hall, which was threatening to run a city street right through their ball park, Johnson delivered the franchise to a couple of well-connected pols, Big Bill Devery and Frank Farrell. Farrell was a professional gambler and pool shark who was in the process of building the city's poshest gambling house. Devery was a former police chief, which means that he was corrupt to the core. An ex-Tammany police chief and the city's leading gambling tycoon. These guys had done business together before.

They established the team in a hastily constructed wooden park, seating 15,000, at Broadway and 168th Street. Because the park was situated at the very top of Washington Heights, it was known as Hilltop Park. The team itself became known as the Highlanders, partly because of the topography but mostly because the name of the club president, Joseph W. Gordon, inspired the more internationally oriented sports writers to make the obvious connection with the Gordon Highlanders, a famous unit of the British army. Which only shows how far Farrell and Devery had strayed from their origins. The biggest support for baseball came from New York's Irish, who were hardly clamoring for an identification with the British military. While the Highlanders remained the team's official name until they moved to the Polo Grounds ten years later, to most of their fans, and indeed most of the writers, they had been either the Hilltoppers or the

Yankees from the very beginning. The *New York Times,* great bastion of conservatism that it is, never called them anything except the Greater New Yorkers, which was a contraction of their corporate name.

Just as in Boston, the name of the game was Names. As manager, Ban Johnson was able to install Clark Griffith, who not only had managed the White Sox to the American League's first championship but, at the age of 34, was still a pretty good pitcher. Johnson had prevailed upon his old friend Charles Comiskey to surrender Griffith by telling him, "We need the best that we have in New York."

The major star and gate attraction was Wee Willie Keeler, whom Ban Johnson had plucked from Brooklyn across the river. Wee Willie goes down in history as "Hit 'Em Where They Ain't," which only means that he hit 'em where they weren't better than anybody else. While playing for the old Baltimore Orioles in 1897, Willie had hit safely in 44 straight games, a record that would not be revived—and never mind that artificial respiration would be necessary—until Joe DiMaggio's record-breaking streak in 1941.

Wee Willie stood 5 feet 4 inches and weighed 140 pounds. He choked his bat almost halfway up, pecked, poked, or slapped at the ball, and went flying down to first base. Willie had a mischievous little leprechaun look about him. There can be no doubt, from the recollections of the players of that era, that he was the most popular player in the game.

The park had been constructed so hastily that there was still a ravine out in deep right field. In the opening game Wee Willie almost went tumbling down into that ravine, never to be seen again, while chasing the first ball that was hit. There was a crew of workmen out there, complete with dirt and shovels, immediately after the game.

Since pitching was what the game was all about in those days when Wee Willie and "inside baseball" reigned supreme, Ban Johnson delivered unto the Highlanders the two pitchers who had taken the Pittsburgh Pirates to the National League pennant in the previous two years—the right-handed Jack Chesbro, and the left-handed Jesse Tannehill. Don't bother to cry for Pittsburgh, though. Why do you think they were called the Pirates?

Changes were taking place in Boston, too. Somers was dispatched to Cleveland to take personal charge of the league's other failing franchise.

The new owner was Henry J. Killilea, a Milwaukee attorney who had been another of Johnson's associates in the Western Association. Killilea was around for only one year, but it was some year. It was attorney Killilea who, as Ban Johnson's surrogate, negotiated the fine-tuning of the peace treaty with Barney Dreyfuss, the owner of the Pittsburgh Pirates.

That wasn't all. By the end of 1903 the sports writers and fans were beginning to press for a championship series between the winners of each league. By coincidence, the pennant winners turned out to be Boston and Pittsburgh, and because of the relationship that had been formed during those treaty negotiations, Dreyfuss and Killilea had no difficulty in working out an agreement to play a nine-game World Series.

The Series proved to be Killilea's undoing. There were rumors of ticket scalping out of the Red Sox office, and they were clearly more than rumors. Betting was rampant. The agreement, as worked out by the two club owners, defined the split of the gate receipts. Killilea kept the club's share for himself while Dreyfuss, who was known as a players' owner, threw his share back into the pot. Killilea can be said to be one of the founding fathers of the World Series, and he was also the owner of the first World Series winner. But the time it was over, he was so universally despised and reviled that there was little for him to do except sell the club and return to Milwaukee.

Needless to say, there was no dearth of Boston interests eager to buy into the team now. Leading the list were the two fiercely competing political factions of the Democratic party. Ban Johnson, who was quite an operator, finessed that one very neatly by selling the club to General Charles Henry Taylor, the owner of the *Boston Globe*. In addition to being the publisher of one of the great Boston newspapers, General Taylor was a Civil War hero and a renowned figure in local political and social life. His son, John I. Taylor, a renowned playboy, was the leading sportsman of the city, a polo-playing, tennis-playing, golfing fool. He also drank a little. General Taylor bought the club for his wayward son, as fathers will, in the fond hope that it would keep him out of trouble.

John I. Taylor became an important figure in the history of the Red Sox. Like Killilea, he won a championship first crack out of the barrel. His first year was so full of drama that it may have been almost as exciting as playing polo in Cohasset.

In their maiden season the Yankees had finished a respectable fourth, which was not exactly what Ban Johnson had in mind. To turn them into contenders he now had to do some shuffling within the American League. So New York added two of the top defensive players at their positions, catcher Red Kleinow and shortstop Kid Elberfeld. To strengthen the pitching he brought in Jack (Red) Powell, a consistent 20-game winner. And when it became clear during the season that the Yankees needed more hitting, he had young Taylor send over Boston's best hitter and most popular player, Patsy Dougherty. In addition to having led the Sox in five different offensive categories during the previous season, Dougherty had won a permanent place in their hearts by belting two home runs in the second game of the World Series.

The uproar out of Boston would have been even greater if Johnson hadn't already arranged a deal, during the course of his preseason shuffling, that brought Jesse Tannehill to Boston in a trade for Long Tom Hughes. As originally formulated, the trade was supposed to turn New York into an instant contender. Long Tom had been the number-three pitcher for the world champions, behind Cy Young and Bill Dinneen, a 20-game winner at the age of 26. Tannehill had been no better than a .500 pitcher for New York, a terrific disappointment. The best-laid plans can not only go awry; they have a way of biting you in the neck. By the time Patsy Dougherty was sent to New York, Tannehill was the leading Red Sox pitcher, and Hughes was about to be shipped to the minors. In Boston, Tannehill would have seasons of 21–11 and 22–9 and pitch a no-hit game.

Jesse Tannehill was the first player ever traded between the two clubs. When you consider the luck the Red Sox were to have in future dealings with the Yankees, he may well have been the best. Until Tannehill injured his arm with 20 games left in the season, he was Boston's winningest pitcher. After that, the 38-year-old Cy Young reestablished himself as the ace of the staff by pitching every second day.

When the Sox boarded the train in Chicago for that final series in New York, Cy had just pitched his second straight shutout while the Yankees were splitting a double-header in St. Louis to give his team that slender half-game lead. Not that Bill Dinneen's contribution can be over-looked, either. From the time of Tannehill's injury, Dinneen went on to win six of his seven starts, bringing his final record up to 23–14 against old Cy's 26–16.

The Yankees were coming back to New York by overnight train from St. Louis. They arrived only three hours before the game and took the field in their blue traveling uniforms to the cheers of 10,000 waiting fans.

There had never been any doubt whatsoever as to who was the ace of the Yankee staff. Without Jack Chesbro and his spitball, the Yankees would not have been within spitting distance of the pennant race. In addition to establishing the won-loss record that has remained unsurpassed in the twentieth century, his 14 consecutive victories remained a Yankee record until Whitey Ford tied it in 1961. He struck out 239 batters, and that too remained a Yankee record until Ron Guidry struck out 248 in 1978. In winning those 41 games he completed 48 of 51 starts.

Happy Jack's nickname came from the deadly scowl of his game face. But there was little reason for him to be scowling by the time the game was over. He pitched the Yankees back into first place with a 3–2 win and was carried back to the clubhouse in center field on the shoulders of his exultant fans.

The reports of the game don't inspire overwhelming regard for the talents of the turn-of-the-century ballplayer.

Each team scored a run in the third inning. The Red Sox scored with two men out on an infield hit, a passed ball, and what was described as "a high ball to the outfield which Anderson tried hard to catch." That was Honest John Anderson, the center fielder, another well-traveled player who had been shuffled over to the Yankees at the beginning of the year.

The tying run scored, "after Keeler had surprisingly struck out," when Kid Elberfeld, the Yankee shortstop, was hit by a pitched ball and scored on a two-out fly by Anderson "which dropped on the left-field foul line for two bases."

New York's other two runs were scored by Patsy Dougherty. In the fifth inning the ex-Soxer got himself a hit on the kind of pop fly that would be called a Texas Leaguer as soon as there was a Texas League around to call it after. He reached third when Candy LaChance, Boston's mustachioed first baseman, dropped the throw from Jimmy Collins, and he scored on a fly to right. The winning run came in two innings later on another error by LaChance, a base on balls, and a single by the Yankee second baseman, Jimmy Williams. (Williams, the hero of the first game along with Chesbro, was going to become the goat—along with Chesbro—in the game that cost the Yankees the pennant.)

Boston got one of the runs back in the eighth. Kip Selbach, the left fielder, walked and was called out when he ran into the second baseman on Freddy Parent's ground ball. This was the age of "inside baseball," and there is always the possibility that he ran into Williams to prevent a double play. There is also the possibility that he was just being clumsy. Parent then went to second on a base hit, moved to third on a groundout, and scored—turnabout is fair play—when Elberfeld fumbled LaChance's grounder.

Candy LaChance is a name that has a boulevardier ring to it. There was, alas, no more to the nickname than meets the eye, tongue, and sweet tooth. The mustachioed LaChance was addicted to striped peppermint candy.

All the Yankees needed now was a split in the final four games. The original schedule had called for a single game on Friday, a double-header on Saturday, and, since there was no Sunday baseball, a final double-header on Monday. But there is a rule in life—remember the wind and sun of '78—which dictates that all good fortune falls upon the certified winner. The Bostons had caught a break. Frank Farrell, who was clearly not blessed with the gift of prophecy, to say nothing of the optimistic spirit one might expect to find in a gambler, had arranged to pick up a couple of extra bucks by renting Hilltop Park to Columbia University for their titanic autumnal struggle against the footballers from Rutgers. And, in the process, he had transferred the Saturday double-header to Boston.

With Chesbro out of the way after the first game, and two of the four remaining games in Boston, winning three out of four was hardly out of the question for the Red Sox.

Having just traveled a full day on the train from St. Louis and pitched a full ball game, Jack Chesbro would seem to have had little need to jump back on a train to Boston for one day and then again the next day for the trip home to New York. Let alone to go to Boston and pitch. But Chesbro had not won 41 games by sitting in a hotel room or loitering in front of a bench.

There are two versions of the ill-considered odyssey of Jack Chesbro. The first version has him screaming at Clark Griffith upon discovering that his name has been left off the traveling list. "What's the matter," he supposedly rails, "don't I work for this team anymore?"

"You just pitched," Griffith protests. "Do you want to pitch them all?"

"Do you want to win the pennant?" asks Chesbro.

The other, and probably more accurate version is that Griffith saw Chesbro looking so forlorn as he was watching his teammates board the train out of Grand Central that he took pity on him and invited him to come along for the ride. Once he was in Boston, Chesbro had insisted on pitching the first game of the Saturday double-header against his old rival Bill Dinneen.

Playing any game in Boston at that time was no picnic for the visiting team, and playing such an important game could be downright intimidating. The Red Sox had a wild and raucous gang of supporters who called themselves the Royal Rooters. The Rooters had evolved out of the Winter League, a group of Boston businessmen who would rush out to the Huntington Avenue grounds after work, take off their hats, and play baseball until it became too dark to see. The president of the Winter League, John Stephen Dooley, was a wealthy cotton broker, and since Boston is a city of tradition, Dooley's daughter, Lib, reigns today as the Number One Red Sox fan. The beneficiary of a permanent box seat at Fenway Park, courtesy of Mrs. Jean Yawkey.

The political leader was John F. ("Honey Fitz") Fitzgerald, who used to be identified as a former mayor of Boston but will slide through history forevermore as John F. Kennedy's grandfather.

The spiritual leader was a saloon keeper with the lovely old name— a period piece of a name really—of Mike ("'Nuf Sed") McGreevy. McGreevy did not exactly run a corner bar. He was a pol himself, and he conducted a lavish establishment that was as much a salon as a saloon. It was the meeting place for politicians and sports figures and that not inconsiderable segment of Boston society that was intimately involved with politics and sports. McGreevy was the final arbiter of all disputes, and once he had handed down his opinion, that was it. 'Nuf sed.

The Royal Rooters roamed around the field before the game, and sometimes during it. They would come running onto the field during the game to give a player a piece of their mind or to argue with the umpire.

For the double-header that Saturday 30,000 wild fans mobbed the Huntington Grounds, and another 10,000, many of whom had been turned away from the ball park, gathered along Newspaper Row in downtown Boston to catch the bulletins as they were being posted.

Every reserved seat had been sold out for a week. The bleacher seats were gone an hour and a half before the game. When the fans stormed the park, temporary seats had to be placed in front of the grandstand to coax them away from the base lines. Beyond that, the overflow crowd was roped off in the outfield. What this meant was that any ball hit into the crowd became a double—a considerable asset for the home team. The leading members of the Rooters held the rope. When one of the Sox hit a fly ball that had a chance of carrying into the crowd, the distinguished citizens holding the rope would all move forward in unison. Need we say in which direction they would move when the ball was hit by an opposing player?

In the middle of that madhouse Jack Chesbro put the first nine hitters down in order, while Dougherty did his usual thing by opening the game with a base hit and eventually scoring. In the fourth inning all those games and innings fell in on Chesbro. Also the roof. Six hits, a walk, and two errors, and there were six runs across the plate before he was willing to admit that maybe he should have stayed in New York.

It was the worst beating Chesbro had taken all year, and only the third time he had been knocked out of a game in 50 starts.

The Red Sox kept hitting, and the final score was 13–2.

The second game immediately became the critical game in the series. If New York won, the Red Sox would have to sweep the double-header back in New York. If Boston won, it would be the Yankees who had to sweep.

Cy Young had reestablished his primacy on the pitching staff after a slow beginning by winning eight of his last nine games. Over that stretch he had pitched four shutouts. Against him the Yankees sent Jack Powell, no stiff. Powell's record was 23–18 as he went out to pitch the most important game of his life.

Red Powell outpitched the great Young, but the great Young won, as the great ones do, 1–0, his third straight shutout. The lone run was scored in the fifth inning on an infield hit over second base by the weak-hitting Boston second baseman Hobe Ferris, a sacrifice, and—here we go again—an error. The error occurred when Ferris took off for third after Cy Young had sent a long fly to center field. Harry Anderson's strong throw got by Wid Conroy in the gathering dusk, and Ferris came in with the only run "amidst deafening cheers," according to the next day's *Times*.

The game was called after seven innings because of darkness. Young had scattered seven hits over those seven innings, and had been kept out of trouble by some brilliant play in his infield. Except for that one unearned run, Powell had never been in trouble.

So back they went to New York for the double-header on Monday that was going to decide it all. Taking the mound for New York, as we know, was our old friend Jack Chesbro. And his opponent, once again, was going to be Bill Dinneen.

But this time, of course, the New Yorks would have the benefit of the home crowd. Well, not necessarily. By going to Boston on Saturday, New York had put the Royal Rooters into play. The Rooters were accustomed to traveling with the ball club for the big games. They rode with them on the same train, and they stayed with them in the same hotel, and in anticipation of just such a finale they had already reserved a whole section of the grandstand in New York, right behind the visitors' bench.

Anybody who doubted the effectiveness, enthusiasm, and sheer lung power of the Royal Rooters had only to consult the Pittsburgh Pirates. In 1903 Pittsburgh had won its third straight pennant and had gone into the Series as the heavy favorite. The first three games were played in Boston, and when the Pirates evened the Series by winning the fourth game at home, they were confident of closing it out before they had to go back.

"And then," as Tommy Leach, the Pirates' great third baseman, related in *The Glory of Their Times*, "they began to sing that damned 'Tessie' song." A rather obscure love song of days gone by, with words that were both simpering and banal:

Tessie, you make me feel so badly,
Why don't you turn around,

Tessie, you know I love you madly,
Babe, my heart weighs about a pound.

The fans had begun to sing it, apparently, as a love song to their ball club. As soon as they started to sing, the Red Sox scored, and so they kept on singing. In the following days they developed lyrics to fit every player on both sides. And every time the air was filled with the strains of "Tessie," the Red Sox would be ignited. "I think the Boston fans actually won that series for them," Tommy Leach said, "with that damn Tessie song."

Well, a couple of hundred Royal Rooters were on hand in New York, including Honey Fitz and 'Nuf Sed and their brass band. They wore big red badges with the emblem "World Champions" pinned to their coats. By common agreement, they were all carrying the same suitcases and satchels they had brought to Pittsburgh the previous year. Also the same megaphones, tin horns, and cowbells.

On Sunday night they roamed through downtown, making pests of themselves, and on Monday they gathered in front of the hotel so they could infuriate the New York fans even further by marching to the ball park behind their band.

Jack Chesbro was pitching in the first game—his third start in four days. The Boston fans had been telling New York fans that Chesbro had shot his bolt when he chose to make the trip to Boston and then taken such a drubbing.

They should not have been so confident. After six innings Chesbro had a 2–0 lead, in part through the hitting of that ex-Boston slugger Patsy Dougherty.

In a way it was as if the 1978 play-off game had been placed in a time capsule and shifted into reverse. In 1904 it was New York, not Boston, that did all the hitting in the early innings and kept blowing its chances to put the game away. And it was Boston, not New York, that was the recipient of every break.

The Yankees' great opportunity occurred in the fifth inning. The bases were loaded twice; there were three straight hits and two bases on balls. Out of it all the Yanks, incredibly, were able to score only two runs.

As the inning had got under way, Jack Chesbro owned the only hit for his ball club. He had tripled to the gate in center field with two out in the third, not necessarily a great idea for a pitcher going out there for the third time in four days.

As he came to the plate in the fifth, with a man on first and two out, the game was halted so that a delegation of fans could come marching onto the field to present him with a handsome fur-lined coat and cap. Here you had the most important game the Yankees had ever played, and they were holding it up for a presentation; they did that in those days. After Chesbro had been taken care of, a delegation of players came off the New York bench to present the club secretary with a gold watch and diamond-studded fob in appreciation of everything he had done for them.

When play was resumed, Chesbro showed his appreciation by rapping out a single. Dougherty followed with another hit to knock in the first run, and the second run came in on a bases-loaded walk.

After all that huffing and puffing by New York, Boston tied the score in the seventh on one solitary infield hit and a couple of errors by the unfortunate Jimmy Williams. His first error came on a ground ball by Hobe Ferris. The second and truly disastrous error came with runners on second and third, one out and the infield drawn in. Bill Dinneen hit an easy ground ball. Williams had the runner cold at the plate, but his throw came in very low, skipped past the catcher, Red Kleinow, and rolled to the backstop. Both runs scored.

The Red Sox had tied the game on two unearned runs. The next wild throw Kleinow saw was going to come from the weary old arm of Jack Chesbro.

In the eighth inning the Red Sox actually rapped out three solid hits, but on the third hit Johnny Anderson threw the pesky Ferris out at the plate. This was not a day when Boston was going to win on solid base hits. This was a day when they were going to win on unearned runs. (If you go back, you will see that the only earned runs the Red Sox scored in the whole series came in the game in which they had clobbered Chesbro.)

In the top of the ninth, with the Royal Rooters filling the air with the sound of music, Lou Criger, who couldn't hit much and couldn't run at all, beat out an infield hit, giving Dinneen a chance to bunt him over to second. Kip Selbach, the left fielder, came to bat, and it looked as if a great story might be in the making. Selbach had started the season with Washington and had been shipped to Boston by Ban Johnson to offset the shuffle that had sent Patsy Dougherty to New York. While he was in Washington, he had led off the opening game of the season by singling sharply off Chesbro, and Chesbro had gone on to set the next 27 men down in order.

Get the picture? Kip Selbach had started the season by spoiling what might have been a perfect game for Chesbro, and he could end it, on his final time at bat, by sending him to his most bitter defeat.

It didn't happen. Selbach grounded out, and Lou Criger went to third.

Slow runner on third, two out, and Chesbro gets two quick strikes on little Freddy Parent. And it is right here, with a count of 0–2 on the batter, that Jack Chesbro unleashes one of the wildest pitches of his generation. Chesbro's spitter goes squirting up into the sky, far over Red Kleinow's head, and Lou Criger comes loping in with the run that is going to win the ball game.

But not yet. The game didn't end on Chesbro's wild pitch any more than the 1978 play-off ended with Bucky Dent's home run. Dougherty, who had been a real pain in the ass to his erstwhile teammates throughout the series, came up to bat in the last of the ninth with two men on—they had both walked—and two out.

Another story in the making. Patsy Dougherty, the one-time Boston favorite who had been handed over to the enemy earlier in the season, was up with the tying and winning runs on base. Like Selbach, he had become a powerful force with his new club. Even more than Selbach, he had been having a powerful series.

Big Bill Dinneen struck him out.

New York won the meaningless nightcap, 1–0, in a 10-inning game that was played in one hour and 10 minutes. Fair enough. Otherwise Boston would have won the pennant by 3½ games, which would hardly have presented a true picture of the season. The game-and-a-half margin was just about right.

It is always written that John T. Brush, the owner of the New York Giants, rejected Boston's challenge to resume the World Series because he felt they were "a bunch of bush leaguers." That doesn't really tell the story.

Brush had purchased the Giants only two months before his fellow owners gave in to Ban Johnson's demands and forced an American League rival down his throat. To Brush the upstarts weren't the Highlanders, the Hilltoppers, or the Yankees. To Brush they were the Invaders.

What made the situation even more galling for him was that he and Ban Johnson were old enemies. When first their paths had crossed, Brush had been the owner of the Cincinnati ball club, and Johnson was a Cincinnati sports writer who was constantly excoriating him as a tightwad, pinch penny, and all-around fool.

And now Brush was in New York. His Giants had won with such ridiculous ease that they had clinched the pennant with a month to go. Very gratifying, to be sure, but hardly an unmixed blessing. The National League pennant race ended so early that all attention had turned to the thrilling battle that was being waged in the American League. The New York sports writers had been drumming up the prospects of the pitching matchups: Chesbro vs. Christy Mathewson (33–12). Powell vs. Joe McGinnity (35–8).

The initial challenge had therefore come not from the Red Sox but from the Yankees, the hated Invaders, and it had come at a time when the Yankees had nosed into first place.

It wasn't until the eve of that final five-game series, two weeks later, that the Giants had felt called upon to respond. And even then, Brush, claiming illness as the reason for the long delay, turned the matter over to his manager, John McGraw. McGraw's statement had the fingerprints of lawyers all over it and was remarkable for its sheer stupidity.

McGraw took upon himself all responsibility "for protecting the honor" of his championship. He reminded the fans of the city that in less than three years he had taken the Giants from last place to first. "Now that the New York team has won this honor, I for one will not stand to see it tossed away like a rag. It is the first I have ever won. It means something to our players and they are with me in my stand." He pointed out that the team had clinched the pennant early, incurring great financial loss. "If we didn't sacrifice our own race to the box office we are certainly not going to put in jeopardy the highest honor in baseball simply for the box office inducements."

And then he added, "If the National League should see fit to place postseason games on the same plane as championship games and surround them with the same protections and safeguards for square sports as championship games then, and not until then, will I ever take part in them."

What was the man saying? John McGraw was a guy who ran with gamblers. Was he saying that the 1903 World Series had come under suspicion? And that Devery and Farrell had a reputation that would not stand close scrutiny. If he wasn't saying that, what *was* he saying?

Immediately after the Sox won the pennant, John I. Taylor issued a statement through the press in which he was careful to give Brush an escape route by declaring that he was not issuing a challenge to the National League champions, but merely making an offer to play a series of games against the New York Giants, with all the receipts to go to the players.

What could Brush do? Having said so emphatically that he would not accede to the wishes of the New York press and fans and play the Yankees, he could hardly agree to play the Red Sox. The Red Sox became the "World Champions by default," and that made them world champions for two straight years.

Brush, having made himself ridiculous, was, well, ridiculed. Especially when his players, in flat contradiction to McGraw's public proclamation of their support, formally petitioned that the Series be allowed to proceed.

The Giants won again the next year, and Brush, in an obvious response to McGraw's earlier call for "protections and safeguards," drew up a list of World Series rules and regulations, including the split in the gate receipts, which are the same rules and regulations that are still in force today.

The Red Sox were the world champions. But they did not in fact play what would have been their second World Series. They would not play in another World Series for eight years.

Within two years they would suffer such a complete collapse that in 1906 they finished dead last, 45½ games behind the leader. The Yankees had done their part in sending them to the cellar by sweeping the opening series. Not that New York was doing much better. For the Yankees, that one year of heightened competition, the year of Chesbro's 41 wins, was almost an aberration. After one more run up to second place in the year of the Red Sox collapse, they fell rapidly out of contention and were never a factor again in what may be referred to as the pre-Ruth era.

There is one highlight during that time, however, that should not pass unnoticed. In 1908 the 41-year-old Cy Young pitched a no-hitter against the Yankees in New York, the third no-hitter of his glorious career.

Nor was it the final flare-up of a career in decline. Pitching for a fifth-place club that year, Cy had a record of 21–11.

At the end of the season the Red Sox traded him to Cleveland.

In 1909, at the age of 42, Cy Young won 19 games for the Indians. To prove that gross lack of sentiment was not restricted to the Boston side of the rivalry, New York gave Chesbro his release a year after the Red Sox bade goodbye to Cy Young.

The Red Sox, with an eye toward the box office possibilities, picked him up immediately so that they could pitch him against the Yankees in the final game of the season.

His old teammates knocked him out of the box.

Sayonara, Jack, and keep smiling.

Jack Chesbro

FISHER AND COLLINS

On May 8, 1915, the Yankees sent pitcher Ray Fisher to the mound. The visiting Red Sox countered with a Ray of their own, lefthander Ray Collins. Though each of these Rays had been their respective team for a handful of years, this was the first—and as it turned out the only—time the two would start against each other in the major leagues. Fisher would earn the win when Collins and a string of Red Sox relievers surrendered 10 runs in the fourth inning. As Grantland Rice explains in this article in *The Washington Post,* published in 1915, this May game was the culmination of a career-long rivalry.

from *BALL FIELD RIVALRIES*
by Grantland Rice

Mention has been made before of the early collegiate rivalry between Eddie Plank, of Gettysburg College, and Christy Mathewson, of Bucknell. But probably in the game no rivalry extends farther back than that between Ray Fisher, of the Yanks, and Ray Collins, of the Red Sox.

These two pitchers were first high school rivals in the box for two or three years. Then Fisher went to Middlebury College, Vt., and Collins went to Vermont University. Here they continued the old fight. In 1906 Fisher came to the Yanks, and Collins at about the same time joined the Red Sox. So through high school, college and the big league the two Rays from old Vermont have been battling against each other on the diamond for more than eleven years, and both still have a number of seasons left in the big corral.

When the 1918 season began, Babe Ruth was a Red Sox pitcher, and Boston was the greatest team in baseball. The Yankees? They were a perennial also-ran outfit. By 1920, Ruth was a Yankee and an outfielder, and New York was on its way to becoming the greatest team in baseball. The Red Sox were mediocre and falling fast. Here baseball historian Allan Wood recounts the events of late April and early May 1918 that led to Ruth's first game as a position player—a day that played a role in changing the course of the rivalry. The selection opens with a quote from an article by Burt Whitman of the *Boston Herald and Journal*.

"BABE RUTH PLAYS THE FIELD"

from *Babe Ruth and the 1918 Red Sox* (2000)
by Allan Wood

"GREATEST VALUATION IN THE HISTORY OF BASEBALL PLACED ON COLORFUL BABE RUTH"

Frazee Rejects $100,000 Offer for Pitcher Ruth

Red Sox Owner Declares He Sooner Would Think of Selling Franchise Than Parting with Big Ace

by Burt Whitman

SINCE THE START OF the championship season, Owner Harry Frazee of the Red Sox has been offered more than $100,000 for one ball player, and of course his name is George H. "Babe" Ruth, colossal southpaw pitcher and hitter most extraordinary. The magnate turned down the offer, saying:

"I might as well sell the franchise and the whole club as sell Ruth. The sum named was three times as much as was paid for Tris Speaker, and of course is far and away bigger than any figure that has been used in baseball. But it is ridiculous to talk about it. Ruth is our Big Ace. He's the most talked of, most sought for, most colorful ball player in the game." Frazee did not care to go into details over the stupendous offer for Ruth. "H. H." was inclined yesterday to belittle the general interest in such an item ... It is a certainty that the offer came from New York or Chicago."
—Boston Herald and Journal, *April 30, 1918*

Late that night, Ruth awoke drenched in sweat, agitated by a nightmare. He dreamt that when he opened his morning newspaper, he discovered he'd been sold by the Red Sox. At Fenway Park the following day, as Ruth warmed up in front of the Boston dugout, Frazee told a group of reporters, "Yes sir, I was offered $150,000 for that Baby, and I would not think of selling him."

(The $100,000 figure quoted in the paper had not been attributed to Frazee. If the offer for Ruth was roughly three times the price paid for Speaker, as Frazee had claimed, $150,000 would be the correct amount.) One writer told Frazee what Ruth had said about his nightmare. He laughed, "Babe's not the only dreamer."

It was a balmy spring afternoon, warm enough for short sleeves, as Ruth made his fourth start of the season. [Senators outfielder] Burt Shotton lined the game's first pitch into right field for a single, but Babe didn't give up another hit until the sixth inning. He finished with a five-hitter and Boston won 5–1. At the plate, he doubled, stole a base and scored two runs.

[Red Sox outfielder] Harry Hooper spoke to [manager] Ed Barrow in a quiet corner of the Fenway Park clubhouse the following Thursday. "Ed, have you noticed that every time Babe pitches, we have a big crowd?" After 3,365 fans watched Ruth's win on Tuesday, attendance for the next two games dipped to 2,150 and 2,725.

"The fans love him," Hooper said. He knew Barrow had invested money in the Red Sox when he accepted the manager's job and that Barrow had an interest in keeping the turnstiles clicking. "He's been the most popular player here almost from the day he arrived. They like to see him pitch—but they love to see him swing that bat. They even cheer when he strikes out! Now that Whitey's sick, we could really use him for the next few days."

[Outfielder] George Whiteman's fever had worsened. When Whiteman arrived at the park that morning, Barrow sent him home and told him he should stay in Boston while the team played in New York and Washington.

"All right, Harry, we'll give it a shot," Barrow finally agreed, more worn down than won over. "But you watch: after the first slump he gets into, he'll be on his knees, begging me to let him pitch again." The Red Sox took their league-leading 11–2 record to New York City that night, flush with confidence. And promptly fell apart.

In 1918, the Yankees and Giants both played at the Polo Grounds in upper Manhattan. (In all five cities that had two major league teams, when one team was home, the other would be on the road.) Joe Bush opened the series in New York on Friday, but never established a comfortable rhythm. He battled into extra innings and even after being hit on the hand by a line drive in the tenth, Bush convinced Barrow to let him stay in the game. One inning later, Bush surrendered three hits and the winning run as the Red Sox lost 3–2.

Ruth didn't play in the first game, but he undoubtedly spent a large part of his Friday night enjoying the excesses of the big city. Yankees manager Miller Huggins heard that Ruth had stumbled back to his hotel around sunrise, and thought he could take advantage of a hungover pitcher. New York scored single runs off Ruth in the first and second innings, and with a runner on in the third, Roger Peckinpaugh pushed a bunt towards the mound. It rolled between Ruth's legs for a hit. Then Frank Baker laid one down. Ruth lunged at it and threw wildly to first base, hitting Baker in the back of the neck. Two runs scored and New York led 4–0. By the end of the afternoon, Ruth handled 13 chances and made two errors.

The Yankees' starter was Allan Russell, a native of Baltimore. He and Ruth had played together in Providence in 1914 and shared a good-natured rivalry. After fanning Ruth early in the game on three pitches, Russell laughed at him.

"Don't get too happy," Ruth called back. "I've got a few more chances today."

In the seventh, Boston trailed 4–1. With one man on and one out, Ruth crushed a ball into the upper deck in right field. It landed about three feet foul. Babe stepped out of the batter's box, tapped some dirt off his spikes with his bat, and turned to home plate umpire Billy Evans. "I'm hitting the next one right back up there," he said flatly, "and it'll be fair this time, no doubt about it."

Ruth stepped back in, his eyes focused on Russell, his hands wringing the end of his bat, waiting for the pitch. He took a huge swing, holding nothing back. As promised, the ball sailed into the top deck, to the left of the foul pole by a wide margin. Ruth tossed his bat aside and went into his first home run trot of the season, taking tiny steps, running on the balls of his feet. When Ruth stepped on the plate, he winked at Evans.

In the ninth inning, many in the crowd of 15,000 were starting for home. It had been a perfect day—the Yankees were ahead 5–3 with one out to go and they'd seen the mighty Ruth belt a home run. But as soon as [Sox catcher] Sam Agnew doubled, a murmur rippled through the stands. Ruth was next. The mass exit slowed. Russell conferred with his infielders behind the mound and the outfielders took several steps back from their normal positions.

Ruth again pounded the ball into the upper deck—he seemed to do it at will—but he had been too anxious and it curved foul. He hit the next pitch harder than he had hit anything all day. [New York's] Armando Marsans was standing nearly 380 feet away in right field; the ball went over his head. Agnew scored and Ruth settled for a double. He was itching to score the tying run, but Hooper made the final out.

The Polo Grounds was shaped like a bathtub, with obscenely short foul lines. The left field line was 277 feet from the plate and right field only 256 feet; a photographer's perch in right put the second deck seven feet closer. The rest of the outfield was a spacious meadow, roughly 440 feet to the alleys and nearly 500 feet to straightaway center. Beyond that was a large scoreboard and the teams' clubhouses. Ruth loved hitting in the oblong park and the fans loved seeing him hit; the Boston papers referred to Babe as "the hitting idol of the Polo Grounds." With his home run off Russell, 4 of his 10 career blasts had come in New York.

On the Red Sox's day off, they traveled to Clifton, New Jersey, for an exhibition game against the Doherty Silk Sox. Harry Doherty, the wealthy silk manufacturer, owned a beautiful park (Doherty Oval) and one of the best semi-professional teams in the country. He also promised five dollars to anyone who hit a home run. So when Boston's pitcher-turned-right-fielder-for-a-day John Wyckoff hit Otto Rettig's first pitch over the fence, he circled the bases and then trotted directly to the owner's box. Doherty handed him a five-dollar bill and Wyckoff jogged back to the bench. After a few innings, Ruth replaced Heinie Wagner at first base. He swung from his heels, but managed only a high flyout and a strikeout. Babe earned no extra spending money in Clifton.

Back in New York on Monday, Ruth finished batting practice, grabbed a towel off the bench and wiped the sweat from his face. Barrow came over and sat down.

"How are you feeling today, Babe?"

"Fine, Eddie. I felt good and loose out there." There was still an electric tingle in his shoulders from his last line drive. "How about letting me pinch-hit again today?"

"I may not need a pinch-hitter, but I do need a first baseman." Ruth perked up. "Really? How come?"

"Hobby's [first baseman Dick Hoblitzel] hands are still bothering him and I've got nobody else. Listen, Babe, you know Harry and I have talked about you helping us out in the field. Maybe it's time to try it. You think you're ready?"

"Are you kidding?" Ruth said. "Where'd I throw my mitt?"

So, in his 174th major league game, Babe Ruth played at a position other than pitcher or pinch-hitter and for the first time did not hit at the bottom of the order. He batted sixth and went 2–4, including a two-run home run off George Mogridge in the fourth inning. At first base, Ruth collected four putouts and two assists, one of them on a double play started by Hooper. Ruth took the relay from right field and fired a strike to Sam Agnew, cutting down a runner at the plate.

Yankees owner Jacob Ruppert watched the action from his private box with his friend Harry Frazee. "Say, Harry, that big kid can do it all—pitch, hit, play the field. How much do you want for him?" Frazee just shook his head and laughed.

According to legend, Red Sox owner Harry Frazee sold rising star Babe Ruth to the Yankees to raise money for his Broadway play *No, No Nanette*. As baseball historian Kerry Keene explains, the truth was considerably more complex.

"THE TRANSACTION: SALE OF THE CENTURY"

from *The Babe in Red Stockings* (1997)
by Kerry Keene

AS BABE AND [his wife] HELEN prepared to head for Los Angeles, an account in the *Boston Herald* declared Babe the world record holder for earnings in baseball for one year. Bob Dunbar chronicled how Babe had earned $2,500 to play in two exhibition games on the 18th and 19th of October. He was scheduled to make $10,000 for his stint in the Pacific Coast League, and then of course his salary with the Red Sox. "Babe's receipts from the Red Sox this last year were $15,000, not $9,000 or $10,000, as reported at various times. He was handed a $5,000 present, bonus, or what ever you call it by Owner Frazee a few days after that wonderful 'Ruth Day at the Fens.'"

Dunbar projected from April 1, 1919 to April 1, 1920, Babe would earn $27,500, surpassing Cobb, Speaker and Johnson as the highest paid player in baseball.

On November 2, 1919, a *Boston Post* front-page story accompanied with a photo of Babe and Helen arriving in Los Angeles, corroborated the Dunbar story. "Babe's income for 1919 will soar to a lofty figure. He has already received $10,000 for his services to the Red Sox team during the regular season. It is said that he also received a bonus from President Frazee at the close of the season for his excellent work during the 1919 campaign."

Babe made an instant impact on the Pacific Coast League. Traveling as a member of Buck Weaver's all-star team, he picked up where he had left off during the season. Smashing home runs at a prodigious rate and in that high-arcing manner that had become his trademark, he instantly had some writers wondering if he would not hit as many as 100 home runs were he to play a full season in the California league.

He was making an impact off the field as well. Demanding a payment of $10,000 before he would even set foot on a movie set did not endear him to the hearts of the Hollywood magnates. It virtually ended his stint at a movie career before it even began. He would have to wait several more years before making his debut as a celluloid hero. This, coupled with the fact that one of his first comments about Los Angeles was that he didn't particularly care for the weather, left fans leery of this young brash ballplayer from the East.

By the time he arrived in Oakland around the 10th of November, he had already been booed by fans at a game in Los Angeles, because he had only doubled in four at bats and struck out twice. It did not take long for Babe to figure out that California was not Boston. In Oakland, rumors began to circulate again that Babe was on the verge of leaving baseball for a career in the boxing ring. This time, there were whispers of a possible title fight with reigning heavyweight champ Jack Dempsey.

The California press had turned out to interview Babe upon his arrival in the Bay city. For most of them, this was their first encounter with the Colossus who had taken baseball by storm. Briefed on his background and home run accomplishments, they waited for their chance to experience Babe first hand. He stunned them when he opened by telling them of his intention to "lick Ty Cobb on sight."

He was furious at quotes attributed to Cobb, which labeled him a "contract violator." Responding to Cobb's allegations, Ruth was quoted in *The Sporting News* of November 13, 1919: "A player is worth just as much as he can get, and Cobb has been paid all that he is worth, believe me, for quite a few years. I wouldn't say anything against Cobb if he held out for $100,000, why should he say anything about me? He ought to be tickled to see any player get as much as he can. I'll settle the question when I meet Cobb." Babe made no bones about the fact that he might substitute his fists for words when he next encountered the Georgia Peach.

At the end of November, the rumors intensified. *The Sporting News* reported that Babe's holdout was "more serious . . . than is generally believed in the East." A world tour was also mentioned, with reports that he would take his show on the road to such far away places as Honolulu and even Australia. Some saw this as just another negotiation ploy, and some were concerned that Babe was genuinely pursuing financial alternatives to playing for the Red Sox. *The Sporting News* viewed the situation in light of Carl Mays' departure from the Red Sox during the 1919 season when they wrote this of Babe's holdout. ". . . He has been analyzing the celebrated Mays case, and has arrived at the conclusion that a contract is not binding on a baseball star who chooses to disregard it and elects to shift to some other club. Some . . . even hint Babe has picked his club, a la Mays, that he too would join the Yankees."

December opened wish a resurgence of talk that Babe would enter the ring. This time, however, there was a new twist. A report out of Los Angeles said that Kid McCoy, a former boxer turned movie actor, would train him for 30 days and then evaluate Ruth as a boxer. If things were favorable, McCoy would then arrange a bout with Jack Dempsey for the world heavyweight championship. Upon hearing of this, Boston sportswriter Neal O'Hara wrote, "If Babe Ruth ever tackles Dempsey, he'll learn he hits a right-hander the same as a southpaw." The same release reported that Babe had officially abandoned his attempt to become a movie actor.

The Boston press did not see this threat to enter the fight game as anything but a ruse in which to gain an edge on Frazee. With his movie career temporarily interrupted and Babe not playing baseball every day, this left plenty of time for golf. Playing 54 holes a day, Babe was honing his game. He often would play with Buck Weaver of the 1919 Chicago White Sox.

It was Weaver who had put together the team on which Babe was playing as they barnstormed the coast of California.

In October, Weaver was one of the eight members of the Chicago White Sox who were in on "throwing" the series to the Cincinnati Reds. It is interesting to speculate on what Babe and Buck may have talked about during their time together on the links and while traveling playing baseball. There is no evidence to suggest that Ruth was aware or became aware of the inner machinations of the 1919 White Sox World Series, however there was a vague reference to an incident that occurred toward the end of the year in a card game in Los Angeles and was reported in the *Boston Post*.

Ironically it was Babe who was portrayed as the villain in this particular circumstance. "There is a little story going around over a little scene that Ruth created over a card game with Buck Weaver of the White Sox as his particular target, which has not added to his [Babe's] popularity in sporting circles as Buck is very well thought of here not only as a ball player but as a Man." There was no mention of the specifics of the incident nor its precipitant, but it is now clear that the careers of Ruth and Weaver were at a crossroads headed in two distinctly opposite directions.

Throughout the month of December, Boston sportswriters speculated on how the Red Sox could improve over their dismal 1919 showing. Their weakness was pitching and would continue to be so, as Babe was now certain to be an every day player. To replace him as a premier left-handed pitcher would be no easy task. Frazee satisfied many when he acquired Harry Harper from the Washington Senators. A 25-year-old left-hander who had showed great promise in his early career, Harper had a terrible year in '19 going 6–21. He had always, however, been very effective against the Red Sox. Paul Shannon of the Post wrote "it could mean the 1920 pennant."

While Babe played golf in California and lobbied for his $20,000 annual salary, Frazee, shuffling back and forth between New York and Boston, had made up his mind and hints of his intentions began to appear. On December 21, the following headline appeared on page one of the sports section of the *Boston Sunday Post*: "BABE RUTH IN MARKET FOR A TRADE."

Two accompanying sub headings read: "Frazee states he will sell or trade any Red Sox player but Harry Hooper" and "Figure Ruth is disturbing element and make club a one-man team." Calling Ruth's contract position "untenable" Paul Shannon stated that neither Frazee nor Barrow would consent to an interview to discuss the matter but offered his view on the possibilities of Babe moving on. "Red Sox fans need not be greatly astonished if the burly batter is allowed to pass on through some deal . . . popular as Ruth is with his mates, as good hearted, generous and open handed as all know . . . the Red Sox have of late become a one-man team and this fact has hurt morale considerably."

New York was mentioned as the potential club involved and Shannon stated that a trade rather than a flat-out sale might better be accepted by the Boston sporting public. He even went so far as to suggest that if the Yankees would give up: "an infielder, an outfielder and first string twirler. . . the fans would endorse the move." Shannon concluded by summarizing where Babe now stood in the eyes of the city; his "attitude, while putting a big dent in his popularity in the Hub, has irritated the Red Sox management, who are beginning to look upon the burly batter as a second Frankenstein."

The Red Sox fans were on notice—"Tarzan," "Hercules," "Cave Man," "The Colossus," "The Mauler," "The Clouter," "The Burly Batter," The Babe, was on the block.

As 1919 drew to a close, many speculated about the value of Ruth. When the St. Louis Cardinals were offered $70,000 plus four players for 23-year-old Rogers Hornsby, the question on everyone's mind was: What is Babe worth? Arthur Duffey of the *Post* answered the question by stating what he felt Ruth was not worth in salary terms. "If Eddie Collins and Ty Cobb are worth $15,000 to the White Sox and the Tigers, is not Babe Ruth worth $30,000 to the Red Sox? He is NOT!!" The idea of a baseball player making that kind of money was thought absurd by most and obscene by many.

Two days before Christmas, the Red Sox sold Del Gainer to Toronto of the International League. Dick Hoblitzell had signed on to manage a minor league team in Akron, Ohio and had signed Jim Thorpe to a contract. Grover Cleveland Alexander declined an offer to become the pitching coach of the University of Illinois baseball team and teach a University course on the science of pitching. On the 30th of December, the aforementioned deal for Harry Harper was struck. The Sox got Harper, infielder Eddie Foster and outfielder Mike Menosky for Bobby Roth and Maurice Shannon.

On the last day of the year, Harold G. Reynolds, the Sporting Editor of the *Boston Post,* wrote a piece from Los Angeles on Babe's current contract situation. Under a headline which read "BABE WILL PLAY WITH RED SOX," Reynolds outlined why Babe would be back in Boston. Calling his talk of retirement, becoming an actor, and a boxer a "bluff," Reynolds wrote the following: "You couldn't keep Babe out of the national game unless you sentenced him to jail, and then probably he would organize a prison league. Ruth is not given credit for possessing any too much gray matter when it comes to business matters, but he is wise enough to know that he is lost unless he is with organized baseball." Within the story there was, however, a foreboding sentence which read in part: "unless Harry Frazee, the owner of the Boston Americans decides to dispose of the slugging star before the season opens." The announcement of the transaction was less than a week away.

Ruth's acquisition by the New York Yankees was front-page news in both Boston and New York. The smallest of newspapers, in hundreds of communities across the country, did not escape without, at least, a tiny blip about the sale. To crystallize the events surrounding the sale of Babe Ruth can best be done by examining and exploring four different and equally important aspects of the deal. They are: Red Sox owner Harry Frazee; the reaction of the media and fans; Babe Ruth himself; and last but certainly not least the gloom that has seemingly hung over the Boston franchise since Ruth's sale which somehow seems to mystically perpetuate as an heirloom to Red Sox fans even today.

Harry H. Frazee: the best that could be said of him is that he was much maligned in Boston. The worst, and closest to accurate, is that he was reviled. Looked upon with scorn and disdain, he may have been the only man that youngsters in Boston learned to hate before they even knew his name. To many he was simply the "Guy who sold Babe Ruth."

Purchasing the Red Sox in November 1916 from Joseph Lannin for, what was reported to be, somewhere between $675,000 and $750,000, Frazee had Ruth in his employ for exactly three baseball seasons. In those three years, the Red Sox finished in second place in 1917, nine games behind the White Sox. First in '18, capturing the World Series and sixth in '19, 20½ games out.

Taking the reigns from Lannin, Frazee, at 36 years old, was the youngest owner in baseball. Initially looked upon warily by Boston writers and fans, he endeared himself to both when by the end of 1916 he offered Clark Griffith of Washington $60,000 for Walter Johnson. Leaving the '16 team pretty much intact—and why wouldn't he—Frazee became very active when [World War I's] call to arms in 1917 decimated the Red Sox. It was the addition of Strunk, McInnis, Schang, and Bullet Joe Bush that was critical to the Red Sox's success in 1918. By the end of the '18 season, Frazee had established himself as a hands-on owner willing to do whatever was necessary to procure a winning franchise.

When Ban Johnson and the rest of the National Commission received the work-or-fight order of 1918, it was Frazee who spearheaded the drive to postpone it from July 1 to September to get in close to a normal season. Frazee was a driving force behind the many ceremonies held throughout the American League, during the 1918 season, in which the proceeds were donated to the Red Cross. It was Harry H. himself who attempted, more than once, during the '18 campaign to set up a World Series to take to Europe and play before the boys at the front in France. Continually rebuked, or ignored, his idea never got off the ground.

Looking at the game as it was in 1918, Frazee had the vision to see the need for a "one-man commission" to sit at the head of Major League Baseball. Acting unilaterally at one point, Frazee offered the job to former President and Supreme Court Justice William Howard Taft. Astute a politician as he was, Taft gracefully declined his offer as not to become entrenched in the inner wars of baseball. Frazee's vision proved accurate, and one need to simply review the state of the game in the 1990s to see how sorely missed was that "one-man commission."

It has been written and chronicled throughout the years that Frazee was in desperate financial straits at the time that Ruth was sold. One story line goes that Frazee sold Ruth so he would have the money to finance a play entitled *No, No, Nanette*. Many a Red Sox fan is raised to understand that this is why Babe Ruth became a Yankee. For some inexplicable reason, this play and the sale of Babe Ruth have for years been linked. The reality is that H. H. Frazee's production of *No, No, Nanette* did not debut until 1924 at a Frazee-owned theater in Chicago and did not reach Broadway until September 16, 1925, two years after he had sold the team to Bob Quinn.

The Boston newspapers from the years of Ruth's tenure with the Red Sox, reveal nothing of financial difficulties on the part of Frazee. The 1918 attendance had dropped off by 138,343 but this was the result of the abbreviated war schedule. Besides, the 1919 attendance had rebounded to 417,291, an increase of nearly 168,000 and was the team's best attendance in the seven year of Frazee's ownership. In short, the notion that Frazee was looking for cash to finance his theatrical ambitions, and he saw Babe as the vehicle to procure that cash, appears inaccurate. It may be a more accurate appraisal of the subsequent sale of the many more who followed Babe to New York and the ultimate sale of the entire team in 1923. Harry's financial squeeze of late 1919 was more of a more immediate nature and would remain veiled until February of 1920.

On February 9, 1920 attorneys for Joseph Lannin, former owner of the Red Sox, and Harry Frazee were in a Boston courtroom. Frazee had given Lannin a note for $262,000 when he had purchased the team in 1916. Lannin asserted that Frazee owed him $125,000 (interesting figure) which was due on November 1, 1919 and had not been paid. An injunction by Lannin was sought and gained, preventing Frazee from "disposing of any of the stock or assets of the club and even from drawing any money out of the club," and an auction date was set for March 3. Frazee's contention was that he only owed $60,000, which he was ready to pay "anytime Lannin is willing to concede to Frazee the amount that is due." Frazee claimed that he had paid roughly $65,000 in debts that were the responsibility of Lannin.

The courts agreed with Lannin, and set March 3 as the date on which Fenway Park would go up for auction. That date would eventually be moved to March 10 and then cancelled as Frazee and Lannin settled their differences out of court and away from the public eye. It was at this time that the public became aware that Frazee's purchase price for the team in 1916 was $1 million.

The idea that Frazee was a tightwad and a skinflint is simply inaccurate.

This especially applies in the case of Ruth. Frazee gave into his contract demands when he signed him in 1919 to a three-year deal. He repeatedly allowed him to play, and receive pay, on barnstorming teams, even though under the conditions of his contract he could have denied him the opportunity to do so. There were even times, during the season, when Babe was allowed to leave the team to participate in an exhibition game in which he would make an extra $500.

Much has been made of the fact and Babe himself so stated, that on Babe Ruth Day at Fenway Park near the close of the 1919 season, Harry presented Babe with a nickel cigar. Frazee himself claimed that when Babe came to him during the 1919 season and lamented the fact that he could not achieve his pitching bonuses because he was playing the outfield, Frazee paid him anyway. Two reports in the Boston papers tell of Babe receiving a bonus from Frazee. One of them even went so far as to print that Frazee presented Ruth with the aforementioned $5,000 bonus for his record-breaking year of 1919. In light of this, does it become difficult to understand that when Babe mailed back his unsigned contract for the 1920 season and demanded, through the newspapers from 3,000 miles away, a doubling of his salary, that Frazee had simply had enough?

Despite Harry's suspected financial woes, there is no reason not to think that when he decided to move Ruth, he still would have preferred players over cash. Evidence to suggest this comes in the fact that Frazee offered Ruth, straight up, to the White Sox for Shoeless Joe Jackson and was refused by Charles Comiskey. This plus the fact that when Frazee went to Barrow for input on players to get from the Yankees it was Barrow who, not believing that any exchange of players would be worthwhile, suggested that he keep it a cash deal.

It is damning indeed that on November 1 Lannin claimed Frazee owed him the exact amount that Ruth was later sold for, however in fairness to Frazee, there is plenty of evidence to show that he did not sell Babe to satisfy his debt to Lannin. To begin with, Frazee had been making payments to the long-defunct Federal League as a result of a settlement to their suit in 1916.

Frazee believed that these should have been Lannin's responsibility as he (Lannin) was the owner at that time the suit was settled. The fact that the courts did not see it that way is no reflection on Frazee's good faith intentions. Secondly, and perhaps most important, Frazee had just completed his most successful year (financially) as owner of the Red Sox.

Frazee was not a stooge and had to be aware that the only reason people came out to Fenway Park to watch his sixth-place team was because of Ruth. He therefore was fully aware that either a Red Sox team with Babe Ruth, or a pennant-contending team without him could well be the best answer to his financial problems. There was no reason not to think, at this time, that Frazee's objective was to build a winning baseball team through the acquisition of players. So when he vowed to take the money and use it to procure players that would again make the Red Sox a contender, no one had cause to doubt him, for he had done it before.

Upon Ruth's sale, Frazee issued what was roughly a 1,500-word statement explaining to the fans his reasons for disposing of Ruth. The *Boston Post* of January 6 printed it in its entirety. "Twice within the past two seasons, Babe has jumped the club and revolted. He refused to obey the orders of the manager and he finally became so arrogant that discipline in his case was ruined . . . He had no regard for the feelings of anyone but himself. He was a bad influence upon other and still younger players."

Frazee continued his scathing attack on Ruth and revealed perhaps how hurt personally he was by Babe's behavior. "Out there on the West Coast, I could have prevented him from playing a single game as his contract signed by him gives me that right. But I allowed him to play unmolested. Then he sends me back his contract in an envelope without a scrap of writing for explanation. This is just a sample of how Ruth respects his written word and his obligations."

Babe's conditioning did not escape Frazee as he made a point to reveal that ". . . Ruth is taking on weight tremendously. He doesn't keep himself in shape. . . . He has a floating cartilage in his knee . . . that may make him a cripple at any time and put him out of baseball." This was as a result of his knee injury that occurred in the fall of 1918, and which had bothered Babe off and on during the '19 season.

The owner concluded his statement by informing the fans of his unsuccessful attempt to procure players for Babe. "Ruth's great value did not appeal to all the other owners. I could not get Joe Jackson for him and I know of at least two other stars that Ruth could not have been traded for. . . . Ruth could not remain on the Boston team under existing conditions."

From the time he had purchased the team in November of 1916 to the time of Ruth's sale, Frazee was an active innovator who was willing to take on the power structure of the game. He had spent money freely to secure players to help the Red Sox win. There was no hint, nor was their any mention of financial problems on the part of Frazee and the Red Sox. Those would surface five weeks later. There was the annual fall rumor of the team's potential sale, but that was generated as much by Ban Johnson as anyone. It must not be forgotten that it was Johnson who had secretly come into Boston in late 1918 in an attempt to find local investors to buy the team.

One accusation made of Frazee throughout the years is that he was an owner whose only concern was to "make a quick buck." It would be ludicrous to suggest that he did not want to make money. What businessman wants to lose it? However, the accusation that it was all he was in it for, appears unfounded. One needs only to look at the fact that he refused to sell the team during the winter of 1918 for $1.2 million. Examine the numbers and decide. In November of 1916, Frazee bought the team for $1 million. Roughly two years later he was offered $1.2 million. Would any businessman who wanted to make a quick buck turn down an opportunity to make $200,000 in a little less than two years?

He had formed a coalition with Jake Ruppert and Charles Comiskey and took on Ban Johnson and the National Commission in an attempt to infuse their vision on the future of baseball. This did not endear him to the hearts of Johnson, the National Commission or certain other American League owners. However, the fact that he had spent freely and had always worked toward strengthening the team on the field created a broad base of support in Boston. At this point in his tenure as owner and President of the Boston Red Sox, Frazee was widely respected and highly thought of by fans and the Boston press. All of that was about to change, for eternity.

There were 11 newspapers in the city of Boston in 1920. The first radio station was still five years away and the idea of sending waves through the air that would turn into pictures on a screen in the living room was considered science fiction by most. The newspaper was the undisputed king of communication.

Obviously, all the newspapers printed this important story, however four newspapers "covered" the story. They were the *Boston Post,* the *Boston Herald,* the *Evening American,* and the *Boston Globe.* The *Post, Herald* and *American* ran stories about the sale for eight consecutive days. It was through these stories that the reaction of the media, the fans, and Babe himself can be felt. The sale of Ruth to the Yankees received far more support than anyone nearly 80 years removed could ever imagine.

The headlines of Tuesday, January 6, 1920 screamed the news that Babe was now a Yankee! Throughout the years, varying dates have been given as the announcement date. All of the newspapers of the sixth refer to late afternoon on Monday, January 5 as the time Frazee announced the transaction. The reported amount of the sale varied, ranging from $100,000 to $150,000. Only the *Boston Post* and the *New York Times* reported the correct figure of $125,000. None of them at the time mentioned the loan of $300,000 that Ruppert gave Frazee, using Fenway Park as collateral. It simply was not known.

The focus of all the stories was the price. Whichever paper reported whichever price, it was clear that it was more than twice as much as anyone had paid for a baseball player. Getting past that sensational aspect of the story, the reactions began.

More than 75 years have passed since Ruth's sale to the Yankees. It is easy to look at the transaction with the hindsight of all those years and ask the obvious question: "How could anyone sell Babe Ruth?" Indeed that was the reaction of many of the time. In the Suffolk Athletic Club just north of the city, men "groaned, hissed and booed" when news of the deal reached them. Shocked was probably the word most often used to describe the initial reaction of the fans.

An editorial in the *Boston Post* on January 6 summed up the feelings of many fans: "The average home patron cannot view with great equanimity the transfer of a star of the first magnitude, the greatest drawing card in the game. Boston fans, therefore, are bound to be disgruntled." Citing that the money secured for Ruth would alone not be enough to lure other owners to transfer players to the Red Sox and adding in the fact that they no longer possessed many players who could be traded for established stars, the editorial proved prophetic when it stated that "the immediate prospects for a winning combination in Boston are not exactly brilliant."

Continuing its prophecy, the editorial concluded: "Cy Young and Tris Speaker went their ways, much to the disgust of the faithful, but the club did not suffer materially. But Ruth is different. He is of a class of ballplayers who flash across the firmament once in a great while. . . . During the past 20 years there have been three such superstars—Wagner, Cobb and Ruth. Wagner stayed with Pittsburgh (sic) . . . Cobb will never play except for Detroit. Money could never buy these two men. But Boston with Ruth is another story."

On the same page as this editorial, *Post* sportswriter Paul Shannon wrote the following:

> "Ruth . . . the biggest box office attraction in the game and the most spectacular player . . . would never have been allowed to leave Fenway Park had it been possible for the Boston club to handle him. Ruth's failure to respect the club's training rules, his unwillingness to submit to any form of discipline, and the bad example he set for the other men formed a combination that President Frazee could no longer endure."

Acknowledging Ruth's greatness as a player, a gate attraction and "the most spectacular player to wear a Boston uniform since . . . Mike 'King' Kelley," Shannon continued, "the regret at his sale will be considerably tempered by the knowledge he was posing as a holdout. And the dear public, wearied year after year by the lack of good faith and unwarranted demands of players who had small consideration for word or contract had rapidly begun to lose patience with the temperamental star. With Ruth gone from the Boston lineup, harmony is sure to be restored."

Concluding, he wrote: "It is believed that practically every man on the Boston team will be pleased at Ruth's sale to New York. Popular as Ruth was, on account of his big-heartedness, the men nevertheless realize that his faults overshadow his good qualities." Paul Shannon had been covering Babe Ruth since he joined the Red Sox in 1914, and his sentiments about Babe being a holdout were echoed in virtually every newspaper in the city.

Referring to Ruth as "Boston's beloved slugger," Ed Cunningham wrote on the front page of the *Boston Herald,* "Mutterings of the storm that will break loose today about the heads of the Boston management were heard last night and fans, almost to a man stoutly oppose the deal." Analyzing he continued, "Baseball fans know little of the internal affairs of a baseball club. They know the players as they act on the playing field and evidently care little of what happens off the field. The fans have their favorites and Ruth captured their hearts by his wonderful batting."

Acknowledging that Babe would probably "smash to bits" his new home run record playing 77 games at the Polo Grounds, Cunningham went on record as being against Ruth's demands from Frazee for a new $20,000 contract. "If that contract was out last season, in all fairness he could ask for an increase to $20,000 and undoubtedly would receive it, but he was not in a position to cast the signed contract aside merely as a scrap of paper." Ironically, Frazee stated that he would have been willing to give Babe a raise "if he had come and requested it in a different attitude then the one taken."

Herald columnist Bob Dunbar talked of Boston fans being "staggered" and "astonished" at the news of the deal. However he did add that "there are two sides to every issue" and that "management is seldom given consideration and generally is censured." Dunbar went on to say that "Frazee believes that he has not been squarely dealt with," then hit the nail right on the head when he concluded, "The departing of Ruth . . . is regretted by all."

It was the *Boston Herald* cartoonist Franklin Collier who penned the famous cartoon portraying for sale signs on the Boston Public Library, the Boston Common and Paul Revere's statue. However Dunbar shed a little light on that as well when he wrote in his column of January 8, "My good friend Franklin Collier is very much upset over the going from here of Ruth. You see Franklin dearly loved to build a cartoon around that delightful 'phiz' of the Colossus . . . instead of having him around every day at Fenway Park Collier will have him but 11 times in the season." Is it possible that Collier's "vision" of the sale was somewhat tainted through the view of a self serving eye?

James O'Leary, writing for the morning edition of the January 6

Boston Globe stated that it would be for "sentimental reasons" that the fans would view the deal with "disfavor." He further stated that if they would reserve judgment "the chances are that they will agree with President Frazee and others that the sale of Babe will eventually redound (sic) to the welfare of the Boston club." O'Leary clearly came down on the side of the Red Sox owner when he stated, ". . . it is hard to see how Frazee could have turned down New York's offer for the star, and it looks as if he had made a good bargain."

O'Leary even wrote an article that appeared on the front page of the January 15 edition of *The Sporting News*. Under a headline which read "FRAZEE FINDS DEFENDER IN HIS RELEASE OF BABE RUTH," O'Leary detailed what he termed Frazee's "many convincing points" and then summarized with, "When it began to look as if Ruth regarded himself as bigger than the Boston club, bigger than the game itself, Frazee made up his mind that there would have to be a change in order to avoid more serious trouble in the future."

Concluding, O'Leary wrote, "The Boston fans are sorry that he goes, there is no mistake about that, but they will have to reconcile themselves to his absence, as they did in the cases of Cy Young, Tris Speaker and others. . . . The old game will go on just the same."

In the evening edition of the *Globe,* John J. Hallahan came out "strongly against the action," yet in his article he stated, "There is no getting behind the fact that Ruth is after the money." Despite not supporting the trade, Hallahan could not come out in support of Ruth's contract maneuvers.

The *Boston Evening Transcript* went so far as to print in their front page story of January 6 that there was "Remarkable unanimity of opinion that the Red Sox made a good deal in disposing of the home run hitter. Nearly everyone agrees that Ruth is too big to stay in Boston." It further stated that the "Red Sox players doubtless will be pleased with the disposal of the incorrigible slugger and team play should be in more evidence." Needless to say, they too were not speaking very favorably of the fact that Babe was demanding a new contract.

The *Boston Evening American* was the most critical of the Red Sox for selling Babe. *American* sportswriter Nick Flatley stated that they had "lost the greatest drawing card the game has ever known, and the esteem of many of thousands of supporters. . . ." Calling Babe "the greatest star ever known to this city where heroes (sic) and pennants . . . have become chronic," Flatley decried what he termed the exploitation of star athletes at the expense of the club's chances of "glory."

He came to Ruth's defense regarding Frazee's contention that Babe was the cause of disturbance on the team. Stating that the only disturbance Babe caused was with his bat, he related that his teammates were as happy as Babe when the home run record fell during the '19 season.

Flatley went so far as to point the finger directly at Barrow as the cause of any dissension on the team. He cited the Carl Mays incident and the fact that "games were lost because pitchers who were getting pounded were left on the hill." He questioned whether Barrow had the "control or experience" to pilot a championship team and suggested that he (Barrow) had blundered in his handling of Ruth. "Ruth is young and his head, doubtless, has been turned a bit by the wonderful adulation his hitting aroused. But . . . he could have been handled in a manner that would have kept him a fixture in Boston."

Flatley continued his diatribe with a reference to Bill Carrigan and his dealings with Babe:

> ". . . he rode him to death and made him play baseball. That system, followed up, would have kept the ideas of movies and prize rings out of the heros (sic) skull. But Ruth got a little out of hand and rather than treat him psychologically, as they say, and bring him back, the Sox have traded him."

Recognizing how unique was Babe as a player, "a bird like Ruth hops into the picture once in a lifetime." Flatley accurately predicted the immediate future of the Red Sox, Babe and the Yankees. "Without Ruth . . . a second division club will not develop into a great money winner here in Boston. Babe will get $20,000 and probably more. . . . He's likely, too, to hammer the Yanks into a pennant promptly."

The next day the *Post* reported that Babe had signed a two-year deal worth $45,000; the Yankees won their first pennant in 1921; and the Red Sox did not see another first division finish until 1934.

Among those who saw Ruth's departure as a positive event was Hugh

Duffy, who had starred with Boston in the National League from 1892 to 1900 and would manage the Red Sox in 1921. Thinking Frazee had made the right move, Duffy said, "No matter how great a star is, he hurts a team if he does not fit with his fellow players."

Fred Tenney, former first baseman and manager of the Braves echoed Duffy's sentiments, "A player that fits an organization is of more value than any star not working in harmony with his club."

Babe had baseball men of equal stature come to his defense in the persons of two former managers, Bill Carrigan and Jack Barry. Barry referred to him as "the most willing member on my team" and said his problem with him was that he wanted to pitch "too much." Stating that the absence of Ruth would leave the Red Sox attack "lamentably deficient" Barry offered that he never "called on Ruth and found him lacking."

Carrigan was equally supportive, stating that he did not regard Ruth as "anywhere near the hard proposition to handle that he was made out to be." Carrigan neglected to mention that on the road he had Babe room right next to him, and Heinie Wagner was his designated chaperone. Charley Lavis a former owner of the same Providence club that Babe played on in the minors in 1914 said, "I figure the Red Sox club is now practically ruined."

The initial reaction of the fans could best be categorized as outrage. It was Babe and his quest for the home run record that had kept them coming to the park in 1919. In a year where the team finished in a dismal sixth place, it was Babe who gave them something to cheer for.

The more prominent members of Boston fandom were also consulted to solicit their opinions. Francis Hurney of the South Boston K. of C., and one of the organizers of the Babe Ruth Day held in September, said, "The management of the Red Sox will have to travel some to get a player . . . like Ruth and I'm sure the gate receipts this year will show a decided decrease now that the true sportsmanship in the game is banished." The Red Sox attendance fell off by less than 15,000 in 1920.

M.T. "'Nuf-Ced" McGreevey, the founder of the Royal Rooters and one of the oldest long-standing Red Sox fans stated that it was the Yankees who were the "gainer[s]" in the deal. Calling Babe "a very big asset,"

McGreevey stated, "I think every real Boston fan will regret his departing." Johnny Keenan, McGreevey's 1920 counterpart was in concurrence with "'Nuf-Ced's' evaluation: "It will be impossible to replace the strength Ruth gave the Sox. The Batterer is a wonderful player and the fact that he loves the game and plays with his all to win makes him a tremendous asset. . . ."

The *Boston Evening American,* for several days after the sale, solicited the fans to write letters declaring their opinions on the sale. All the letters they printed came with a byline attached. The bylines said such things as "DID WISE THING," "BIG MISTAKE MADE," "DISCORD STORY BUNK," "BABE WORKING FOR RUTH," "ANOTHER RAW DEAL" and "FRAZEE HARMED SELF." The newspaper concluded after reviewing all the letters received that: "The Babe Ruth controversy is still about fifty-fifty." They summed up the fans' feelings thusly, "The fans think that Ruth is some ball player . . . who can help out any team . . . when he is so inclined . . . they do not all believe Ruth was working for the best interests of the Boston Red Sox last summer."

It is interesting to note that nowhere in any newspaper over the eight-day period in which this story dominated the sports pages, was there one comment printed attributed to a teammate of Babe's. There could be a simple explanation for this, however it does seem a bit peculiar. Jack Barry made it a point to voice his comments to his local paper in Worcester, Massachusetts. Bill Carrigan made contact with the media from his home in Lewiston, Maine. Yet not one of Babe's mates had any comment that made its way into any Boston newspaper at the time of the sale.

The initial reactions emanating from Ruth himself were two. The first came in the form of a telegram to his business manager Johnny Igoe dated January 5. It read simply, "Will not play anywhere but Boston, leaving for the East Monday." The second was a small article written by Gene Doyle and printed in the *Boston Post* of January 6 in which Doyle claims, "Ruth knew nothing of the deal until he was told by me." Stating that "the news surprises me a bit," Babe went on to say, "I think it's a dirty trick of Frazee to sell me to the New York team. If it is true . . . I will still hold out for a salary of $20,000 and I may demand part of the purchase price." Babe's first in-depth reaction to the trade came in the *Boston*

Evening American of January 7. Holding back nothing, he blasted Harry Frazee. Saying he was "not good enough to own any ball club, especially one in Boston," Ruth accused Frazee of doing "more to hurt baseball in Boston than anyone who was ever connected to the game in that city. The Boston people are too good for him, and it will be a blessing when he steps out or is ousted."

Continuing his salvo, Ruth hit at Frazee in regard to his contract. "Because I demanded a big increase in salary, which I felt I was entitled to, he brands me as an ingrate and a troublemaker. . . . Any fair-minded fan knows that my efforts on the Boston club last season warranted a larger salary and I asked for it. I have always hustled as hard as any man on the diamond . . . doing everything I could to make the club win."

In closing, Babe commented that as much as he liked Boston and its fans, he was glad to be rid of him. For were it not for Frazee, Babe would have been content to play with the Red Sox to "the end of my baseball days."

Lost on Babe was the fact that back in Boston he received little, if any, support on his attempt to double his salary. His staunchest supporters—and there were throngs of them—felt he should honor the three-year deal he had signed at the beginning of the '19 season. No one doubted nor disputed the fact that he was the best player in the game. A large contingent recognized him already as the greatest slugger in the history of the game. Many even felt he was worth the $20,000 he was requesting. However, in the matter of his holdout, the vast majority of writers and fans sided with Frazee.

This was due, in large measure, to the fact that Babe had demanded a new contract while under an existing agreement. Fifty or so years removed, this action would be called "renegotiation," and would become fairly common practice among professional athletes. However, in 1920 it was totally unacceptable to even Babe's most ardent admirers. Even in New York, where they were welcoming him with open arms, W. J. Macbeth wrote for the *New York Tribune,* "Ruth's attempt to flaunt the Red Sox to the face despite an unexpired contract called for a showdown as a matter of discipline."

Walking the Municipal Golf Links on Wednesday, the 7th, with Bill

James of the White Sox and Gene Doyle of the *Post,* Babe continued his offensive against Frazee. Reacting to a comment attributed to Frazee which said that as a star Babe "would be an obstacle to the club winning pennants." Ruth responded, "I have been with the Red Sox six years . . . and we won three pennants, not so bad . . . I am not or never have been a disturbing element . . . I have always played for the interest of the public and the players."

Claiming that Frazee cared "nothing about the Boston people" and predicting that he expected Frazee to sell the team very soon, Babe again stated his intention to get a piece of the purchase price, and the following day sent a telegram to Frazee requesting $5,000 from the proceeds of the sale. He even went so far as to say that he would not report to New York without it. Frazee, making good on his earlier intent to not give Babe "so much as an old straw hat," gave him nothing.

On January 9, Babe took a more organized approach to his offensive against Frazee. Visiting the telegraph office in Los Angeles, he dispatched four telegrams to Boston. One each to the sports editors of the *Boston Herald,* the *Boston Post,* the *Boston Globe* and the *Boston American.* Each was printed in its entirety in each of the newspapers. Of differing lengths with varying details, they were all of the same flavor. Babe hit back hard at Frazee.

Calling Frazee's statements "absolute falsehoods . . . meant to poison the minds of the Boston people against me," Babe challenged the Red Sox owner to find one player on his team who felt Babe was a disturbing element and stated he would give Frazee $100 for every player found. Accusing him of "putting me on the pan as a means of covering himself for my sale to New York" Babe stated, "This propaganda has been sent out to try and pacify Boston people over the sale. It is a rank injustice to both them and me, for there is not any of it true."

This was an underlying theme in all of them. It seems that Babe could tolerate just about anything but being fingered as a source of discontentment with his teammates. He was deeply hurt by the sale, and his hurt turned to anger at the contention that he was the source of trouble on the team. Denouncing again and again the truth of Frazee's statements, Babe threatened to "file suit for damages. . . . He is trying to injure me with the Boston fans and I will not stand for this. The people know me and I am just as strong for the fans of Boston as they are for me."

He gave tribute to the fans of Boston saying they have "no superiors." He credited them for their loyalty to the home team combined with fairness to give "due credit to visiting players." Calling his six years playing in a Boston uniform "pleasant ones," Babe said good-bye to Boston. "I regret having to leave Boston. . . . When I come back . . . in a New York uniform it will be like coming home."

In Boston, people waited for the "other shoe to drop" in the form of a major Red Sox acquisition or as some suspected, the actual sale of the team. Frazee failed in an attempt to get Happy Felsch from the White Sox, and the reality that it was easier to sell a big star than to buy one began to set in. Interestingly, Felsch along with Joe Jackson, Buck Weaver and others would play their last years in 1920, then be banned for life for their involvement in the 1919 World Series "scam."

With the initial furor dying down, the fans of Boston were willing to give Frazee time to make good on his promise to obtain more players. As much as they revered Ruth, and as great a player as everyone knew that he was, the fans sympathized with and supported Frazee's contention that Ruth was wrong for not living up to the three-year contract he had signed prior to the 1919 season. Besides, they had seen star players come and go before yet the success of the team on the field had continued. They knew that teams could survive the loss of major stars and re-emerge as contenders. They had seen it before; Cy Young left and they still won. Speaker left in 1916, and the pennant still flew at Fenway. Frazee had stated he had talked with Detroit, Chicago and St. Louis and expected to make a deal soon. The fans were willing to wait, the Red Sox's new star could not be far away.

As the outcry diminished, the posturing in the newspapers ceased. Babe never returned from the West Coast until the middle of February. On the same day that the attorneys for Lannin and Frazee were arguing before a Boston judge, Babe announced his intention to seek $15,000 of his purchase price from Frazee. He also stated he would "exceed" his home run record of 1919. Although he never got a dime or even "an old straw hat" from the $125,000 Frazee received for him, he did make good on his home run prediction.

Scattered reports had him signing for various amounts of money. He actually played for the $20,000 he sought in 1920. He would get $30,000 in 1921 and by 1922 he was earning an ungodly sum of $52,000 a year, or as Babe liked to think of it, $1,000 a week.

Both teams gathered up and headed South for spring training. Babe went to Jacksonville, Florida, where he would make his first headlines by going after a heckling fan in the stands. The Red Sox returned to Hot Springs, Arkansas, and when they left, the fans were still waiting for the arrival of the new players Frazee had promised.

The questions of the Red Sox fans regarding who Frazee would acquire were answered on March 27 when an announcement came out of New York stating that Frazee had purchased the Harris Theater on Broadway. No price was given, however it was reported that it had been built at a cost of $500,000, and only weeks before, a theater on the same block had sold for $650,000. So much for the money from Ruth going to purchase new players.

The Red Sox opened the 1920 season with four wins in a row, including a doubleheader sweep of the Yankees on Patriots Day, April 19. Over 35,000 people showed up to welcome home the Babe, and they broke down the fence in rightfield in their eagerness to get to the ball park. Playing centerfield and batting fourth for Miller Huggins, Babe went 3–8 in the doubleheader with a double and two singles. Cheered and given a "hearty hand," Babe's appearance at Fenway in enemy garb, to many, signified the official passing. Babe was gone.

Babe pulverized the record books in 1920, setting new major league records in runs scored, RBI, walks, slugging percentage, and as he predicted, home runs. His 54 home runs were more than every other TEAM in the league. He also led the Yankees in stolen bases with 14 as New York finished in third place, three games behind Cleveland.

Boston finished in fifth place, 25½ games behind the leaders. The outfield, which had been anchored by Hooper and Ruth, was now made up of Hooper, Menosky and Hendryx. Hooper, having his usual solid year, led the team with seven homers.

Frazee took over the Harris theater in July, redecorated, renovated, and called it the "Frazee." The ultimate indignity came in late November when a report out of Chicago cited a transcript from the Suffolk County court-house in Boston, Massachusetts which stated that on May 25, 1920, "there was executed by the organization controlling the Boston American League Baseball Club a mortgage for $300,000 in favor of Jacob Ruppert et al." Not only did Ruppert have Ruth, he basically owned Fenway Park as well. The book on Babe Ruth and the Red Sox was closed. As the year drew to a close, Babe's golfing buddy from the previous winter, Buck Weaver, was making plans to take a one-man play to vaudeville houses designed to "prove his innocence of complicity in the alleged conspiracy to 'throw' the 1919 World Series." Harry Frazee's dream of a "one-man commission" came closer to reality as Ban Johnson appointed a committee of three to meet with a National league committee and Judge Kenesaw Mountain Landis.

Rumors in Boston had the team being sold to a group that included Boston College football coach Frank Cavanaugh and again, a young Boston banker named Joseph P. Kennedy. A cloud hung over Frazee as questions of the propriety of one owner carrying a mortgage on the other's ballpark were being looked into by Ban Johnson and the American League. The cloud would only grow darker—so dark that nearly 70 years after his death, it still hovered.

As for Babe, he stood on the threshold of immortality, poised to do what he'd always done—take the game of baseball to a level it had never known before.

CONTINUED FALLOUT AND WHAT MIGHT HAVE BEEN

The record is there to be examined, analyzed, and dissected, but the question that fans and historians alike are left to consider is, "What if Babe Ruth had not been sold, and spent his entire career with the Red Sox?"

While Babe Ruth played with the Red Sox from 1914 through the 1919 season, they compiled a record of 514 wins and 359 losses. In that same time frame, New York was a mediocre 430–445. Boston won the World Series in 1915, '16 and '18. They finished second in 1917 and slipped to sixth in 1919. New York, on the other hand, had finished in sixth place twice, fifth once and fourth once before rallying to a third-place finish in 1919.

In 1920, the Yankees finished with a record of 95–59, completing the most successful year in their history. In 1921 they won their first American

League pennant and repeated the effort in '22 and '23, becoming only the second American league team to win three consecutive pennants.

The fortunes of both of these organizations turned when Harry Frazee peddled Babe Ruth to Jake Ruppert. The fact that many of Babe's Boston teammates followed him to New York in the early twenties (including the entire pitching staff) had as much to do with the teams' immediate reversal of fortunes as anything else. However, nearly 80 years later, the sale of Babe Ruth still casts a shadow that hangs, at times, like gloom over the Red Sox and their fans. *Boston Globe* sportswriter and Massachusetts native Dan Shaughnessy wrote lightheartedly of this gloom in his 1990 book *The Curse of The Bambino.* Before the book, in the early 1980s, tee-shirts were sold outside of Fenway Park which read "Boston Red Sox: 1918 World Champs." Part of the vendor's sales pitch was that the Red Sox were indeed under a curse and it would last until the year 2018, a 100-year sentence to frustration and heartbreak for selling the "Colossus." Witches were called to Fenway in the 1970s to cast out demons and put an end to curses.

Virtually every Red Sox team that has won and proceeded to post-season play has had to deal with an onslaught of media asking them about "the curse" and the Red Sox propensity to lose big games in bizarre, unimaginable ways. With most of them not from Boston and lacking the firsthand knowledge of Red Sox history, players would often become perplexed, which at times gave way to irritation and then to anger.

Although in Babe's last year in Boston the team finished in sixth place with a record of 66–71, it seems highly unlikely that they would have fallen to the depths they reached in the 1920s if he had remained in the fold. This was their first losing season since 1908. They were a proud franchise with a tradition of winning, having captured five of the first 15 World Series, three since Babe joined them in 1914.

If Babe had remained, one might assume that Barrow would have remained as well. Therefore, the aforementioned sale of Babe's teammates may not have transpired either. There is no reason to think that Boston's dominance would not have re-emerged and continued into the 1920s. Perhaps additional success would not have placed Frazee in the financial state where he felt it necessary to sell his players, and there may have been no sale to Bob Quinn in 1923.

Quinn owned the team from 1923 until 1933. In that dismal decade, the Red Sox won 671 games while losing 1,075, for a winning percentage of .384. Their best season came in 1931 when they won 63, lost 91 and finished in sixth place, 45 games behind Philadelphia. Without that decade of desolation, there may have been no sale in 1933 to Thomas A. Yawkey. Thirty-three at the time he bought the Red Sox, Yawkey may have purchased some other franchise in the American League, or perhaps even a National League team. Maybe he would have even chosen a team in the emerging National Football League instead of a baseball team.

With no sale of Ruth, there may have been no Quinn. With no Quinn, there may have been no Yawkey. The benevolent Yawkey was known for being very good to his players—some said too good. He established such a relationship with Ted Williams that it was Ted who spoke on his behalf when he was posthumously inducted into the Hall of Fame in 1980. Carl Yastrzemski states flatly that Thomas Yawkey was the reason he signed with Boston instead of Philadelphia. No sale of Ruth, no Quinn, no Quinn, no Yawkey, no Yawkey, no Yaz, and maybe no Williams. Ted's tempestuous ways may have been treated differently by another owner, and perhaps he would have been traded or worse yet, sold. Without Tom Yawkey owning the Red Sox, would Joe Cronin have ever been bought from Washington in 1934 for $250,000? Would Jimmie Foxx ever have made it to Fenway Park, where he slugged 35 of his 50 homers in 1938? Would Lefty Grove have won his 300th game in some other uniform than Boston's? Maybe the Red Sox ticket office would today be located at 4 Frazee St. instead of 4 Yawkey Way.

By the mid-1920s, the Red Sox pitching corps that had once sported the names of Ruth, Leonard, Mays, Shore, Foster, Pennock, Bush and Jones had been replaced by such stalwarts as Collins, Ehmke, Wingfield, Wiltse, Harris, Weltzer, and Zahniser. It is debatable if even Babe could have lifted them from their forlorn fate. However, it seems doubtful that such a fate would have befallen them had he remained. Frazee had, up to the point where he sold Ruth, spent his money to acquire quality ballplayers. There is no reason not to think that if he had it, he would have continued to do so.

That the landscape of baseball history would have been radically altered had Babe remained with Boston is obviously indisputable. Indeed, an entire book could be written on the ripple effect it would have had on the way baseball is perceived worldwide. What is interesting to speculate about, however, is how Babe's own career may have changed had he continued to play for the Red Sox. Would his home run numbers have been quite so prolific? Yankee Stadium was tailor-made, or one could say custom-designed for his long, high rightfield drives. Would he have had as much success in Fenway with its relatively spacious rightfield? In 1918 when he led the A.L. in home runs with 11, all of them were hit on the road. In 1919, when he again led in homers with 29, 20 of them were hit on the road.

The greatest impact Babe had on the game was that he hit the ball higher, harder, and farther than it had ever been hit before. The baseball public marveled at how high his infield popups went. They would often be delighted if they happened to be present when Babe hit a long flyout during the course of an 0 for 4 afternoon. There is no way of knowing how many of Babe's Yankee Stadium home runs would have been outs at Fenway Park. With the way that Babe hit the ball, it does not seem as if there would have been many. Regarding the "House That Ruth Built," might it not have even been built in 1923 with no Ruth, and the success he had helped to bring?

Throughout the history of Fenway Park, there have been many left-handed hitters who have had greater success due to its leftfield wall, with Fred Lynn and Wade Boggs as two more recent examples. With Babe's adroitness with the bat, it seems likely that he would have adapted well to its presence. There was the time in July of 1918, when he spent the morning with Barrow working on hitting the ball to left, then proceeded to bang three hits that afternoon to leftfield. It could be expected that Babe would have honed his off-field hitting skills, and before long would have been hitting opposite field home runs with startling frequency.

In all probability, Babe would have hit about the same amount of home runs. His talent and skills as a power hitter were unprecedented in the history of the game, and it seems implausible that they would have been contained by the dimensions of the park in which he played.

There are several other points to ponder regarding Ruth's imagined continuation in a Red Sox uniform. In 1929, numbers on the back of uniforms came into fashion, with Babe's number "3" signifying his third position in the Yankee order, the method most, if not all teams used to number their players. Having been firmly entrenched in the cleanup spot in the Red Sox order by 1919, it is logical to assume that Ruth may have worn number "4" on a Boston uniform. Today, in Fenway Park's rightfield corner, the numbers 9 - 4 - 1 - 8 are displayed to honor four retired greats from the team's history. Had Ruth spent his entire career in Boston, might the number "4" be displayed in honor of him rather than Joe Cronin?

As Ruth's career was winding down, it was well known that he coveted a major league managerial position. In finishing his career with the Red Sox, would it have been a natural transition for him to have taken over as skipper of the team? If so, would he have taken a protege such as Ted Williams or some other young slugger under his wing?

Our final, lasting image of Babe Ruth alive, is an aged and shriveled figure standing in a baggy uniform at home plate for one final time two months before his death in 1948. Had he spent his career with the Red Sox, that heart-rending, poignant scene would likely have taken place at Fenway Park.

Despite his relatively brief tenure, Babe's mark remains in Boston and New England. In May of 1968, there was a street and park named after him in South Boston, where his first wife, Helen, lived, and where he was a member of the Knights of Columbus. Red Sox fans of New England in 1983 voted him the starting left-handed pitcher on their all-time Red Sox team. In 1995, he was one of the original inductees into the Boston Red Sox Hall of Fame, and around that same time a local baseball fan and historian spearheaded a drive that led to a plaque being dedicated on the spot where Babe played with the Providence Grays in 1914, commemorating his final minor league stop.

Yet somehow Boston remains almost apologetic about Babe's time spent with the Red Sox. Shocked that he left, saddened and disgusted by what transpired in the decade that followed his departure, and broken-hearted over three generations of some of the most noteworthy failures in the history of the game, Red Sox fans have incorporated into their psyche an expectation of failure that becomes increasingly difficult to shake with the passage of each baseball season.

Even though he was one of the original inductees into their Hall of Fame, the Red Sox organization itself appears somewhat reluctant to call attention to the fact that Babe played for them at all. In this current age of the Internet and cyberspace, anyone with a computer can communicate with the Boston Red Sox. Greeted with an attractive home page, fans can peruse a myriad of areas of interests. Among them is a section labeled "Legends." Listed in this section are the following names in order of their appearance: Cy Young, Tris Speaker, Smoky Joe Wood, Tom Yawkey, Joe Cronin, Jimmie Foxx, Johnny Pesky, Ted Williams, Bobby Doerr, Carl Yastrzemski, Rico Petrocelli, Carlton Fisk, Luis Tiant, Fred Lynn, Jim Rice and Dwight Evans. Conspicuous by its absence is the name George H. "Babe" Ruth. It is almost as if they would rather pretend that he was never there than acknowledge that they sold him.

The past cannot be altered, and only through acceptance can it be resolved. The time has come for the Boston Red Sox and their fans to embrace the time that he spent in Boston, to step out from the shadow of his sale and celebrate the time that he was among them. For before he became a Yankee and made his rendezvous with destiny, he had redefined the game of baseball as The Babe in Red Stockings.

Babe Ruth and Stuffy McInnis sign their 1918 Red Sox contracts
(*From left:* Ed Borrow, Babe Ruth, Harry Frazee, Stuffy McInnis)

Whenever the Red Sox have developed a really good player, he has soon been transferred to New York, all to the discouragement of the Boston customers, who are the most naïve and durable customers in baseball."

—Westbrook Pegler of the *Chicago Tribune*, May 1932

THEY SAID IT...

Some claimed that the Red Sox were cursed, that they were doomed to their decades of failure as punishment for Sox owner Harry Frazee's sale of Babe Ruth to the Yankees in 1920. Even those who put no stock in the so-called "Curse of the Bambino" can't deny that one group of New Englanders truly was cursed by the Ruth sale—the descendants of Harry Frazee who had to live with his name.

"STILL FRAZEE
AFTER ALL THESE YEARS"

from *Yankee Magazine* (June 2000)
by Spencer Frazee

IN THE SUMMER OF 1976 I was a rookie patrolman with the police department in Manchester, Connecticut. On a warm Sunday afternoon, I pulled over an old Nash with Massachusetts plates for running a red light. The driver was a polite, spry old man in his eighties. I remember thinking, I'd hate to have to tangle with this guy: he's in good shape for an old codger.

As I returned to the car with his ticket, the old man said. "Son, this is the first ticket I've received in 65 years of driving, and I want to thank you very much. There's no doubt I deserved it, and everyone needs an occasional reminder when he gets careless."

Not too many people say that when you hand them a traffic ticket, so when the old man began to reminisce, I listened politely. It was a slow

Sunday afternoon anyway, and I love to hear stories of the "old days," especially from someone who lived them.

In his early years, the old man played a little professional baseball, raced cars and motorcycles, and played the horses. He went on to tell me how he'd married five different women over the years and outlived them all. Suddenly he looked at my name tag and said, "Frazee? The acorn doesn't fall far from the tree, does it?"

"Excuse me?" I asked, not understanding. "I said, the acorn doesn't fall far from the tree. You're related to Harry Frazee." It was a statement, not a question.

"Never heard of him." I wasn't about to admit I'd heard the stories a hundred times from my grandmother.

"Oh, you're related to him all right. It's in the eyes."

"Who is he?"

The old man took a deep breath. "Harry Frazee bought the Boston Red Sox just before World War I. After winning the 1918 World Series, he sold every decent player they had to the New York Yankees."

"Still never heard of him."

"Yeah. Well, Harry had bought the Red Sox in 1916 with his profits as a Broadway producer. He led the Red Sox to their last world championship in 1918 and then promptly sold all his best players to Jake Ruppert of the New York Yankees. Harry's Broadway plays were bombing, and he needed the cash to pay his creditors.

"I knew him. Everyone did. Hated him, too. Frazee single-handedly created the Yankee dynasty by selling them Babe Ruth, Herb Pennock, Everett Scott, Wally Schange, Carl Mays, and Waite Hoyt. In fact, in the Yankees' 1923 World Series win, 11 of their 24 players were from the Red Sox."

I'd heard the story too many times as a youth. My ancestor was a very famous guy, at least around Fenway, where Frazee is a name that goes with Benedict Arnold and Lizzie Borden.

I can't remember the old man's name now. But I do remember what he said before he drove off. "Harry destroyed the Red Sox for a hundred years, and now another Frazee has destroyed my perfect driving record."

The Boston Red Sox spent much of the 1920s and 1930s in the lower half of the American League standings. New York, with a lineup full of legends like Babe Ruth and Lou Gehrig, was in nearly perennial pennant contention. But in 1938, the Red Sox believed they were ready to leave behind two decades of poor play and challenge New York. The season was still in its early months when Boston player-manager Joe Cronin decided he was done letting the Yankees push him around.

"BAD BLOOD INFUSION: IN 1938, CRONIN-POWELL BRAWL SPARKED DECADES OF HOSTILITY"

from *The Boston Globe* (April 2, 2004)
by Bob Ryan

MEMORIAL DAY, 1938. THE Yankees–Red Sox climate that now produces exhibition game tickets being hawked on eBay starts here.

It starts with the largest crowd ever to see baseball played in Yankee Stadium and it features—what else?—a classic brawl. Forget anything else you have read or heard. The Yankees and Red Sox as we know them today began on May 30, 1938, in the fourth inning of the first game of a Memorial Day doubleheader in a massively overcrowded Yankee Stadium. That's when Joe Cronin and Jake Powell put up the ol' dukes, both on and off the field. When it was over, both men had been ejected; Sox player-manager Cronin would have deep scratches on his face, as well as bruises and welts all over his body; the Yankees would have swept a pair, and the history between the franchises would never be the same.

Until this day, there had been no rivalry, simply because there had been no real competition. Once Harry Frazee was through dismantling the team that won World Series in 1915, 1916, and 1918, the Red Sox were an abomination, finishing eighth and last eight times, seventh once, and sixth once between 1923 and 1932, during which time the Yankees were winning seven American League pennants and four World Series. What basis could there possibly have been for a rivalry?

Tom Yawkey bought the club in 1933 and immediately began buying ballplayers. Playing in a rebuilt Fenway Park, the Red Sox finished fourth at 76–76 in 1934. It was Boston's first break-even team since 1918.

By 1938, the Red Sox finally had a real ball club. For the first time since the Babe Ruth sale, they were ready to challenge the mighty Yankees. In fact, so were a few others. On the morning of May 30, Cleveland (22–12) was in first place, followed by Boston (19–14), Washington (21–17), and (gasp) New York (17–14).

The Yankees were under siege and the fans of New York had taken note. Bobby Doerr, then a second-year player, was Boston's starting second baseman that day, and he recalls the afternoon vividly. "There were eighty-three million, five hundred thousand there," he chuckles.

The actual figure will never be known. Gerry Moore of the *Boston Daily Globe* claimed there were "84,000 persons who filled nearly every available breathing space in the vast Yankee Stadium." John Drebinger of the *New York Times* put the official attendance at 83,533 (81,891 paid) and claimed there were precisely 511 additional fans who were refunded their money "because they could find no place of vantage to see anything but the backs of the necks of earlier arrivals." The official box score posted an attendance figure of 82,990, which would make this a major league record, period, eclipsing the inaugural crowd of 80,284 at Cleveland's Municipal Stadium five years earlier.

What remains beyond dispute is that this was the largest crowd ever to witness baseball in the 81-year history of Yankee Stadium, which in its second configuration, cannot even hold 60,000.

The great crowd had come with one hope—to see the two-time

defending world champions give the back of the hand to the upstart gang from Boston, an aggressive bunch that took its cue from Cronin.

The feisty skipper/shortstop sent Lefty Grove to the mound in the first game, and the crusty lefthander did not have his best stuff. It was 5–0, Yanks, by the time there was one out in the Yankee fourth. Cronin relieved Grove with 27-year-old lefty Archie McKain, who gave up RBI singles to Bill Dickey and Myril Hoag on his first two deliveries to make it 7–0. That brought up left fielder Alvin Jacob "Jake" Powell, a player about whom everyone had an opinion.

The *Globe's* Moore: "Whether by intent or from not having been sufficiently warmed up, McKain's ensuing effort nearly beaned Powell and sent the eccentric Yankee diving into the dust. He had taken a similar trip to escape a high hard one from Grove in the previous inning. On neither of these occasions did Powell pay any attention to the pitcher, but when McKain plinked him squarely on the thigh with a following throw, instead of walking to first base, the onetime Senator stormy petrel headed straight for McKain."

The *Times'* Drebinger: "Powell fell to the earth to duck the first pitch, which seemed aimed squarely at his head, and the second one struck him a glancing blow to the stomach. On picking himself up, Jake marched belligerently to the pitching mound. McKain seemed more than willing enough to meet him halfway."

McKain was hardly noted for being a head-hunter. "A very fine person," asserts Doerr. "A lefthanded pitcher. Not a hard thrower."

"A little lefthander," confirms 91-year-old Broadway Charlie Wagner, who was in the bullpen while all this was going on, and who would pitch the eighth inning for the Red Sox. "A darn good pitcher. Didn't throw hard, but hard enough. He could pitch. He had the guts of a daylight burglar."

Powell was a major piece of work. Did you notice? *Eccentric? Stormy petrel?* Or go with Doerr's description. "Kind of a maverick type of a guy," he declares. "One of those players it didn't take much to start a fight with."

At age 30, Jake Powell was in the middle of a 688-game major league career, the highlight of which was a 10-for-22 outburst against the Giants in the 1936 World Series. He had good skills, but he was ornery and, to be blunt, a very outspoken racist and anti-Semite who had been accused of deliberately breaking Hank Greenberg's wrist during a violent collision that cost the great Detroit first baseman just about all of the 1936 season, and who would twice be suspended by commissioner Kenesaw Mountain Landis for spewing racial venom on the radio, once after proclaiming that one of his favorite duties as an offseason policeman was "beating up [n-words] and then throwing them in jail."

That brought him a 10-day suspension. In one of the more interesting trades of the day, the Senators swapped him to New York for outfielder Ben Chapman, another legendary racist who would attract attention 11 years later for being one of the most vitriolic hecklers of Jackie Robinson. This, amazingly, while managing the Philadelphia Phillies.

Troubled to the end, Powell would shoot himself to death at age 40 while being questioned by Washington police for a bad check charge. So here was Powell going out to confront McKain, when, according to Moore, "hardly had these two grabbed each other by the arms when Cronin hove to the scene. Joe came running in from his shortstop position, pushed McKain out of the way and started swinging on Powell almost in one motion. This fracas was quickly halted by the umpires, and other players."

Drebinger: "But before they had a chance to mix, manager Cronin dashed over from his shortstop position and decided to take an active hand. In fact, he opened fire on Jake, and, with the latter retaliating, there was a spirited struggle until umpires and players pulled the combatants apart."

Cronin and Powell were ejected, but their business was not finished. In those days both teams had to use the runway adjacent to the Yankees' third base dugout in order to reach their respective clubhouses. Umpires Bill McGowan, Cal Hubbard, and Ed Rommel, each a legendary arbiter, collectively failed their essential duty, which was to monitor the departure of the battling duo. For when Cronin entered the runway, Powell was waiting.

Moore: "Following a few words, they went at it and weren't separated until the umpires hastened down from the field to intervene. The immediate damage wrought came in the form of several deep scratches on Cronin's face."

Red Sox pitching coach Herb Pennock (who had played for both teams): "Joe had several gouges on his face that didn't come from punches and the best information I could gather was that he had a headlock on Powell and was just about ready to give him the business when a bunch of Yankees pulled Joe off and somebody grabbed his face in the process. The only Yankee who tried to break it up, from what I could learn, was Joe DiMaggio." Of course.

One on one, Joe Cronin could take care of himself, against Jake Powell, or anyone else. The Irishman from San Francisco was a noted scrapper. "He was a pretty aggressive type," says Doerr. "He would do anything to protect his players."

"The guy would be there in a minute if anything was wrong," agrees Wagner, who is back in a Red Sox spring training uniform, just as he's been since 1938. "The minute you saw Powell charge our player, you knew he'd be there."

But as tough as he was, he couldn't handle the whole Yankee team, or, at least, a significant portion of it. "That was terrible, the way the Yankees beat up on Joe," says Doerr. "It was one of those things. We should have made sure we had some of our players go down the runway with him."

The Yankees won that game, 10–0, and they won the second game, 5–4. Cronin and Powell would get 10-game suspensions. The Yankees would win the pennant over Boston by 9½ games, but they would know Boston was around to stay. Archie McKain would be traded to the Tigers, where he would earn a World Series ring in 1940. Jake Powell would remain a controversial character. Cronin would manage the Red Sox until 1947 and would go on to be their general manager, the president of the American League, and a 1956 Hall of Fame inductee.

And Bobby Doerr will always remember the awesome crowd at Yankee Stadium. "It was just a constant rumble," he says. "All day long, just a constant rumble."

Not to mention the rumble in the runway.

A Constant Rumble. That sums up the Yankees and the Red Sox ever since, wouldn't you say?

"I would rather beat the Yankees once than any other team twice.... They were the best, and they were cocky, particularly in New York with those Yankee pinstripes on. It was as if you ought not to beat them. You ought to just go out there and rather politely lose."

—1940s Red Sox pitcher Tex Hughson

THEY SAID IT...

New York Times editor Mary Cantwell was not a hard-core baseball fan as an adult—she admits as much at the start of this essay. But she never forgot what legendary hitter Ted Williams and the rest of the Red Sox meant to her during her childhood, or what Joe DiMaggio and the Yankees meant to her sister.

"HATING DORIS"

(1993)
by Mary Cantwell

IN TRUTH, I AM not a fan. I don't know the names of the players and I am confused about what city has what franchise, and the leagues have been split into divisions that I choose not to recognize. Recently, I read something about a possible Japanese purchase of some share of some team. "The gall!" some people said, but I could summon no more than a yawn. The game will stay a game, won't it? It will still be nine men trying to outhit and outcatch nine other men, and afternoon shadows darkening the playing field until the floods come on and make the paling sky look sick.

My colleagues are mostly males, and on opening day a few of them don't show up at the office. Later they say they had to go to their grandmother's funeral, and then there are great bursts of laughter and an all-round jabbing of elbows. But I distrust the ho-ho-hos and the nudges to the ribs. I think they are simply observing a ritual, honoring an old custom. Showing up for the season's first pitch is one of the ways they know they are men. A real fan, I figure, is a fan for all innings. A real fan doesn't wait for the World Series, as my colleagues do, to start ho-ho-hoing again.

Once in a while, though, around the end of August, when I am flipping through the sports pages on my way to the crossword, a headline catches my eye. The Red Sox are in second place. Or third place. Or maybe even in first. Then I feel as I do when the drums roll and the high-school kids lift their cornets at the start of my hometown's Fourth of July parade. My stomach flutters, my eyes get damp around the edges, and my ribs get tight around my heart. "Maybe this time," I say to myself, knowing all the time that I know better.

Now I can scarcely believe it, the way it was for me on the hot summer mornings when we—my parents, a friend of theirs, and my sister, the Yankees fan—headed north on Route 1. Past Pawtucket, shabbiest of mill towns, we went, and Narragansett Race Track, and the two Attleboros, and the shallow ponds and skinny trees that lined the glory road to Boston. Glory Road because Boston was the home of Fenway Park: the "jewel box," my father called it. That's what everybody called it, the jewel box, a box that was crammed with emeralds because everything at Fenway Park was green, green, green. There was no advertising, nothing to detract from the game and the color of summer.

Leaving my house we would have seen, as we would have seen every morning that Boston was playing a home game, a woman named Miss Kellogg waiting for the bus. Miss Kellogg, a schoolteacher in her fifties, would travel the seventeen miles to Union Station in Providence. Then she would travel, by train, the forty miles to Boston. Then, by hook or by crook but probably another bus, she got to Fenway Park. Miss Kellogg was a real fan.

We all were, except for my grandfather, who adulated the Yankees, and my sister, who adulated him. Together they sat by his big radio, he with his right ear to its gothic facade, and cheered on their team. If their team was playing the Red Sox, we cast them into outer darkness. Ours was a civil household, no plates crashed against the walls. But we were serious about the Sox. The Red Sox were ours as surely as if they'd been based at

Guiteras Field, up in back of the junior high, and my grandfather and sister were incomprehensible to us. In casting their lot with the Yankees they were turning their backs not only on our team but on New England in general and Rhode Island in particular. To Rhode Island we gave the affection one gives the runt of the litter. We were infatuated with its size; we thought our state adorable.

It was also the best of all possible worlds in that, though in a sense it had declared its independence from Massachusetts centuries ago, Rhode Island had kept Boston for its own. The Hub is less a nickname than it is a fact; and the Sox belonged to us as much as they belonged to Lynn, or Dorchester, or Southie. Why neither my family, nor anyone else within earshot, ever evinced a similar passion for the Braves I do not know. Perhaps it had something to do with the National League. Perhaps it was simply Ted Williams.

Ted Williams was the first famous person I had ever seen and, unlike every famous person (but one) that I have seen since, he looked the part. Curiously, I have no memories whatsoever of him at bat, only of him standing alone in left field, as isolated by his celebrity as by his position. I don't recall his ever smiling or, for that matter, any expression crossing a face that was as soberly beautiful as Buster Keaton's. Today I flinch from photographs of a grinning Williams, fearing they'll efface my memory of that stern, solitary presence. His austerity precluded my ever having a crush on him, although I had just reached the age of falling in love with movie stars and he was handsomer than any of them. It would have been like having a crush on a monk.

I liked Bobby Doerr, too, as much for the solid thunk of his name as anything else. And Johnny Pesky's name, I figured, was what made him the scrambler that he was. As for Dom DiMaggio, a "little professor" was peculiarly suited to the Athens of America. Better yet, he was, my father claimed, the greatest of the DiMaggios even if it was his brother that got all the press. In fact Dom, standing for Boston, and Joe, standing for New York, symbolized the way in which we New Englanders defined the two cities. The one was class, the other mass.

Along the road to Boston my father pointed out landmarks from his personal, rather peculiar Baedeker. There was the diner where you could get the best buttered toast in the world, for instance, and the town that gave birth to America's plug-ugliest congressman. Above all there was the house on the Fenway, the house with the shamrocks carved into the shutters, in which lived James M. Curley, the former mayor of Boston. Like generations of New Englanders, my father had that weakness for scamps that made, and still makes, local politics a wonder of the universe—and that may explain the Red Sox' seemingly permanent place in local hearts.

It was when the car reached Commonwealth Avenue and its squatty six-story apartment houses that Boston began for us: and at the Hotel Somerset that we finally pulled in. Our pregame lunch at the Somerset was why my sister and I were dressed for baseball as formally as we would have been for church. As my brother-in-law, who is still hanging on to his Jimmie Foxx–autographed baseball, says, "You had to look nice for the Somerset."

From the hotel it was only a short walk to Fenway Park. Boston is hot in summer, hotter even than New York, and our faces were red and our upper lips beaded with sweat by the time we reached our box. But not for long. The green, that all-enveloping green, acted like air-conditioning.

The Sox jogged onto the field . . . and it is here that the film freezes. In my mind's eye, Ted Williams is in left field, forever fixed in place. Maybe I looked at him too intensely; maybe I was as blinded by him as I would have been had I stared too long at the sun. I cannot see more. The reel doesn't start unwinding until we are back in the car, and heading for home. The sky is streaked with red now and the air slouching through the car's open windows seems exhausted by the heat. My sister, who is younger than I by eighteen months, has fallen asleep.

That was my summer of the Red Sox. It was, I believe, only one summer and to this day I cannot account for there not being more. It must have been Ted's entering the Navy, though, and my father traveling all the time during World War II. The trips to Boston ended, and my sister and I were pretty much stuck in our small town. She crouched in the bushes outside our house scanning the skies for Stukas; I kept an eye on the harbor and imagined periscopes.

Still, I kept up with the team—in Rhode Island, it would have been impossible not to—and wept when Ted married a woman named Doris.

Too young for carnal longings, and ignorant besides, I was made uneasy by this capitulation to sexual affection. I was, in fact, like the boys at the Saturday matinee who squirmed and booed when it looked like the cowboy might kiss the lady.

Through junior high and high school, I went on rooting for the Red Sox but never went to another game. Even so, I saw Ted Williams again, this time in a novel—in Theodore Dreiser's *An American Tragedy.*

Charting the life and times of Ted Williams was a constant preoccupation of the *Providence Journal* and the tabloid *Boston Daily Record,* so just as I was aware of Ted's having eyesight just this side of Superman's so I also knew that his mother belonged to the Salvation Army, and that he had spent part of his childhood skulking behind a big bass drum as she, playing a cornet, marched her family through San Diego. When I opened *An American Tragedy* for the first time I was startled to read something I was sure I had read before.

It is "Dusk—of a summer night," and a man carrying a portable organ, a woman carrying a Bible and several hymnals, and their three children are walking through "the commercial heart of an American city." The man sets down the organ, the boy sets down a camp-stool for his older sister, the organist, and the mother says, "I should think it might be nice to sing twenty-seven tonight—'How Sweet the Balm of Jesus' Love.' . . .

"The boy moved restlessly from one foot to the other, keeping his eyes down, and for the most part only half singing. A tall and as yet slight figure, surmounted by an interesting head and face—white skin, dark hair—he . . . appeared indeed to resent and even to suffer from the position in which he found himself." The boy is Clyde Griffiths, as tragic a character as there is in American fiction, and in his childhood he is Ted Williams to the life.

Since Williams's mouth is legendarily foul, I should not like to hear his response to so purely literary an observation. But there it is. When Ted Williams wrote in *My Turn at Bat* that "I was embarrassed about my home, embarrassed that I never had quite as good clothes as some of the kids, embarrassed that my mother was out in the middle of the damn street all the time," he is the young Clyde Griffiths lamenting that his family was always "hard up," poorly dressed and "deprived of many comforts and pleasures which seemed common enough to others."

The famous, provided they are famous long enough to become embedded in the public consciousness, are always hung with bits and pieces of their admirers' selves. They become, in effect, armatures for dreams. My passion, and that is not too strong a word, for Ted Williams was only partly informed by enthusiasm for the home team and its most prominent player. Mostly it was fueled by the imagination of a bookish little girl who saw in him a Galahad incarnate. That, later, I saw in him the young Clyde Griffiths made him even more magic. To me Williams was human only when he opened his mouth and confirmed—again and again—my conviction that idols should seldom, if ever, speak.

Joe DiMaggio, on the other hand, was draped in love: my sister's love for our grandfather. Joe was her hero because he was his hero. If the Yankees were trailing, hopelessly trailing, and Joe had no more turns as bat, their hands would reach as one to turn off the radio.

It was on another hot morning that, years after the summer of the Red Sox, we set out for New York and Yankee Stadium and the treat of my sister's life. Bobby Feller was pitching against Joe DiMaggio and my father wanted us to see the contest. He wanted us to see everything there was to see in the world that we were soon to claim and that he was too soon to leave. He couldn't show us Chartres, he couldn't shepherd us across the Equator-those things we would have to do on our own—but, by God, he would, while he could, show us some great baseball. So we set forth, on a day that would melt marble, along the Merritt Parkway to Yankee Stadium.

We feared New York, feared it the minute my father told us to lock the car doors because we were entering the kind of neighborhood in which you had to be careful. This wasn't Commonwealth Avenue, these were slums whose blind windows were hung with limp curtains and slanted shades. Nor was this Fenway Park, this enormous stadium that had us climbing and climbing until our mother bade us stop because the heat and height were going to her head. This was everything I had ever heard about New York and its Yankees, this hugeness and this heat and, conversely, this chilling impersonality.

"Now I want you to watch the way Joe coils himself around the bat when he swings," my father said, joyous because New York was his town even if the Yankees were not his team. Yankee Stadium was no jewel box, but had we ever seen so many people in one place before? Of course we hadn't. We were shrinking to pin-dots.

As it was with Ted, so it was with Joe: I couldn't take my eyes off him either. Like Ted, he looked the part of a famous person. The isolation, the sense that he stood in a space that repelled invaders, was the same. But there was a difference. I could track Joe out of the outfield and into the batter's box. He got a hit off Bobby Feller, and he did indeed coil himself around the bat.

So now we had them. My sister had Joe and I had Ted, and we could both die happy because we had seen them in the flesh. "You musn't forget this day," my father said. "You musn't forget that you saw Joe DiMaggio *and* Bobby Feller." So we didn't, any more than we would have forgotten seeing Lee surrender to Grant, or David bean Goliath.

That was my last baseball game. My mother's, too, and my father's because he died the next year. Not my sister's: she kept it up, and she never deserted the Yankees. But it was not the last time I saw Joe DiMaggio. Once he passed me on Fifth Avenue, a tall, sallow man in a black raincoat, irrevocably separate from the crowd. "Guess who I saw today?" I crowed when I called my sister, jubilant because it was I, not she, who had nearly touched the hem of his garment. Thus, I said, is treachery rewarded. I hadn't forgotten how she cheered on the Yanks.

Now I watch baseball only on television, and only during those rare times when the Red Sox are in third place. Or in second. Or even in first. Then I wonder why I gave it up. I like this game; I like its lucidity. If I were to return, however, it would be out of nostalgia. Nostalgia is dangerous. If I followed the Red Sox long enough, before I knew it I'd be listening for *The Lone Ranger* and *Jack Armstrong, the All-American Boy*.

I like to look at photographs of Ted Williams, though: so young, so gaunt, so terribly handsome. Sometimes I like to talk about him as well. A few years ago, for instance, I was reminiscing with a friend who was growing up in Boston at precisely the same time that I was growing up in Rhode Island. She sees me as having been permanently ensconced in the local library and I see her as permanently languishing in a swanboat or in a box at the old Opera House, so we were both surprised when we both confessed to having kept Ted Williams scrapbooks. We talked about his batting average and the Boudreau shift and of how the service gypped him of his greatest seasons and then she said it, the thing that all little New England girls, however far from puberty, said about Ted Williams. "My God," she said, "how I hated Doris!"

Joe DiMaggio, Ted Williams, Dom DiMaggio

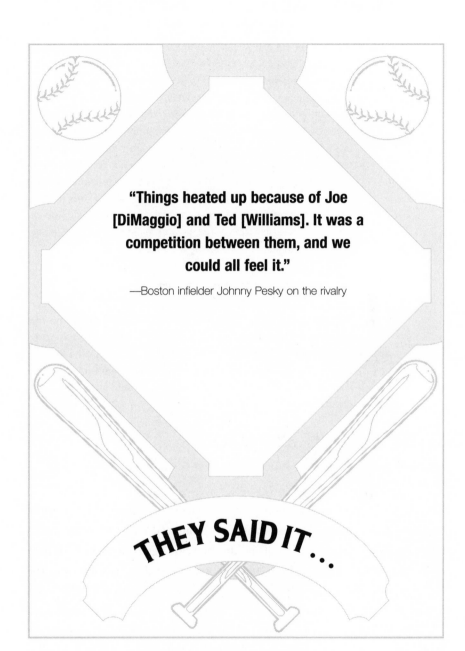

"Things heated up because of Joe [DiMaggio] and Ted [Williams]. It was a competition between them, and we could all feel it."

—Boston infielder Johnny Pesky on the rivalry

THEY SAID IT...

By 1946, World War II was over and so, it seemed, was the era of Yankee domination over the Red Sox. Boston coasted to the American League pennant that year with such ease that many baseball writers and fans believed they were witnessing the dawn of a Red Sox dynasty. But the Yankees were still the Yankees and the Indians and Tigers fielded strong teams in the late 1940s as well. In 1947, the Yankees reclaimed the pennant, and Detroit edged the Red Sox for second place. Still, high hopes remained in Boston. The seasons that followed all seemed to come down to the wire in the American League. Each year Pulitzer Prize–winning sportswriter Red Smith was on hand to describe the action. The following articles describe three pivotal Yankees–Red Sox games from three memorable seasons.

THREE BY RED SMITH

The final scheduled game of Boston's 1948 season had no real meaning for their opponents, the Yankees—Boston had knocked them out of the playoff hunt just the day before. But the Red Sox were still alive. They could force a one-game playoff for the American League pennant with a win—*if* Detroit beat Cleveland a half a country away.

"THEY PLAYED IT BY RADIO"

From the *New York Herald Tribune* (October 4, 1948)
by **Red Smith**

BOSTON—IT WAS A day when malice lay over everything, thick as mustard on a frankfurter, and you could reach out and feel it like something tangible. The Yankees, killed off by the Red Sox yesterday, were out here in Fenway Park to gouge back an eye for the one they had lost, and the Red Sox, inspired by the loftiest sort of cupidity, wanted that World Series money so badly they could taste it.

The 31,354 specimens penned in the park had a sort of shine on their faces, the sweatily eager look that a bullfight crowd wears when the bull is five runs ahead of the matador in the ninth inning.

It was the third inning and the Red Sox, who had been two runs behind, had scored three times and had two runners on the bases, with one out and Bill Goodman at bat. Chuck Dressen, the Yankees' opulent coach, was out in the middle of the diamond talking to Bob Porterfield, the rookie pitcher, and the crowd started to scream.

At first, the notion was that the customers were only trying to work on Porterfield, hoping to shake the kid's unnatural poise. But there was a different sort of note in the crowd's voice. People behind the Boston dugout were standing and cupping hands to mouths and shouting things to the players, and after a little while it was apparent what was happening.

There were portable radios in the stands and the customers had just heard about that third inning in Cleveland. The word had reached the press box. The Tigers had a run home and the bases filled with one out. Then another flash came "Wakefield doubled."

You should have seen that crowd. Everybody was on his feet, and everybody was screaming, but the ball players acted as though they hadn't heard anything. Goodman singled, driving in Boston's fourth run.

The crowd made a fair fuss about that, but that was nothing. The small, unseen man who lives in the scoreboard swung a panel open and took down the number of the Cleveland pitcher and put up another. He took down 19 and put up 26, which meant that Bob Feller had been replaced by Sam Zoldak.

You should have heard that crowd. They weren't watching the Red Sox, who were scoring another run just then on a force-out by Birdie Tebbetts. They were watching the scoreboard, where the figure 5 went up for Detroit. That was a mistake, and a moment later the sign was changed and the number 4 was posted, the real Detroit score for the third inning.

Now the third inning was over up here. The Red Sox were in front, 5 to 2, and out in Cleveland the Tigers were leading, 4 to 0. Everybody knew Hal Newhouser was pitching for Detroit. Everybody knew that if Boston could stay ahead, there would be a tie for the American League pennant. Nobody thought for a moment that Newhouser would blow a four-run lead.

Of course he didn't. And of course the Red Sox won, setting up the first play-off the American League has had. But it wasn't easy. The Yankees have a guy named Joe DiMaggio. Sometimes a fellow gets a little tired of writing about DiMaggio; a fellow thinks, "there must be some other ball player in the world worth mentioning." But there isn't really, not worth mentioning in the same breath with Joe DiMaggio.

That guy, DiMaggio, had hit a double in the first inning and driven in New York's first run. He had grounded out in the third, but in the fifth Phil Rizzuto singled. Bobby Brown doubled Rizzuto to third, and then Joe came up. There were two runs on the bases and DiMaggio was the tying run at the plate.

First base was open. Up in the press box, people said, "I don't care how wrong it is to put the tying run on base. They have got to put this guy on."

But Joe McCarthy didn't. Heaven knows, the Red Sox manager is aware of what DiMaggio can do. The champ did it often enough for McCarthy when they were together on the Yankees. But McCarthy let Joe Dobson pitch to the guy. So, naturally, the guy hit another double, slamming the ball to the left-field fence and dragging his dead left leg stiffly as he ran to second base while two runs came home.

He had now driven home three of New York's four runs. He had twice made a contest of this game. He brought the Yankees up close enough to scare the daylights out of the Red Sox, until Joe's brother Dom hit one over the wall in the sixth.

Joe went on to make four hits in five times up, in his last game of the year. When he singled in the ninth, Bucky Harris sent Steve Souchok in to run for him. Maybe Bucky wanted the guy to walk off by himself, so he could get a personal tribute from the crowd instead of just going off, unnoticed, along with eight other guys. Because Harris thinks of things like that. Or, maybe, Bucky just wanted a sound runner on first base.

Anyway, Souchok went in and DiMaggio limped off, and the crowd stood up and yelled for the guy who had done more damage to Boston than any ten other guys they could mention. He tipped his cap and disappeared into the runway leading to the clubhouse.

That's all, except for one small story. Last night, Joe and his brother Dom dined together. Joe said, "You gave us hell today, but tomorrow I'll hit my fortieth home run."

His little brother said, "I don't think you will, but I'm gonna hit my ninth."

One of them had to be right.

Cleveland beat Boston 8–3 in the one-game playoff for the American League pennant.

The Yankees and Red Sox met under similarly tense circumstances again the following September. Just a week remained in
the 1949 season. By the time the game was over, the Red Sox had
climbed past the Yanks and into first place in the American
League . . . and the Yankees had learned the downside of fielding
a short shortstop.

"A QUARTER-INCH AWAY"

from the *New York Herald Tribune* (September 27, 1949)
by **Red Smith**

AT 5:18 P.M. YESTERDAY, guys in gray flannels erupted from the Red Sox
dugout and charged across the lawn of Yankee Stadium to beat upon Ellis
Kinder's spine with jubilant paws. Johnny Pesky flung a headlock on Al
Zarilla and hugged the outfielder to his small bosom in one of the great
love scenes of modern drama. The Yankees walked off the field, and
maybe out of the pennant race.

After three hours and eighteen minutes of frantic and untidy striving,
the Yankees had lost a ball game by one run and a quarter of an inch; they
had lost first place in the American League for the first time since the
season opened last April 19; Ralph Houk, a former major in the Rangers,
had lost a desperate engagement with the most sweetly forgiving umpires
on earth; 66,156 witnesses had lost their voices.

The game that put the Red Sox in first place and the Yankees second
turned upside-down on a line drive which failed by the width of Phil
Rizzuto's little finger to become a triple play. Dom DiMaggio hit the ball
in the eighth with two Bostonese on base, none out, and the Yankees
leading, 6 to 3. Rizzuto leaped. The ball smacked the very tips of his
gloved fingers, seemed to lodge there for a fragment of time, then tore
loose and dribbled into left field for a single.

The count had been three balls, two strikes on DiMaggio, so both runners were away with the pitch. Both were far off their bases, could have
been retired easily had Rizzuto held the ball. Instead, the inning lasted
until Boston had scored four runs and won the game.

When Pesky slid under Houk with the winning run on a squeeze play, the Yankee pennant bubble and the Yankee catcher exploded. It is just barely possible that Major Houk saw more violent action in the Battle of the Bulge than that which followed.

Shrieking, he hurled himself from Willie Grieve, the plate umpire, and clawed at the honorable stomach. Joe Page, the pitcher, threw his glove aloft and rushed in, howling imprecations. White uniforms converged in a noisy swirl, and with them came Mr. Grieve's colleagues—Cal Hubbard, Charley Berry and Joe Paparella.

Mr. Hubbard, the largest peacemaker on the Eastern Seaboard, patted the major's breastbone with vast, placating paws. The major circled Mr. Hubbard, boring in upon Mr. Grieve. Mr. Berry, once an All-America end at Lafayette, over-shifted to the left and got a propitiating clutch upon the major's sleeve. Pigeons circled in affrighted flocks overhead, dropping olive branches.

At length something that might be loosely described as peace descended. Because their toleration is as great as their big, warm hearts, the umpires didn't chase anybody. The game went on and the last New York hope vanished when Zarilla, who had plucked a fly by Johnny Lindell out of the right-field seats in the second inning, made a running leap in the ninth and grabbed a drive that Tommy Henrich had aimed at a client's wishbone.

It will be written that the game was played in a bona fide World Series atmosphere. That isn't altogether true. During the more exciting moments, members of the Stadium Club who pay hundreds of dollars for season tickets stood at the bar and drank, listening to the game by radio. During a World Series, they sit at tables and play gin rummy.

There was something of the World Series attitude in the dugouts, though. The Yankees had all the carefree joviality to be expected of a team that had squandered a plushy lead by losing four of the last five games. The Red Sox grinned and Joe McCarthy, their keeper, relaxed in his office.

Casey Stengel had asked Henrich to try to play right field and Tommy, gently fingering the damaged vertebrae which he keeps wrapped in a straitjacket, had said, "I will for you, Case." Now somebody recalled the powerful throw with which Zarilla had retired Henrich at the plate Sunday in Boston.

"Did you ever see a better throw, Tommy?"

"I didn't even see that one," Henrich said.

McCarthy was laughing and spinning yarns in the small room which he used to occupy as manager of the Yankees. Casually he brought up a recent report in a Boston paper that he would be let out after this season, win or lose.

"He fired me," he remarked of the reporter who wrote the story. "There's just one thing I know; he won't get the job."

"Reminds me," he chuckled, "of Bill Dahlen when he managed Brooklyn. He's leaving the park one day when a fellow comes running up and says, 'Well, Bill, I hear you're losing your job.' 'I dunno,' Bill says, 'but you ain't gonna get it, you slob.'"

The Yankees lost this game, and with it their lead in the American League, but there were still five games left in the season. Dave Anderson describes the 1949 season, including the furious race to the finish, later in this anthology.

By 1950, talk of a Boston dynasty was dying away—but the Sox refused to go quietly.

"THE VACANT CHAIR"

From the *New York Herald Tribune* (September 24, 1950)
by Red Smith

HALF AN HOUR BEFORE the people giving an automobile to Lefty McDermott threw out the first polysyllable, amplifiers outside Yankee Stadium were warning the crowds that all reserved seats were exhausted. This was erroneous. During the first game of the itsy-bitsy World Series between the Yankees and Red Sox, the seat reserved for Casey Stengel remained unoccupied. It was Casey that got exhausted.

Before the game, the doughty field marshal of the Yankees did deign to sit down, if you can call his posture sitting. While the players warmed up he assumed a characteristic pose, in which the only part of him in contact with the bench was a spot on the back of his neck about the size of a silver dollar. Disposed thus in defiance of all natural laws, he plaited his legs into a long braid and, folding his arms, hugged himself tightly, as though wrapping himself up in himself against the afternoon's gray chill.

It was Yogi Berra who called attention to the weather. His comely features were unshaven and somebody remarked about the thick shrubbery on his jaw.

"I'm wearin' it to keep warm," Yogi explained sensibly. "I got a little cold."

Physicists were still studying this when Ed Lopat went to work on the pitching rubber. Thereafter, Marshal Stengel covered more ground than both DiMaggios. A witness watching nobody but Casey could have told pretty accurately what was happening on the field.

When Dom DiMaggio opened the first inning for Boston by cowtailing a fraternal triple over the head of J. DiMaggio in center field, Casey clutched for support and got hold of an upright supporting the dugout roof. He stood frozen. So did Dominic as Lopat retired Johnny Pesky, Ted Williams and Junior Stephens in order.

Nobody knew it then, but that brotherly belt of Dominic's was to be the only loud hit off Lopat all day. It was almost as loud as the boos which welcomed Sir Williams on his first time at bat in the Stadium since early July.

In the Yankees' first inning, Berra's beard hissed in the breeze as he rushed down to first base in time to beat a double-play throw which would have retired the side. Then Joe DiMaggio took one pitch for a ball and sliced a fly into the first row seats in right field. Joe's hit traveled about 310 feet, his kid brother's approximately 450. The big guy got two runs, junior got exercise. In baseball, there is no substitute for experience and savvy.

As the ball leaped from Joe's bat, Mr. Stengel leaped from the dugout. His cap was off and he was springing about in such a whirling frenzy he looked like several Hopi Indians in a tribal sun dance. He swung his cap again and again in an encircling gesture that said: "All the way around! All the way!"

In the second inning, Bobby Doerr tied into a pitch and lashed it on a line over second base. Clean, stand-up double, one would say as it started.

Joe raced in on a long angle to his left, thrust out his glove, palm up like a landlord taking a pay-off under the table. The ball snuggled into the pocket.

Casey stood on the dugout step, his face blankly agape. His chin, which is fairly long in repose, touched his breastbone.

In the third inning, Joe charged into left field, reached up and plucked a drive by Dominic out of the air. Casey shoved his paws into his hip pockets and strutted the length of the dugout, his chest out. A few minutes later he was straining across the bat rack, his jaw waggling so fast it was a mere blur. Joe Paparella, the plate umpire, had called a strike against Bill Johnson and Mr. Stengel was offering a suggestion.

Johnson walked, Phil Rizzuto doubled and Joe DiMaggio was purposely passed, filling the bases. John Mize hooked a single into right for two runs. This flushed Yankees out of the dugout like a covey of quail, but this time Mr. Stengel indulged in no theatrics. His manner was that of a commander whose operations were proceeding precisely according to plan.

He responded similarly when Hank Bauer followed with a double good for the fifth New York run. Casey popped up the steps so he could follow the ball's flight into right field, then relaxed, planting an elbow on the dugout roof and leaning there at peace with the world.

By this time early returns were in from Cleveland and the scoreboard recorded the beginning of Detroit's ordeal out there. With the Tigers headed for defeat and Lopat breezing along on a five-run cushion, just ambling toward his fourth shutout of the season, Mr. Stengel was relatively content.

As the afternoon darkened and New York prospects brightened, he did a good deal of pacing, shouting, wigwagging and leaping about. But his carriage was jaunty now, with just the proper touch of swagger for the manager of a club leading its league by a game and a half, with a three-game bulge on the Red Sox.

If he frowned, ever so slightly, it was in concentration, thinking of today's game.

The Yankees would win the 1950 pennant, and 12 of the next 14 AL pennants besides, before sliding into mediocrity in the mid 1960s. For Boston, 1950 was the end of an era. The club wouldn't finish another season within ten games of first place until 1967.

Three pennant races stand out in the 100-year rivalry of the Yankees and the Red Sox. The first was 1904, the most recent, 1978. In between there was 1949.

"1949"

from *Pennant Races* (1997)
by Dave Anderson

JOE DiMAGGIO HAD SIGNED baseball's first $100,000 contract in 1949, but ten weeks into the schedule he had not earned a penny. Even before the Yankees assembled in St. Petersburg, Florida, for spring training, he complained that his right heel felt "like it had a nail" in it. During a Dallas exhibition game about a week before the opener, he limped to the dugout.

"The pain's unbearable," he said.

Dr. George Bennett, the Baltimore orthopedist who had performed bone spur surgery on the heel several months earlier, recommended X-ray treatments and salt injections to dissolve calcium deposits. But the season had begun with DiMaggio on crutches, wearing a camel's hair coat instead of his pin-striped uniform. The healing process had continued to be slow. Now, in the Yankee clubhouse at Fenway Park before a June 28 night game, manager Casey Stengel, surrounded by New York and Boston sportswriters, was waiting to learn if his thirty-four-year-old centerfielder was finally ready to play.

"If he tells me he can play, he'll play," Stengel said.

"Why didn't he come up today on the train with the team?"

"He stayed in New York this morning to see if he could find a trick shoe to take some of the strain off his heel. He took an afternoon plane."

"How's he looked in batting practice?"

"He's been working out now about a week and a half and he says it feels pretty good," Stengel said. "We told him from the first to do it his way. You don't have to worry about a man like him. He'll give it to you when he's got it. The real trouble with a man like him is keeping him from trying to do too much too soon."

Joe DiMaggio had not yet earned any of his $100,000 salary, but he had earned Casey Stengel's description as "a man like him."

Over his Hall of Fame career, the stately slugger known as the Yankee Clipper would hit .325 with 361 homers and 1,537 runs batted in despite Yankee Stadium's vast valley in left-centerfield, despite losing three seasons during World War II to Army service. In 1941 he had hit safely in a record fifty-six consecutive games. One of eight children of an Italian immigrant-fisherman, he had a sixty-one-game streak with his hometown San Francisco Seals of the Pacific Coast League in 1933 as an eighteen-year-old rookie. But the true measure of his importance to the Yankees was their success. In his thirteen seasons, the Yankees would win nine World Series and ten American League pennants. With his dignified manner and dignified dark suits, white shirts, silk ties, and glossy black shoes, he popularized the word *class* in baseball.

"When he walked into the clubhouse," Yankee clubhouse man Pete Sheehy once said, "the lights flickered."

Now, with Casey Stengel talking to the writers in the Fenway Park clubhouse, Joe DiMaggio arrived. As he changed into his uniform, he realized that the manager was peering at him through a gap in the writers. Peering back, DiMaggio caught Stengel's gaze and nodded. As if on cue, Stengel looked around at the writers.

"I've just been told the man can play," he said. "So he's in the lineup, batting fourth."

Not that anybody was expecting much. The night before, after more than a week of batting practice mostly against Al Schacht, the former major league pitcher and baseball clown who owned a midtown Manhattan restaurant, DiMaggio had popped up four times against Kirby Higbe's knuckleball in a mayor's charity exhibition game with the New York Giants at Yankee Stadium. And tonight he would be facing the flaming fastball of Mickey McDermott, a rookie lefthander with a 2–0 record who had blanked the St. Louis Browns on three hits in his previous start.

"Not the ideal pitcher to come back against," DiMaggio told teammate Tommy Henrich. "I haven't faced a lefthander since spring training."

But on his flight to Boston, he had explained to a friend, Dick Allen, a Boston businessman, that he intended to play because of Fenway Park's nearby leftfield wall, alias the Green Monster, alias the Wall.

"You don't get a chance to swing at that wall too often," DiMaggio said. "I've already missed three of our eleven games in Fenway this year."

Even without DiMaggio, the Yankees were in first place with a 41–24 start, four and one-half games ahead of the Philadelphia Athletics, five games ahead of the Red Sox. But with ten victories in their last eleven games, if this Red Sox team managed by Joe McCarthy, whose Yankees had won seven World Series and eight pennants, could sweep the three-game series, the race would be on. That hope had attracted 36,228 customers, a Fenway Park record for a night game. Quietly, all those Red Sox rooters were hoping that if DiMaggio was rusty, the Yankees might slump. But when he walked up to the plate to lead off the second inning, he received a standing ovation from the Red Sox fans, who always seemed to admire him as much as Yankee fans did.

"McDermott kept throwing his fastball and I kept fouling them off, swinging late," he would say years later. "I must've fouled off six or seven pitches."

On the next swing, DiMaggio drilled a single into leftfield and scored on Hank Bauer's three-run homer. The next inning, he slammed a two-run homer into the net atop the Wall for a 5–4 lead. But with two out in the ninth, Ted Williams was up.

"Joe would appreciate it," catcher Yogi Berra said to Williams, "if you would end this game by hitting a nice easy fly."

Williams did just that, lifting a fly ball to center that DiMaggio caught. "That fly was hit just right to catch," DiMaggio said later. "Ted sometimes hits sinkers which are tough, but this one had a nice loft to it." And the Yankee slugger's voice had a nice lilt to it. "My legs tightened up on me in the late innings. The heel doesn't bother me now, but it probably will in the morning." If it did, it didn't affect him in Wednesday afternoon's game. After the Red Sox knocked out lefthander Tommy Byrne in the first and took a 7–1 lead, DiMaggio hit a three-run homer in the fifth off righthander Ellis Kinder just over the top of the Wall into the screen.

"Flukiest homer I've ever hit," DiMaggio would remember. "He threw me a pitch that broke on the outside. I was fooled, but with two strikes I was protecting the plate. I just tried to get a piece of it. If a bird had been perched on the fence above the 379-foot sign, the ball would've hit it."

Usually stoic, DiMaggio was smiling as he approached home plate, maybe because of that "flukiest" homer. Charlie Silvera, the next batter, greeted him at the plate. So did base runners Phil Rizzuto and Tommy Henrich, who draped their arms around him as they trotted to the dugout. Gene Woodling's three-run double in the seventh created a 7–7 tie, then DiMaggio hit another homer in the eighth off lefthander Earl Johnson.

"That was off a curveball," DiMaggio remembered. "It hung there waiting to be smacked."

After that 9–7 victory, one of the Yankees welcomed the Boston writers with "Here come the undertakers from the Red Sox burial." And the Red Sox would lose again Thursday, 6–3, when DiMaggio hit another three-run homer, a towering shot in the seventh off lefthander Mel Parnell that clanged against a metal light tower in left-centerfield above his youngest brother, Red Sox centerfielder Dom DiMaggio.

"On that one," DiMaggio recalled, "I really caught all of it."

Over the three games, DiMaggio hit four homers and a single, scored five runs, and knocked in nine. All this after having missed the first ten weeks of the season. All this against the rival Red Sox in their own ballpark.

"I really surprised myself," DiMaggio would say years later. "We shocked 'em. They didn't say a word. Not even my brother."

Suddenly the Yankees had opened an eight-game lead on the third-place Red Sox, and Joe DiMaggio had opened Williams's old wounds. "The Red Sox," *Boston Herald* sports columnist Bill Cunningham wrote after the second game, "have no one great dynamic personality who can lift them bodily by his very presence and his tremendous performance. In short, they have no Joe DiMaggio. He's a pressure player, a money player and a clutch player. Anytime he walks up to the plate, the game walks up there with him. The Red Sox counterpart is Ted Williams and the record is beginning to say in disturbing repetition that Mr. Williams does not come through in the clutch. Not against major opposition. Not when the blow means the lead or the game. He didn't do it in the 1946 World Series. He didn't do it in the all-important playoff game with Cleveland last year. He didn't do it [in this series]. This is no attempt to ride Mr. Williams. His batting average is always beautiful. His r.b.i.'s are impressive. He hits magnificent home runs. He generally gets on and he usually scores. But we're talking in terms of the prime Power Man who, even if crippled, can limp up there as New York's famed Yankee Clipper did and turn the contest around with a mighty swing of his mace. We're furthermore talking about the type of nonpareil who is expected to do it, who can be depended upon to do it. The Yankees have one, and they now have him back."

Williams was accustomed to being roasted by Dave Egan, the *Boston American*'s vitriolic sports columnist. But now, with Cunningham's words stuck in their slugger's craw, the Red Sox took a midnight train to Philadelphia where the loss of a July 4 doubleheader dropped them twelve games behind the Yankees.

Most people in Boston had surrendered, but Joe McCarthy hadn't. After those two losses in Philadelphia, the Red Sox manager said, "We can still win the pennant. I'm not saying we're going to, but we can." Even though his pennant-winning Yankee teams with Babe Ruth, Lou Gehrig, and Joe DiMaggio had usually torn the American League apart by September, cigar-smoking Marse Joe had always been too successful to surrender. He knew he had a team good enough to win, virtually the same team that had lost a pennant playoff to the Cleveland Indians the year before. Williams, Dom DiMaggio, and Al Zarilla in the outfield. Billy Goodman at first base, future Hall of Famer Bobby Doerr at second, slugger Vern Stephens at shortstop, Johnny Pesky at third. Birdie Tebbetts catching Mel Parnell, Ellis Kinder, Joe Dobson, and Chuck Stobbs. And soon McCarthy's patience was rewarded; the Red Sox surged. Even when they lost a September 11 doubleheader in Philadelphia, McCarthy wasn't discouraged.

"Whether we won or lost today didn't make much difference," he said. "We'd still have to beat the Yankees in those five games at the end of the season."

Those five games: two in Boston on September 24 and 25, a makeup game in New York the next day, and the final two in New York on October 2 and 3. But if those five games were to mean anything, the Red Sox had to be within striking distance by then. Although the Yankees' spirits had been lifted by DiMaggio, relief lefthander Joe Page and shortstop Phil Rizzuto had kept them atop the standings.

"The Yankees have pitching, and they have Joe Page," said Zack Taylor, the St. Louis Browns' manager. "If Joe McCarthy had Page, the Red Sox would be ten games in front."

Joe Page had emerged in 1947 after a scolding by DiMaggio for his nocturnal habits. Pitching poorly, Page appeared on his way back to the minors. To console himself after a bad game, he stayed out long after midnight before returning to the hotel room he shared with DiMaggio.

"What the hell are you doing?" DiMaggio had snapped. "The way you live, you're letting the team down and you're letting yourself down."

Page's world turned. That season he produced a 14–8 record with a 2.48 earned run average and seventeen saves. In the 1947 World Series against the Brooklyn Dodgers, he was credited with the victory in the decisive seventh game after having saved another triumph. In 1948 he skidded to 7–8 with a 4.26 earned run average, creating the since disproved theory that a relief pitcher cannot be effective two years in a row. But in 1949, when Americans hummed the songs from Rodgers and Hammerstein's *South Pacific,* he would have a 13–8 record with a 2.59 earned run average and twenty-seven saves. He would never be this good again, but now, as the Yankees moved through September, he was the man coming out of the bullpen whenever starters Vic Raschi, Allie Reynolds, Ed Lopat, or Tommy Byrne faltered.

"Joe Page," said Casey Stengel, "is a relief pitcher who provides relief."

Phil Rizzuto provided other elements: sure hands on a ground ball, an accurate arm, an underrated bat, deft bunts, and flawless base running. At five-six and 150 pounds, he had grown up in Brooklyn but was dismissed as too small at Dodger and Giant tryouts. Casey Stengel, then the Dodger manager, told him, "Go get a shoeshine box." But a Yankee scout, Paul Krichell, signed Rizzuto and now, ironically, Stengel was the Yankee manager.

"I wouldn't want you to repeat this to my owners," Stengel told the writers, "but I'd gladly pay my way around the circuit following this team just to watch my shortstop perform. He can do everything. He makes unbelievable plays. He can hit a long ball when he wants to. He can beat out bunts to both sides of the plate. One or two shortstops may beat him in the RBI column, but that's all. He leads in every other department."

Rizzuto would bat .275 and score 110 runs as a leadoff man for the first time in his career, one of Stengel's many moves in showing that he was more manager than comedian.

When the Yankees finished third in 1948, general manager George Weiss fired Bucky Harris and hired Stengel, who would be the most famous manager in this famous franchise's history: seven World Series titles (including a record five straight) and ten pennants in his twelve seasons. But the choice surprised most baseball people. In nine seasons directing the Dodgers and the Boston Braves, his teams had finished as high as fifth only twice. In his twelve seasons as a minor league manager, his teams had won only two pennants, twenty years apart. At the Yankee news conference announcing his hiring, fifty-eight-year-old Charles Dillon Stengel justified his reputation.

"I want first of all," he began, "to thank Mr. Bob Topping for this opportunity."

Dan Topping was the Yankee co-owner, not his brother Bob, but the mix-up was understandable. Bob was in the headlines then for his marital problems with Arlene Judge, the film actress who had once been Dan's wife. Not that Dan Topping was annoyed. He laughed along with everybody else. Laughter was to become the most common reaction to the

Yankee manager over the next twelve seasons. Laughter at his syntax. Laughter at his philosophy. And his laughter on his way to the bank with all those World Series shares. But in 1949 he had not yet convinced anybody that he was a shrewd manager.

"There'll be some changes, but we'll go slow," he said. "You can tear down a club a lot quicker than you can build it up."

Stengel's primary change was installing a platoon system, notably with Bobby Brown and Billy Johnson at third base, with Hank Bauer and Gene Woodling in the outfield. Stengel believed that righthanded batters hit better against lefthanded pitchers, and lefthanded batters against righthanded pitchers. The players didn't agree, but they couldn't disagree with the results: the Yankees were in first place. And sometimes even the players agreed that Stengel had a mystic touch.

"In the middle of one game," Bauer remembered, "the old man put Cliff Mapes in rightfield, moved me to leftfield, and we both threw a guy out at the plate. But he never told us who was playing and who wasn't. We had to check the lineup card every day."

Stengel's lineup card also had future Hall of Fame catcher Yogi Berra, whose throwing had been polished by coach Bill Dickey, a Hall of Fame catcher himself. In one of his first inspired one-liners, Berra acknowledged, "Bill Dickey learned me his experience." Nobody had to learn Berra how to hit. He would wallop twenty homers and drive in ninety-one runs. Tommy Henrich, moved to first base from rightfield after DiMaggio's return, would whack twenty-four homers and knock in eighty-five runs. Henrich had been impressed with Stengel early in the season on a train about to leave Philadelphia after a loss. Even before the train pulled out, four Yankees were sitting around playing "Twenty Questions," then a popular radio game show. But when Stengel realized what the four players were doing, he glared.

"I got a question for you guys," the new manager snapped. "Which one of you ain't going to be here tomorrow?"

But on September 18, with the Red Sox now only two and one-half games behind, the Yankees had gathered for a Sunday afternoon game with the Indians when they learned that DiMaggio was ill. He remained in his Elysee Hotel suite that he shared with his good friend George

Solotaire, a New York ticket broker. Up in Boston that afternoon the Red Sox routed the Chicago White Sox, 11–5. Williams hit his thirty-ninth and fortieth homers and drove in 6 runs for a total of 153, Vern Stephens hit his fortieth homer for 150 runs batted in, and Ellis Kinder coasted to his twenty-first victory. But the Yankees also won, 7–3, with Joe Page pitching the last three innings.

"DiMaggio is running a high fever," Yankee publicist Arthur (Red) Patterson told the writers. "He might miss tomorrow's game too."

It was more than a high fever. Soon the diagnosis was changed to the flu, then to viral pneumonia. "I'd flood the sheets with perspiration," DiMaggio would say years later. "The chambermaid had to redo the bed every few hours." Monday, with the Red Sox idle, lefthander Ed Lopat, who relied on junk-ball pitches, stopped the Indians, 6–0, on a five-hitter. The Yankees were three games up. Tuesday the Yankees won again, 3–1, as Page preserved Allie Reynolds's 17–5 record. The Red Sox won, 5–3, after Joe McCarthy disrupted Bob Lemon's no-hit bid by complaining to plate umpire Cal Hubbard that the Indian righthander was fingering the peak of his cap between pitches.

"Look at his cap," McCarthy demanded.

Soon after Hubbard ordered Lemon to discard his sweat-stained cap for a new one, Mel Parnell's sixth-inning single spoiled Lemon's no-hitter and sparked a five-run rally. Parnell's twenty-fourth victory tied the Red Sox record for a lefthander set by Babe Ruth, who was 24–13 in 1917 before switching to the outfield. At dinner that night in a Boston restaurant, Lemon noticed a gray fedora behind the bar.

"Who's hat is that?" Lemon asked.

"Tom Yawkey left it here one night," the bartender said.

"Let me borrow it for a day."

When the next day's game was about to start, Lemon, wearing the gray fedora instead of his Indian cap, sauntered behind home plate and stared at Hubbard.

"This cap all right?" Lemon asked.

"Fine," the umpire said, smiling.

That afternoon the Red Sox, after trailing, 3–1, rallied to win, 9–6, on Williams's forty-first homer into their bullpen off Steve Gromek. When the Boston writers arrived in the Red Sox clubhouse, Williams stared at Bill Cunningham.

"Can't hit in the clutch?" Williams said with a sneer.

That afternoon in New York the Yankees had taken an early 8–1 lead. All the Red Sox players had left their clubhouse by the time equipment manager Johnny Orlando hurried into McCarthy's office.

"The White Sox beat the Yanks, nine to eight," Orlando said. "Gus Zernial hit a three-run homer off Page in the ninth."

Calmly flicking the ashes off his cigar, McCarthy looked up and said, "What am I supposed to do? Jump out of my chair?" Even though Page had failed, for a change, McCarthy knew that he had nobody in his bullpen like the Yankee lefthander. To preserve that afternoon's victory, McCarthy had used his ace righthander and legendary drinker, Ellis Kinder, for the last three innings. Credited with the victory, Kinder was now 22–5. Since the Red Sox were not scheduled Thursday and Friday, he was still McCarthy's choice to start Saturday against the Yankees in the first of those five games that presumably would decide the pennant.

"I'll be ready Saturday," he had said. "This was just a workout. The arm feels great. I only threw fifteen pitches in the bullpen."

Thursday the Yankees were rained out in Washington, creating a doubleheader Friday afternoon. They lost the opener, 9–8, in the tenth inning when righthander Sid Hudson's pop fly off Page fell between Henrich, who had backed off the ball, and second baseman George Stirnweiss, who lunged too late for it. The Yankees won the second game, 7–1, behind righthander Fred Sanford, so they remained two games up. But when they arrived in Boston the next morning they were still without Joe DiMaggio.

"His temperature is nearly normal and his appetite is good," Dr. Jacques Fischl reported. "He's better, but he's not ready to play."

True to his word, Kinder was ready to pitch. His six-hitter blanked the Yankees, 3–0, as Williams slammed his forty-second homer twenty-six rows deep into the wing of the rightfield grandstand. With his curveball creating four called third strikes in his thirteenth consecutive victory, Kinder was now 23–5, including 4–0 against the Yankees, whose lead had been sliced to one game. But when McCarthy was congratulated, he shrugged.

"What for?" the Red Sox manager said. "It's just another game. There's another tomorrow."

Sunday's game produced another Red Sox victory, their ninth straight, and a tie for first place. Johnny Pesky slashed a double in the first, knocked in two runs with a single in the second, and his seventh-inning single off Allie Reynolds preceded Williams's forty-third homer. Parnell spun a four-hitter, 4–1, for a 25–7 record.

"You pitched a great game, boy," McCarthy said.

"Thank you, Mr. McCarthy," the lefthander said.

Up in the press box, Bill Cunningham began typing an apology to Ted Williams for what the *Herald* sports columnist had written about him during DiMaggio's midseason return. In the clubhouse, the photographers were asking Williams to pose with Parnell and Pesky.

"Just one shot," the slugger told them.

After the first flashbulb popped, Williams turned and strode to his locker. Soon the Red Sox were boarding a train at the Back Bay station for Monday's makeup game at Yankee Stadium, the start of the season's final week. When the Red Sox went on to Washington for three games, the Yankees would remain at the Stadium for three against Philadelphia. Then they would finish the season Saturday and Sunday in New York against each other. But now, with the two teams tied for first place, Monday's game attracted 66,156 to the House That Ruth Built, the Babe Ruth the Red Sox had sold to the Yankees in 1920, the Babe Ruth whose departure from Boston created the title of Dan Shaughnessy's 1990 book about the Red Sox' frustrations, *The Curse of the Bambino*.

With first place at stake, Monday's pitchers were Mickey McDermott and Tommy Byrne, two wild lefthanders, in what developed into a wild game.

To protect a 6–3 lead, Stengel called for Page in the fifth, but by the eighth the lefthander had lost his fastball. Tebbetts led off with a single, and pinch hitter Lou Stringer walked. Dom DiMaggio singled off Rizzuto's glove for one run. When Stirnweiss muffed Pesky's grounder, another run scored. Williams's grounder was ruled a hit when Page forgot to cover first. Stephens's sacrifice fly drove in the tying run. Doerr dropped a squeeze-play bunt toward Henrich, who threw to catcher Ralph Houk, but plate umpire Bill Grieve ruled Pesky safe. Houk and Stengel protested so vigorously that umpire Cal Hubbard had to push them away.

After the 7–6 loss dropped the Yankees a game behind, outfielder Cliff Mapes yelled at Grieve, "How much did you have on the game?"

Grieve whirled. "There's never been an umpire found guilty of anything like the ballplayers, throwing games and like that," he shouted, alluding to the Black Sox scandal. "You. . . ," but Cal Hubbard and Charley Berry moved him toward the umpires' room.

Mapes would be fined $200 by American League president Will Harridge and ordered to apologize to Grieve, which he did. Houk and Stengel each were fined $150 for their outbursts. Houk kept insisting that he had blocked Pesky from the plate. Pesky disagreed.

"Houk seemed to have frozen for an instant," the Red Sox third baseman said. "When he did tag me, it was on the hip after my feet had touched the plate."

Virtually forgotten were rightfielder Al Zarilla's two sensational catches. With two on in the second, he leaped high above the 344-foot sign on the low rightfield wall to snatch Johnny Lindell's slicing drive. In the ninth he made a diving, toppling catch of Henrich's low liner to help Kinder preserve the victory. The day before, Zarilla had nailed Henrich at the plate with a perfect on-the-fly throw to Tebbetts. With what would be a .277 average and ten homers, Zarilla had more than justified McCarthy's appraisal of him as a "hustling, lively type of player who can run and throw" after his May 5 arrival from the Browns in a trade for outfielder Stan Spence and $100,000.

Tuesday afternoon Vic Raschi dominated the A's, 3–1, for his twentieth win. That night the Red Sox, prevented from taking batting practice by a steady drizzle in Griffith Stadium, strafed the Senators with twelve hits, 6–4.

Wednesday the Yankees won again, 7–5, on Rizzuto's squeeze bunt off lefthander Alex Kellner for the go-ahead run. Before that game, Joe DiMaggio, pale and drawn after losing eighteen pounds in his slow recovery from viral pneumonia, took batting practice. He was hoping to be ready for the two weekend games with the Red Sox at the Stadium, especially the Saturday opener, which would be "Joe DiMaggio Day." Still weak, he took only fifteen swings, hitting only one ball into the leftfield stands. He hurried to the clubhouse.

"I'm going right back to my hotel and rest, but I'll be out again tomorrow," he said. "At the end of that workout, it felt as if the bat was swinging me."

In Washington, the Red Sox had put together a run against right-hander Ray Scarborough, their 1948 nemesis. They were hoping to protect that 1–0 lead as Chuck Stobbs went to the mound for the ninth, but singles by Roberto Ortiz, Eddie Robinson, and Al Kozar tied the score. McCarthy waved to his bullpen for Kinder as Parnell continued to warm up. Sam Dente's single loaded the bases, then Senator manager Joe Kuhel sent up Buddy Lewis, a lefthanded batter, as a pinch hitter. McCarthy called for Parnell.

With a one-one count, Tebbetts suspected a squeeze play, signaled for a pitchout, and tagged Robinson for the second out as Kozar moved to third. With a ball and two strikes on Lewis, Parnell's curveball bounced away from Tebbetts for a wild pitch as Kozar scored. The Red Sox had lost, 2–1.

On hearing that score, Tommy Henrich knew the Yankees had a chance. Not only had the Red Sox dropped into a tie for first place again, but two Senators involved in that rally, outfielder Al Kozar and shortstop Sam Dente, had once been Red Sox teammates, along with two other Senators, outfielder Sam Mele and lefthander Mickey Harris. "Tomorrow," Harris promised, "I'll beat 'em myself." Thursday it rained in both Washington and New York, postponing Harris's opportunity until Friday and altering the Athletics' pitching.

When the A's assistant manager, fifty-nine-year-old Earle Mack, the son of owner-manager Connie Mack, received several telegrams and letters criticizing his naming Phil Marchildon as Friday's pitcher, he announced that Dick Fowler would start.

"They aren't going to point any fingers at us," Earle Mack said. "Look at all these letters and telegrams. They even accuse us of lying down. It's damned nasty terrible stuff. We'll try to keep these letters from Dad, but I think he did see some of them."

Still wearing the high starched collar popular at the turn of the century, eighty-six-year-old Connie Mack had returned to Philadelphia with an upset stomach. Although Earle Mack had played only five major league games as a catcher-first baseman-third baseman, all for his father's team, he had been an A's coach for decades.

"Some of these letters," Earle Mack said, "even say we're not trying because Dad gave out a story one day picking the Yankees to win."

Marchildon had a 19–9 record in 1947 for the A's, but a sore arm had contributed to his 0–3 record for the fifth-place A's in 1949, provoking the telegrams and letters. He hadn't pitched for nearly three months before returning in late August. In his second start, he didn't last the first inning as the Red Sox scored five quick runs. Fowler had been knocked out by the Yankees in the third inning of Tuesday's game but he had a respectable 14–11 record.

"If Fowler can't do the job," Earle Mack said, "Carl Scheib will be next. And if Fowler and Scheib can't stop them, we'll come in with Bobby Shantz, Lou Brissie, and Joe Coleman."

Fowler did the job. He completed a four-hitter, 4–1, after first baseman Ferris Fain hit a three-run homer off Lopat in the third. "That shows 'em," Earle Mack said. "I just tore up a telegram that said, 'Don't pitch tired Fowler. Use your ace, Kellner.' " In Washington, meanwhile, McCarthy had to use his ace, Ellis Kinder, in relief to assure an 11–9 victory after Mickey Harris and the other Senator pitchers had issued fourteen walks. In the ninth Kinder was strafed for two doubles and a single before he walked two to load the bases with one out, but he got Sam Mele to bounce into a game-ending double play.

As the Red Sox hurried for their train to New York, they again had a one-game lead. All they needed was a victory either Saturday or Sunday out of these pitching matchups: Parnell-Reynolds, Kinder-Raschi.

But the question the Yankees couldn't answer yet was: Would Joe DiMaggio play and if he did, how well would he play? Before Thursday's game had been rained out, he reported, "I feel much better." Friday he took batting practice again and announced, "I might be able to play." Not long after DiMaggio arrived for Saturday's game, Stengel asked, "Can you take one turn at bat?"

"Sure," he said. "I'll try to play three innings."

DiMaggio took batting practice. To stay warm in the cloudy chill during the Joe DiMaggio Day ceremonies, he wore his navy blue Yankee jacket as he stood with his seven-year-old son, Joe, Jr., near home plate for nearly an hour. Two of his brothers, Dom in his Red Sox uniform and Tom, stood behind him. When their mother, Rosalie, was introduced, she walked past Joe and hugged Dom.

"I saw Joseph yesterday," she explained later. "I hadn't seen Dominic."

With his words booming out of the scoreboard loudspeakers, the Yankee Clipper acknowledged the gifts: an automobile for himself and another for his mother, a twenty-two-foot Chris-Craft powerboat, and dozens of other presents. He would donate nearly $50,000 in cash gifts to the Damon Runyon Cancer Fund and the New York Heart Fund. Then he looked around at the 69,551 spectators.

"When I was in San Francisco," he said, "Lefty O'Doul told me, 'Joe, don't let the big city scare you. New York is the friendliest town in the world.' This day proves it. I want to thank the fans, my friends, my manager Casey Stengel and my teammates, the gamest fightingest bunch that ever lived. And I want to thank the good Lord for making me a Yankee."

He turned toward Joe McCarthy, who had presented him with a scroll signed by the Red Sox.

"They're a grand bunch too," he said. "If we don't win the pennant, I'm happy that they will."

Soon the game was on. The Red Sox jumped on Reynolds for a quick 1–0 lead. Dom DiMaggio singled. Williams singled. DiMaggio moved to third on a wild pitch and scored on Stephens's fly to left. With one out in the third, Reynolds, overthrowing in his determination, walked Pesky, Williams, and Stephens before Bobby Doerr sliced a single past second baseman Jerry Coleman for a 2–0 lead. Stengel didn't hesitate. He waved to the bullpen for Page even though it was only the third inning. At the mound Stengel stared at him.

"How far can you go?"

"A long way," Page said.

"Then get going."

Page walked Zarilla, forcing in a run. He also walked Goodman, forcing in another run. But the husky lefthander's rising fastball struck out Tebbetts and Parnell. With the Yankees trailing, 4–0, DiMaggio trotted in from centerfield, caught Stengel's eye in the dugout, held up his right hand, and waved five fingers: he would play through the fifth inning.

As the Red Sox moved to their positions with a four-run lead and Parnell pitching, they could almost taste the champagne stored in a Stadium Club refrigerator. Especially the talkative Tebbetts.

When Rizzuto fouled off a pitch in the bottom of the third, he heard Tebbetts say, "Tonight we'll be drinking champagne and tomorrow we'll pitch the Yale kid. Think you can hit a kid from Yale, Rizzuto?" During the season the Red Sox had signed righthander Frank Quinn off the Yale campus. In eight appearances, Quinn had worked a total of only twenty-two innings, all after games had been decided. Deterred by arm trouble, Quinn would never win a game in the majors (or lose one, for that matter), but the Yankees were angered by the wisecrack they remember although Tebbetts doesn't.

In the dugout, Rizzuto grumbled, "That Tebbetts, you know what he told me: that their Yale kid will be pitching tomorrow." His teammates had never seen him so furious.

"It wasn't like Phil created a pep rally," Henrich would say years later. "But it was something that annoyed us, it maybe helped us put some runs together against Parnell."

In the fourth, Joe DiMaggio, who had fanned in the first, sliced a ground-rule double into the rightfield stands. Johnson struck out, but Bauer singled, and the Yankees finally had a run. Bauer moved to third on Lindell's long single and scored on Coleman's fly ball to Dom DiMaggio to make it 4–2. In the fifth Rizzuto opened with a single. Henrich bounced a grounder toward the mound. Another pitcher might have turned it into a double play, but the ball skidded through Parnell for an infield hit. Berra's single scored Rizzuto and, with Joe DiMaggio up, McCarthy called for righthander Joe Dobson.

DiMaggio slashed the ball back at Dobson. Again, another pitcher might have turned the hot grounder into a double play, but the ball skidded off Dobson's glove and rolled onto the grass behind the mound. DiMaggio beat it out. With the bases loaded, McCarthy preferred to keep his infielders in their normal position. Johnson bounced into a double play as Henrich hurried across the plate, tying the score at 4–4. When the inning ended, DiMaggio's five innings supposedly were up but he never even looked at Stengel in the dugout. He hopped up the concrete steps and trotted to centerfield.

Page and Dobson maintained the 4–4 tie into the eighth. Hoping that lefthanded pinch hitters might have better success against Dobson's curveball, Stengel had Bobby Brown bat for Johnson and Cliff Mapes bat for Bauer, but the Red Sox righthander got them out.

With Johnny Lindell the next batter, Stengel had another left-handed pinch hitter available, Charlie Keller, but the manager decided to let Lindell swing. As a righthanded batter, Lindell was in the lineup only because Parnell had been the Red Sox starter. Over the season the thirty-three-year-old leftfielder hadn't done much except annoy general manager George Weiss with his nocturnal adventures as the club rogue.

"I wish," Lindell often said, "that Weiss would give me all the money he spends to have detectives follow me around."

For all his size and strength at six-four and 217 pounds, Lindell was batting only .238 with only five homers and only twenty-six runs batted in. Once a successful righthanded knuckleball pitcher in the Yankee farm system (23–4 at Newark in 1941), he had been transferred to the outfield two years later by Joe McCarthy, then the Yankee manager. In 1944 he hit .300 for the Yankees with eighteen homers and 103 runs batted in, but in Stengel's platoon system, he was only a part-time player. This was only his seventy-eighth game of the season, only his sixty-fifth in the outfield. Now, as Lindell dug into the batter's box, Tebbetts called for a high fastball.

Dobson pitched. Lindell swung. The ball rose higher and higher, soared over Williams's head and landed in the lower leftfield stands. Home run.

"It's all McCarthy's fault," Lindell later told the Boston writers. "When I came up to the Yankees, he switched me to the outfield."

The Yankees were ahead, 5–4, and after Joe Page mowed down the Red Sox in the ninth, the two teams were tied for first place. Despite their disappointment, the Red Sox knew that they could still win the pennant by taking tomorrow's season finale. And for all of the Yankees' elation in their clubhouse, they knew that they still had to win tomorrow.

"It's not done yet," Joe DiMaggio kept telling his teammates. "Don't forget that. It's not done yet. We've got to win tomorrow."

DiMaggio was smiling. His double and single had generated the pair of two-run innings that erased the 4–0 deficit, and he had remained in centerfield for all nine innings. But he was weary. "I was just playing from inning to inning," he told the writers. "The last few outs my shinbones were getting cramped. My legs feel hard and swollen." In his small office off the clubhouse, Stengel, wearing only his gray sweatshirt, said, "That DiMaggio is a wonder. How about him playing the whole game?" But now the writers were asking questions.

"Who's your starter tomorrow?"

"It'll be Raschi tomorrow, and it'll be Reynolds tomorrow, and it'll be Page tomorrow."

"Who's your starter in the World Series opener?"

With an exaggerated wink, Stengel said, "There will be a slight delay on that one." In the Red Sox clubhouse, nobody was joking with Joe McCarthy about his World Series starter. At his locker Williams looked up when he realized some of the Boston writers had just walked over from the Yankee clubhouse.

"Who's pitching for them?" Williams asked.

Reading from his notebook, one of the writers said, "Stengel told us, 'It'll be Raschi tomorrow, and it'll be Reynolds tomorrow, and it'll be Page tomorrow.' " Hearing that, Pesky smiled.

"How about Lopat?" he said.

Vic Raschi, known as the Springfield Rifle because he grew up in that western Massachusetts city, didn't throw quite as hard as Reynolds, but hard enough. Swarthy and often silent, the thirty-year-old righthander was a tough competitor. Asked once by pitching coach Jim Turner how he intended to pitch to a certain hitter, he replied, "Hard." Although never so hard as to throw at a hitter's head. As a youngster, his brother Eugene had been blinded when beaned in a sandlot game. That memory haunted the Yankee righthander. But for him Sunday's showdown had a hard meaning. The year before, he had been bypassed by manager Bucky Harris during the final crucial weekend in Boston after having lost all four of his starts against the Red Sox that season. Ignoring Raschi's 19–8 record,

Harris had used rookie Bob Porterfield, who didn't survive the third inning as the Yankees were eliminated.

With the 1949 pennant at stake, Stengel never thought about not starting Raschi, just as McCarthy never thought about not starting Ellis Kinder.

Coincidentally, in that final series with the Yankees the year before, Kinder had been bypassed when McCarthy chose Joe Dobson to start the Saturday game. But now Kinder was the American League's best pitcher, and its most surprising success story. Out of the hills around Jackson, Tennessee, he spent World War II in the Army and didn't get to the big leagues with the Browns until 1946, when he was thirty-one. Traded to the Red Sox, he put together an ordinary 10–7 record in 1948. But as he took the subway downtown to the Commodore Hotel after Saturday's game, he had a 23–5 record, six shutouts, and a streak of thirteen victories. He was 7–2 against the Yankees over his career and 4–0 this season, including a 3–0 six-hitter in his previous start eight days earlier and two innings of shutout relief in Monday's makeup game. In his thirteen relief appearances, he had earned four saves. But his teammates knew he was their most devoted drinker. Devoted mostly to bourbon.

"Take him out tonight," Vern Stephens, who knew Kinder from the Browns, told Arthur Richman, a *New York Daily Mirror* sportswriter. "We don't want Ol' Folks doing anything different."

Around eleven o'clock that Saturday night, when Red Sox batboy Johnny Donovan checked the Commodore room that Kinder was sharing with Dobson, both pitchers were there. By midnight Dobson was alone. Kinder had departed to meet his friend Arthur Richman in one of the nearby Lexington Avenue bars close to the *Mirror* office.

"He didn't talk much about Sunday's game," Richman, later an executive with both the Mets and Yankees, would remember. "He hadn't lost in months. He had every confidence. We stayed out until the bars closed at four in the morning."

Kinder returned to the hotel with a female companion, got a few hours' sleep, phoned room service, and grunted, "Get some coffee up here." He took the Lexington Avenue subway to the 161st Street station with some of the early arrivals in the crowd of 68,055, then walked around to the players' entrance of Yankee Stadium, where he would be pitching the game that would decide the pennant. When his teammates saw him, they smiled. Ol' Folks looked perfectly natural: a little hung over, a little sleepy. Just like he had looked before every other start in his sensational streak. But in the Yankee first, leadoff man Phil Rizzuto slashed a liner down the leftfield line. The ball, hugging the base of the box seats, rolled into the rain gutter.

Running toward second base, Rizzuto realized that the ball had squirted out of the gutter past Williams. He hurried to third for a triple.

With the Red Sox infielders back in their normal positions on McCarthy's orders, Rizzuto knew he could score on an infield out. Henrich knew it too. He always had trouble hitting Kinder, whose pitches seemed to travel at nine different speeds. His plan was not to swing hard, to stay flat-footed, get in front of the pitch, and hit it to the right side. He bounced a grounder to Bobby Doerr who threw to Billy Goodman as Rizzuto raced across the plate for a 1–0 lead. With two out, Joe DiMaggio tripled, chugging into third base on his sore and swollen legs.

"I was puffing like a steam engine," he would say later.

Now, with Kinder about to pitch, DiMaggio started to take a short lead when he heard third-base umpire Bill Summers yell, "Time." DiMaggio retreated to the bag, wondering why time had been called and why Summers had taken a few steps toward him.

"I thought I'd give you a breather, Joe," the umpire said.

DiMaggio nodded his appreciation. Summers waved his arms. The game resumed. Through seven innings Rizzuto's run would be the only run as Kinder dueled Raschi for the pennant. With one out in the eighth and Kinder due to bat, McCarthy sent up Tom Wright as a pinch hitter. Wright, just up from the minors, had appeared in only four games, three others late in the 1948 season. In his six major league at-bats, he had two hits, a double and a triple. When he walked, the tying run was on first, but Dom DiMaggio bounced into a double play.

Without a dependable relief pitcher, McCarthy had been forced to use Kinder and Parnell out of the bullpen down the stretch. With the first two Yankee batters in the eighth, Henrich and Berra, both left-handed, McCarthy waved for Parnell, but the twenty-five-game winner was weary.

He hadn't lasted six innings as Saturday's starter after his ninth-inning wild pitch in Wednesday's loss in Washington had wasted eight shutout innings. Now he threw to Henrich, who swung and missed. He had been trying to hit to leftfield, away from his power. Behind him, he heard Joe DiMaggio's voice.

"Go for it," DiMaggio was yelling to him.

Henrich went for it, swatting a curveball into the rightfield stands for his twenty-fourth homer.

Now it was 2–0, a big difference from 1–0.

When Berra singled, McCarthy changed pitchers again. With DiMaggio coming up, the Red Sox manager called for Cecil (Tex) Hughson, a thirty-three-year-old righthander who hadn't pitched for three weeks. Hughson had once been the ace of the Red Sox staff. He had a 22–6 record in 1942 and after returning from military service, a 20–11 record in 1946. Arm trouble limited him to a 3–1 record in 1948 and, after surgery in the off-season, he started only twice in 1949 before being relegated to McCarthy's doghouse, an afterthought in the bullpen. Summoned now to keep the Red Sox alive, he was even more surprised than his teammates were. Quickly, he got DiMaggio to bounce into a double play.

One more out and maybe the Red Sox, down by only 2–0, could do something in the ninth. But the Yankees weren't through with Hughson, who would be pitching in the big leagues for the last time. Yesterday's hero, Lindell, singled. Billy Johnson singled and when Williams bobbled the ball, Hank Bauer, who was running for Lindell, hurried to third. With second base open, McCarthy decided to walk Cliff Mapes, a lefthanded hitter, so that Hughson could pitch to Jerry Coleman, the skinny second baseman.

As the eighth hitter in the batting order, Coleman, a rookie who got his chance when George Stirnweiss suffered a severely spiked hand on opening day, had a .274 average, but not much power: twenty doubles, five triples, only two homers. Having grown up in San Francisco, where Joe DiMaggio was an idol, Coleman once glanced out to centerfield and realized he was playing second base with Joe DiMaggio out there behind him. Now, with the bases loaded and the pennant at stake, Coleman didn't even look back to see if a pinch hitter was behind him. He knew that with the Yankees ahead, Stengel would stay with his best defensive players.

On a high inside fastball, Coleman looped the ball toward rightfield. Doerr ran out. Zarilla ran in and dove, but couldn't quite catch it.

"He only hit it with half his bat," Zarilla said later. "The ball didn't go quite high enough. I didn't touch it. Missed it by inches."

Bauer and Johnson scored easily. When third-base coach Frank Crosetti noticed that Zarilla had landed hard in diving for the ball and couldn't retrieve it, he waved Mapes home for the third run and a 5–0 lead before Doerr's throw cut down Coleman at third.

"I just kept going," Coleman would say later. "Anytime another runner was trying to score, Casey wanted you to draw the throw."

But the Red Sox didn't go quietly. Pesky fouled out, but Williams walked and Stephens singled. Doerr lifted a long fly that Joe DiMaggio chased but, in his weariness, couldn't run down. Williams and Stephens scored on the triple. Now it was 5–2 with a runner on third. Out in centerfield DiMaggio had to make a decision.

"I should've had Doerr's ball in my hip pocket," he would say years later. "My legs felt like lead. In the best interests of the Yankees, I knew I had to take myself out."

Seeing DiMaggio trotting toward the dugout, Stengel waved Cliff Mapes to centerfield from rightfield, moved Hank Bauer from leftfield to rightfield, and inserted Gene Woodling in leftfield. Zarilla flied to Mapes but with two out, Goodman singled. Now it was 5–3 with a runner on first and Birdie Tebbetts, the potential tying run, at bat. Henrich walked toward the mound with the ball, but Raschi glared at him.

"Give me the goddamn ball," Raschi snapped, "and get the hell out of here."

Turning away, Henrich smiled. Same ol' Raschi, tough as nails. Moments later Tebbetts lifted a pop foul along the first-base line. Henrich caught it. The Yankees had won the pennant with a 97–57 record. They would win the World Series from the Brooklyn Dodgers, four games to one. But the Red Sox, for the second straight season, had produced a 96–58 regular-season record, which would win most pennants. And for the second straight season they had lost the pennant in their final game, the only major league team ever to do that. Some of their loyalists second-guessed McCarthy's decision to remove Kinder for a pinch hitter, but in the Red Sox clubhouse Tebbetts defended his manager.

"He had to," Tebbetts said. "You're one run behind in the eighth. You've got one out and your pitcher's coming up. You've got to use a pinch hitter."

That basic baseball strategy did not appease Ellis Kinder. At his locker he looked up at his friend Arthur Richman, clutched his throat, and growled, "Shit in the neck again," his way of saying that for all their statistics, the Red Sox again had been unable to win the biggest game of the season. Williams had led the league with forty-three homers and 159 runs batted in, losing the triple crown when George Kell, the Tiger third baseman, edged him for the batting title, .3429 to .3427. Parnell won twenty-five games, Kinder twenty-three. The Red Sox had a 61–16 record at Fenway Park (only 35–42 on the road). Despite the two losses in Yankee Stadium, the Red Sox had a 61–22 finish.

"Two exasperating endings in two years," Ted Williams would say years later, referring to the 1948 and 1949 seasons. "We should've won both of 'em."

But over the last four games in Washington and New York, three of which the Red Sox lost, Bobby Doerr was their only player to get a hit in each game. Williams had one hit in twelve at-bats, Pesky none in fifteen, Tebbetts none in twelve, Stephens two in ten, Dom DiMaggio three in seventeen. Even so, Kinder blamed McCarthy more than anyone else for the game that meant the pennant. He believed he would have blanked the Yankees in the eighth and ninth while those three Red Sox runs in the ninth would have meant a 3–1 victory. Not that the Yankees agreed. To them, if Vic Raschi had needed to pitch a 1–0 shutout, he would have done just that.

"In my mind," Tommy Henrich told the writers, "nobody was going to beat Raschi in this game."

When the Red Sox were returning to Boston by train, Kinder, fortified by bourbon, stormed into Joe McCarthy's compartment and derided the manager. But more than anyone else, Red Sox owner Tom Yawkey understood why the Red Sox lost.

"Two teams," he said, "can't win the same pennant."

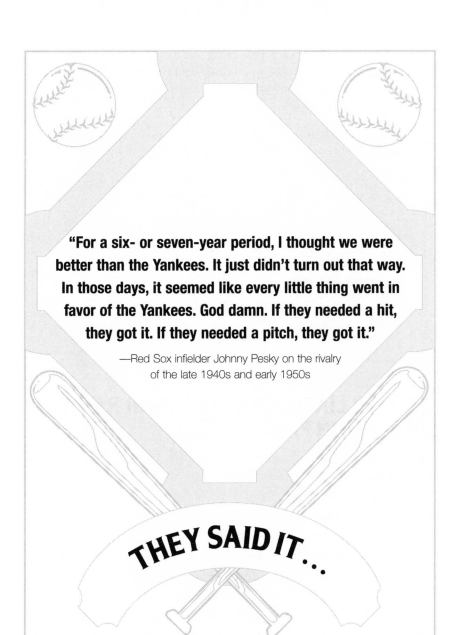

"For a six- or seven-year period, I thought we were better than the Yankees. It just didn't turn out that way. In those days, it seemed like every little thing went in favor of the Yankees. God damn. If they needed a hit, they got it. If they needed a pitch, they got it."

—Red Sox infielder Johnny Pesky on the rivalry of the late 1940s and early 1950s

THEY SAID IT . . .

Red Sox great Ted Williams retired from the major leagues in 1960, and passed away in 2002. Unlike so many of Boston's best players, he did not leave mid-career to play for the Yankees . . . at least not yet.

"TED WILLIAMS: SOX FANS FEAR REVIVED SPLINTER IN PINSTRIPES"

from the *Atlanta Journal-Constitution* (July 10, 2002)
by Mark Bradley

OPENING DAY, 2060. THE crowd at the Fleet Financial Showplace & Baseball Field—the park formerly known as Fenway—falls silent. The terrifying vision is about to become real. The first two visiting hitters have reached base, and now the New York left fielder steps in. It's his first at-bat for his new team, his first at-bat of the 21st century.

The Red Sox pitcher, Derek Lowe III, is struggling with his hereditary sinker. He throws two pitches in the dirt. Then a called strike. (The New York left fielder is renowned for taking the first strike.) Lowe throws again, and the left fielder drives the pitch the wrong way, toward the glassed-in luxury suites stacked atop one another in left field. (The Green Monster has been slain in the name of commerce.) The ball smacks the Plexiglas and rattles around in the corner. Two runs score. The New York left fielder should have a double, but he stops at first base. He's winded. He should be. He's 141 years old.

All New England is aghast. The sainted Teddy Ballgame lies not in state but in really cold storage. His body is in an Arizona warehouse, chilled in liquid nitrogen, preserved for the purpose of . . . what? To produce another .400 hitter via cloned DNA? Or, spookier still, to be revived when medical science finally gets its act together?

All New England is appalled. This is affront to human decency, cry the Nor'Easters. In death, the sainted Teddy Ballgame has been taken hostage by son John Henry Williams, a crass sort who had the misfortune of being named after two mythological figures. Can't somebody do something? Can't somebody swoop in—Johnny Havlicek, maybe—and steal the remains?

What none of New England will dare admit is that its concern transcends medical ethics, transcends the concept of human decency. There's something else at work here. There's the fear that Ted Williams will be resuscitated, will be restored to something approximating health, will do what Red Sox heroes always do.

Become a Yankee.

Babe Ruth did it. The Red Sox sold the Bambino for cash and rue it still. Wade Boggs did it. The champion of chicken cuisine took his batting titles to the Bronx, where he played on a World Series winner. Roger Clemens did it. The greatest pitcher in Sox annals now wins games and plunks hitters as a hated Yankee. This outbound stream of indignity is why Sox fans are the most fatalistic zealots on the planet. It was thought that their pessimism knew no bounds, but here's a sight even dour New Englanders never considered.

The Splendid Pinstriped Splinter.

On Sept. 28, 1960, Ted Williams took his last swing and hit a home run off Jack Fisher. Who could have known that, owing to John Henry and liquid nitrogen, there might be more swings left? Who would have believed that the consensus Greatest Hitter Who Ever Lived might live on after life has apparently ceased? Who could have guessed that another Triple Crown might be just a thaw away?

Give it 50 or so years. Give biotech a chance to figure something out. Then wake Ted Williams, pump him full of steroids—surely Donald Fehr

Jr. and the Players Association won't have agreed to testing so soon—and watch what happens. The sweet swing returns. Steinbrenner's heirs come calling. The greatest hitter who ever lived winds up where every big-ticket free agent winds up. And all of New England gets to forget Bucky Freakin' Dent and ponder a deeper outrage.

Ted Williams, Yankee.

Teddy Frozen Ballgame.

"Boston fans are experts at predicting disaster. They should be nationalized to predict earthquakes and hurricanes and tornadoes, particularly in October."

—*New York Times* columnist George Vecsey

THEY SAID IT...

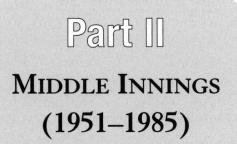

Part II

MIDDLE INNINGS
(1951–1985)

PART II
MIDDLE INNINGS
(1951–1985)

THE POWERFUL YANKEES DOMINATED the American League in the 1950s and early 1960s. In those years, the perennially pitching-poor Red Sox rarely gave New York much of a fight. But the Yankee dynasty fell to pieces during the mid-1960s, brought down by aging stars, young talent that failed to develop, a new baseball amateur draft that meant the Yanks couldn't fix their problems by throwing money at prospects, and, not least, by New York's reluctance to sign many black players—a mistake also made by the Red Sox.

By the late 1960s, the Yankees were no longer contenders. The Red Sox managed a surprise pennant in 1967, but that success proved hard to repeat when Jim Lonborg, their best pitcher, suffered knee and arm injuries.

The rivalry finally returned to the forefront in the mid-to-late 1970s. Boston won the 1975 American League pennant, then New York took the flag in 1976 and 1977. In 1978, the Red Sox and Yankees ended their regular season schedule tied, forcing a one-game playoff. For the first time since the late 1940s, both teams were pennant contenders at the same time, and Yankee–Red Sox games were once again among the highlights of the American League season.

"It's always nice to beat the Yankees.
You need everything you've ever had
all the time—plus luck."

—Red Sox pitcher and noted Yankee-killer
Mel Parnell

THEY SAID IT...

Most seasons are remembered for their thrilling finishes. But for the Yankees and Red Sox of 1967, the most telling game came very near the start—the New York Yankees home opener, Boston's third game of the regular season. The rivals had claimed the bottom two spots in the American League in 1966, and little was expected of them in 1967. True to the predictions, New York would finish the '67 season in ninth. But the Boston Red Sox captured the American League pennant. The season became known as "the impossible dream" in Boston. For a young pitcher and catcher, the dream began on April 14, when each made his major league debut.

BOSTON RED SOX vs. NEW YORK YANKEES

from *Lightning in a Bottle: The Sox of '67* (1992)
by Herbert F. Crehan with James W. Ryan

FRIDAY, APRIL 14, 1967, dawned sharp and clear in New York City. The sun's ray fought with the lingering cold of winter to produce a typical spring baseball day in the Northeast.

The weather may have been typical but the events of the day would be anything but. For rookie catcher Russ Gibson and rookie pitcher Billy Rohr just waking up in the Biltmore Hotel in Manhattan was an adventure. The fact that they would both be making their major league debut at Yankee Stadium that afternoon seemed quite implausible.

Gibson had learned late Thursday that he was going to catch for Rohr against the Yankees shortly after manager Dick Williams finished castigating the team in the clubhouse for its 8–5 loss to Chicago. Williams was particularly upset because his players had committed five errors and gave up five unearned runs in the top of the ninth. Third baseman Joe Foy caught a lot of the steam for his two errors. The loss put the Red Sox at 1–1 for the early season.

"Dick came over to me after the meeting and told me that I was going to catch the next day. This was after Mike Ryan had caught for the team in the first two games against Chicago. The next day meant the Yankees in New York. I could only say, 'Great!' The fact was that I couldn't wait to get into the lineup and see major league action."

Actually Gibson was glad that Williams hadn't started him in Boston because the few days off helped to settle him down and shake off any nervousness about playing in the majors.

"Dick was smart that way, the way he handled his players. He had a lot of confidence in me. Knew how I played and I had all that experience from the minors, but still he let me unwind by sitting out our first two games. To tell you the truth, I was glad that I didn't catch the opener at Fenway. All the hometown crowd, the family and friends who'd be up from Fall River [Massachusetts]; I'd probably have been very nervous. Yeh, I really was glad."

For Fall River native Gibson, it was a dream that seemed impossible just two short years earlier. Not that he lacked the tools to do the job behind the plate at the major league level. That was never in doubt. Sure you would like to see a little quicker bat and a bit more power. But Russ Gibson could call a game with any of them and he could handle pitchers. That was a given.

Two years earlier, in 1965, Gibson had been a victim of the Red Sox depth chart at catcher. He was invited to spring training with the major league club coming off an outstanding year at the Red Sox Triple-A club in Seattle. He had batted a solid .276 with seventeen homers and anchored a young pitching staff for 130 games behind the plate. After eight years of riding buses in the bushes, Gibson was more than ready for "the show."

The newly-married Gibson put on a show of his own in Florida. Still a few months shy of his twenty-sixth birthday, he was in his prime and he showed it with his defensive ability and with his bat. Surely the top brass on Jersey Street couldn't ignore his performance.

But ignore it they did. Six foot four Bill Tillman had batted .278 in 131 games for the Red Sox the year before and he was pencilled in at number one before spring training even started. Mike Ryan, another local boy, from Haverhill, Massachusetts, was two years younger than Gibson, a little bigger than him and the brass wanted to see what he could do in the Bigs. Besides, the new manager [of the Sox farm club in] Toronto, Dick Williams, was only thirty-five years old and could benefit from the presence of a seasoned veteran. And if Russ Gibson was anything, he was an organization man to the core. Ryan would go north to Boston and Gibson would go farther north to Toronto.

It's a long ride from central Florida to Toronto, Ontario. And it's even longer when you've just sent your new bride home alone. Home as in Fall River, Massachusetts, just an hour drive from Fenway Park, home of the Boston Red Sox. Your home team.

To get to Toronto from Florida you have to go through North Carolina and if you're Russ Gibson you think about 1959–61 in Raleigh and Winston-Salem. As you head further north into Pennsylvania and New York you think about Corning, New York, in 1957 and York, Pennsylvania, in 1962. Certainly Toronto is a lot closer to Fenway than Seattle was in 1963 and 1964. But in April of 1965 the locals would be much more interested in hockey star Frank Mahovlich of the Toronto Maple Leafs than the arrival of journeyman catcher Russ Gibson.

A five-day car ride gives a man a lot of time to think. Especially if you've already logged as many miles on the highway over eight years in the minors as your average Greyhound bus driver. In a very short time Gibson had gone from the dead of winter in Fall River to the false spring of Winter Haven, Florida. As the seasons reversed themselves again and he headed back to the lingering winter in Toronto, Gibson had come to a difficult conclusion.

Two years later, Gibson was standing in the lobby of the Biltmore thinking about the game with the Yankees that afternoon. He could look around and see veterans like Carl Yastrzemski, Rico Petrocelli, and Tony Conigliaro who thrived on the limelight of New York. He could look over and see fellow rookies, Mike Andrews and Reggie Smith, who had been teammates on last year's championship Toronto club. And he could see rookie manager Dick Williams, who had been his manager and mentor in Toronto for the past two years. In some ways, Williams was the man who was most instrumental in Gibson's starting assignment that day.

When Gibson arrived in Toronto in April of 1965, he reported directly to manager Williams' office. Almost the first words out of his mouth were, "If I can't make it to the majors after eight years in the system and the spring I had, I think it's time to hang them up." Williams responded with, "Look, I'm new at this job and I need some help. I want you to stay here as a player-coach. I expect that my time will come in Boston and if I can, I'll take you with me. Take a few days off to play golf and then come back and let's get to work."

Gibson played a little golf—you can get some good drives off when the ground is still frozen—and thought it over. He came back and helped Williams and Toronto to two consecutive championships. Now he was getting ready for Opening Day in Yankee Stadium and he knew he had made the right decision. Gibson never talks about his first game in the majors without recalling a humorous anecdote. "All those years in the minors, Corning, Lafayette, Waterloo . . . Raleigh and Winston-Salem, York and then on to Seattle and Toronto . . . no matter where we went to play, it was almost always by way of bus. Every type of bus you can imagine. Now, finally, I'm in the big leagues, the majors, and I'm imagining that wherever the team goes, it'll be first class and by air. So what happens? When I'm told that I'm to catch the next day in New York against the Yankees, the Red Sox take a chartered bus at night to go down to the big town. Boy, what a letdown. It's 1967 and we're going to New York for their season opener and there I am back in the bus, for Pete's sake!"

When the Red Sox went out to Yankee Stadium Friday, Gibson, a husky six-footer with hands like bear paws, felt calm and confident, ready to do the job. It was his first major league start, but the Red Sox were away from home and as always puffed up to do battle with their traditional foes, the pinstriped Yankees.

"It didn't bother me that I was going to catch because we were in New York and I'd be more relaxed, at least that's what I thought until I walked into Yankee Stadium. As soon as I came out of the dugout and could see the size of the field, all I could think was, 'God, this is unbelievable!' They had all the plaques of the great Yankees . . . Ruth, Gehrig, DiMaggio, all those guys and the size of it. And all the fans who were out for the opener. It was beautiful! Fantastic! But it's like everything else, believe me. I'm a pro and as soon as the National Anthem was over, I knew I had a job to do and looked forward to it."

Gibson knew his pitcher, Billy Rohr, would be subject to the jitters. Like Gibson, it was his first major league start. Russ, though, had ten years playing time in the minors against many top caliber players who had gone up to major league teams, so he wasn't so overawed by big leaguers and the crowd.

Rookie southpaw Billy Rohr's route to the majors was much less bumpy and had almost no U-turns. Rohr had been a high school phenomenon at Bellflower High School in Garden Grove, California. His portfolio in his senior year included three no-hit games. The Pittsburgh Pirates signed the seventeen-year-old Rohr for $40,000 immediately after graduation. Serious money in those days.

Rohr and Gibson took very different paths through the minors. Gibson reported directly from graduation to Corning, New York, in the New York/Pennsylvania League. He got four hits in his first two games and was told to report to Lafayette in the Midwest League. Corning wanted to use someone else as their catcher. Rohr reported to Kingsport, Tennessee, in the Appalachian League and was told that he was too valuable to pitch in games. His routine was to pitch batting practice and then watch from the stands. The Pirates were trying to hide him. The Red Sox weren't fooled. When the Pirates failed to protect him by putting him on their expanded major league roster, the Red Sox snapped him up for $8,000. It would appear that Pittsburgh paid $32,000 to provide Kingsport with a batting practice pitcher! Strange places these major leagues.

While Gibson had to work his way up the minor league rungs over ten years, Rohr was assigned immediately by the Red Sox to their Triple-A farm club in Toronto. Once again, the system's depth chart had come into play. The pitching-thin Red Sox were ready to throw any strong, young left-handed arm into the breach. Rohr showed a great deal of promise in Toronto but he was a long shot to stick when he arrived in Winter Haven in the spring of 1967. A strong showing in Florida and Dick Williams' belief in his potential had earned him the starting nod for opening day in Yankee Stadium.

"I could tell from his initial practice throws that he was nervous and it was up to me to settle him down. Hey, he was just this tall, skinny kid . . . part Indian, Cherokee, if I remember . . . and it was just a matter of talking to him. Billy had shown a lot of good stuff in spring training and he and I had talked about the batters we'd be facing and how he should pitch to each one. I went out to talk to him. 'Just put 'em between the lines, Billy, and we'll take each out as it comes along.' "

Gibson reminded Rohr, whose best pitches were a fast sinking ball and sharp curve, that Yankee Stadium was a great park for him to pitch in, particularly where it was his first major league start. Even 400 foot fly balls could be caught for easy outs, a fact Dick Williams was well aware of when he assigned Rohr to pitch against the Yankees.

Gibson recalled, "Billy's ball moved a lot. He had a sharp curve that came in on the hitter and a fastball away. In fact, the ball moved so much that it looked like it was right over the plate. But by the time you took a cut at it, swung away that is, it was down and away. Billy, that day, once he got his rhythm, had them hitting a lot of ground balls, ones our guys could easily scoop up."

Gibson had one edge over the typical rookie debuting in New York. As a teenager, he had been a three-sport start at Durfee High in Fall River, Massachusetts. Sports consumed this old New England town—they still do—and Russ was the superstar of his era. He quarterbacked the football team, turning down several football scholarships to join the Red Sox immediately after graduation. Gibson was a sparkplug on the Durfee High basketball team, leading them to the New England schoolboy championship in his junior year. But his first love was baseball and his natural position was behind the plate.

In the fifties, the Hearst Corporation sponsored an all-star series throughout the United States starting at the local level. This culminated in a national all-star game bringing the 50 best high school ball players in the U.S. together. Gibson excelled at all regional levels and three hits at Fenway Park earned him a trip to the Nationals. The game was played at the old Polo Grounds in New York and Gibson was on the receiving end of three innings of shutout baseball thrown by Mike McCormick, who went on to a distinguished career with the San Francisco Giants.

If Gibson was a little nervous, Rohr was nearly a basket case. Rohr had sought to prepare for his moment of glory by switching roommates from catcher Bob Tillman to staff ace Jim Lonborg. Lonborg took him out for dinner to go over the Yankee hitters. According to Lonborg, "We were there for two hours, and for an hour and three quarters, he didn't say a word. I talked and he just listened."

Rohr took a sleeping pill but he was up and about at 7:00 A.M. the next morning. "We talked about their hitters some more, had breakfast, then went to the park. I knew he was nervous," said Lonborg.

Rohr's teammates sensed his nervousness. Pitcher Dennis Bennett quipped, "If he gets by the first inning he'll be okay. But he's a nervous wreck right now."

The opening day crowd was small by New York standards: only a shade over 14,000 fans. But there was an ample mix of celebrities. Jacqueline Kennedy was there with her [seven]-year-old son, John Jr. Quincy-born movie star Lee Remick was there. The late Tony Conigliaro sent her a note before the game suggesting that if she wanted to date a real star she should meet him after the game.

The 1967 Yankee team will not go down in the annals with the 1927 Yankees, or the 1936 team or even the 1961 Yankees. There were no Ruths, no DiMaggios, not even a Phil Rizzuto. But there were some decent bats in the lineup. Tom Tresh and Joe Pepitone could still swing a bat. Ellie Howard was nearing the end of a distinguished career, but as he would later dramatically prove, he could still get around and the sight of No. 7, Mickey Mantle, pinch-hitting in the eighth inning would strike fear in the heart of Russ Gibson.

"All right, Billy-baby, settle down. Easy out there. Just keep it between the lines," Gibson yelled through his mask to his battery mate atop the mound. Despite his nerves, Rohr got the Yankees one, two, three in the first inning and began to relax because by then the Red Sox had a 1–0 edge off Reggie Smith's lead-off homer.

Once the game began, the only real sign of nervousness from Rohr was the rapidity with which he pitched. Gibson remembers "every pitch was right at my target . . . I didn't even have to move. His control was unbelievable and his fastball was really sinking. They couldn't do anything with him."

Gibson could sense his pitcher settling down as he retired the first ten

Yankees in the giant stadium before walking a man. "Yeh, he was still a little nervous, but you could almost see the wave of confidence taking over him," Gibson recalled. "He was remembering what Jim Lonborg had told him about the hitters and the stuff about them that we'd discussed before the game and between each inning as we went along. 'Course because you got 'em out with one type of pitch one time, didn't mean that you'd call for the same pitch against him every time. You sort of have to pitch them a little different every time. If you get a hitter out on fastballs, you can't throw him ten of them in a row. He gets the big picture and soon will hammer one away. No, you have to mix it up."

Gibson has some success at the plate as well. Facing the wily veteran Whitey Ford, Gibson was prepared for anything in his first at-bat. Gibson remembers that "Whitey's ball moved a lot. I got one that I could handle and lined it right up the middle." Not a bad start for a guy who was ready to give up the game two years earlier.

Gibson was too concerned about keeping his pitcher under control to think about his own situation. "Fact was I really wasn't nervous, especially after a couple of innings of play. Sure it was the Yankees and we were on their home turf, but it was easy for me by then. I began to think of it as any other ballgame where I always wanted to win. When we got the lead on Reggie's homer, and I got a hit my first time at bat it helped a lot. Meanwhile, Billy was just pitching a hell of a ballgame."

Rohr had the ability to throw the ball where he wanted it to go. "It was unbelievable," Gibson recalled, "I couldn't believe it for a kid like that in his situation. He had such good control. The only pitch that got away that I can remember is the one in the ninth."

After five innings, both teams and the fans became aware of what was transpiring. With each succeeding inning, the tension built in the stands. As is baseball tradition, no one on the Red Sox bench mentioned even the words "no-hitter." Gibson concentrated on going over the hitters between innings. It was a tight game and there was no time to focus on individual glory, just the task of winning the game.

Rohr entered the sixth inning without anything against him even resembling a basehit. And he was nursing a slim 1–0 lead. To pitch a no-hitter you need outstanding "stuff" and a great deal of luck. There is more than one pitcher in the Hall of Fame who never put that combination together. But Rohr was working so quickly that it appeared the game would soon be over. And he was about to catch a bit of luck.

The first ball hit hard off of Rohr was a line drive from the bat of Horace Clarke. It was a solid smash, but it went on a line to Carl Yastrzemski. A portent of more good fortune to come later.

There was even greater drama in the sixth inning. Bill Robinson was pretty much a journeyman ballplayer, but he could hit some. And hit one he did in the sixth. Hit one right off Rohr. Baseball is the game that has benefited the most from the instant replay. Plays of multiple dimensions happen in a flash and given the game's elegant pauses, there is time to freeze-frame the action and figure out what really happened.

Picture Rohr's eighty-five miles an hour fastball reaching Robinson in a second. Imagine Robinson's bat responding in milliseconds. His grounder goes directly back at Rohr with twice the speed of the pitched ball. It careens directly off Rohr's shin and in less than one second it has been redirected to Joe Foy at third base. Foy grabs it and fires it to George Scott at first base and Robinson is out by an eyelash. Less than five seconds have elapsed from the time the ball has left Rohr's hand. Miraculously, it seems Rohr's flirtation with immortality has been preserved. Such is the perfection of baseball's dimensions and the combinations that are played out.

Gibson was already headed for Billy, who was dancing around the mound in pain. Right behind him came Williams and trainer Buddy LeRoux. Elsewhere in the stadium, the crowd roared its appreciation for the great out.

Williams recalled later that he "asked the kid to roll down his stocking. He was on television. He has the skinniest legs you ever saw. I knew he was hurt. I was thinking of taking him out but I left him in."

"I had mixed feelings on my way," Gibson said. "I was happy for Foy's great play but also very concerned for Billy. That ball had ricochetted like a cannonball off his leg. But he sort of waved us off. Kept saying he was okay. Williams was not completely convinced. He thought maybe Billy should come out because he might hurt his arm by favoring his leg. Billy said it wouldn't be a problem. He wanted to stay in. Dick cautioned me to let him know immediately if Billy began to favor his leg and he'd have to pull him."

After taking a few pitches, Billy signalled that he was okay to pitch. The crowd gave him a big hand while Gibson scrutinized his pitching performance.

"He looked good to me. Far as I was concerned he was tossing better pitches than before that grounder hit him. I told Dick that when we came off the field and he left him in."

From Rohr's perspective, it was the ultimate "bang-bang" play. He told Cliff Keane of the *Boston Globe* after the game, "I never saw the ball come back at me. It hit my leg and it hurt. I looked and saw Joe Foy take the ball by third base with his bare hand and he threw out the runner."

When a pitcher goes five innings without a hit, everyone gets interested. You're past the halfway point. When a pitcher reaches six innings without a hit, everyone gets serious. Only nine more outs to go: a very manageable number. Two-thirds of the way there.

Gibson said that he first became a believer in a Rohr no-hitter after that sixth inning. "I think everybody by then was having thoughts about such a possibility. You just had to know it was a possibility, but no one said a word about it. We just kept going along through the seventh and eighth innings and Billy just kept setting them down."

There was a certain amount of tension on the Red Sox bench but after all these were all professional athletes not schoolboys. Their primary focus was on squeezing out a victory. Gibson recalls being very aware of the no-hitter in progress, but he was more concerned about being on the right side of a tight 1–0 lead. He continued to go over the hitters with Rohr and to urge him to bear down. The ultimate pros find a no-hitter in progress to be a distraction. Their only interest is in putting a "W" on the board.

When the Red Sox failed to score in the top of the seventh, the New York crowd rose for the traditional home seventh inning stretch. While they were Yankee fans, their sentiments were clearly with Rohr as he marched to the mound and towards history. Rohr faced the meat of the Yankee order and he dispatched them just as quickly as if he were still pitching for Bellflower High School against a local nine. Three up, three down and only six to go.

This was getting very serious. Gibson had to shift his attention from the eighth inning Yankee lineup to his turn at bat. He would leave young Mr. Rohr in the capable hands of pitching coach Sal Maglie.

Catchers will tell you that they don't hit for higher averages because they have to concentrate so much on the defensive part of the game. Yankee pitcher Whitey Ford had Gibson's full attention on this at bat, however. Gibson knew that Whitey remembered he had thrown him his best pitch on his first at-bat and had been burned with a hit. He figured Ford would try something else so he went up "thinking curve." Curve him Whitey did and Gibson touched him for his second hit.

Perched on first base, Gibson had to be glowing. He had toiled ten years in the minors to get to this place. Now two hours into his first game he's hitting .500—off of Whitey Ford, no less—and catching a no-hitter. Which direction is Cooperstown anyway?

Reggie Smith failed to advance Gibson, who represented a cushion for their 1–0 lead. Young third baseman Joe Foy a native of the Bronx, stood in against Ford. No respecter of future Hall of Famers, Foy sent a Ford delivery smartly into the left field bleachers. The Red Sox bench, sensing victory, jubilantly welcomed local boy made good Foy. With a three-run margin, the tension was eased a little.

There is a lot of evidence that it is "easier" to pitch a no-hitter in a tight ballgame than a blowout. For example, in the American League there were twelve no-hitters thrown during the 1960s. Nine of the twelve games were settled by a margin of four runs or less and eight of them were two-run margins or less. In a close game, the pitcher has to bear down on each and every hitter. There is no margin for error. With a lead of five runs or more, a pitcher may look to "save" a little for his next start and give up a few.

Rohr appeared to be ideally positioned as he took the mound in the bottom of the eighth inning. With a three-run lead, he could go for the "perfect pitch." If he cut it too fine a bases empty home run would still leave him with a two-run lead. Not only that but he was working to the lower third of the Yankee batting order.

With shortstop John Kennedy due up to the plate, catcher Gibson was startled by the loudest roar from a crowd that he had ever heard. He looked beside him to see a large number seven and the most imposing looking hitter he had ever seen. The legendary Mickey Mantle had been announced as a pinch hitter. Mantle wasn't huge—5' 11½"—by any standard, but he looked as if he had been carved from clay and fitted with

Yankee pinstripes. If anyone could put an end to Rohr's epoch effort, Mantle could. But twenty-one-year-old native Californians are not awestruck by New York legends—at least not young Mr. Rohr. Mantle, whose days of terrorizing American League pitching were several years behind him, flied out routinely to Tony Conigliaro in right field. Another major threat had passed and Gibson breathed a sigh of relief.

As Rohr walked off the mound at the end of the eighth inning, reality began to set in everywhere in Yankee Stadium. The reality to the fans that he was only three outs away from immortality. The reality among his teammates that the kid might just do it. Nowhere was reality more in evidence than in the press box. Reporters were flipping through record books to see if any rookie had ever pitched a no-hitter in his first game. Phone calls were made back to the sports desks in New York and Boston. Someone said, "How about Bobo Holloman?" That turned out to be wrong. Holloman had pitched a no-hitter for the St. Louis Browns in 1953 but he had made one previous three-inning relief appearance. No one had a nominee, not even the most senior reporter, but no one had a definitive answer either.

Dick Williams was interested in Rohr's no-hitter but he was much more concerned about getting an insurance run or two. After all this was his New York debut as a manager and he had promised that his 1–1 team would win more than they would lose. This wasn't the Yankees-Red Sox of *The Summer of '49*—the teams had finished one-half game apart in tenth and ninth places respectively in 1966—but this was an important game to his young team.

"Then there we were at the top of the ninth," Gibson recalled, "and all our guys went down in rapid fire order. But it was okay because we led 3–0. And Billy and I looked at each other and without a word we walked up from the dugout. Boy, for a kid, he sure had a serious expression on his face. It was strange; everyone was standing to watch Billy go to the mound but no one was cheering. It was like no one wanted to do anything that might snap the no-hitter, even the Yankee fans."

Gibson reviewed the three Yankee hitters due up in the top of the ninth. The three best Yankee hitters. Tom Tresh, batting in the third spot, was only about a .250 hitter but he had power. He had hit twenty-seven home runs in 1966 and he was good in the clutch. Tresh could be the one to stop it. Joe Pepitone was worrisome. He was another .250 hitter with power and he was unpredictable. He might strike out or he might hit one into the right field bleachers. Joe was a problem. Elston Howard was a cause for concern as well. Although Howard was thirty-eight years old, he had been a tough out for thirteen years in the big leagues. He had hit .313 as recently as 1964 and he had the experience of playing under pressure in forty-seven World Series games. Ellie was a real threat. Three tough outs: all pitchable but not one sure thing in the bunch.

Standing tall and thin atop the mound, the young Boston lefty looked about like some imperial potentate on his lowly subjects, checking to be sure all eight were positioned to his taste. Each in turn gazed back at him as though he was some demi-god who was about to perform a magical feat that would bring them all lasting fame.

"Their leftfielder, Tom Tresh, was first up for New York," Gibson said. "I give Bill the signal for his fast sinking ball and he lets it go and Tresh catches it clean and hard on his bat and it takes off like a rocket to left over the heads of the infielders. I cursed. There was no way that ball was going to be caught. It was a white blur on a course to rip right over Yastrzemski's head. There goes the no-hitter!"

Yaz, however, wasn't buying it. While the crowd groaned, he took off like a shot towards the fence on a line with the white blur that was headed right for the space far above him. He was running all out when he leaped like a yearling deer into the air to spear Tresh's ball with his splayed glove.

Yaz came to earth with a thump and absorbed the impact by going into a full somersault. The crowd held its breath! Did he have the ball? He rose triumphantly to hold the ball safely in his glove for all to see. It was a catch for the record book and all the more so in such a game. The cheers from the crowd seemed to swell in their numbers.

Three to nothing, Boston. Last of the ninth. One out. Now only two outs away from an historic no-hitter. The thunderous roars and applause was not only for Yaz but mostly for Rohr's working no-hitter which he had saved. The genie was out of the bottle. The forbidden word was being spoken: NO-HITTER! All hoped that they'd see history happen right before them that day.

"Billy was more relaxed, looking good," Gibson said. "The grim look had faded with Yaz's spectacular catch. He was beginning to believe that he might just pull off the unthinkable—a no-hitter in his first major league game. We were working very good, getting the pitches right down the middle."

The next batter up for the Yankees was rightfielder Joe Pepitone, who hit a fastball in the air to right field. Tony C. hardly had to extend himself to make the catch. The crowd again sundered the air with their whoops of delight. A historic moment lay ahead and they would be part of it for the ages.

With two outs in the bottom of the ninth and losing 3–0, catcher Elston Howard, a solid, muscular slugger who had gone zero for three at-bats, prepared to face young Billy Rohr. Before he got to the plate, Williams hurried to the mound to caution Rohr to watch his first pitch, "Howard's a dangerous batter on the first pitch."

Now there wasn't a sound to be heard but the encouraging chatter of the Red Sox players as they hovered expectantly about their positions in anticipation of Rohr's initial pitch. The count went to two and two on fastballs and the stadium was set to explode. The unthinkable was going to become reality. Get ready for it!

Rohr would up, all arms and legs whirling about, and threw his next pitch. "It was a strike! Right on!" Gibson said. "It was the final out of the game. Then, I couldn't believe it."

But believe it he had to. The umpire, Cal Drummond, called Billy's toss a ball to bring the count to three and two. Gibson though to this day says he will go to his grave convinced that the umpire blew the call. "It was that close between our rookie battery and the veteran batsman. He obviously felt that he had to give it to Howard."

Gibson only mildly contested the call. "I knew Billy was thinking three and two and that he really wanted to get on top of the curve ball and get it over good to put Howard away. Up to the ninth we hadn't thrown a curve at him. Billy figured it was time to toss one up. It fooled Howard, making him swing in the dirt for it. Now with the three and two count we figured it was time to throw him another one."

Rohr appeared so confident on the mound that Gibson never went out to speak to him at any time during the ninth. "His control was just that good. We had Howard to three and two and agreed on the second curve. Billy would up and threw the ball but I knew immediately that he held it too tight and it sort of squirted out on him. What the hell! One pitch that hung a fraction too long!"

When Howard hit the ball to right toward Tony C., Gibson knew it was in there, a clean base hit. The good thing was that there was no doubt about it. It was a solid, well-stroked hit, leaving Tony without any chance of making a play.

"It was sort of a letdown," Gibson said, "but what the hell, we're still in a 3–0 game and you can't let down too much because I've seen games turn around pretty damn fast. Once the no-hitter was gone, the idea was let's win the game and get out of here."

As for the young lefty for Boston, he hardly changed expressions as he watched Howard's single bounce into right field. If he was disappointed, he didn't show it. His attitude like Gibson's was matter-of-fact like, "Hey, that's baseball. Next batter."

While Gibson and Rohr stood silently with nonplussed expressions, the throng in Yankee Stadium howled in dismay at the loss of "their no-hitter." Hometown hero Elston Howard was the villain although he was only doing what he was paid to do—hit the ball. The boos filled the huge expanse of the stadium. Later Howard would recall that "my job is to hit the ball and I've three kids to feed and that's what I do. I looked over at Rohr when I got to first base and I could see that he was hurting, but I wasn't sorry a bit." After reflecting for a moment he said, "That's the only time I've ever been booed in Yankee Stadium for getting a base hit."

With Howard at first base, Charley Smith, New York's third baseman, came up to the plate. The fans' boos continued to wrack the air. Smith took his cuts and soon was retired for the final out. Rohr had a one-hitter.

Almost instantly, the roars of disapproval directed at Howard for getting a hit before his hometown crowd turned to cries of congratulations for Billy Rohr. The fans were baseball lovers first before partisan diehards and showed their appreciation for his great pitching effort with their sustained applause.

Rohr and his fellow players dashed toward their dugout only to run into their own teammates who rushed out to congratulate their pitcher. All were soon swept away into the dugout and the clubhouse by hordes of policemen, the media and fans who had broken through police lines. In the midst of all the excitement and whooping, Jackie Kennedy and her son came by to congratulate Rohr.

When things began to calm down and some sense of order was restored, Rohr told press people that he first "thought about a no-hitter about the fifth or sixth inning. Nobody on the bench talked about it and neither did any of the Yankees." In ironic acknowledgment of Howard's lone hit, he added, "Sure I'm a little disappointed that Howard got the hit. But he gets paid more to hit than I do to pitch, so how can you begrudge him one. When he was on first I looked over at him. Yeh, I was disappointed but I wasn't mad at all."

Howard disagreed with the Red Sox contention that he should have been struck out on the 2–2 pitch. "If the kid thought one of them curves was a strike up to the last one he wasn't right," said Howard. "Them other pitches were too low and Drummond can't call them strikes because they're balls." He was a far better hitter than a post-game quote-maker.

According to Gibson Red Sox manager Williams was "happy about the win. He congratulated us on a good game. His attitude was to win a game any way you can. No-hitter or one-hitter, it still went into the books as a win. And Dick was determined the team was going to win more than it lost in '67." Rohr, of course, was "on top of the world," according to Gibson. "It was a great thrill for him. I'm sure he definitely wanted the no-hitter, but as a professional you do the best you can. And Bill certainly had on that day."

When Gibson was informed by Williams that he wouldn't be catching again until Sunday, he joined Yaz, Mike Andrews and the pumped up Billy Rohr on a trip downtown to a Wall Street pub.

"We were all on a high, coming off such a spectacular win over the Yankees in New York. We felt like we owned the town. A radio broadcast truck came by and we flagged it down."

They told the driver that they wanted a lift downtown to a Wall Street restaurant. When he demurred, Gibson said to the driver while pointing at Billy, "You know who you got here? Billy Rohr, the Red Sox pitcher who threw the one-hitter today at Yankee Stadium. Only tossed 122 pitches against your big guy, Whitey Ford. Billy here, it was his first major league outing. Your guy, Ford, was making his four hundred and thirty-second."

Once the truck crew realized the quality of their catch they insisted on taking the Red Sox players to their radio station for a live interview. Only then did they transport the Boston quartet to their eatery on Wall Street.

High on the list of congratulatory messages Rohr received was a telegram from Boston mayor John Collins: "You gave Boston an unforgettable day. Red Sox fans everywhere salute you and congratulate you on a fine pitching performance. May today's victory be the first of hundreds in your major league career."

Sadly, it was not to be so for the lanky lefthander. For though Billy Rohr was swept victorious off the mound with his one-hitter that day in Yankee Stadium, he was to win only one other game in 1967, ironically against the Yankees again in Boston, and an additional game in 1968. Incredibly, Rohr's career began and peaked on that cold April day. Today, he is a successful lawyer in California.

In another ironic twist, Yankee catcher Elston Howard, who got the lone hit off Rohr in the 3–0 Boston victory, was traded late in the season to Boston and made a successful contribution to their miracle finish. By the time he joined his Boston teammates in August, young Billy Rohr had been exiled to the minors.

This most improbable of starts on opening day in Yankee Stadium was the first clue that this was perhaps a team of destiny. Time and time again they would be counted out only to rise again from the canvas. It would take another 159 games, however, to determine how the drama would be played out.

Today, Russ Gibson lives in Swansea, which is not far from his boyhood home in Fall River, and works as a regional salesman for the Massachusetts State Lottery.

"It's still incredible," he says, "when I think of the game that Billy pitched. To pitch a one-hitter and then win your second game again against the Yankees. And then not to win another game until 1968 and only one and then he disappears. He was traded to Cleveland the next year and couldn't perform on the mound."

Gibson surmises that "when you're a sinker ball pitcher like Billy, you lose your sinker ball if you don't throw hard. Billy didn't really throw that hard. He threw fairly hard, but he lost his sinker. When he lost that his ball stayed flat. They killed him because with his best pitch, the ball moved. When he stayed on top, the ball sank. Once he lost whatever he lost, the sinker went in straight. The same thing happens to a lot of pitchers in the majors. With Billy, bingo, he's gone! He's out of baseball two years later. How do you figure it?"

Gibson himself remained with the Red Sox through the "Impossible Dream" year and all of 1968 and 1969. "I was probably as close as anyone to being a regular catcher, playing in eighty to ninety games each of the last two years. My hitting was improving, .225 in 1968 and .251 in 1969."

Unfortunately for Russ, when Dick Williams was unceremoniously fired in late 1969, Gibson's days with the Red Sox were numbered. What price glory, heh? "When I heard that Dick got fired I knew I was gone. He, in effect, had been my mentor going back to Toronto, and it was just a matter of time."

Gibson's time came in at the end of spring training in 1970 when he was "leading the team in hitting in the Grapefruit League. I was the top catcher, headed for my best season ever. I remember that I was hitting something like over .400."

Despite his great spring, the Red Sox traded Gibson to the San Francisco Giants. To add insult to injury, he was traded for a player to be named later and that old Red Sox nemesis—cash. "Hell, they didn't even trade me for anybody. What a comedown."

What has it meant to Russ Gibson all the years since he was a member of that wonderful winning team of 1967? "I can only tell you that something like that changes your life as far as the way you live. Everybody knows you no matter where you go. People are always sending you cards, letters, whatever, asking for autographs. They want you to speak at banquets. People act like the 1967 season was just yesterday. Actually, most of the people hereabouts can recall better than I can just what I did that season. You play in so many games for so many years, including the minors and they all begin to blur. Still, I like to go and talk to the fans and tell fun stories. The ins and outs of the team. People though, they still remember things I have no recollection about."

Ultimately, Gibson said, "It's like a love affair because we shared so much together that season . . . a love affair not only with the fans but with the players who shared so many ups and downs with you and who became a close bunch of guys."

A final reflection about Russ Gibson: if the house next door to you is for sale, see if Gibby is interested. Russ Gibson is perhaps as nice a man as you will ever meet. He is everybody's ideal next door neighbor.

"Every time I come back to Boston, I'm remembered. They used to say, 'I saw you pitch.' Now they say, 'My dad saw you pitch.' When they start saying, 'My granddad saw you pitch,' I'm not coming back."

—Billy Rohr,
more than 30 years after the end
of his brief major league career

THEY SAID IT...

By the mid-1970s, the Yankees and Red Sox were fighting each other in the standings for American League East Division titles. They also were fighting each other on the field in a more literal sense. The teams didn't get along, and it occasionally came to blows. Two pairs of players in particular couldn't stand each other, according to then Red Sox second baseman Jerry Remy. Boston pitcher Bill Lee feuded with Yankee third baseman Graig Nettles, and Yankee catcher Thurman Munson didn't see eye-to-eye with Red Sox catcher Carlton Fisk. The following pair of articles examine these rivalries within the rivalry.

FISK VS. MUNSON: A TRUE WAR

from ESPN.com [July 23, 2003]
by Peter Gammons

CARLTON FISK AND I broke into the big leagues at the same time, September 1971. I grew up in the small New England town of Groton, Mass., up on the New Hampshire border. Fisk grew up on the banks of the Connecticut River in western New Hampshire, in the town of Charlestown.

To Red Sox fans who suffer the insecurities of growing up in the shadow of the Yankees, Fisk was one of them. The Red Sox are often called "The Olde Towne Teame" because they are the team of New England—not just Boston—and its history of town teams that played on the weekends from the 1860s until World War II, a tradition that still carries on in places like Maine's Pine Tree League with the Norway-South Paris Twins, the West Paris Braves and the Mexico Reds. They were the real Yankees—the New England Yankees who don't much like anything about New York.

If you go back to all the fire and hatred between the Red Sox and Yankees in the 1970s, you go back to Fisk. Boston vs. New York, Fisk vs. Thurman Munson.

It started in a meaningless September game in 1971. Munson was jammed and fell back as he hit a ground ball wide of first. Carl Yastrzemski, playing first base, grabbed it on the run and fired to Luis Aparicio, who was coming across the second-base bag. To Aparicio's surprise, he looked up, expecting not to have a play, but there was the rookie Fisk beating Munson down the line. Aparicio threw a changeup and Munson was safe at first.

But Fisk had beaten Munson down the line. There began the rivalry of the '70s. Thurman Munson hated Carlton Fisk because he was jealous of him—the chisled, handsome Fisk, in contrast to the dumpy, stubbled Munson. On Aug. 1, 1973, the two teams were tied for first place. It was the ninth inning, one out, Munson at third, Felipe Alou at first, Gene Michael batting, John Duffield Curtis III pitching.

As Curtis let his first pitch go, Munson broke for the plate. Michael tried to bunt, and missed. With Munson coming, the scrawny Yankee shortstop tried to step in Fisk's way, but Carlton elbowed him out of the way and braced for Munson, who crashed into him as hard as he could. Fisk held onto the ball, but Munson tried to lie on top of him to allow Alou to keep rounding the bases.

Fisk kicked Munson off him and into the air, and swiped at him with his fist. Michael grabbed Fisk, and as Curtis grabbed Munson—his former Cape Cod League roommate—Fisk threw Michael down with his left arm and fell to the ground. "Fisk had his left arm right across Stick's throat and wouldn't let up," said Ralph Houk, the Yankees manager at the time. "Michael couldn't breathe. I had to crawl underneath the pile to try to pry Fisk's arm off his throat to keep him from killing Stick. All the while he had Michael pinned down, he was punching Munson underneath the pile. I had no idea Fisk was that strong, but he was scary."

Fisk fought it out with Dirty Al Gallagher of the Angels, and got into it with Frank Robinson. In 1975, he returned after missing the first 2½ months with a broken arm and immediately homered and led the Sox to three victories in four games against the Yankees in a series that turned around the season and led to a Red Sox pennant.

Then, in 1976, came the great brawl. It started when Lou Piniella crashed into Fisk at the plate, feet first. Both players came up swinging, and when the brawl was over, Bill Lee had injured his shoulder after getting in fights with Mickey Rivers and Graig Nettles. Two years later, "Fisk Eats Rice" T-shirts were on sale outside the Stadium. "It wasn't just Red Sox–Yankees, it was Yankees-Fisk," Graig Nettles once said. "Then [Rick] Burleson said he hated anyone in a Yankee uniform. But Fisk was it."

How bad was it with Munson? One day, Yankees PR director Marty Appell included in the media notes all the categories in which Munson led AL catchers. He also put that Munson was second among AL catchers in assists. That day, Yankees pitchers struck out seven batters. On every one, Munson dropped the ball, threw it to first for the assist, then gestured toward the press box.

New Englanders looked at Fisk and saw themselves. So when he is enshrined in the Hall of Fame on Sunday, it will be small town New England's day. When his 27 goes up on the right-field roof aside Joe Cronin's 4, Ted Williams' 9, Carl Yastrzemski's 8 and Bobby Doerr's 1, it will be the first time a New Englander's number will hang in the home of The Olde Towne Teame.

A quarter-century after their famed fight, Red Sox pitcher Bill Lee and Yankee third baseman Graig Nettles see no reason to patch things up.

"LEE VS. NETTLES: TIME HASN'T HEALED SORE FEELINGS"

from the *Hartfort Courant* (May 20, 2002)
by Paul Doyle

AMID THE SCRUM AT the plate, Bill Lee's left arm was numb.

In the May 20, 1976 brawl that defined the rivalry between the Red Sox and Yankees, Lee was body-slammed by Graig Nettles. When Lee got up, with no feeling in his arm, he charged Nettles. The response from the Yankees third baseman: a punch that left Lee with a black eye.

The bruise subsided, but Lee's pitching career was derailed. He did not regain full strength in his left arm until 1978. In 1979, he won 16 games for the Expos, pitching as well as he ever had.

But don't think for a moment that Lee has forgiven Nettles. On the 25th anniversary of the Yankee Stadium brawl, Lee remains his feisty self as he recounts the details of the scrape.

Over the years, Lee has never discussed the fight with Nettles and says he has no interest in a conversation.

"No, you can't talk to a Neanderthal like that," Lee said from his home in Vermont last week. "He doesn't really communicate very well. This guy is so politically incorrect you wouldn't want to waste your time. So, no, I don't talk to him."

The last time they exchanged meaningful words, in fact, was on the field 25 years ago. When Lee realized how badly his shoulder was hurt, he charged Nettles, screaming obscenities.

Lee tried to punch Nettles, but he couldn't lift his arm. Nettles responded with a right hook that left Lee with the shiner.

"Tensions were running high," Nettles said.

Indeed, the brawl was the residue of a 1973 tangle between Carlton Fisk and Thurman Munson. After that fight, Lee said the Yankees were "like a bunch of hookers, swinging their purses."

As the dislike between the teams grew, Yankees players remembered Lee's quote. And as the outspoken Lee became one of the better left-handers in the American League, he was not popular with opponents.

So when Lou Piniella collided with Fisk in 1976, it was inevitable that Lee would become a target.

"Lee would make the opposition very angry," former Red Sox third baseman Rico Petrocelli said. "He would throw that slow curve to strike somebody out, then he'd prance around the mound like he was real happy about it."

Said former Red Sox infielder Denny Doyle: "Lee's personality was the type the Yankees loved to hate. Not only that, but he was semi-fearless. He didn't care where he was or who he was pitching against."

Lee was backing up the plate when Piniella and Fisk began to wrestle and he initially tried to stop Otto Velez from entering the pile. He was thrown from Velez and punched by Mickey Rivers.

Dazed from the punch, Lee was picked up by Nettles and tossed to the ground. Nettles later said he was trying to keep Lee out of the fight.

But reached at his California home last week, Nettles admitted the Yankees were trying to make a point to Lee.

"A couple of their players had scratches [in 1973]," Nettles said. "And Lee said something like, 'You know you're in a fight with the Yankees because you get hit with [fingernails] and purses.' And I remembered it. He was always taking shots at us like that unnecessarily. So I pulled him off and I wanted to make sure he knew he wasn't getting hit with a purse."

Later, the purse thing passed through Nettles' mind as he delivered the punch to Lee's left eye.

"He just tried to sneak around the pile and he came at me, started jawing at me, getting in my face, so, again, I wanted to make sure he wasn't hit with any purse," Nettles said. "I got several thank-yous from their players after that happened, thanking me because they said, 'Now we don't have to put up with him for the next three months.'"

There was a sense that Lee brought some of the problems on himself. Some Red Sox players and coaches said Lee was instigating the fight by calling the Yankees various names.

"I just remember they were clearing out and Lee was in there yapping away," former Red Sox coach Johnny Pesky said. "That was Bill, though. He was like that. He was a competitor."

Said former outfielder Rick Miller: "A lot of us were a little bit peeved at Bill Lee for starting that fight up again. Here he was injured and he came out and tried to start that fight with Nettles again. Didn't do any good."

As for the notion that Nettles was simply trying to keep Lee out of the fight, Lee laughs.

Lee has spoken with Rivers over the years, although he now calls him "a cheap-shot artist." But he also says he likes Rivers, who was an active participant in the brawl.

"I know Bill Lee," Rivers said from Florida. "A lot of things happen and they pass over. I don't dwell on it or live in the past. There's no animosity between me and Bill Lee."

There was animosity between the teams 25 years ago, as the rivalry reached an emotional peak. The Yankees hated Fisk, whom they felt overshadowed Munson. And whether Lee was an instigator or not, the Red Sox did not like the way Nettles conducted himself during the brawl.

Meanwhile, the fight became fodder for the fans. When the Yankees came to Fenway Park, Rivers was heckled and had objects thrown at him. Yankees fans had no use for Lee, who compared Billy Martin and the team to the Nazis.

Again, his views have not changed.

"That was the type of behavior you'd expect from the Brown Shirts," Lee said last week.

Lee had won 17 games in '73, '74 and '75, but his career with the Red Sox was never the same after the brawl, as it took two years before his arm strength returned. By then, he was in Don Zimmer's doghouse. He was missed in '76, when the Red Sox finished 15½ games behind the Yankees. In 1977, the Red Sox won 97 games but finished 2½ games behind the Yankees. Lee was 9–5 in 27 games.

Lee, 54, continues to play on barnstorming teams, and he often runs into former teammates and opponents. Lee and Rivers played together in the Senior League in the early 1990s.

Nettles, who scouts for the Yankees, has seen Lee at various old-timers' games. One of Lee's close friends, former Expos teammate Steve Rogers, once hit Nettles with a pitch in an old-timers' game. Lee loved that, but only wishes he could face Nettles one last time.

"I've been looking to play against him," Lee said. "And I still am."

On October 1, 1977—the last day of baseball's regular season—the Boston Red Sox pursuit of the Yankees and the American League East title ended in failure. On October 2, Yale professor and Red Sox fan Bart Giamatti wrote that baseball breaks his heart, that it is designed to break hearts. His essay appeared in *Yale Alumni Magazine* the following month. Twelve years later, Giamatti became commissioner of Major League Baseball—a dream job for the passionate baseball fan. But again the game would break his heart, this time in a way it was never designed to do. As commissioner, Giamatti was forced to suspend baseball legend Pete Rose for life for gambling. Giamatti died of a heart attack just days after the suspension was announced.

"THE GREEN FIELDS OF THE MIND"

from *Yale Alumni Magazine* (November 1977)
by A. Bartlett Giamatti

IT BREAKS YOUR HEART. It is designed to break your heart. The game begins in the spring, when everything else begins again, and it blossoms in the summer, filling the afternoons and evenings, and then as soon as the chill rains come, it stops and leaves you to face the fall alone. You count on it, rely on it to buffer the passage of time, to keep the memory of sunshine and high skies alive, and then just when the days are all twilight, when you need it most, it stops. Today, October 2, a Sunday of rain and broken branches and leaf-clogged drains and slick streets, it stopped, and summer was gone.

Somehow, the summer seemed to slip by faster this time. Maybe it wasn't this summer, but all the summers that, in this my fortieth summer, slipped by so fast. There comes a time when every summer will have something of autumn about it. Whatever the reason, it seemed to me that

I was investing more and more in baseball, making the game do more of the work that keeps time fat and slow and lazy. I was counting on the game's deep patterns, three strikes, three outs, three times three innings, and its deepest impulse, to go out and back, to leave and to return home, to set the order of the day and to organize the daylight. I wrote a few things this last summer, this summer that did not last, nothing grand but some things, and yet that work was just camouflage. The real activity was done with the radio—not the all-seeing, all-falsifying television—and was the playing of the game in the only place it will last, the enclosed, green field of the mind. There, in that warm, bright place, what the old poet called Mutability does not so quickly come.

But out here on Sunday, October 2, where it rains all day, Dame Mutability never loses. She was in the crowd at Fenway yesterday, a grey day full of bluster and contradiction, when the Red Sox came up in the last of the ninth trailing Baltimore 8–5, while the Yankees, rain-delayed against Detroit, only needing to win one or have Boston lose one to win it all, sat in New York washing down cold cuts with beer and watching the Boston game. Boston had won two, the Yankees had lost two, and suddenly it seemed as if the whole season might go to the last day, or beyond, except here was Boston losing 8–5, while New York sat in its family room and put its feet up. Lynn, both ankles hurting now as they had in July, hits a single down the right field line. The crowd stirs. It is on its feet. Hobson, third baseman, former Bear Bryant quarterback, strong, quiet, over 100 RBIs, goes for three breaking balls and is out. The goddess smiles and encourages her agent, a canny journeyman named Nelson Briles.

Now comes a pinch hitter, Bernie Carbo, one-time Rookie of the Year, erratic, quick, a shade too handsome, so laid back he is always, in his soul, stretched out in the tall grass, one arm under his head, watching the clouds and laughing; now he looks over some low stuff unworthy of him and then, uncoiling, sends one out, straight on a rising line, over the center field wall, no cheap Fenway shot, but all of it, the physics as elegant as the arc the ball describes.

New England is on its feet, roaring. The summer will not pass. Roaring, they recall the evening, late and cold, in 1975, the sixth game of the World Series, perhaps the greatest baseball game played in the last 50 years, when Carbo, loose and easy, had uncoiled to tie the game that Fisk would win. It is 8–7, one out, and school will never start, rain will never come, sun will warm the back of your neck forever. Now Bailey, picked up from the National League recently, big arms, heavy gut, experienced, new to the league and the club; he fouls off two and then, checking, tentative, a big man off balance, he pops a soft liner to the first baseman. It is suddenly darker and later, and the announcer doing the game coast to coast, a New Yorker who works for a New York television station, sounds relieved. His little world, well-lit, hot-combed, split-second-timed, had no capacity to absorb this much gritty, grainy, contrary reality.

Cox swings a bat, stretches his long arms, bends his back, the rookie from Pawtucket, who broke in two weeks earlier with a record six straight hits, the kid drafted ahead of Fred Lynn, rangy, smooth, cool. The count runs two and two, Briles is cagey, nothing too good, and Cox swings, the ball beginning toward the mound and then, in a jaunty, wayward dance, skipping past Briles, feinting to the right, skimming the last of the grass, finding the dirt, moving now like some small, purposeful marine creature negotiating the green deep, easily avoiding the jagged rock of second base, traveling steady and straight now out into the dark, silent recesses of center field.

The aisles are jammed, the place is on its feet, the wrappers, the programs, the Coke cups and peanut shells, the detritus of an afternoon; the anxieties, the things that have to be done tomorrow, the regrets about yesterday, the accumulation of a summer: all forgotten, while hope, the anchor, bites and takes hold where a moment before it seemed we would be swept out with the tide. Rice is up, Rice whom Aaron had said was the only one he'd seen with the ability to break his records, Rice the best clutch hitter on the club, with the best slugging percentage in the league, Rice, so quick and strong he once checked his swing halfway through and snapped the bat in two, Rice the Hammer of God sent to scourge the Yankees, the sound was overwhelming, fathers pounded their sons on the back, cars pulled off the road, households froze, New England exulted in its blessedness, and roared its thanks for all good things, for Rice and for a summer stretching halfway through October. Briles threw, Rice swung, and it was over. One pitch, a fly to center, and it stopped. Summer died in

New England and like rain sliding off a roof, the crowd slipped out of Fenway, quickly, with only a steady murmur of concern for the drive ahead remaining of the roar. Mutability had turned the seasons and translated hope to memory once again. And once again, she had used baseball, our best invention to stay change, to bring change on. That is why it breaks my heart, that game—not because in New York they could win because Boston lost; in that, there is a rough justice, and a reminder to the Yankees of how slight and fragile are the circumstances that exalt one group of human beings over another. It breaks my heart because it was meant to, because it was meant to foster in me again the illusion that there was something abiding, some pattern and some impulse that could come together to make a reality that would resist the corrosion; and because after it had fostered again that most hungered-for illusion, the game was meant to stop, and betray precisely what it promised.

Of course, there are those who learn after the first few times. They grow out of sports. And there are others who were born with the wisdom to know that nothing lasts. These are the truly tough among us, the ones who can live without illusion, or without even the hope of illusion. I am not that grown-up or up-to-date. I am a simpler creature, tied to more primitive patterns and cycles. I need to think something lasts forever, and it might as well be that state of being that is a game; it might as well be that, in a green field, in the sun.

The 1978 season is perhaps the most famous in the history of the Yankees–Red Sox rivalry. Boston streaked to a 14-game lead over the reigning World Champion Yanks by late July. But New York came storming back and by early September was just four out heading into a four-game set in Boston.

"THE BOSTON MASSACRE"

from *Sports Illustrated* (September 18, 1978)
by Peter Gammons

THE MAN HAD ON a gray Brooks Brothers suit, which made him look for all the world as if he were Harvard '44, and he was leaning over the railing of the box next to the Red Sox dugout. "Zimmer!" he screamed, but Don Zimmer just stared dead ahead. The score at that point in last Friday night's game was 13–0 in favor of the Yankees and except to change pitchers a few times the Red Sox manager hadn't moved in three hours. He had stared as Mickey Rivers stood on third just two pitches into the game. He had stared as, for the second straight night, a Yankee batter got his third hit before Boston's ninth hitter, Butch Hobson, even got to the plate. He had stared as the Red Sox made seven errors. And now he stared as the man kept screaming his name.

"I've been a Red Sox fan for twenty years," the man hollered. "A diehard Red Sox fan. I've put up with a lot of heartaches. But this time you've really done it. This time my heart's been broken for good." Finally Zimmer looked up, just as security guards hauled the man away.

From Eastport to Block Island, New Englanders were screaming mad. Only a couple of weeks before, the Red Sox had been baseball's one sure thing, but now Fenway Park was like St. Petersburg in the last days of Czar Nicholas. Back in July, when Billy Martin still sat in the Yankee manager's office and New York was in the process of falling fourteen games behind the Sox, Reggie Jackson had said, "Not even Affirmed can catch them." But by late last Sunday afternoon, when the 1978 version of the Boston Massacre concluded with New York's fourth win in a row over the Red Sox, the Yankees had caught them. And the Yanks had gained a tie for first in the American League East in such awesome fashion—winning sixteen of their last eighteen, including the lopsided victories that comprised the Massacre—that Saturday night a New Yorker named Dick Waterman walked into a Cambridge bar, announced, "For the first time a first—place team has been mathematically eliminated," and held up a sign that read: NY 35–49–4, BOS 5–16–11. Those figures were the combined line score of last weekend's first three games. The disparity between those sets of numbers, as much as the losses themselves, was what so deeply depressed Red Sox fans. "It's 1929 all over again," mourned Robert Crane, treasurer of the Commonwealth of Massachusetts.

The Red Sox and Yankees began their two-city, seven-game, eleven-day showdown in Boston last Thursday—it will continue with three games this weekend in New York—and it quickly became apparent that this confrontation would be quite different from their six-game shoot-out in late June and early July. On that occasion the Red Sox had beaten the Yanks four times and opened up a lead that appeared insurmountable. Back then the Yankees had so few healthy bodies that catcher Thurman Munson was trying to become a right fielder, and one day a minor league pitcher named Paul Semall drove from West Haven, Connecticut, to Boston to throw batting practice. Had the New York brass liked the way he threw, Semall would have stayed with the Yankees and become a starter. By midnight, Semall was driving back to West Haven, and soon thereafter injuries became so rife among New York pitchers that reserve first baseman Jim Spencer was warming up in the bullpen.

Rivers, the center fielder and key to the Yankee offense, had a broken wrist. Both members of the double-play combination, Willie Randolph and Bucky Dent, were injured and out of the lineup. To complete the up-the-middle collapse, Munson was playing—sometimes behind the plate and sometimes in right—with a bad leg, and the pitching staff had been reduced to *Gong Show* contestants. Paul Semall got gonged. Dave Rajsich got gonged. Larry McCall got gonged. Catfish Hunter, Ed Figueroa, Dick Tidrow, Ken Clay, Andy Messersmith, and Don Gullett were all hurt or soon to be injured. Only the brilliant Ron Guidry stayed healthy. Almost singlehandedly he kept the bottom from falling out during July and early August.

Then, as the regulars gradually began getting back into the lineup, the blow—up between owner George Steinbrenner and Martin occurred. Martin resigned on July 24, and the next day Bob Lemon, who had recently been canned by the White Sox, took over. "The season starts today," Lemon told the Yankees. "Go have some fun." Considering the disarray in New York during the preceding year and a half, that seemed a bit much to ask. So was catching Boston. No American League team had ever changed managers in midseason and won a championship. "Under Lemon we became a completely different team," says Spencer. "If Martin were still here, we wouldn't be," snaps one player. "We'd have quit. Rivers and Jackson couldn't play for him. But Lemon gave us a fresh spirit. We kept playing. We looked up, and Boston was right in front of us." The fact that a suddenly revived Hunter had won six straight, that Figueroa had regained health and happiness, that Tidrow had again become hale and that rookie right hander Jim Beattie had returned from the minors with his self-confidence restored didn't hurt.

And while the Yankees arrived in Boston 30–13 under Lemon and 35–14 since July 17—the night they fell fourteen games behind—the Red Sox had been stumbling. They were 25–24 since July 17. Their thirty-nine-year-old leader, Carl Yastrzemski, had suffered back and shoulder ailments in mid-July, and then he pulled ligaments in his right wrist that left him taped up and in and out of the lineup. He had hit three homers in two months. Second baseman Jerry Remy fractured a bone in his left wrist on August 25 and had not appeared in the lineup thereafter.

Catcher Carlton Fisk had been playing with a cracked rib, which he said made him feel as if "someone is sticking a sword in my side" every time he threw. Third baseman Butch Hobson has cartilage and ligament damage in both knees and bone chips in his right elbow. The chips are so painful that one night he had to run off the field during infield practice; his elbow had locked up on him. When New York came to town, he had a major-league-leading thirty-eight errors, most of them the result of bad throws made with his bad arm. Right fielder Dwight Evans had been beaned on August 29 and was experiencing dizziness whenever he ran. Reliever Bill Campbell, who had thirty-one saves and thirteen wins in 1977, had suffered from elbow and shoulder soreness all season.

The injuries tended to dampen Boston's already erratic, one-dimensional offense, which relies too heavily on power hitting even when everyone is healthy. They also ruined the Sox defense, which had been the facet of play most responsible for giving the Red Sox a ten-game lead over their nearest challenger, Milwaukee, on July 8. No wonder the pitching went sour, with Mike Torrez going 4–4 since the All–Star Game, Luis Tiant 3–7 since June 24, and Bill Lee 0–7 since July 15. And as Boston awaited its confrontation with the Yankees, it lost three out of five to Toronto and Oakland and two of three in Baltimore. The Sox' only lift came in Wednesday's 2–0 win over the Orioles. Tiant pitched a two-hitter that night, and Yaz, his wrist looking like a mummy's, hit a two-run homer. It was one of only two hits the Sox got off Dennis Martinez.

As play began Thursday night at Fenway Park, the Red Sox lead had dwindled to four games with twenty-four to play. "We'll be happy with a split," Lemon said. By 9:05 P.M. Friday—during the third inning of Game 2–Lemon turned to pitching coach–scout Clyde King and said, "Now I'll only be happy with three out of four." Right about then the *Washington Post*'s Tom Boswell was writing his lead: "*Ibid.,* for details, see yesterday's paper." The details were downright embarrassing to the Red Sox.

The embarrassments had begun with a Hobson error in the first inning Thursday. Then a Munson single. And a Jackson single. Zap, the Yankees had two unearned runs. After giving up four straight singles to start the second inning, Torrez went to the showers. Munson had three hits–and the Yankees seven runs—before Hobson got his first at-bat in the bottom of the third. After the seventh inning, someone in the press box looked up at the New York line on the scoreboard—2–3–2–5–0–1–0—and dialed the number. It was disconnected. When the game ended, the Yankees had twenty-one hits and a 15–3 victory.

New York's joy was tempered by two injuries. Hunter left the game with a pulled groin muscle in the fourth, too soon to get the victory, though the Yanks were leading 12–0. "The bullpen phone rang and six of us fought to answer it," said Clay, who won the phone call and the game. Hunter, it turned out, would probably miss only one start. In the sixth inning, Munson was beaned by Dick Drago. Though dizzy, Munson said he would be behind the plate Friday. "He smells blood," Jackson said.

The next night, the Yankees not only drained Boston's blood but also its dignity. Rivers hit rookie right hander Jim Wright's first pitch past first baseman George Scott into right field. On the second pitch, he stole second and cruised on into third as Fisk's throw bounced away from shortstop Rick Burleson. Wright had thrown two pitches, and Rivers was peering at him from third base. Wright went on to get four outs, one more than Torrez had; he was relieved after allowing four runs. His replacement, Tom Burgmeier, immediately gave up a single and walk before surrendering a mighty home run by Jackson.

Beattie, who in his Fenway appearance in June had been knocked out in the third inning and optioned to Tacoma in the sixth, retired eighteen in a row in one stretch, while the Red Sox self-destructed in the field. Evans, who had not dropped a fly in his first five and three-quarters years in the majors, dropped his second one of the week and had to leave the game. "I can't look up or down without getting dizzy," he said. Fisk had two throws bounce away for errors. Rivers hit a routine ground ball to Scott in the third and beat Scott to the bag, making him three-for-three before Hobson ever got up. The game ended with a 13–2 score and the seven Red Sox errors.

"I can't believe what I've been seeing," said King, who has watched about forty Red Sox games this season. "I could understand if an expansion team fell apart like that, but Boston's got the best record in baseball.

It can't go on." On Saturday afternoon, Guidry took his 20–2 record to the mound. It went on.

This was to be the showdown of the aces. Dennis Eckersley, 16–6, was 9–0 in Fenway and had not been knocked out before the fifth inning all season. He had beaten the Yankees three times in a twelve-day stretch earlier in the year. When he blew a third strike past Jackson to end the bottom of the first, he had done what Torrez and Wright had not been able to do—shut the Yankees out in the first inning.

"It looked like it was going to be a 1–0 game, what with the wind whipping in and Eckersley looking like he'd put us back together," said Zimmer. After Burleson led off Boston's first with a single, Fred Lynn bunted. Guidry, who could have cut down Burleson at second, hesitated and ended up throwing to first. Then Dent bobbled Jim Rice's grounder in the hole for an infield single. Two on. But Guidry busted fastballs in on the hands of Yastrzemski and Fisk, getting them out on a weak grounder and called third strike, respectively. Despite leadoff walks in the next two Boston at-bats, the Sox hitters were finished for the day. Rice's grounder would be their second and last hit of the afternoon.

Yastrzemski seemed to lift his catatonic team in the fourth with a twisting, leaping catch on the dead run that he turned into a double play. But three batters later, with two on and two out, all that Yaz and Eckersley had done to heighten Boston's morale unraveled when Lou Piniella sliced a pop fly into the gale in right center.

"It must have blown a hundred feet across, like a Frisbee coming back," says Eckersley. Lynn came in a few steps but he had no chance. Burleson made chase from shortstop, Scott took off from first. The ball was out of reach of both. Rice, who was playing near the warning track in right, could not get there. Frank Duffy, the second baseman, did, but when he turned and looked up into the sun he lost sight of the ball. It landed in front of him. It was 1–0. After an intentional walk to Graig Nettles, Dent dunked a two-strike pitch into left for two more runs. "That broke my back," said Eckersley. By the time the inning had ended, Eckersley was gone. There had been another walk, an error, a wild pitch, and a passed ball. Seven runs had scored. "This is the first time I've seen a first-place team chasing a second-place team," said NBC's Tony Kubek.

Guidry had not only become the second left hander to pitch a complete game against the Red Sox in Fenway all season, but also was the first lefty to shut them out at home since 1974. "Pitchers are afraid to pitch inside here," he said. "But that's where you've got to."

The victory brought Guidry's record to 21–2, his earned-run average to 1.77, and his strikeouts to 220; it also brought the New York staff's ERA to 2.07 over the last twenty-six games. "They must be cheating," said Lynn. "Those aren't the same Yankees we saw before. I think George Steinbrenner used his clone money. I think those were Yankee clones out there from teams of the past."

"These guys are—I hope you understand how I use the word-nasty," said Jackson. "This is a pro's game, and this team is loaded with professionals. Tough guys. Nasty."

"This is two years in a row we've finished like this, so it must say something about the team's character," Tidrow said. Before Lemon took over, the only times the word "character" was used in the Yankee clubhouse it was invariably followed by the word "assassination."

With the 7–0 loss figured in, the Red Sox had lost eight out of ten. In those games they had committed twenty-four errors good for twenty unearned runs. Twice pop-ups to shallow right had dropped, leading to two losses and ten earned runs.

Tiant had been the only starting pitcher to win. Evans, Scott, Hobson, and Jack Brohamer, who most of the time were the bottom four in the batting order, were twelve for 123–or .098. "How can a team get thirty-something games over .500 in July and then in September see its pitching, hitting, and fielding all fall apart at the same time?" wondered Fisk.

After being bombarded in the first three games, all that the Red Sox could come up with in their effort to prevent the Yankees from gaining a first–place tie on Sunday was rookie left hander Bobby Sprowl. In June, while the Sox were beating the Yankees, Sprowl was pitching for the Bristol Red Sox against the West Haven Yankees.

Clearly he was not ready for their New York namesakes. He began by walking Rivers and Willie Randolph, lasted only two-thirds of an inning, and was charged with three runs. The most damaging blow came after Sprowl gave way to reliever Bob Stanley, who promptly yielded a single to

Nettles that drove in two runners whom Sprowl had allowed to reach base. The Yankees would build a 6–0 bulge before coasting to an eighteen-hit, 7–4 victory. Suddenly, New York not only had a psychological edge on the Red Sox, but it also had pulled even with them in the standings.

"It's never easy to win a pennant," said Yastrzemski. "We've got three weeks to play. We've got three games in Yankee Stadium next weekend. Anything can happen." He stared into his locker. Anything already had.

"The intensity begins before the game.
You kind of sense electricity in the air."

—Yankee outfielder Gary Thomasson on
Yankees–Red Sox games in 1978

THEY SAID IT . . .

The 162–game season was not enough to determine a winner in the American League East in 1978. When the schedule reached its end, the New York Yankees and Boston Red Sox had identical records of 99–63. It would come down to a one-game playoff in Fenway Park.

"BASEBALL'S FINEST HOURS"

from the *Washington Post* (April 1, 1979)
by Thomas Boswell

> *"Our playoff with Boston last year was the greatest game in the history of American sports."*
>
> —George Steinbrenner,
> owner of the New York Yankees

BASEBALL IS A GAME of frozen paintings, huge murals locked in the mind's appreciative eye.

It is also the sport which, within this broad tableau, focuses its attention on individuals and their deeds with an isolating, skewering radiance.

Baseball never confuses those who love it, nor protects those who play it. Ultimately, it is the game without veils, the sport created for analysis and rumination.

Of all baseball's murals in the last quarter-century, none can surpass the American League East playoff last October between the world champion New York Yankees and the born-to-sorrow Boston Red Sox.

A baseball game, at its best, can be like an elaborate and breathlessly balanced house of cards. Tension and a sense of crisis build with each inning. Each deed of the game, each player, finds his supporting role.

Last year that house of cards was built not for one afternoon, but for an entire six-month season. By closing day each player seemed to carry with him a nimbus of symbols, an entire personal history like some Athenian warrior whose exploits against Sparta were memorized by an entire community.

In fact, that one game served as an almost perfect microcosm of 75 years of baseball warfare between the Apple and the Hub—a distillation of the game's richest, longest and most Homeric rivalry.

In the history of baseball, only one other moment—Bobby Thomson's home run to end the '51 playoff between the New York Giants and the Brooklyn Dodgers—has provided such a monumental house of cards as the bottom of the ninth inning of this Yankee victory.

When that impossible distinction "best game ever" is being thrashed out in heaven, these games must be mentioned first. Perhaps they should each have a crown—best in the annals of their respective leagues.

The '51 playoff, marvelous for its fireworks and confetti, was the epitome of baseball's age of innocence, a game that any child could grasp.

The '78 playoff, however, pitted teams of darker and more complex personality in a far subtler game—a contest for the student of inside baseball. Is there any other kind?

The '51 classic ended in raw pandemonium, the '78 masterpiece in utter profound silence. Certainly, it is possible to prefer the latter in such a matter of taste.

It must not be held against last year's masterpiece that it merely ended a divisional race, that the Yanks still had to upend two more pretenders before they could keep their World Championship for a second consecutive year.

New York needed just four games to eliminate Kansas City in the American League playoffs, and only six to lick Los Angeles in the World Series. Neither joust reached a moment of primitive emotion.

To beat the Bosox, the Yankees bled for six months, only to find themselves tied after the 162nd and last game of the regular season. Their final margin of triumph—5–4 in this one-day sudden death showdown—was thin as smoke, a distinction almost without a difference between the two most powerful teams in the sport.

Even now, that concluding moment of delicious indeterminance remains as fresh as the crack of the first line drive of spring. Baseball returns. But the Yankee–Red Sox playoff of 1978 lasts.

The sun is warm in Winter Haven now, the Florida orange trees nod their full branches over the outfield fences of the Red Sox spring training retreat.

But for Carlton Fisk, and many another Sox and Yanks, the air still seems crisp, the sky a dazzling autumn azure and one solitary popup hangs high over Fenway Park.

The final split seconds of that playoff afternoon are one of baseball's indelible frozen paintings. Let Fisk speak about the moment when the air burst from a balloon that had been blown ever larger for 163 games.

"I knew the season would be over as soon as Yastrzemski's popup came down," said the tall, patrician catcher with his hair parted in the middle like Henry Mencken.

"It seemed like the ball stayed up forever, like everything was cranked down into slow motion. I was trying to will the ball to stay up there and never come down . . . what a dumb thing to have run through your mind.

"Even the crowd roar sounded like a movie projector at the wrong speed when everything gets gravelly and warped.

"After the last out, I looked around and the crowd was stunned. Nobody moved. They looked at each other like, 'You mean it's over now . . . It can't be over yet . . . oh, nuts . . .'

"It had only been going on for half a year, but it seemed like a crime for it to end."

The buildup to that final crescendo actually began more than 24 hours before. The great playoff of '78 was, in reality, two days of absolutely contrasting atmosphere and mood.

Boston's Fenway Park is normally best on the worst days, in raw misty spring and foggy fall. The streets around the Fens are crowded, narrow and damp. Taxis blow their horns at the herds of Soxers in Lansdowne Street.

That's the way it was on the first day of October—the last day of the regular season.

A healing rain caressed that ancient, indescribably delicious ball-yard—a rain of balm and absolution. In that soft October drizzle the Sox of Boston were washed clean.

Just as New England was ready to give up hope, the prayers of Red Sox fans were answered. On that final Sunday, Boston won and the New Yorkers, playing 300 miles away in Yankee Stadium, lost.

The most spectacular and sustained pennant race in American League history had reached the only climax worthy of it—the two best teams in baseball each had 99 victories. One of them would have to win a 100th.

Just two weeks before, the Red Sox had finished one of the most ignominious collapses in history—losing 17½ games in the standings to the inexorable Yankees, blowing all of a 14-game lead and falling 3½ games behind with only 14 to play.

If Cotton Mather had been alive, he would have been a Bosox fan. And he would have been mad.

In other towns, the incipient collapse of a beloved team might bring forth prayers and novenas, as Brooklyn once lit candles for the Dodgers. In fickle Fenway, however, the faithful reacted as though the Sox had deliberately knelt in the hallowed Fens and licked the Yankees' boots.

The Red Sox have long memories. It is their curse. They are an imaginative team—more's the pity—susceptible to hauntings and collective nervous breakdowns. They prove that those who cannot forget the past are also condemned to repeat it.

The evil that the Bosox do lives after them. The good is oft interred with their moans. Somewhere it must be written that the Carmine Hose shall suffer.

When the Sox are winning, every player is a minor deity. When the angels fall, they are consigned to the nether regions.

So, that final-day victory, Boston's eighth in a row and 12th in 14 games over the last two weeks, was like an emotional reprieve from the gallows.

The entire final week of the season was summarized in that final chilling Sunday. Each day Boston would throw an early lead on the scoreboard, hoping to shake the New Yorkers' faith in their tiny one-game lead. And each day the Yankee dreadnought would send its message back via the radio waves with an answering victory.

A new punishment had been found to fit the Sox felony of squandering a huge lead—torture by victory. A sense of fatality or inexorable and well-deserved punishment seemed to hang over the Sox. The Prayer to St. Jude, patron saint of lost causes, was tacked to their bulletin board.

Finally, the ghost was all but given up. Brave talk ceased. Predictions of a playoff were swallowed. During that Sunday morning batting practice, the Sox were grim.

Then the spirit of mischief seemed to enter Fenway. Toronto's flaky outfielder Sam Ewing snuck through the open door in the scoreboard and posted a fictitious "8" next to the name of the Yankees' opponent—Cleveland.

The early-arriving crowd went into a tizzy that did not stop for three hours. Bizarre echoing eruptions rumbled through the stands whenever word of the Yankee demise arrived by radio.

All afternoon, Sox relief pitcher Bob (Big Foot) Stanley kept a transistor radio to his ear in the bullpen, leaping to his feet to lead hundreds of fans in ovations for Cleveland runs.

Slowly, a ripple, and finally a roar would erupt from 32,000 people as, one-by-one, the blessed message was passed like a fire bucket.

Before the game even ended—with Boston ahead, 5–0, and New York behind, 9–2—the scoreboard exalted: "Next Red Sox Home Game Tomorrow."

This was the afternoon that made '78 unique in baseball's century.

Two other teams had suffered breakdowns comparable to Boston. The New York Giants of 1915 got the rubber bone for blowing a 15-game Fourth of July lead to the Miracle Braves of Boston, and eventually losing by a craven 10½ games.

And the '51 Dodgers had a 13-game lead on August 11, only to be tied on the last day of the season, then beaten.

But no team had ever looked into the abyss of absolute self-betrayal and recovered from it, come back to finish the season—despite injuries—like a furious hurricane.

At their nadir, the Sox had lost six straight September meetings with the Yankees by a score of 46–9. They were outhit, 84–29. "It was so lopsided," said Boston pitcher Mike Torrez, "that you wouldn't have believed it if it had happened to the original Mets."

The real victims of the Boston collapse were, in part, the Yankees. The Horrid Hose were so disgraceful that they drained the glory from the Yanks' great comeback.

"Never sell the Yankees short," said Boston coach Johnny Pesky, who has hated pinstripes for 40 years. "They played great the last three months [52–22]. They'll never play that well again as long as they have a-------."

While other teams are too tight to breathe in a crisis, the Yankees spit their tobacco and smooth the dirt with their spikes.

The Yanks, with their almost unsinkable raw talent, their polished passion for the game once the contest begins, and their partial immunity to the pandemonium that swathes them, have gradually come to resemble a sort of leviathan with hiccups.

In midseason the champions were hemorrhaging in Boston. There are other New England sharks than the mythical Jaws of Amity. The pearly white teeth snapping around them on those moon-bathed nights at Fenway were the healthy and rapacious Sox.

"If Boston keeps playing like this," said New York's Reggie Jackson, "even Affirmed couldn't catch them. We'll need motorcycles . . ."

Every day and every night in those final hours of troubled manager Billy Martin the scene around the Yankees was the same. The crowds in the hotel lobbies, at the ticket windows and outside the players' entrances were huge, pummeling the players with kisses and curses.

Meanwhile, the Sox read their press clippings. Everyone from Ted Williams to the cop in Yawkey Way said these Sox were the best edition since '01.

What blighter would point out that the Fenway Chronicles show an almost inexorable baseball law: A Red Sox ship with a single leak will always find a way to sink. For documentation, see the Harvard Library. Doctoral theses are on file there.

In other seasons, the Sox self-immolation was a final act consonant with the team's public image for generations—a green wall at their backs, green bucks in their wallets, green apples in their throats.

Red Sox fans had come to view their heroes with the skepticism of a Hawthorne or Melville searching for the tragic flaw. No team is worshiped with such a perverse sense of fatality. "Human, all too human," that's the Red Sox logo.

Ever since the day 60 years before when dastardly Harry Frazee sold Babe Ruth to the Yankees, fortune had forsaken the Sox. The axis of baseball power swung south with Ruth. Since Boston last raised a Series banner in 1918, the Yankees have been champions 22 times.

This grim heritage, however, was an unfair burden to the '78 Sox, who were the antithesis of their predecessors. If the Sox had a critical flaw, an Achilles heel, it was their excess of courage, their unquestioning obedience to the god of guts. This, they swore to a man, was the year for that eternally receding World Series Triumph. Let the '80s be damned.

The Sox scapegoat was easy to find—doughty little manager Don Zimmer, the man with the metal plate in his head whom pitcher Bill Lee contemptuously called "the gerbil."

Zimmer was publicly seen as a hard guy who was given a high-strung, high-octane Indy race car and kept the pedal to the metal as though he were driving an old dirt-track stocker. Naturally, the engine blew and the Sox coasted to a dead stop.

However, the Yankees also had catastrophic pitching problems, constant injuries for the first 100 games and a manager who had to be fired for his own health's sake.

Why were the Yankees so good at cutting their losses, while the Red Sox were so poor at minimizing theirs? Why did the Yankees have the restraint to let their injured heal in June, when the Sox were pummeling them, while the Sox exacerbated their miseries by going full throttle?

It's all tied up with history and that old Yankee fear. It's axiomatic in the Northeast that no Red Sox lead is safe. And it is cradle lore that no Boston team ever has faced up to a Yankee challenge in September.

Therefore, Zimmer had little choice but to push his delicately balanced powerplant until the black smoke poured from the exhaust. Mythology forced his hand. Only a 20-game lead would suffice.

The Sox pushed that lead to 14, but then the black flag waved the Sox into the pits, while the Yanks kept circling the track.

The hordes of invading Yankee fans even took to taunting the Sox in their own lair. In the tunnel under the Fenway stands, Yankee fans set up a cheer each night as they passed the doors of the Boston locker room.

"Three, three, three . . . two, two, two . . . one, one, one . . . ZERO, ZERO, ZERO," they counted down the dwindling Boston margin each night as the Yankees swept the famous four-game series that will live in lore as The Boston Massacre.

Perhaps a philosopher would not be surprised at the Zenlike manner in which the Red Sox reunified themselves. As soon as the massacred Bostonians, the despair of eight states, threw in the towel, gave up the ghost and tossed in the sponge, they pinned the Yankees' ears back in their seventh-and-last September meeting.

That, of course, is the visceral clubhouse definition of choking. If you can't tie your shoelaces under pressure, but play like a world-beater as soon as it's too late, that's worse in the dugout world than being a no-talent klutz. That is called taking the apple.

Even if Boston's sweet fruit of victory had a bitter pit of self-knowledge at its center, the hard swallow was medicinal.

One day the Sox were pathetically cornering reporters, asking, "Tell me, what's wrong with us?" Soon, it seemed, they would be asking that sorrowful question of lampposts and parked cars.

But a small thing like one victory over New York, even one that seemed meaningless, broke the grip of the curse.

So, when the Yankees arrived at Fenway on Playoff Day, they no longer came either as June victims or September conquerors. They came as October equals—very worried equals.

The house of cards was finally built. And it was monstrous. Which way it would fall no player claimed to know.

At baseball's showcase World Series games, the batting cage is as congenial as a Kiwanians convention. Teams arrive for fame and fun; no grudges fester. Before the playoff, the Yankees and Red Sox circled each other like lions and leopards around the same African watering hole. Their only words were taunting barbs disguised as light humor.

Some celestial handicapper must have written out the lineup cards. They were too symbolic to have been penned by mortals named Don Zimmer and Bob Lemon, the Yankees' caretaker manager.

Each team spotted the other a Golden Glover as both Evans and New York's Willie Randolph were sidelined. But far better for symmetry were the starting pitchers: Torrez against Ron Guidry, the man called Lou'siana Lightnin'.

Just a year before Torrez had been the Yankees' World Series pitching hero, winning two games. Then the Sox signed him at free agent auction for $2.7 million—their loud pronouncement that they would match the Yankee pocketbook.

Just four days before, Torrez had emerged from the emotional low point of his career. If one player's failure epitomized the charge of gutlessness made against all the Sox, it was Torrez. For 40 days down the stretch when he was desperately needed, he had not won a single game, while losing six.

The Sox feelings about the great Guidry were simply summed up. "We have the home field. We have the momentum. They . . ." said short-stop Rick Burleson, pausing, "have Guidry."

Guidry's feelings were even more elemental. Asked if a mere one-game playoff were fair, the left-handed executioner answered, "One's enough. I can only pitch one."

Discovering Guidry in the Yankee locker room is like stumbling over a cat in a dog show. His story is the hidden moral kernel in the vain bluster of the Yankee saga. Imagine, if it can be done, a player amid these New Yorkers who has the innate confidence of an only child, the proud self-containment of a Lou'siana Cajun and the strong silences of a small-town boy raised on hawk hunting and walking the railroad tracks.

No star player is so invisible on his own team, whether loping across the outfield or lounging in the dugout. But for the playoff, no player approached Guidry for being conspicuous. The reason was cogent—

Guidry entered the game with the best record of any 20-game winner in the history of baseball: 24–3.

Every game needs a call to arms, but this one started with trumpet blasts.

A brilliant fall light—a painter's vivid stark light—bathed Fenway as Torrez began the day by throwing his first four pitches to Mickey Rivers low, high, inside and outside. The Yankee speedster waited only one pitch to steal second base.

"So that's it," the throng seemed to say by its sigh. It was going to be just like last time, when New York jumped to leads of 12–0, 13–0, 7–0 and 6–0 in four Fenway days.

When the long history of the Sox sorrows is written, those horrific first innings in September would rank infernally high. Each game came complete with the same chilling footnote: "Ibid. . . . for full details, see previous night's game."

Would it be so again? Always, it was Rivers beginning the psychic unraveling, stealing second as though it had been left to him in old Tom Yawkey's will. That sad lopsided spectacle seemed under way again when Torrez made an egregious error—throwing Reggie Jackson a fastball strike on an 0–2 pitch with two outs.

The ball climbed to the level of the left-field light towers, climbed until it seemed to look in the faces of the teenagers who had scrambled atop the Gilby's Gin sign beyond the wall. The Yankees would lead, 2–0, Guidry would breeze. The great day would be a dud. But the groaning crowd had forgotten the Fenway winds.

Whenever the Sox and Yanks meet in Boston, the first order of business is to inspect the flags. The Yankees, a predominantly left-handed hitting team, desperately want an inward breeze to enlarge the confines of the cozy Fens.

The Sox, designed along Brobdignagian lines, with seven home-run hitters, would settle for dead calm. Only when the flag points toward the plate do they droop.

When the Yanks arrived in early September, for four straight days the Sox grumbled as the wind blew, sometimes 30 miles an hour, straight in from left. Betrayed again, even by Fenway Park.

So, when Jackson's blast was suddenly stymied by the wind and fell almost straight down, nearly scraping the wall as it fell into Carl Yastrzemski's glove, a marvelous sense of irony swept over the Boston dugout.

The Yankees had been robbed by the same fates that had bedeviled Boston.

"That was no wind," said Lee later. "That was Mr. Yawkey's breath."

It is a unique quality of baseball that the season ticketholders who see all of a club's crucial games believe they can also read the minds of the players.

Each team's season is like a traditional 19th-century novel, a heaping up of detail and incident about one large family. After 162 chapters of that tome, the 163rd chapter is riddled with the memories, implications and foreshadowings of the thousands of previous pages. Any play which rises above the trivial sends a wave of emotion into that ocean-size novel of what has gone before.

Since everyone is reading the same vast book, the sense of a collective baseball consciousness can become enormous. With each at-bat, each pitch, there is an almost audible shuffling of mental pages as the pitcher, hitter and catcher all sort through the mass of past information that they have on one another.

Just this sort of extended personal history existed between the Yankee star Guidry and the Boston captain Yastrzemski to begin the second inning. In a word, Yaz was harmless against Guidry when the left-hander was at, or even near, his best.

So, when Yastrzemski rocked back on his heels on the second pitch of the second inning to thrash at a fastball in his wheelhouse (up and in) it should have been a feeble mistake. Instead, it was a home run—a hooking liner that curled around the rightfield foul pole by less than a bat-length. Yaz had turned the Lightnin' around.

Suddenly, the afternoon bristled with potential.

Guidry was at his weakest. Torrez, who was to strike out Yankee captain Thurman Munson three times with nibbling, teasing sliders, was at his best. In other words, they were even.

"When these teams play," Fisk had said two weeks before, "it is like a gigantic will controls the whole game. And it's either all behind one team, or all behind the other."

But this day the forces of the game could not make up their minds. It was a beautiful ambivalence.

The crowd seemed to be in the grip of angina, the cheers caught in their nervous throats. The Keep Your Sox On faithful sat silent in their fireman caps decorated with the nicknames of their undependable deities: Boomer and Butch, Soup and Scooter, Rooster and Pudge, Eck and Looie, Big Foot and Spaceman, Dewey and Yaz.

By the end of the fifth, the day's work more than half done, the ballpark was so silent that those in the rooftop seats could hear Blair pleading to his Yankees, "Let's go, man. Let's go."

For this single afternoon to achieve permanence, it had to be a miniature of the entire season, a duplication of the same emotional roller coaster.

So, in the sixth, the Sox scored again, Burleson lining a double over third and Jim Rice clipping an RBI single to center. As Rice's hit, his 406th total base of the season, bit into the turf, it seemed that the game, the year and a Most Valuable Player duel between Rice and Guidry had all been decided on a single pitch.

More folly. Any historian knows that a 2–0 lead after the sixth is the quintessential Red Sox lead—just enough to merit euphoria, just enough to squander. After all, in the seventh game of the 1975 World Series Boston could taste its incipient upset over Cincinnati, leading 3–0. And that turned to dust.

Every seesaw needs a fulcrum, and Lou Piniella quickly provided one for this game.

A ground out and an intentional walk put men on first and second, two outs, and Fred Lynn at bat. When fragile Freddy yanked a Guidry slider into the rightfield corner, every dugout mind had the same thought: "Two runs."

Piniella, however, materialized directly in the path of the ball. He was so far out of normal Lynn position that he ought to have had a puff of magical smoke curling up behind him.

"It was a ridiculous place for him to be . . . about 20 yards from where he normally plays me," said Lynn.

"I talked to Munson between innings," said Piniella afterward. "We agreed that Guidry's slider was more the speed of a curveball and that somebody could pull him."

Even so, Piniella was stationed in a sort of private twilight zone.

"It was a 100–1 shot any way you look at it," said Lynn. "He plays hunches out there. The man's just a gambler."

At bat, Piniella says, "I've guessed on every pitch that was ever thrown to me . . . don't do too bad, do I?"

To those in the stands, the play looked routine, like so many in baseball: a blistered line drive directly at an outfielder standing a few feet in front of the fence. It was the hallmark of this game that its central plays reflected the true daily life of the inner sport. They were not flamboyant and egalitarian, but exclusive and subtle. Baseball's well-kept secret is that it has never been solely a democratic national pastime, but an elitist passion as well.

The Babe and the Iron Horse will never understand what happened next. Big Ed Barrow and Col. Jacob Ruppert will take a lot of kidding in baseball heaven when tales are told of the tiny home run hero of The Playoff.

Since the roaring '20s, the diamond nine from New York that wore gray pinstripes has meant heartless hegemony, monolithic muscle.

Bucky Dent, though he bats last in the Yank order, nonetheless is a symbol of power himself—the power of cash. For two seasons George Steinbrenner was obsessed with getting Dent away from the Chicago White Sox. Finally, a trade was made.

When Dent dragged his bat to home plate with two out and two men on base in the Yankee seventh, then fouled the second pitch off his foot, hopping out of the batter's box in pain, he looked as ineffectual and inconspicuous as a CIA agent with a bomb in his briefcase.

Normally, the worrywart Fisk uses such delays to visit his pitcher with admonitions, or to demand warmup pitches. "Fisk is out at the mound so much," needles Lynn, "that I've threatened to change the number of Carlton's position from '2' to '1½.'"

But for Dent, what's the worry?

As Dent was administered a pain-killing spray, on-deck hitter Rivers, who had forgotten his sunglasses and butchered a flyball earlier, suddenly became uncharacteristically observant. He saw a crack in Dent's bat and fetched him another of the same style.

Of such minutiae is history made. That and fastballs down the middle.

"After Dent hit it," said Fisk, "I let out a sigh of relief. I thought, 'We got away with that mistake pitch.' I almost screamed at Mike.

"Then I saw Yaz looking up and I said, 'Oh, God.'"

Several innings before, the wind had reversed and was blowing toward the leftfield corner.

Yastrzemski watched that boosting wind loft the ball barely over the wall, fair by 80 feet. As the three-run homer nestled in the net, Yastrzemski's knees buckled as though he had been hammered over the head with a bat.

The Yankees erupted from their dugout like souls released from Hades.

What followed seemed as inexorable as a shark eating the leg after it tastes the foot.

Quicker than you could say, "Rivers walks and steals second again," Torrez was leaving the game. Though he had fanned the next hitter—Munson—three times, Zimmer waved in Stanley. Naturally, Munson doubled to the wall for the inning's fourth run.

When Reggie Jackson, the Hester Prynne of sluggers who walks through the baseball world with a scarlet dollar sign on his chest, knocked a home run into the centerfield bleachers in the eighth, it seemed like mere hot doggery. And when Jackson slapped hands with Steinbrenner in the box seats before greeting any of his mates to celebrate the 5–2 lead, it was just another of Reggie's compulsive theatrical gestures.

Little did the crowd suspect what all the players knew—that the war had not ceased.

Beyond the Fenway fences, the trees of New England were tinged with reds and oranges. They might as well have been tears.

This game, like the entire season, was about to be salvaged by the sort of Red Sox rally against fate that had no historical precedent.

If Torrez and Guidry went down as the pitchers of record—the official loser and winner, then Stanley and that ornery Goose Gossage were the pitchers of memory.

In the eighth Jerry Remy grounded a double over the first-base bag off Gossage and scored on Yastrzemski's crisp single to center. Yaz followed Remy home when Fisk and Lynn cracked singles, using their quick strokes to combat Gossage's numbing speed.

The bear trap was set for the Yanks—men on first and second with only one out, and the lead down to 5–4.

The great book of the season had, however, been turned to the wrong page to suit Boston.

Gossage mowed down Butch Hobson and George Scott—low-average sluggers with long, looping swings. Neither could get untangled quickly enough to handle his rising fastballs.

Never mind. The stage has been set for the bottom of the ninth with Gossage protecting his 5–4 lead.

From the press box, baseball is geometry and statistics. From the box seats, it is velocity, volume and virtuosity. From above, Gossage is a relief pitcher. From ground level, eye-to-eye in his own world, he is a dragon.

Nevertheless, the brave Bosox started beating on Gossage's ninth-inning door. The feisty Burleson drew a one-out walk.

Winning is an ancient Yankee story, a heritage of talent mixed with an audacious self-confidence and an unnerving good fortune. Losing is an old sadness for the Sox, a lineage of self-doubt and misfortune. All those threads of history and baseball myths were about to come together in one play.

The 5-foot-6 Remy slashed a liner to right when the Goose's 0–2 fastball laid an egg.

The assembled parishioners sang "Hallelujah," then groaned their eternal "Amen" as they saw the ball fly directly toward Piniella.

Little did they, or Burleson on first, know that only one person in the park had no idea where Remy's liner was—Piniella.

"I never saw it," he said. "I just thought, 'Don't panic. Don't wave your damn arms and let the runner know you've lost it.'"

So Piniella the Gambler stood frozen, trusting, as he has so often, to luck.

While Piniella waited for the streaking ball to hit at his feet or hit him in the face, Burleson waited between bases, assuming Piniella had an easy play.

A throw of the dice, said Mallarmé, can never abolish chance. The exception seems to be the New York Yankees, who abolish chance with their poise, letting luck fall about their shoulders like a seignoral cloak.

"I never saw it until the ball hit about eight feet in front of me," said Piniella later, drenched with champagne. "It was just pure luck that I could get my glove on the ball and catch it before it went past me. If it had gone to the wall, those two scooters would still be running around the bases."

Had Burleson, after stopping in his tracks, tried to go first-to-third, he would have been a dead Rooster. Piniella's throw was a one-hop strike to the bag.

Had Piniella not had the presence of mind to fake a catch, Burleson would have reached third easily. From there, he could have scored to tie the game on Rice's subsequent fly to Piniella. From second, he could only tag and go to third.

If Dent's homer has been discussed throughout America, then Piniella's two gambles—his out-of-position catch on Lynn and his blinded grab on Remy—are still being dissected in every major league dugout.

"It's the play I'll always remember," said Graig Nettles.

Steinbrenner will never forget either. "I have a tape cassette of the whole game in my office," said the owner. "I don't know how many times I've watched that game. And I always stop at the Piniella play and run it over and over. What if Jackson had been out there? He's left-handed, so the glove's on his other hand, the ball gets by him, Remy has an inside-the-park homer and we lose.

"It's annoyed me that our playoff game seems to have been over-shadowed by us beating the Dodgers in the Series for the second year in a row," said Steinbrenner. "Don't people understand? Somebody wins the Series every year. There's only one game like that in a lifetime. I'd call it the greatest game in the history of American sports, because baseball is the best and oldest game, and that's sure as hell the best baseball game I ever saw."

If any game ever brought 75 years of animosity to a climax, this was it.

"When they had two on in the ninth with Rice and Yaz coming up," said New York's Roy White, "I was just holding my breath. You wanted to close your eyes and not see 'em swing. The wind was blowing out and I could feel that Green Monster creeping in closer."

"All I could think of was Bobby Thomson and that '51 playoff," said Nettles. "I figured if anybody was going to beat us, those were the guys."

This playoff lacked only one thing: a time machine. When Captain Carl, Boston cleanup man, stood at the plate facing Gossage with the tying run dancing off third and the winning run on first, that moment should have been frozen.

The 32,925 standing fans, the poised runners, Yaz's high-held bat, Gossage's baleful glare: for once baseball had achieved a moment of genuine dramatic art—a situation that needed no resolution to be perfect.

A game, a season and an entire athletic heritage for two cities had been brought to razor's edge.

"I was in the on-deck circle, just like I was when Yaz flew out to end the '75 Series," said Fisk.

"You know, they should have stopped the game right then and said, 'Okay, that's it. The season is over. You're both world champions. We can't decide between you, and neither of you should have to lose.'"

Sports' moments of epiphany are written on water. The spell of timelessness must be shattered, the house of cards collapse. Yaz cannot stand poised forever, waiting for the Goose, like the characters on Keats' Grecian Urn. Art may aspire to fairness, but games cannot aim that high. They must settle for a final score.

"I was thinking, 'Pop him up,'" said Nettles. "Then Yaz did pop it up and I said, 'Jeez, but not to me.'"

When the white speck had fallen into Nettles' glove, the Fenway fans stood in their places. For long minutes no one moved, as the baseball congregation drank in the cathartic sweetness of the silence. Proud police horses pranced on the infield, waiting to hold back a crowd that never charged.

"They should have given both teams a standing ovation," said Nettles. But he was wrong. This was better.

Finally, the whir of a public address recording began. Gently, softly, the music of an old-fashioned melancholy carrousel drifted through Fenway Park.

The sun was going down, so we all went home, bearing with us canvases for a lifetime.

Bucky Dent

The much-celebrated 1978 one-game playoff between New York and Boston to decide the winner of the American League East takes on a special poignancy when viewed through the eyes of a dedicated Red Sox fan.

"A DAY OF LIGHT AND SHADOWS"

from *Sports Illustrated* (February 26, 1979)
by Jonathan Schwartz

> *I didn't feel much pressure the night before the game, when the manager told me that even if Guidry went only a third of an inning I'd be the next guy out there. But I felt the pressure when I actually came into the game. More pressure than I've ever felt. Even in my personal life.*
>
> —*Goose Gossage*

IN THE KITCHEN IN upper Manhattan, Luis Tiant appeared to be in charge of the Red Sox' 162nd game of the year. Boston had widened a small lead over Toronto to five runs, and Tiant's impeccable control compelled even the restless woman roaming through the apartment to stop at the kitchen door and admire his performance, as one would admire an exquisitely bound volume of dense theological writing in another language.

In the bedroom, the Yankees had fallen well behind Cleveland and were hitting pop-ups, always a sign late in and game that things are out of hand.

The woman was restless because her quiet Sunday afternoon was being assaulted by the babble of baseball and by what she perceived as yet another increase in my furious tension. She had retreated to the living room to sit sullenly among the Sunday editions of *Newsday*, *The Washington Post* and two interim New York papers born of a strike that was now in its eighth week. She had been told that this was positively *it*; that there was *no* chance that the Red Sox would advance past this Sunday afternoon; that the baseball season would be over by sundown. She had been told that there would never be a repetition of my impulsive flight to Los Angeles after the Yankees' four-game Fenway Park sweep three weeks before. I had simply up and left the house during the seventh inning of the last humiliating defeat. I had taken nothing with me but a Visa card and $50. I had called home from Ontario, Calif., having pulled my Avis Dodge off the road leading to the desert, though I realized it was well after midnight in New York. "I am filled with regret," I said from a phone booth without a door. "Over what?" I was asked.

Her question meant this: Was I filled with regret because the Red Sox had lost four consecutive games, or was I filled with regret because I had up and left without explanation and had not bothered to call until the middle of the night—and if you want this relationship to work you're going to have to work at it?

I replied above the roar of traffic from the San Bernardino Freeway that I was regretful about leaving, and about my insensitivity and my inability to put baseball in perspective. "A trip of this kind," I said severely, "will *never* happen again."

The truth: I was regretful because the Red Sox had lost four consecutive games, had blown an enormous lead and had handed the championship of the Eastern Division of the American League to the Yankees.

Three weeks later, the phone rang for an hour after the Sunday games were over. Congratulations! From California. Palm Springs, Brentwood, San Francisco. From Stamford, Conn. and Bridgehampton, N.Y. From 73rd Street and 10th Street in Manhattan. Congratulations!

Returning from oblivion, the Red Sox had tied for first place on the last day of the season, forcing a playoff game in Boston the next afternoon. Somehow this development had moved people to seek me out with warm feelings, as if my control had been as superb as Tiant's and had contributed to the unexpected Red Sox comeback. My control, of course, had vanished after Labor Day, leaving me infuriated and melancholy. And yet I accepted congratulations that Sunday afternoon as if my behavior during September had been exemplary. In fact, I had wept and raged. I had participated in two fistfights, had terminated a close friendship and had gone out in search of a neighborhood 15-year-old who had written RED SOX STINK in orange crayon on the back window of my car. I had set out after him with vicious intent, only to return home in a minute or so, mortified. The psychiatrist, whom I immediately sought out, said to me. "This is *not* what a 40-year-old should be doing with his time. *Comprendez-vous?*"

On the triumphant Sunday evening I drank Scotch and talked long distance. I was asked, "Are you thrilled?" I was thrilled. "Can they do it?" I doubted they could. "Are you going to the game?" Well, maybe.

I had actually thought of trying to use my connections as a radio broadcaster to round up some kind of entree to Fenway Park for the next afternoon, but the prospect of tracking down people in their homes on a Sunday night was depressing. And there would be the scramble for the air shuttle, an endless taxi ride in a Boston traffic jam, no ticket or pass left at the press window as promised, and a frantic attempt to reach Bill Crowley, the Red Sox' cantankerous P.R. man, on the phone—"Bill, the pass was supposed to have been . . . and no one's seen it and they can't . . . and is there any possibility that I could . . ."

No, I would watch at home, alone. I would have the apartment to myself all day. I would stand in the bedroom doorway and watch with the sound off to avoid Yankee announcer Phil Rizzuto's ghastly shrieking. At home, in the event of a Red Sox victory, I would be able to accept more congratulatory calls, this time for the real thing. "To me, it's the division championship that means the most," I had often said reasonably to whoever would listen. "After the division it's all dessert."

And yet. Had there been a more significant athletic event held in this country during my lifetime? The World Series, like the Super Bowl, is public theater, designed to entertain. Women and children gather around. Aren't the colors on the field pretty? Isn't that Howard Baker?

The NBA playoffs, even the Celtics' wild triumphs of the '60s, are local affairs, presented for small numbers of people in the heat of May. And what, after all, can be seriously expected of a major professional league that has a hockey team in Vancouver?

It occurred to me that perhaps one event had been as significant as the Yankee–Red Sox playoff—the Bobby Thomson game of 1951. The circumstances had been similar: a playoff involving intense rivals home-based in relative proximity; personalities that occupied the mind at four in the morning; and startling rallies through August and September, the '51 Giants having wiped away a 13½-game Dodger lead and the '78 Yankees having fought from 14 back of the Red Sox. The difference in the two games seemed to be a small one: for the Dodgers and Giants it had been the third of a three-game playoff; for the Red Sox and Yankees it would be one game, sudden death.

In February, with a cable-television bill, a notice had arrived: COMING ATTRACIONS, EXCITING BASEBALL ACTION. RED SOX BASEBALL ON CHANNEL F.

The notice had said nothing else, but it had stopped my heart. Having lived in New York and having been a Red Sox fan since childhood, I had spent hours sitting in parked automobiles on the East Side of the city where reception of WTIC in Hartford, which carries Red Sox games, was the clearest. Eventually I had obtained through a friend in Boston an unlisted air-check phone number that tied directly into WHDH broadcasts. Form anywhere in the world one could hear whatever it was that WHDH—and, subsequently, WITS, with a different number—was airing at any moment of the day or night. WHDH was—just as WITS is—the Red Sox flagship station, and one had only to be prepared for an exorbitant phone bill to listen to any Boston game, or season. Between 1970 and 1977 I had spent nearly $15,000 listening to Red Sox broadcasts. In a hotel in Paris I had heard George Scott strike out in Seattle. From my father's home in London I had heard George Scott strike out in Detroit.

From Palm Springs, Calif. I had listened to at least 100 complete games, attaching the phone to a playback device that amplified the sound. One could actually walk around the room without holding the receiver. One could even leave the room, walk down the corridor and into a bathroom to stare glumly into one's eyes in a mirror and still pick up the faint sound of George Scott slamming into a double play in Baltimore.

The most significant athletic event in my lifetime.

$15,000 in phone bills.

Endless Red Sox thoughts on beaches, and in cabs, and while watching movies with Anthony Quinn in them.

And most of the summer of 1978 spent in a darkened kitchen with Channel F.

I got on the phone to a guy who works at ABC, the network that would televise the playoff game. Their truck was up there now, I assumed, with everyone's credentials in order.

The guy at ABC owed me $150 and a copy of Frank Sinatra's rare *Close to You* album that I had lent him for taping six months before. The guy at ABC was at home asleep.

"I'll try. I'll do my best," he said, "but it's slim city."

He called me at eight in the morning. A press pass would be waiting in my name at the front desk of The Ritz Carlton Hotel in Boston. "If anyone asks, you're with Channel 7 in New York," he said. "But you've got to be dignified, or I'm in the toilet."

"Have I ever not been dignified?" I asked.

"Yes," he said. "Yes," he repeated softly.

LOU PINIELLA: *We had dinner around eight. Me and Catfish and Thurman. After dinner, we went over to a watering hole, Daisy Buchanan's. We had a couple of drinks, and we talked about the game. I remember that we all thought it was ironic justice that these two good teams should wind up like this after 162 games. Like it was just meant to be. Some of the fans in there, they recognized us, and they ribbed us about how we were going to get beat and all. But, you know, we all felt pretty confident because of the series in September when we came up to Fenway and beat 'em four straight. We all love to play at Fenway Park, and we talked about it that night.*

In the morning I got up early, around nine, and had my usual breakfast: corned beef hash, three eggs over lightly, an order of toast, orange juice. I like to play on a full stomach. It's just the way I am.

I got to the park around noon. I felt nervous, but it's good to feel nervous. It puts an edge on things. In the clubhouse about 12 guys played cards. It kind of relaxed us. I thought about Torrez. I never hit him too well.

I talked to Zimmer before the game. I wished him good luck. He's a very close friend of mine. He lives in Treasure Island, and I live in Tampa. I remember thinking during batting practice, what a beautiful autumn day in Boston. It was a beautiful day. You know?

"It's a game that blind people would pay to hear," Reggie Jackson once said of the prospect of a Frank Tanana–Ron Guidry matchup.

That comment flashed through my mind while I was riding in a taxi to Fenway Park. The season did, too. Specifies: an extra-inning loss to Cleveland in April that concluded a Sunday afternoon doubleheader at 8:46 P.M.; opening day in Chicago, and the next afternoon there; two games in Texas a few weeks later. All told, five losses that came in the closing inning. Had the Red Sox held on to but one of those games, there'd be nothing cooking at Fenway today—no tie, no playoff. The Yankees would be scattered across the country like the Montreal Expos, and the Red Sox would be in a Kansas City hotel lining up tickets for friends.

I had bought the papers at The Ritz Carlton after picking up my pass, but I hadn't read them and wouldn't now as I approached Kenmore Square. After all, who wanted to stare at Ron Guidry's stats on Storrow Drive?

I arrived on the field at 1:10, exhilarated, the papers left in the taxi, my pass in hand.

I took a look in the Red Sox dugout. At the far end Ned Martin, the team's chief radio announcer, was fumbling with a small cassette recorder while, next to him, manager Don Zimmer waited patiently in silence. I have known Martin for 15 years and discovered early in our relationship that he has no mechanical aptitude. The tap in a kitchen sink would break away from its stem at his touch. A zippered suitcase would open only in the hands of a hotel maintenance man. The cassette machine, though it was used daily to tape the pregame show with the manager, was apt to defy Martin at any time, before any game. I saw at once that it was defying him now, on this most crucial of crucial afternoons.

Crouching on the top step of the dugout, I stared down at the two men. Perhaps three minutes elapsed, enough time for Zimmer to take notice of me. "Who's that?" he said to Martin, who was tangled in the tape of a broken cassette.

Ned looked up. "Holy Christ," he said, aware that someone who knew him well was scrutinizing his difficulties.

"I'll deal with you later," I said to him.

"Christ," Ned repeated, an utterance that to this day remains the first word on the last pregame program that Martin, a Red Sox announcer for 18 years, would conduct on the team's radio network.

Munson was hitting. Around the batting cage were the faces of the New York press, and those of some Boston writers I had gotten to know through the years. One of the Boston writers told me that moments earlier, in the clubhouse, Carl Yastrzemski had confided that he was "damned scared." A New York broadcaster, who was there only for the pleasure of it, said to me somewhat confidentially, "This is a gala occasion."

Always, when I think of baseball games that have been played, I see them as if they had taken place in the light of day. I have spent a lot of time mentally reshuffling two-hitters and leaping catches that occurred at 10 or 11 in the evening, so that they return to me grandly in afternoon sunshine. The fact that baseball is part of my daily procedure, like getting up for work or eating lunch, inspires me to conjure up sunlight for its illumination.

Forty-five minutes before the 2:30 start, I realized as I looked around the park that in all my years of journeying to Fenway, on all the summer afternoons spent peacefully in the many corners of the stadium, I had never experienced a day of such clarity, of such gentleness. Fluffy cirrus clouds appeared to have arrived by appointment. The temperature of 68° was unaccompanied by even the slightest trace of wind, which made the day seem 10° warmer than it was. For such a majestic encounter there had been provided, despite a less-than-optimistic forecast the night before, a shimmering neutral Monday, as if God, recognizing the moment, had made some hasty last-minute adjustments. It was the afternoon of my imagination, the handpicked sunlit hours during which my perpetual baseball game had always been played.

After a while I made my way up to the press room, which is on the roof of the stadium, behind the press box and the three enclosed rows of seats that stretch down both foul lines. They had been desirable seats to me as a child, because they allowed easy access to foul balls. One had only to lurk in the doorway of one of those roof boxes and await the inevitable. Other lurkers in other doorways were the competition—kids my age, ready to spring into action.

"Here it comes!"

We were off. Under or over a green railing (now red). Across the roof to the brick wall. A slide, a leap, a grapple. A major league baseball in your pocket; if not this time, the next. You always had a shot at getting one on that roof. If I competed 50 times, and surely that is a conservative guess, I emerged from my adolescence with at least 15 souvenirs—and one chipped tooth (the railing).

Before entering the press room, I looked around for a moment. I could see myself outside doorway 25–27 wearing a Red Sox cap. Oh, how quiet it had been when I raced across the top of Fenway Park—just those other feet and the whistling wind shooing me ever so gradually through the years to this very afternoon, to this very press room that I had aspired to for so long, to the tepid piece of ham and half a ring of pineapple that I would be served, to the unexpected sight of Phil Rizzuto making his way toward my table.

"You huckleberry," he said to me with a smile. "I heard what you said."

The morning before, on my radio program in New York, I had spoken harshly of Rizzuto's announcing. "He is shrill," I had said, which is true. "He roots in an unfair and unacceptable way for the Yankees," which is true.

"I heard you," Rizzuto repeated, extending his hand. "You got a nice calm show. I like it," he continued, surprising me.

Rizzuto is a charmer, an attractive, graying man with the eyes of a child. One imagines that his attention span outside a baseball park is short, but one would like to be included in whatever spare moments he has available. My distaste for his broadcasts was muted at once by the warmth of his radical innocence. Getting up from my seat, I touched his cheek in friendship. I had never met Rizzuto before and had often imagined myself dressing him down before a large and approving assembly. Instead, when he departed to make his way to the radio booth, I found myself regretting the fact that I hadn't told him that I had never come upon a better or more exciting shortstop. Never.

MIKE TORREZ: *I had my usual breakfast, just tea and a piece of toast. I don't like to pitch on a full stomach. As I drove to the park, I thought about a couple of games during the year. After those games I had thought that I didn't want them to be the deciding thing. Like a name in Toronto that Jim Wright pitched. It was extra in-nings. We got a few guys on. I think with no outs. We couldn't score and we got beat. And there was a game in Cleveland when we came back with four in the ninth. Yaz hit a homer, but we blew it. You think about those things.*

When I was warming up in the bullpen I felt good. I had good motion. I didn't throw hard until the last two minutes. I looked over at Guidry and waved to him. I wished him good luck and all that. He did the same to me. And I thought about Rivers and Munson. They're the keys. And then the national anthem was played. And then we started to play.

A photographers' box is suspended beneath the roof seats along the first-base line. One descends a metal ladder that is difficult to negotiate. One stands throughout the game, because the early arrivals have captured the few folding chairs scattered around.

As Mickey Rivers, the first batter, approached the plate, I said out loud to no one, "If Torrez gets Rivers right here, the Red Sox will win." I have a tendency to think and speak such notions. "If this light turns green by the time I count three, I won't catch the flu all winter."

Rivers walked on four pitches and promptly stole second. "If Torrez gets out of this with only one run, the Red Sox have a shot," I said aloud.

Torrez got out of it unscored upon, striking out Munson with commanding determination. I was elated. My hands were shaking. I moved to the right corner of the box and stood by myself in a small puddle of water left over from a rainstorm the night before.

Instilled in me from childhood is an awful fear that Whitey Ford created: the fear not only of not winning, but of not even scoring, of not even stroking a modest fly ball to an outfielder. Grounders and strikeouts, and the game would be over in an hour and 40 minutes. Done and done.

Ron Guidry is a slim man with shocking velocity and a devastating slider. One does not imagine that one's team will defeat Guidry, or score on Guidry, or make even the smallest contact with Guidry's pitches. What caught my eye in the first three innings as I hung above the field, clasping my hands together to prevent the shaking, was that the Red Sox were not futilely opposing him. The outs were long outs. The hitters were getting good wood on the ball.

I was astounded when Yaz connected with an inside fastball for a leadoff second-inning homer, a blast that from my vantage point looked foul. Fisk and Lynn followed with fly-ball outs, Lynn's drive propelled to deep centerfield. I reasoned that Guidry, after all, was working on only three days rest, that he was a fragile guy, that maybe there was a shot at him. . . . Maybe there was a shot at him.

Torrez was getting stronger as the game moved along. When the fourth inning began, my nerves were so jumbled that I felt it impossible to continue standing in that puddle staring out at the field. I wanted to break away from it, soften its colors, lower its volume.

I climbed up the metal ladder and went into the men's room, a separate little building with one long urinal and two filthy sinks above which was written in large, well-formed blue Magic Marker letters and numbers FATE IS AGAINST '78.

In the press room the ABC telecast was playing to an empty house. I sat down to watch an inning or so and was joined a moment later by Ned Martin, whose partner, an amiable, childlike man named Jim Woods, was handling the fourth. Woods' usual innings were the third, fourth and seventh. Knowing of this arrangement. I had hoped for Ned's appearance. Someone so close to it all, so immersed in it all for so many years, would have the answer. He would reassure me, calm me down.

"Well," I said.

"Torrez," he said.

"Do you think?"

"Can't tell."

Ned is usually more loquacious than he was that afternoon. He is as articulate and as creative a sportscaster as there is in the country. He is often poetic and moving. "The Yankee score is up," he had observed late in September from Toronto, where scores remain only momentarily on the electric board. "Soon it will be gone," he had continued in his usual quiet tone. "It will flash away like a lightning bug into the moist and chilly Canadian night."

From Chicago a number of seasons ago—I wrote it down at the time: "The dark clouds approaching from beyond leftfield look to be ambling across the sky in no apparent hurry. They know what trouble they are and are teasing the crowd with their distant growl."

We sat in silence through the rest of the inning.

"Well," I said finally, hoping for an encouraging word.

"You never know," Ned said.

I walked him back toward the radio booth. On the catwalk outside the visitors' radio booth, Buddy LeRoux, one of the Red Sox' new owners, was in conversation with two men wearing dark suits. I heard LeRoux use the word "cautious." He, too, was wearing a suit, pinstriped and ill-fitting. It was a baggy garment that did not complement a man of position.

I studied his eyes. This same fellow, with a younger, pudgier face, had, as the Celtics' trainer, sat next to Red Auerbach throughout my adolescence, attending thoughtfully to some of the heroes of my youth. His face is lined now, his demeanor formal, suggesting high finance. An owner. What did he know of shaky hands and midnight calls from Ontario, Calif.? There he was in conference, having missed the fourth inning—or so I imagined. I thought: If an owner can take the fourth inning off, what is so important about it all, anyway?

I returned to the puddle for the fifth and sixth innings. The Yankees stirred around against Torrez, but didn't break through. The Red Sox sixth produced a run on a line single by Jim Rice.

It also produced the play that changed the game.

Fred Lynn came to bat with two runners on two outs and a 2–0 Red Sox lead. It was clear that Guidry was not overpowering. With Torrez so formidable, another run might put the game away. At that moment, it seemed possible to me that the Red Sox would actually win, that the nightmare would end at last.

I paced half the length of the photographers' box. With every pitch I moved a few feet to my right or left, winding up at the foot of the ladder for Guidry's 3–2 delivery.

RON GUIDRY: *I was a little tired and my pitches were up. I threw him a slider on the inside. He must have been guessing inside, because he was way out in front of it and pulled it.*

LOU PINIELLA: *Guidry wasn't as quick as usual. Munson told me that his breaking ball was hanging, so I played Lynn a few steps closer to the line than usual. I saw the ball leave the bat and then I lost it in the sun. I went to the place where I thought the ball would land. I didn't catch it cleanly, but kind of in the top of my glove. It would have shorthopped to the wall and stayed in play. Without any doubt two runs would have scored. But it was catchable.*

I watched the ball, trying to judge how deep it was but I realized it didn't quite have it, but I envisioned a double. Piniella seemed confused. I wanted the two runs. I felt 4–0 in my heart.

Piniella's catch was an indignity. He had appeared bollixed and off-balance, lurching about under the glaring sun in the rightfield corner. That Lynn had unleashed so potent a smash and would go unrewarded, that *I* would go unrewarded, that the game itself would remain within the Yankees' reach, struck me as an ominous signal that things would not, after all, work out in the end. The game and the season—the losses in Toronto, Butch Hobson's floating bone chips, Rick Burleson's injury just before the All-Star break, a thousand things that had created this day in the first place—all had spun through the early autumn sky with the ball that Lynn had struck, the ball that Piniella held in his bare right hand all the way in from rightfield, across the diamond, through the third-base coach's box and into the dark sanctuary of the visitors' dugout. He had caught it, he had held on to it, he held it even now, sitting there on the bench. The play could not be called back. The score still stood at 2–0.

In the top of the seventh inning I went into the solitary phone booth on the first-base side of the roof. I dialed my secret air-check number, realizing it was the first time I had ever sought it out as a local investment.

It was a Jim Woods inning, which frightened me all the more. Woods, like a child fumbling with a lie, cannot hide the truth of any Red Sox situation. One can tell immediately if Boston is in a favorable or thorny position, if the game is lost or won, or even tied.

Even with a 2–0 lead, Woods was somber. For Pittsburgh, New York, St. Louis, Oakland and Boston, Woods had been broadcasting baseball games ever since Dwight Eisenhower's presidency. The importance of Piniella's catch had not eluded him. Then he was presented with singles by Chris Chambliss and Roy White that brought the lead run to the plate. I had dialed in for the security of the radio's familiar rhythm and was suddenly faced with potential disaster.

I hung up on Woods and ran back to the photographers' box, taking the steps of the ladder two at a time. Jim Spencer was pinch-hitting for the Yankees. I remembered a Spencer home run earlier in the year. Could it have been against the Angels? Jim Spencer, of all people. Spencer hit the ball fairly well to left, but Yaz was with it all the way.

Two outs.

Bucky Dent.

I had a fleeting thought that, through the years, Yankee shortstops had hurt the Red Sox at the plate. Inconsequential men—Fred Stanley, Gene Michael, Jim Mason—no power, .230 hitters. Shortstops.

Bucky Dent.

I leaned way over the railing, as if trying to catch a foul ball hit just below me. I was motionless, except for my shaking hands.

Dent fouled the second pitch off his shin.

Delay.

I studied Torrez. He stood behind the mound rubbing up the new ball. He did not pace, he did not turn to examine the outfield. He just rubbed up the new ball and stared in at Dent, who was bent over to the left of the plate, his shin being cared for.

MIKE TORREZ: *I lost some of my concentration during the delay. It was about four minutes, but it felt like an hour. I had thought that they'd pinch-hit for Dent with maybe Jay Johnstone or Cliff Johnson. I felt good. I just wanted to get going. That first inning really helped. My concentration was there, especially on Munson. During the delay, I thought slider on the next pitch. But Fisk and me were working so well together, I went along with his call for a fastball. When Dent hit it, I thought we were out of the inning. I started to walk off the mound. I could see Yaz patting his glove.*

I watched, hanging over the railing. I had seen too many fly balls from the roof seats on the first-base side to be fooled now. This fly ball by a Yankee shortstop with an aching shin was clearly a home run. I had no doubt from the start.

When the ball struck the net, Yastrzemski's whole body trembled for an instant. Then he froze, every muscle drawn tight in excruciating frustration.

I said out loud, "God, no! God, no!"

In minutes the Yankees had scored another run.

I climbed the ladder and walked slowly to the press room. I went into the lavatory, closed the door to the one stall and sat on the toilet with my head in my hands, wishing there was a lid on the seat. It was entirely quiet, as if I were alone in the stadium.

"You are emotionally penniless," a girl had shouted at me years before from behind a slammed and locked bathroom door.

That is what came into my mind in my own locked cubicle.

I also thought to leave the park, to take a walk, to just go away. Instead I decided to change locations, to venture to the far reaches of the leftfield roof, out near the wall.

A couple of kids were running mindlessly around, chasing each other as if they were on a beach. They pushed their way through clusters of writers and photographers who were all standing, because there were no seats to be had. I sat down on the roof and crossed my legs. I was no more than a foot from the lip, which was unprotected by a railing or other barrier.

The wind had picked up. Shadows dominated the field, except in right and right center. I noticed that the clouds were just a bit thicker. A rain delay. Would the game revert to the last complete inning? A seven-hour delay and finally a decision. Red Sox win 2–0. I saw it as the only possibility. It had to rain right at this moment. Torrentially. Monumentally. Before the new Yankee pitcher could complete this last of the seventh. The new Yankee pitcher was Gossage, and Bob Bailey was preparing to pinch-hit against him.

Bob Bailey!

I bowed my head.

GOOSE GOSSAGE: *When I saw Bailey coming up, I said to myself, with all respect to Bob, "Thank you."*

Bailey looked at strike three and went away, out of my life, off the team, out of the league, out of the country, away, away.

Reggie Jackson homered in the eighth. I affected bemusement as I watched him round the bases. I thought: Let's see, just for the fun of it, how big it's going to be. What does it matter, anyway? It's only a game.

Official bemusement on the leftfield roof.

A leadoff double by Jerry Remy in the bottom of the eighth. How nice.

A Rice fly-ball out.

Five outs left. It's only a game.

Three consecutive singles.

The score was 5–4, Yankees' favor, with Red Sox runners on first and second. Hobson and Scott, two righthanded hitters, would now face the righthanded Gossage. My bemusement vanished. I stood.

I felt that Hobson had a real crack at it, that he is a good two-strike hitter and that he would surely be hitting with two strikes before very long. I felt that if they let Scott hit I would leap from the roof in a suicidal protest. The Boomer vs. Gossage was too pathetic for me even to contemplate.

Hobson's fly-ball out to right set up the Boomer vs. Gossage. I did not leap from the roof. I sat down and rested my chin on my knees. I believe I smiled at the Boomer. I know I said aloud, "Surprise me, baby."

The Boomer did not surprise. Gossage took only a minute or so to strike him out.

I remained motionless as the teams changed sides and as they played the top of the ninth, about which I can remember little. It seems to me that Paul Blair got a hit and Dick Drago pitched. There was base running of some kind, activity around second. I know there was no scoring.

Just before the start of the last of the ninth, I imagined myself swimming in an enormous pool. I was in the desert in early summer. I thought that it was the dry heat that enabled me to move through the water so rapidly. I hardly had to move my arms or legs in order to cover the length of the pool. It was possible to swim forever.

I spotted Dwight Evans striding quickly, intensely to the plate. For whom was he hitting?

He was hitting for Frank Duffy, who had replaced Jack Brohamer, who had been hit for by Bailey. Duffy had played third in the top of the ninth, and I hadn't even noticed.

Evans was hitting for Duffy.

Why hadn't Evans come to bat instead of Bailey in the seventh?

And where was Garry Hancock? A lefthanded hitter, a slim Gary Geiger kind of guy. Where was Garry Hancock?

It looked to me as if Evans nearly got ahold of one. He missed, by God knows how small a portion of the ball, and flied routinely to left.

Gossage walked Burleson as if it had been his intention. That would give Rice a turn at bat, providing Remy stayed out of the double play.

Remy lined a shot to right. My thought was . . . double play. Piniella catches the ball and throws to Chambliss with Burleson miles off first.

LOU PINIELLA: *I didn't want the ball hit to me. It was a nightmare out there in the sun. I kept telling Blair in center to help me. When Remy hit it, I saw it for a second and then lost it. I knew it would bounce, so I moved back three steps to prevent it from bouncing over me to the wall. I moved to my left a piece. I decoyed Burleson. I didn't want him to know I couldn't see it. If Burleson had tried for third, he would have been out. There's no doubt about it. My throw was accurate and, for me, it had good stuff on it.*

JERRY REMY: *I think Burleson did 100% the right thing. It would have been very close at third. He had to play it safe. I knew I had a hit, but Rick had to hold up for just a moment between first and second. So why gamble?*

I knelt on the roof. I thought, is this actually happening? First and second, one out, last of the ninth. And Rice and Yaz. Is this actually happening?

GOOSE GOSSAGE: *I tried to calm myself down by thinking of the mountains of Colorado, the mountains that I love. I thought that the worst thing that could happen to me was that I'd be in those mountains tomorrow. I had once hiked to a lake in the mountains. It was really quiet. I had pictured seats on the mountainsides. Thousands and thousands of seats looking down on a ball field next to the lake. I imagined myself pitching in front to all those people in the mountains.*

I didn't think Yastrzemski had a chance. I thought about it being late in the day, about his being fatigued, about how he wouldn't get around on Gossage's fastball. My hopes rode with Rice.

Lou Piniella: *I played Rice in right center, not deep. It cut the angle of the sun. I saw the ball clean. I caught it maybe 25 feet from the fence.*

Goose Gossage: *When I was warming up before I came in the seventh, I imagined myself pitching to Yaz with two outs in the ninth. The Red Sox would have a couple of guys on base, and it would be Yaz and me. When it turned out that way, I thought, here it is. It was ESP. Really, I'm not kidding.*

I screamed at Yaz from the leftfield roof. "Bunt, goddam it!" I even waved my arms, thinking that I might catch his eye. He'd call time out and wander out to leftfield. "What did you say?" he'd shout up at me. "Bunt!" I'd yell back. "Interesting," he'd say.

Then Yaz would lay down a beauty.

Burleson, who had taken third after Rice's fly ball, would easily score the tying run.

Carl Yastrzemski, nearly my age.

I gazed down at him through tears.

I thought: Freeze this minute. Freeze it right here. How unspeakably beautiful it is. Everyone, reach out and touch it.

The Red Sox might have won their playoff game against the Yankees in 1978, if not for a single fateful decision made many years earlier. In the following essay Boston pitcher Bill Lee considers what might have been.

"WHAT IF...BUCKY DENT"

from *The Little Red (Sox) Book* [2003]
by **Bill Lee**

MAY 9, 1961, 10-year-old adoptee Russell Earl O'Dey was practicing the piano. The weather outside was sunny and inviting. Wafting through the open window on the waves of warmish air, Russell could hear the faint, disjointed voices of his friends as they chose up for a game of baseball on the vacant lot next door to his Savannah, Georgia, home. Russell felt restless. He enjoyed the piano, but he also enjoyed baseball. And he played both very well. Small for his age, he nevertheless was a good fielder and reliable hitter, but he had little or no power. Those same soft hands that marked him as a piano prodigy also made him the best defensive shortstop of his age-group in Savannah. Young Russell had two parallel dreams: to hit a pennant-winning home ran in the major leagues and to win international acclaim as a pianist.

He left the keys and went to sit by the window. He watched the team

194

selection play out according to the timeless rules of youth. Finally someone said, "Hey, where's Bucky?" They turned toward his house to see him looking back from the window. They shouted for him to join them. He paused and looked at the piano then he looked back at the ball field. He appeared to be weighing something in his mind. After a long pause he shouted, "Sorry guys, I'm trying to learn a piano piece for the school concert Friday night." With that he walked purposefully back to his piano and began to play, inexpertly but persistently. Through the window, his friends could hear the halting but recognizable chords of "Take Me Out to the Ball Game." They rolled their eyes at such a blatant waste of God-given baseball talent and returned to their game.

Seventeen years later, the Boston Red Sox and the New York Yankees met in the 163rd game of what the schedule makers had designed as a 162-game season. In actual fact, the Red Sox had already gone through three distinct seasons in the past six months. Season one was April to mid-August. They started as the hottest team in baseball, compiling a seemingly insurmountable first-half record of 47–26. Season two ran from mid-August to September 16 and featured something called the Boston Massacre. During this period, they swooned as dramatically as any jilted heroine of the silent screen, squandering a seven-and-a-half-game lead in no time flat. Before the dust had settled, the Yankees were three-and-a-half games in front. Season three was from September 17 to the end of the 162-game marathon. To their everlasting credit the Sox fought back and won every one of the last eight regular-season games to end in a dead heat with the Bronx Bombers. Now came season four, the cruelest season.

The single-game playoff was played at Fenway Park. In the seventh inning, the first two Yankees hitters reached base with the Red Sox still leading, 2–0. Shortstop Fred Stanley, a .219 hitter with one home run, came to the plate. For a moment it looked as if Yankees manager Bob Lemon would lift him for a pinch hitter, but Zimmer was thinking ahead. He walked to the mound, patted Torrez on the butt, and signaled right-handed sinkerball specialist Bob Stanley in from the bullpen. Stanley versus Stanley. Stanley's sinker was among the "heaviest" in baseball, and the Portland, Maine, native was at his best. On a 2–1 count, Stanley the pitcher threw his best sinker. The bottom fell out of the pitch as it crossed home plate, and Stanley the batter swung and popped the ball toward Red Sox shortstop Rick Burleson. Rooster gloved the ball on the second bounce and smoothly flipped it to Jerry Remy at second, who gunned it to Scott at first to complete the tailor-made double play. The inning over, the Red Sox still clung to a 2–0 lead. They were now six scant outs away from capturing the American League pennant in this roller-coaster-from-hell season.

The eighth and ninth innings would be a challenge. The always-pesky Mickey Rivers singled and stole second. Stanley, rattled by the presence of the hyperactive Rivers, threw Munson a fat pitch, and the surly catcher promptly singled to drive in the Yankees' first run of the game. It was 2–1 and after a hasty discussion with pitching coach Al Jackson, Zimmer ordered the bullpen into action. One right-handed pitcher and one southpaw quickly began warming up. The next batter grounded to short and Burleson froze the runner before rifling the ball to first base for the second out of the inning. It was October 3 and up came the man they called Mr. October—Reggie Jackson.

As Reggie came to the plate, Zimmer strode to the mound once again and signaled for the lefty. At first, I didn't respond, thinking there must be some mistake. I was, after all, the man who publicly and repeatedly called Zimmer a gerbil. I was low man currently in the gerbil's doghouse. I was the man who helped to found the Buffalo Head Society, an organization apparently dedicated to making Zimmer's life a living hell.

I entered to a questioning buzz from the crowd, followed by recognition, applause, and the sound of 65,850 raised eyebrows. I had lost seven starts in a row at one point in the season and had thus earned my banishment to the bullpen. I was now being given a chance at re-entry into an atmosphere thick with tension.

On my first pitch, Reggie swung from his heels and pulled a screaming foul ball into the Boston dugout, scattering Red Sox players in all directions. He examined the bat, found it cracked and walked toward the dugout. Mickey Rivers came to the top step and offered him his bat, Reggie declined, saying: Why would I take the bat of a .265 hitter with a 65 IQ?" My next offering was an inside slider. The batter turned on it, driving the ball high and deep but just to the right of Pesky's pole. Strike two.

I walked behind the mound and paused as thirty thousand fans took a collective breath. Two stinging fouls does not instill confidence in fans burned way too many times. I had thrown two inside fastballs and both had been crushed by Jackson, who would feast on fastballs like George Scott at the postgame buffet. I hesitated, having an internal argument with myself. My last post-season appearance had been in Game 7 of the 1975 series, when I unleashed a blooper pitch that the Cincinnati Reds' Tony Perez promptly blooped over the Green Monster. The Red Sox went on to lose that game and the Series. I looked in for the sign from catcher Carlton Fisk. I shook him off once, twice, three times. Fisk then asked for time and trotted to the mound; his stiff gait was reminiscent of Frankenstein with arthritis setting in. We were arguing and Fisk was not a happy man. We could not have been more different in attitude and approach to the game. Fisk was a conservative, hard-nosed stolid New Englander with old-fashioned values and work ethic. I was a southern California liberal who appeared to go out of his way to create controversy and then glory in the spotlight. We had only one thing in common: we both loved baseball and we both had an unfettered will to win. Don Zimmer came to the top step of the dugout and glared toward the mound. He was about to come to the mound when Fisk and I came to a compromise, and Fisk ambled back behind the plate.

Would I throw the blooper again? Thirty thousand fans silently asked the question. Reggie Jackson, a historian of the game and an intelligent man who boasted an IQ of 160, also asked that question. This was, after all, the Spaceman, and you could never tell with me. I had brawled with the Yankees and called them Brown Shirts.

I went into my windup and released a sidearm slider that started for Jackson's letters, freezing him, and then broke across the plate low and away for a called third strike.

In the World Series that followed, the Red Sox played the Brooklyn Dodgers. The Dodgers outfield included Reggie Smith, a one-time center fielder in the fearsome Red Sox outfield of Yastrzemski-Smith-Conigliaro.

Still numb from their playoff win, the Red Sox lost Game 1, 11–5, in Los Angeles on homers by Dusty Baker and Davey Lopes. Yaz responded with a home run, but it was too little too late. Game 2 was closer, but the Red Sox lost again, 4–3. The difference was a home run by Dodgers third baseman Ron Cey.

Back in Boston, the Red Sox hitters came to life, pounding 10 hits off Dodgers ace Don Sutton and relievers Lance Rautzhan and Charlie Hough. Leading the way for Boston were Carl Yastrzemski, Freddie Lynn, and Jim Rice.

Meanwhile, as the Red Sox organist John Kiley was playing "The Hallelujah Chorus," and Red Sox fans were cavorting around the bases with the players, somewhere in a Vienna opera house virtuoso pianist Russell Dent joined fellow musicians in a stirring rendition of a fugue from his idol Johann Sebastian Bach's "The Well-Tempered Clavier." Dent was so enamored of Bach's work that he was often referred to jokingly as Johann Jr. When he finished the piece with a flourish, Dent received a standing ovation for a performance that the music reviewer for the *International Herald Tribune* called "more than just a hit. It was a home run in ivory." Dent's patron, Herr Brennerstein, was ecstatic. Of course there was inevitable grumbling from competing pianists, including one disgruntled German named Torrezstein, who played in the wrong pitch. Torrezstein was managed by impresario Herr Don Zimmer-Frei. Zimmer-Frei hated the works of Bach as much as he despised Russell Dent. In a classic case of "pianist envy" he drove his Volkswagen back to the Rhineland uttering frustrated, disbelieving cries of "Bach und Dent . . . Bach und fugueing Dent!"

SPEAKING OF BUCKY

Assorted thoughts on the Bucky Dent homer that helped New York win the one-game playoff for the 1978 American League East division title . . .

"The silence was deafening. It was the eeriest sound I've ever heard at a ball game. All over Fenway Park after Bucky hit that homer, you could have heard a pin drop."—Yankee second baseman Willie Randolph

"When Bucky hit the ball, I told the folks, 'It was a fly ball to left field. Oh, it's a home run.' I gave Bucky a tape later and I said, 'I'm sorry Bucky, I said it's just a fly ball to left.' And he said 'That's all it was.'" —Radio broadcaster Ernie Harwell

"I see [replays of] it a lot on TV. I know one of these days we're going to win that game." —Former Red Sox second baseman Jerry Remy

"Every time I see Bucky Dent, I almost want to go over and kick him in the foot." —Boston outfielder Mike Greenwell, who was 15 in 1978

"Were you bitter? . . . Do you still hate me?" —Bucky Dent's questions to a pair of Red Sox fans sitting near him in Fenway's "Monster Seats," not far from where Dent's home run had cleared the stadium's left-field wall 25 years earlier.

Histories often focus on the famous. But the story of the Red Sox–Yankees rivalry isn't just the story of DiMaggio and Williams, Schilling and Jeter. Sometimes lesser talents play the key roles. The following essay recounts the experiences of two ballplayers of modest abilities. While these men had only brief careers in New York and Boston in the 1970s, they managed to embody the essence of their respective teams.

"A TALE OF TWO DOYLES"

adapted from *Ninety Feet from Fame:*
Close Calls with Baseball Immortality
by **Mike Robbins**

WHAT IS IT THAT makes the Red Sox the Red Sox? What is it that makes the Yankees the Yankees? On October 22, 1975, an otherwise forgettable ballplayer named Denny Doyle helped answer the first of those questions. Three years later his younger brother, Brian, helped answer the second.

On June 14, 1975, the Boston Red Sox purchased the contract of second baseman Denny Doyle from the California Angels. The transaction was of only passing note to baseball fans. Doyle wasn't a star. He was a 31-year-old infielder who'd managed a career batting average of just .245 in five seasons with Philadelphia and California. He'd recently lost his starting job to a rookie named Jerry Remy.

Everything changed for Doyle when he landed in Boston. He went from a bench player on a bad team to a starter on a good one. He embarked on a 22-game hitting streak and compiled a .310 batting average for Boston during the remainder of the season. "It's like a dream," Doyle told the press.

Thanks in part to Denny Doyle, the Red Sox reached the World Series that year. And thanks in part to Doyle, who hit safely in every game of the Series, Boston was on the verge of winning game six and pushing their October showdown with the heavily favored Cincinnati Reds to a decisive seventh game. Then everything changed for Doyle once again.

Game six was tied at six apiece in the bottom of the ninth. No one was out. Denny Doyle was on third, just 90 feet from recording the game-winning run. Red Sox outfielder Fred Lynn lifted a fly ball to short left—too short, clearly, to score Doyle. Yet when the catch was made, Doyle sprinted for the plate. The play wasn't even close. Doyle was out, and the game rolled into extra innings. It was later revealed that Boston third base coach Don Zimmer had yelled "No, no," to Doyle. Doyle heard "Go, go" and nearly ran the Red Sox out of the Series. Fortunately for Doyle, the Red Sox won the game anyway, on Carlton Fisk's home run in the 12th. The Series went to a seventh game, and Doyle's baserunning blunder became nothing more than a footnote.

Through the early innings of game seven, it again seemed that Doyle's dream season would end with a championship. Boston led 3–0 as the game rolled into the fifth. Boston starter Bill Lee had made the Big Red Machine sputter through the first four innings, but Dave Concepcion opened the fifth with an infield single. Ken Griffey, up next, hit the ball right to Doyle—and right through Doyle for an error. The usually sure-handed second baseman had made an error on one of the most important plays of his career.

Once again he got away with it. Despite the error, Lee worked out of the inning without allowing a run. Only Doyle had one more mistake in him. In the top of the sixth with one out, a man on first, and the score still 3–0 Boston, Cincinnati catcher Johnny Bench hit an apparent double play grounder to short. Rick Burleson flipped the ball to second baseman Doyle, who avoided the sliding runner but threw too high to first. Bench was safe and the inning continued. This time the Red Sox wouldn't escape Doyle's gaff. Tony Perez, up next, hit a two-run homer. Lee was forced from the game by a blister in the seventh, Cincinnati plated two more runs, and Boston lost game seven 4–3. Denny Doyle had averaged just 12 errors per season for the past four years. In the biggest game of his life, he'd committed two.

Oddly, Boston fans chose not to tar-and-feather Doyle for his miscues. He remained with Boston for two more seasons, hitting .250 in 1976 and .240 in 1977. He was released shortly before the 1978 season when the Red Sox acquired Angels second baseman Jerry Remy, the same man who had replaced Doyle in the California lineup three seasons before. Denny Doyle would never play another game in the major leagues—but another Doyle would.

Brain Doyle didn't expect to be a major leaguer in 1978. The Yankee farm hand hadn't been invited to play with the major leaguers during spring training, and when the season began, he wasn't even starting for his minor-league club. But when Yankee infielders Willie Randolph and Bucky Dent went down with injuries early in the year, Denny Doyle's younger brother landed in the show.

Brian's major league career got off to a slow start. Though he was on the Yankee roster for much of the season, he played sparingly and hit a paltry .192. But with Randolph injured and on the shelf in October, the sure-handed Doyle became New York's starting second baseman for four out of six games in that year's World Series.

In his first two Series starts, Brian Doyle performed about as expected—he managed just one hit in seven at-bats. But New York's other option at second, Fred Stanley, was no more productive in his two starts, so with the Dodgers and Yankees all even at two games apiece, weak-hitting Brian Doyle got the starting nod the rest of the way.

All the Yankees wanted was solid defense at second base. They got much more. With a championship on the line, Doyle played the best baseball of his life. He went six for nine the rest of the way, scored four runs and fielded his position flawlessly as the Yankees took two straight for a six-game Series win. Brian Doyle's World Series total of seven hits nearly matched the 10 he'd produced in the entire regular season. His .438 average was the highest in the Series of any player who had more than four at-bats. "Who's the MVP?" Reggie Jackson shouted after the final game. "Brian Doyle! How about Brian Doyle?"

"It's unbelievable," said Doyle. "It really is."

It was also unsustainable. The 1978 World Series would be Brian Doyle's only moment in the sun. In his three remaining seasons in the majors, he never played in more than 34 games in a year or hit above .173. He managed just one career homer. Brian Doyle's career batting average of .161 in only 199 regular season at-bats average pales beside his brother's .250 in 3,290 at-bats. Yet Brain Doyle would forever be remembered as a winner, his brother as a loser.

The Doyle family thus sheds light on a deep truth concerning two of the American League's most storied franchises. Two men were taken from the same gene pool and sent to the World Series. The one with the greater talent was assigned a Red Sox uniform, the one with lesser abilities the Yankee pinstripes. The Red Sox player committed a series of crucial mistakes; the Yankee hit .438 and fielded flawlessly. "For all you Red Sox fans," wrote Brian's son Kirk years later, "the curse is real . . . It not only infected a team but also went after brothers." These days Denny and Brian live within a few blocks of each other in Winter Haven, Florida. They run the Doyle Academy, a baseball camp, with the help of a third brother, who didn't play in the majors. Sometimes Denny and Brian don their old major league uniforms for the campers. When Denny sees Brian in his Yankee pinstripes, wrote the *Orlando Sentinel* recently, he's been known to make a jibe or two about the team that much of America loves to hate. In response, Brian just raises his right hand, shows off his World Series ring, and says "Twenty-six," referring to the number of Yankee World Series victories. Denny Doyle had a substantially better career than his brother, but his big moment came with the Red Sox, so things went wrong when it mattered most. Brain's ring wins all arguments.

"I don't like the Yankees," Denny recently told a reporter. "And you can quote me on that."

There is a very fine line between rooting for the Red Sox and rooting against the Yankees. The author of *Diary of a Yankee-Hater*, then a New York resident, crossed that line willingly and never looked back. He didn't much care who won so long as the Yankees lost. In 1980, he'd get his wish, as the Yankees won the American League East, but were swept by the Royals in the playoffs. The selections included here focus mainly on New York's interactions with Boston.

SELECTIONS FROM "DIARY OF A YANKEE-HATER"

[1981]
by **Robert Marshall**

Friday, November 9, 1979. Every year New York gets a new skyscraper, a defecting Russian ballet star, a previously unheard-of ethnic-day parade and, thanks to George Steinbrenner, a couple of free agents. This year Steinbrenner set a record with the speed in which he signed Bob Watson and Rudy May. And he's still fishing for the biggest catch of the year, Nolan Ryan. Steinbrenner landed the first big-money free agent, Catfish Hunter, five years ago and has continued to add big names to the Yankee roster every year since: Reggie Jackson, Don Gullett, Rich Gossage, Tommy John, Luis Tiant. He is quick to point out that he's not responsible for the system—and equally quick to imply that so long as the system is there, you're stupid (or, worse, poor) if you don't take advantage of it. But the success of a team like Baltimore makes you think that there is more to winning baseball than assembling the best team money can buy.

The Watson signing, and the Yankee first-base situation in general, show how Steinbrenner and free agency are combining to destroy even the illusion of team loyalty that used to be part of the popular image of baseball. Bob Watson had played fourteen years for one club, the Houston Astros. When they decided that at age 33 he couldn't hit anymore, Boston took a chance on him and he proved he still could, at least in the American League, to the tune of .337. Now that he has proved his value, Steinbrenner has coaxed him away from the Red Sox, just as he did with Luis Tiant. Sure, the Red Sox had the chance to match the Yankees' offer, but what club in its right mind will pay a part-timer $375,000 a year—not just this year, but until he's 37 years old. But Steinbrenner "just looked over our budget for this year and realized that two and a half million people came out to see a fourth-place team . . . and gave us their hard-earned money." The ticket prices jumped up the year they signed Reggie and more people than ever showed up. Jack the prices up another dollar and bring in some more free agents. If Watson's hits net one win for the Yankees and they win their division by that one game, the signing will be a huge success financially, for Steinbrenner as well as for Watson.

But Watson has left the club where he enjoyed his best years, and he has left the club which gave him a second life. He has joined the ranks of baseball's ronin, the wandering samurai without a master, an identification, a loyalty. Bob Watson will never be a Yankee. He will be an Astro winding down his career in New York. He will never get the applause for a home run that Roy White has gotten for a mere appearance as a pinch runner.

Baseball fans are loyal, first to the team they support, second to the players who make up that team. Ideally, the two loyalties reinforce each other. A kid in Los Angeles would say that he likes Steve Garvey because he's a Dodger, and he likes the Dodgers because they have Steve Garvey. When a Tommy John leaves, it wrenches this civic identification, and the player and the team suffer in the public esteem. With some players, the identification is so strong that you hope they can stay with the team until it's time to quit—and you hope they know when that time comes.

A Yankee fan's loyalty is primarily to the organization. It has to be. The only current Yankee player, Roy White aside (where he will be soon), who has come up with the Yankees and has no other team identity is Ron Guidry. Steinbrenner must believe, no doubt correctly, that fans would rather win with purchased goods than come in second with homegrown stuff. He has assigned no value in his calculations to years of service in pinstripes. This was never clearer than last week when he unloaded Chris Chambliss for light-hitting catcher Rick Cerone from Toronto. Chambliss, of course, started with Cleveland, but in six years in New York he played day in, day out and became the closest thing to a fixture in the Yankee lineup of the '70s. His performance was more than routine: his home run against Kansas City to win the 1976 playoffs was one of the most dramatic in Yankee history. But he became "expendable" the moment backup first baseman Jim Spencer signed a four-year contract at $300,000 a year.

If Spencer couldn't beat out Chambliss for the job on the field, how was he able to do it in the off-season? My hunch is that Spencer gave up his shot at the free-agent market for less money than Chambliss would have wanted next year, when he would be eligible to go that route. And Steinbrenner didn't want to lose Spencer this year and be forced to pay Chambliss twice as much next year or see him leave without a thank-you. Steinbrenner has lived by the free-agent sword long enough that he guards against its coming back to nick him. He knows he won't be able to appeal to any player's sense of team loyalty to stick with the Yankees. Loyalty didn't keep John with the Dodgers, Tiant with the Red Sox or Gullett with the Reds.

Saturday, May 24, 1980. On a softball field in Central Park, I finally ran into the man who bet me five dollars last year that Ron Guidry would win more games than Dennis Eckersley. Actually, I was the one who forced the bet on him, and it was a follow-up to our more complicated bet in 1978 that Eckersley and Mike Torrez would win more games for the Red Sox than any two Yankee pitchers. Eckersley was a favorite of mine from his three seasons at Cleveland, when he practically had to pitch a no-hitter, which he did once, to be assured of winning. Cleveland was the first team in my sports lifetime to beat the Yankees, and I have rooted for the Indians in gratitude ever since. And although I have received little recompense for this choice since 1954, the Indians have generally managed to produce one pitcher—Herb Score, Cal McLish, Sam McDowell, Gaylord

Perry, Eckersley—whom I could root for with some likelihood of success, no matter how badly the rest of the team was doing. With the Red Sox' hitting behind him, Eckersley was a sure 20-game winner. That's exactly what he won, but Guidry had his phenomenal 25–3 season, and the surprising Tommy John added 21 wins, five more than Torrez.

In '79 I knew Guidry couldn't repeat his previous success and I thought Eckersley would. For half the season I had a lock on the five dollars. Guidry volunteered for bullpen duty after Gossage sprained his thumb and Eckersley built up a five-win lead. Then in August Eckersley started to come up empty and Guidry began an eight-game winning streak. For me the tension climaxed on September 3 when the Yankees, by this time fourteen and one-half games behind Baltimore, faced off against the Sox for a three-game series, and Eckersley and Guidry were named the starting pitchers.

As I turned on the radio to listen, I knew in my gut that Eckersley would not pull it off—and when he was knocked out in the second inning, I consoled myself that he'd at least get plenty of rest before his next start. My hopes were then pinned on Guidry's not getting the win, and they were still alive when Boston narrowed New York's lead to 6–5 in the top of the eighth and knocked out Guidry. I made a deal with the Radio Devil, one of the few superstitious forces in my life: let the Red Sox score again and I will agree to let the Yankees ultimately win the game. The deal went through all right, but I had left a large loophole. The Red Sox scored their sixth run in the ninth—but only after the Yankees had added four insurance runs in the bottom of the eighth. Guidry picked up the win, which provided his season margin of one over Eckersley.

By the time the season ended, however, the Yankee fan I bet with had switched jobs. It is probably just as well that we didn't meet again until this week. By then only a fool would have bet a third time against Guidry, or John. As if to confirm this analysis, Guidry improved his record to 5–0 last night. This time when I turned on the radio and heard Wille Randolph homer to lead off the game and the Yankees take a 3–0 lead in the first inning, I didn't even bother to call on the Radio Devil. With the Yankees playing Toronto, I had no chips to negotiate with.

Monday, June 23. "Wanna go to the Red Sox game tonight?" one of my Boston friends asked me on the phone this afternoon. After first ascertaining that he was not offering an extra ticket in the owner's box or some equally select and protected area, I quickly and righteously declined. If Old-Timers' Day yesterday brought out the best in Yankee fans, the appearance of the Red Sox in Yankee Stadium tonight is sure to bring out the worst. The two teams may or may not hate each other now that Thurman Munson can no longer resent All-Star votes for Carlton Fisk and now that Bill Lee has taken the shoulder that Graig Nettles separated and his diatribes about "Nazis" Steinbrenner and Martin to the National League. But even if Mike Torrez came out and embraced Reggie Jackson in centerfield, where Jackson does his limbering up exercises before each game, the vendors selling Boston Sucks T-shirts would be assured of their brisk sales, for the battle in the stands has a life of its own.

When the Yankees visit Fenway Park, thousands of students from New York who are attending colleges in and around Boston go out to Fenway Park and cheer the Yankees like liberators arriving in Paris. They also thumb their noses and collect their bets from the fanatical Red Sox fans they find themselves living among for eight months of the year. And when the Sox come to New York, they prompt a pilgrimage to Yankee Stadium of every young working male who grew up in Massachusetts and who has come to the Big Apple to pursue a career. With the exception of a perverse minority of Yankee fans, everyone in New England is a Red Sox fan, and anybody leaving New England has to go through New York.

The crowds at Yankee–Red Sox games are not your Family Night, your Ladies' Day or your Senior Citizens crowds. They are not even the innocently destructive under-fourteens that fill up the Stadium for Bat Day, Helmet Day or Jockstrap Weekend. These are fans who want to see the other team lose. They are crowds of men who are young, who are out to impress the world and who drink a lot of beer. Add to this the normal collection of rowdies who like to be where the action is, who like the atmosphere of yelling, screaming and chanting obscenities, cap stealing, banner ripping and beer throwing, and you have a good idea of why I prefer to stay home and watch the Yankee–Red Sox games on TV.

Oh, one more thing: tonight's game has been delayed a half hour to accommodate the folks from ABC, who decided over the weekend that we would rather watch this game than the boring Dodgers against the Astros (who were pitching Joaquin Andujar, not Ryan or Richard). This should give the yahoos an extra half hour of lubrication before the game even begins. Last fall I attended the first Monday Night Football game ABC televised from Shea Stadium. Starting at nine o'clock, the Jets and Vikings played a game that would have put me to sleep except that fights kept breaking out in the stands—even though everyone was rooting for the same team. The game ended with a guy bouncing on the baseball backstop and people in the upper stands throwing beer down on him. New York has been well in the forefront of a fifteen-year trend toward unruly sports crowds. And I'm not talking violent sports, like hockey, boxing and roller derby. I am referring to such formerly genteel sports as tennis and golf. Forest Hills used to attract moderate crowds of suburban tennis players, who would rarely whistle when a close call by a linesman went against their favorite player. Then, with no little help from such bad actors as Ilie Nastase and Jimmy Connors and the increasing commercialization of the sport, the scene changed. On my last visit to Forest Hills, 10,000 fans stood and chanted, "We won't go," when management canceled a scheduled match so as not to interfere with a separate-admission evening program. Last year, with the Open shifted to Flushing Meadows, across the subway tracks from Shea Stadium, a crowd riot not only forced the umpire to change a call, it also forced the tournament director to change the umpire.

New Yorkers were able to show off their golf etiquette last week when the U.S. Open was played at northern New Jersey's Baltusrol Club. Television viewers could watch Jack Nicklaus sink a fifteen-foot birdie putt to win the event—and almost get trampled as a result. One section of the crowd swarmed like the Italian army across a sand trap even as Nicklaus lined up his putt.

Some sports commentators tried to turn this rowdiness into a spontaneous outpouring of affection for the veteran Nicklaus. There was some of that talk, too, when the Shea Stadium infield was torn up after the Mets won the pennant in 1973. But it was pretty hard not to recognize wanton destruction and disrespect of other human beings as the sheer ugliness it is when this strain of behavior reached a peak of sorts in the 1976 playoffs at Yankee Stadium. That was the year that Steinbrenner brought the Yankees their first pennant in 12 years. They did it in the fifth game of the play-offs against Kansas City, when Chris Chambliss led off the bottom of the tenth with a home run. Onto the field poured a swarming mass of fans—seemingly all 20-year-old males bent on acquiring souvenirs from Yankee players, including Chambliss, who was still rounding the bases. Halfway to third he realized his predicament, and he started knocking people down. He came home like a fullback trying to get through the Atlanta Falcons and we will never know whether he ever touched home plate (one story was that he went back out an hour after the game just to make sure). What should have been the greatest moment of his sporting life, a majestic sweep around the bases with the pennant-winning run, became instead a moment of terror.

Since then at Yankee Stadium, the players know that when a big game is over, you grab your glove, your hat and your glasses and run to the dugout and save the congratulations for the locker room. The "spontaneous exuberance" of the fans is usually plotted well in advance and is fortified by three hours of beer drinking. It is no more a part of the game than having your tires slashed while your car is in the Stadium parking lot. My solution would be to station machine gun–carrying special forces on the foul lines after the game with instructions to open fire at knee level the moment anyone stepped on the field. Leftover liberals might not like it, but I suspect that it would do the trick.

Monday, June 23. Tonight, I hope, was the first day of the rest of the season, as the Red Sox brought the Yankees a bit closer to earth, not to mention Milwaukee, with a 7–2 trouncing. The Yankees' second loss in a row was filled with delicious moments. For starters, Eckersley beat Guidry. Yastrzemski hit a majestic two-run homer to right. Bobby Brown misplayed two balls in center field. Randolph threw high and wide to the plate, allowing one run to score and setting up another. Tony Perez, the Red Sox' replacement for Bob Watson, drove in two runs to increase his league-leading total to 53. Reggie was stifled, hitting two easy grounders and a broken-bat single. The only Yankee runs were solo shots in the first and eighth by Joe Lefebvre: after the first Eckersley tossed the resin bag and smiled, after the second he just shrugged. The Yankees can't use the absence of Dent, Jones and Murcer as an excuse, either, for Boston was playing without Rice, Fisk and Remy and with a hamstrung Hobson limited to DHing. Before last night I had never even *heard* of two players in the Boston starting lineup—Stapleton and Hoffman.

Even though, or maybe because, the Yankees were losing badly, the fans behaved about as I expected, prompting Howard Cosell to give a little lecture on "rowdyism" and prompting Boston rightfielder Dwight Evans to don a batting helmet to ward off unfriendly missiles in right field, including a lead sinker.

Reggie was not completely shut out of the national spotlight. After he walked in the first inning, he pulled some candy in an orange wrapper out of his pocket and had a snack while standing on first base. Please don't tell me it was a Reggie bar!

Tuesday, June 24. "Boston's rivalry with New York is total," my Irish friend from Melrose, Massachusetts, explained to me as we watched the Red Sox play the Yankees on TV. "Ever since New York passed Boston as the dominant port city on the East Coast, Boston has felt itself in competition with New York. But while New York grew huge and adopted a worldly-wise, money-can-buy-anything attitude, Boston remained a backwater. It was parochial in its worldview. But the people in Boston always felt that while New York was bigger, Boston was better. Unlike New York, Boston had class.

"The Boston sports fan is a purist, too. He takes his sports very seriously. And the team managements find players who relate to the city. Look at the guys who are stars in Boston—Carlton Fisk, Dave Cowens, John Havlicek. They are dedicated athletes who give everything to their sport and are part of the community. They appear at Jimmy Fund fund raisers and speak at Little League dinners. Compare this with New York. The stars here are guys like Joe Namath, Walt Frazier and of course Reggie, guys who drive Cadillacs and Rolls-Royces and hang out in East Side bars.

"Every kid in the Boston area is a Red Sox fan. You start when you play in Little League and your team goes to Fenway Park and you sit together out in the rightfield stands. Then you go to college in Boston and you sit with all the college kids in the bleachers. Look at the two ballparks. At Fenway you're right on the field, you can see the players, it's a personal, friendly, family atmosphere. Yankee Stadium is like New York: it's big, impersonal and cold.

"The attitude toward the Yankees used to be tinged with awe, back in the '50s and early '60s when the Yankees were so good. Ever since the Sox won in '67, however, Boston thought it could beat the Yankees, and there has been a lot of frustration when the Red Sox lost. I don't have to tell you about the last couple of years."

And why do Yankee fans, with their established dominance and cosmopolitan worldview, care so much about beating Boston? First is the presence of so many Red Sox fans in New York. Everyone knows at least one fanatical Red Sox fan who will lord it over him if Boston beats the Yankees. And there are always enough Red Sox fans at the Stadium to goad the macho Yankee supporters into louder obscenities and ruder behavior. Second is the fact that the Red Sox have had a genuinely competitive team on the field. While Baltimore may have had a better record than Boston over the last fifteen years, the Orioles have not had the superstars—like Yaz, Rice, Lynn and Fisk—that Yankee fans could recognize as individual rivals for their own heroes.

And so tonight there were again more than 40,000 fans at Yankee Stadium screaming and chanting as the Yanks turned the tables with a 10–5 win that included a game-turning pop-fly home run by Cerone and a predictable three-run coup de grâce by Reggie. And oh yes, there was also a smoke bomb thrown onto the field and wildly jubilant fans who ran out during the game to meet Reggie and try to borrow Gossage's cap while he was pitching.

Sunday, September 14. The Boston Red Sox have given me so many thrilling moments in the last six years that I do not want to be too hard on them now. For me, Rooster Burleson and Pudge Fisk are the very models of what a major league shortstop and catcher should be. Butch Hobson is a throwback to the storied twenties, a player who ignores constant pain for the chance to bat in a clutch situation. Fred Lynn is the only centerfielder of the last decade who can stand comparison to the Mays-Mantle-Snider triumvirate. Dewey Evans has kept alive the tradition of a rightfielder with an arm that is a defensive weapon, à la Clemente and Kaline. And Carl Yastrzemski, Captain Carl, is one of the great clutch players of all time, a hero who earned his way into the Hall of Fame in 1967 and is playing with the same determination, albeit not the same body, thirteen years later. So I salute the Red Sox for the successes they have had, for the great team they almost became. And I will not grow bitter over the four games they just lost to the Yankees, or the excruciating fact that in the seven games the two teams played in Boston this year, the Sox didn't win a one.

Each baseball game has its own character, and there is no reason to expect two teams to follow the same script two days in a row. Yet all seven of these games had a depressing sameness: the Yankees got off to an early lead, the Red Sox chipped away for a run here and there to make it close, then Davis or Gossage came in to shut them down in the late innings, preserving a—to take the scores from this weekend—4–2, 4–3 or 5–2 win.

The rational analyst of this pattern would probably cite pitching, which the Yankees have and the Red Sox don't. The emotional analyst might point to a Boston stubbornness that bordered on stupidity. Don Zimmer, no one's favorite manager, called on reliever Bob Stanley to pitch to Bob Watson three games in a row, resulting in two singles, a home run and five RBIs; after proving that Dent and Rodriguez couldn't touch his curve, Dennis Eckersley threw them both inside fastballs, the only pitch they could conceivably hit onto the leftfield screen, which they both did, for four runs and today's victory. Believers in the preternatural, meanwhile, would merely hark back to October 2, 1978, and explain, with ample justification, that the two teams are caught in the mold of the greatest regular-season game ever played, that the Red Sox, like Tantalus, are doomed to come close, but always fall short, for as long as Yaz wears an 8 on his back.

Sunday, September 21. The Yankees finished off a 10–3 year against the Red Sox today in a dull game decided in the first inning, when all the runs in New York's 3–0 win came home. Some ever vigilant statistician pointed out that this loss mathematically eliminated Boston from the 1980 division race. That's nothing. "In the sweep of four games [last weekend]," according to the *Boston Globe,* "the Yankees put an end to the era 1975 supposedly began. With this final degradation, the Yankees finished five years of beating the Red Sox *any time they had to.*"

And just as the Yankees dominated the opposition on the field, their traveling circus held sway in the off-the-field arena, and the *Globe,* for once, was not too proud to send a reporter to cover it. *Globe* columnist Leigh Montville interviewed the twenty fans who hung around the lobby of the Sheraton Boston for Yankee autographs their first day in town. Not all players cooperate in this ritual, and in fairness to their point of view, these kids are not looking for a once-in-a-lifetime thrill; they are more professional pests, who will sell any extra autographs they can get. Still, the difference in players' attitudes would be instructive if it weren't so expected. The nicest team, according to this article, is the Orioles; they will sign anything over and over. At the other extreme is former Yankee pitching coach Art Fowler. "He told me to go play in the traffic," one young fan said.

The biggest game of all, no surprise, is Reggie Jackson. "He just signs 'Reggie' most of the time," complained one expert, without speculating whether that's to annoy the collectors or simply to indicate his greatness. This day, when he descended from the coffee shop, he was in control. He told the youthful entrepreneurs that he was signing once this trip, today was it, and he did not want to see any of the same faces for the rest of the weekend. "You got it?!" As 14-year-old Keith Nashawaty explained: "You have to get Reggie when he's feeling good. He said to me once, 'Do you know I have to do this every day of my life?' I told him, 'Reggie, a guy has an obligation to his fans.' He looked at me and said, 'Not to you, kid.'"

Saturday, October 11. The newspapers today are covering the NBA season, which opened yesterday, and the NHL season, which opened the day before. The baseball season still has two weeks to go, in what I hope will be a good World Series between the Royals and the Astros, two deserving teams whose time has come and whose new blood is appreciated—by me, if not by NBC. And if somehow the Phils can come back, I would certainly not begrudge a World Series victory for the only one of the original 16 teams that can still say it has never won a World Series.

But with the Yankees' loss to the Royals, the 1980 baseball season in New York is over. There are some award announcements to come, but they shouldn't involve the Yankees this year: Steve Stone is the Cy Young winner and George Brett the MVP, without any doubt in my mind. The newspaper writers whom I have relied on all year will have some final thoughts, but when one team loses eight of twelve regular-season games then three straight playoff games to another team, the postmortems need not look too far for a cause of death.

When Frank Messer aad Bill White shook hands and wound up the TV broadcast, while Fran and the Scooter were saying so long on the radio, I, too, took my leave from this 1980 season. I got what I wanted, I guess, a Yankee defeat at the hands of the Royals—repaymeat, if somewhat late and inevitably incomplete, for the Yankee playoff wins in 1976, 1977 and 1978. But after the first moment of "pure elation" (Quisenberry's reaction to Brett's homer), I sank into thoughts of nostalgia for the season and was overcome by a feeling of emptiness, for the baseball-less winter ahead.

On last night's postgame show, the briefest one of the year, Messer observed that Steinbrenner will undoubtedly start making some changes. That picked my spirits up. Will George go after Winfield? Will Howser be back? What will happen to Murcer and Piniella? What about Reggie's contract? What about the Yankees' 40-year-old pitching staff? Their aging third basemen? Will Steinbrenner ever want to see Spencer and Soderholm again? Will the rookies, and the players I scouted in Nashville, get a chance? What about . . .

But that is next year. This year's diary is closed.

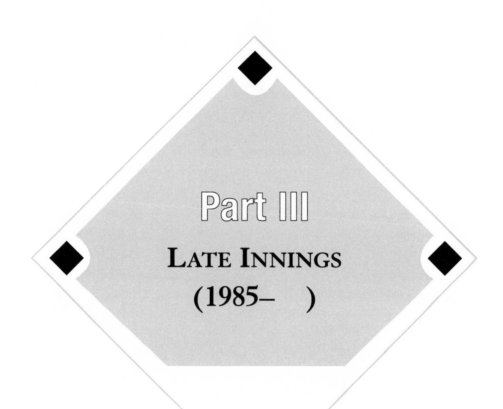

Part III
LATE INNINGS
(1985–   )

PART III

LATE INNINGS

(1985–)

THE 1980S AND EARLY 1990s are remembered as a dark era in Yankees history. The Yanks fell to the Dodgers in the 1981 World Series, then didn't reach the postseason again until 1995. The late 1980s and early 1990s are remembered as a time of heartbreaking near-misses in Red Sox history. Boston fielded some strong teams in those years, and made the playoffs several times. For once the Yankees weren't in the way—yet Boston couldn't seem to get out of its own way when it mattered most. The Red Sox failed to win a World Series, though they came within one strike of doing so in 1986 before losing to New York's other team, the Mets.

By the mid-1990s, it was clear that both baseball and the Boston–New York rivalry had seen better days. The Toronto Blue Jays were the dominant team in the American League East. A prolonged strike wiped out the 1994 postseason just when it seemed New York was on the verge of returning to the top. Many baseball fans were becoming disillusioned with the sport, but the rivalry endured. More than 4,000 fans turned out for a spring training game between New York and Boston in 1995—even though the Yanks and Sox players were still on strike, their places taken by mostly anonymous career minor leaguers. When the real players returned in 1995, the Red Sox edged out the Yankees for the division title—but both clubs made the playoffs, thanks to the new wild-card rule, which allowed a second-place team in each league to slip into the postseason.

New York won both the American League East and the World Series in 1996. As in the 1920s, when Boston's best players ended their careers wearing pinstripes and winning championships in New York, the Yankees' third baseman that year was former Sox star Wade Boggs. Roger Clemens, another former Red Sox star, would soon win a couple of World Series with the Yanks as well.

As the 1990s drew to a close and the new century began, the Yankees seemed to own the top spot in the American League East; the Red Sox seemed to end each season in second. But the wild-card rule meant that finishing second didn't preclude a trip to the playoffs, and New York and Boston now had the opportunity to face off in the American League Championship Series, doing so in 1999, 2003, and 2004. New York claimed the first two meetings. Boston exacted its long-awaited revenge in 2004.

Exhaustive media coverage has helped make the Yankees–Red Sox rivalry *the* baseball story in recent years, much to the chagrin of fans of the league's other 28 teams. Early-season meetings between the clubs are played in a postseason atmosphere. Crowds in Boston launch into taunting chants about the Yankees in the middle of winter. Wearing a Red Sox cap on the streets of New York has become a risky proposition. Even non-baseball fans can't help but know when the Yanks or Sox are in town.

The rivalry has escaped the bleachers and become part of our culture.

Late in the 1978 season, the New York Yankees flew into Boston
and swept the Sox in a four-game series. The wins pulled New York
into a tie with Boston for the lead in the American League East. Ten
years later, New York once again traveled to Boston for a four-game
set in mid-September, trailing the division-leading Red Sox by four
games in the loss column. The echoes of 1978 weren't lost on concerned Sox fans, particularly when New York beat Boston ace
Roger Clemens in the first game.

"YANKEES GO HOME"

from *Sports Illustrated* (September 26, 1988)
by Ron Fimrite

THE INSTANT THE BALL left Mike Pagliarulo's bat, a sense of grim
inevitability settled like some poisonous vapor on old Fenway Park, on all
of old New England, for that matter. Yes, fainthearted Boston Red Sox
fans were telling themselves, it was happening again, just as it had 10 years
ago. The New York Yankees were going to lay remorseless waste to
another September of hope and promise. Indeed, there was Pagliarulo's fly
ball sailing through the cool air last Friday night in an obvious home run
arc to the seats in rightfield, transforming yet another apparent Red Sox
win into a foredoomed loss. But let us set the scene:

> The Yankees came to Boston for a four-game series last week 4½ games behind the
> Red Sox in a tightening American League East race. Sound familiar? New York had
> been four back when it hit town in September 1978; it then trashed Boston in four

221

straight by a cumulative score of 42–9, took a share of the divisional lead and finally won the pennant, 5–4, in the postseason Fenway playoff game in which Bucky Dent hit his famous—infamous in New England—seventh-inning homer into the net beyond the leftfield wall.

The eerie similarity between the circumstances then and those of last week set Red Sox fans off on a veritable rampage of dread and self-loathing. It was as if they felt only another Boston Massacre could release them from this terrible angel. *Boston Globe* columnist Mike Barnicle wrote on Thursday of a recurring nightmare he had been enduring, in which Dent, "this short, beady-eyed guy with the Daytona 500 haircut," stood in the on-deck circle, "a broken bat in his hand and an evil gleam in his eye."

And so, when the Yankees won the first game of the series last Thursday 5–3, driving Sox ace and American League strikeout king Roger Clemens from the mound, Bostonians nodded in miserable acknowledgment of their fate. The Yanks were now 3½ out and closing. If Clemens, who had tossed a one-hitter in his previous outing to break an 0–5 pitching slump couldn't win, what now? Clemens didn't pitch badly, but he was humiliated by a homer and a key double from Pagliarulo, who had been hitting .096 in his last 16 games and, to make matters worse, hails from nearby Medford, Mass. He had also been hurt by a Claudell Washington steal of home made possible, Washington said, by Clemens's habit of ducking his head before going into his motion. Even so, it took five Yankee pitchers, from starter Rick Rhoden to closer Dave Righetti, to finish off the Sox. But then, Yankee pitching had been something of a group grope lately, anyway.

With his ace beaten, Boston manager Joe Morgan turned on Friday night to Wes Gardner, a former reliever and former Met (remember 1986!). Gardner gave up hits to the first three batters he faced—Rickey Henderson, Washington and Don Mattingly—and two runs, but he shut the Yankees down from there until the eighth inning. The New York starter, rookie left-hander Al Leiter, lasted only 27 pitches before retiring with a twinge behind his shoulder blade. The Sox jumped on his successors—Steve Shields, Dale Mohorcic and Lee Guetterman—for seven runs, five of them coming in a riotous fifth inning that included a bases-loaded walk to a rookie, Carlos

Quintana, in his first major league at-bat. Quintana was hitting for the storm-tossed Jim Rice, who this season had already been given a chilly reception by the Fenway faithful for his tired play, punished for shoving his manager and mocked as he closed in on the league career record for hitting into double plays; then, on Friday, he was hit on the left knee by a Leiter pitch that forced him to the sidelines, out of harm's way. Rice was just one of seven batters, six of them Red Sox, hit by pitchers in the first three games of this bitter series.

Boston had a comfortable 7–2 lead when New York came to bat in the eighth. Gardner gave way to Dennis Lamp after a walk to Rafael Santana and a single by Washington. Dave Winfield scored both of them with a missile off the wall. And when Jack Clark walked, the tying run came to the plate in the suddenly dangerous person of Pagliarulo. Morgan called on his hulking reliever, Lee Smith, who threw one pitch to the Massachusetts Yankee, a fastball "out over the plate," as Pagliarulo described it. Pags connected, and he "knew" the ball was out of the park. "How could it not be?" he asked later. "I hit it better than the one last night."

As the crowd fell silent, Yankee manager Lou Piniella was doing a little dance in the dugout and Sox rightfielder Dwight (Dewey) Evans was retreating, tracking the ball. Then, suddenly, Evans stopped just inches short of the wall, reached up and caught the ball one-handed. He didn't even have to leap. There would be no Yankee sweep this time. And, said Boggs, tweaking a horde of "negative" reporters afterward in the clubhouse, "there'll be no 1978 now. Sorry, fellas."

The fact is that this New York team, for all of its vaunted firepower, is not up to 1978 snuff. The defense is uncertain and the pitching is in disarray. The latest pitching coach, Clyde King, currently in his third term at that job, looks upon his staff much as Bonaparte must have viewed *la Grande Armée* on its retreat from Moscow. "Our bullpen is worn out," King said after watching a total of seven relievers go to the front Thursday and Friday. "We're using three, four, five guys a game. That's because we have to approach every game as if it were the last of the season. People malign our pitching staff. Well, if you look at the ERA [4.35 through Sunday], maybe it's deserved. But we have guys who, while they're not exactly hurting, are just a little tired."

King has been on the job for only five weeks and is the third Yankee pitching coach of the season; owner George Steinbrenner apparently considers men in this position as expendable as his managers. And in fact King would rather be back up in the front office as special adviser to the boss, the job he held before being called on to help out below. "Heck, since I've been here, I've been everything but owner," says King. That's one job, rest assured, he can forget about.

Both Piniella and Morgan entered this critical if not exactly historic series feeling they had to earn at least a split. Both wanted more, of course, especially Piniella, who looked red-eyed and sorrowful after Pagliarulo's near homer on Friday. Time, he knew, was running out on him. He has only this weekend's three-game series with the Sox in Yankee Stadium to make up the ground lost in Boston. Morgan, who comes across as a funnier, faster talking and certainly more profane Pa Kettle, was as relaxed and cheerful during the weekend as his team's fans were overwrought and fearful. He spent hours before every game regaling newsmen with recollections of his days as a "career minor leaguer."

"I was a Triple A player, period," he said. "But what the bleep. I got more bleeping stories and I know more people—including some I dont' want to know—so what the bleep. I played for five major league teams, and all that added up to was a year and a half and about 30 hits [36, to be exact]. But what the bleep. I was going to write a book about all this. I'd have called it *How's Your Old Tomatoes?* That was a signal for the squeeze play I learned from Joe Schultz when he managed me at Triple A in Atlanta. Joe would coach third and say to the runner. 'How's your old tomatoes?' And that runner would go."

In the fourth inning on Saturday, Morgan called his own squeeze play without the tomato code, but for all the good it did him, he might as well have said, "How's your old man?" With the game scoreless, Mike Greenwell on third and Todd Benzinger at bat against the Yankee's Charles Hudson, Morgan flashed the sign. Greenwell broke for the plate, but Benzinger, transfixed, only vaguely attempted to bunt. New York catcher Don Slaught had Greenwell trapped, but instead of throwing the ball, he tried to run him down between home and third. Slaught finally caught up with him just short of third but dropped the ball attempting a diving tag.

Greenwell never did score, though, and that's only fitting because he had no business being on third base in the first place. He got to first after he struck out on a Hudson pitch in the dirt that got away from Slaught. Boldly, he tried to steal second, and when Staught, having one of those innings, threw the ball into centerfield. Greenwell reached his final stop at third. To complete his awful sequence, Slaught struck out leading off the next inning. So it goes for the Yankees, the 1988 model.

The Red Sox did get a run in their half of the fifth, but not without controversy. Baby-faced Jody Reed, whose mustache makes him look like a kid dressed up for Halloween, doubled and reached third on Rich Gedman's sacrifice. Then Wade Boggs lifted a high fly down the leftfield line. A fan, leaning out of the stands that angle out almost to the playing field, had a shot at catching the ball but missed. Henderson did catch it, falling awkwardly backward against the wall, while Reed tagged and scored easily from third. Piniella rushed onto the field in a rage, claiming correctly that third base umpire Ted Hendry had called fan interference, but incorrectly that the run, therefore, should not count. Umpire crew chief Jim Evans said Reed would have scored in any event, and the run counted, whereupon Piniella announced that the game was being played under protest.

The freak plays could not detract, however, from a magnificent pitching duel between Hudson—starting in place of Tommy John, who had a stomach virus—and Bruce Hurst, who over the last two months has stood in for Clemens as the ace of the Boston staff. Hudson had allowed only one run and two hits going into the eighth when Evans led off with a rising drive into the screen, which proved to be the game-winning run. The packed house rocked, and even the most devout disbeliever was now shouting hosannas. The homer gave Evans 100 RBIs for the season, the third time in a distinguished 16-year career he had passed the century mark. Benzinger scored a gravy run on Larry Parrish's double but this was Citizen Hurst's game. He allowed only three hits and a run, white walking two and striking out nine. It was his 18th win against five losses, his ninth win in his last 10 decisions and his 13th this season in Fenway, the supposed graveyard of left-handers. "I think this team has come to realize that pitching is an important part of our game," he said, earnestly emphasizing the obvious. "And Roger [Clemens] is a big reason for that. He's been a dominant force." But not as dominant lately, Hurst was too modest to say, as Bruce Hurst has been.

On Sunday, Boston sent the Yankees packing with a 9–4 thrashing as the Sox pounced on poor Ron Guidry—now a sorry imitation of his once invincible self—for six runs in just 1½ innings. A three-run homer by Ellis Burks in the first and a two-run shot by Evans in the second led an early attack that put the game out of reach for the now dispirited New Yorkers. They had come to town confident of repeating history. They left 6½ out, in fourth place, with their pennant hopes all but dished.

The Sox may well have exorcised forever the demons of 1978. But they're not without some sorcery of their own: Out of character though it may seem. Morgan keeps a little metal witch on his desk, professing, however, that he attaches no importance to the talisman. "Some woman sent it to me," Morgan says. "I don't know what it is—the wizard of bleep, maybe." Besides, he says, he doesn't need anything exorcised, least of all the ancient events of '78. "I can't even remember the '70s," he says. "I was in the minor leagues." But after last weekend at Fenway, one could hazard a guess that '88 might just possibly have some meaning for him.

Five of the seven teams in the American League East would finish the 1988 season within three-and-a-half games of first place. But thanks to Boston's 5-2 record against the Yanks in September, the Red Sox would prevail. The Red Sox were swept by Oakland in the playoffs.

What's a Red Sox fan to do when his daughter roots for the Yankees? *New York Times* editor Stephen Engelberg was forced to consider that question.

"THE HOME TEAM"

from the *New York Times Magazine* (July 4, 1999)
by Stephen Engelberg

MY WIFE HAD PREPARED me for it, but the sight was nonetheless arresting. Standing at the door was my oldest daughter, Ilana, her face a gap toothed vision of joy as she sported her newest possession: a Yankees pinstripe jersey, emblazoned across the back with the name Clemens.

I felt a swell of pride that my daughter was embracing my passion for baseball. But her choice of teams and idols was deeply unsettling, to say the least.

For three decades, I have lived and (mostly) died by the travails of the Boston Red Sox. Reared in a Boston suburb, I became, as is natural in New England, a rabid Yankees-hater.

Toronto's signing in 1996 of Roger Clemens, Boston's best pitcher since, well, Babe Ruth, was bad enough. The pain deepened this year when he was traded to the Yankees. With typical Red Sox fatalism, I imagined the coming season in which Clemens would defeat the Red Sox in a championship game, cheered on, no doubt, by my daughter.

When Ilana was born six years ago, I was sure she would take up the family tradition. But growing up in the long shadow of Yankee Stadium, she has fallen victim to dubious influences. Tino Martinez. Derek Jeter. David Cone.

I became a baseball fan in the magical season of 1967, when the underdog Boston team got every break imaginable and won the pennant on the last day.

My daughter became a baseball fan in another magical year. Unfortunately, it was 1998, the year the Yankees repealed all rules of baseball logic and won 125 games and the World Series. For me, it was torture. Aren't you just loving this, coworkers would ask after each daily Yankee victory?

Actually, no. I wasn't loving it at all.

I came by my dislike of New York teams honestly. As a 6-foot-3, gangly 13-year-old, my idol was Bill Russell, the Boston Celtics player who overcame teenage awkwardness and became basketball's dominant center. The flashy, shorts-grabbing Knicks of Walt Frazier were the enemy.

Then there was baseball. The Red Sox were frequently out of contention by fall, and I would scour the papers for Yankee losses that might lift my spirits.

Boston did make it to the World Series in 1975, taking on the Cincinnati Reds. Unfortunately, I was attending a British boarding school with a 10 P.M. curfew.

No problem. I sneaked into a bathroom with a radio, tuned in the Armed Forces Network and shivered in the cold as Boston fell behind in Game 6. I gave up at 4 A.M., missing Carlton Fisk's game-winning homer in the 12th inning.

Two days later, I learned of Fisk's heroics and the Red Sox's Game 7 defeat from a one-paragraph item in a London paper.

In 1978, I was in Britain in August and read the *International Herald Tribune* with mounting horror as the Sox squandered a 14-game lead to, whom else, the Yankees.

And then there was the unspeakable disappointment of 1986. I bore witness to the Red Sox World Series collapse against the Mets at a party full of raucous New Yorkers. One strike away, dear God, one strike.

I had planned to share this misery with my children. When Ilana asked me for "Daddy stories," I would tell her about my trips to Fenway Park, about a day when a Red Sox outfielder ended pregame warm-ups by throwing me the ball.

Even so, after her first visit to the House That Ruth Built, she was hooked. I wondered, Is it an act of betrayal or fatherly love to school your child in the lore of a team you despise?

The finer points of baseball are passed from generation to generation. My love of the game came from my father, whose family fled Hitler's Germany for Brooklyn. He was force-fed English at school, a 10-year-old enrolled in a class of kindergartners. The Brooklyn Dodgers were his first American love and he maintained his loyalty for years, even after the Dodgers abandoned Brooklyn for Los Angeles. But when my brother and I lost our hearts to the 1967 Red Sox, he quickly and permanently shifted his allegiance.

I faced a similar quandary last year. Hours before Game 6 of the league championship between the Yankees and the Indians, a colleague called to offer two tickets.

I hesitated. If the Yankees won, I would witness their pennant-clinching victory. Hell on earth, or heaven, depending on your perspective. Still, how could I deprive Ilana?

We went and stood atop our seats in the rain, screaming with everyone else as the Yankees fell behind and then rallied. The Yankees' closer retired the final Indians' batter and police horses charged onto the field. Confetti filled the air. I held my daughter above my head, cheering wildly with the crowd in an instant of untrammeled joy. Her face was creased with a beatific grin, and for a just a moment, or maybe for the rest of our lives, we were Yankee fans together.

Go Clemens.

"It doesn't matter if you win or lose . . .
well, it didn't when I was on
the Red Sox."

—Yankee pitcher Roger Clemens, presenting
"The Top 10 Things Baseball Has Taught Me"
on *The Late Show with David Letterman,*
June 16, 2003

THEY SAID IT . . .

A Yankee fan and a Red Sox fan live together as man and wife. . . .
It might sound like the premise for a new ESPN reality show or the
setup for an off-color joke, but this modern version of the mixed
marriage really does occur, for better or for worse.

"IRRECONCILABLE DIFFERENCES"

from *The Boston Globe* (October 9, 2003)
by Don Aucoin

MARK CROUGH, A COHASSET native and devout Red Sox fan, was
instantly attracted to Kerry Carle when they met on Easter weekend four
years ago in a Killington, Vt., ski shop. But Carle was harboring a dark
secret Crough would not discover until four months later, when they
moved together to Boulder, Colo.

Upon arriving in their new home, Carle opened her suitcase to
unpack. Suddenly, before her swain's astonished eyes, out tumbled a . . .
Yankees hat. "I didn't know," recalls Crough, 35, who married Carle this
year. "It killed me. There I am, having to go out on hikes in public with
her wearing a Yankees cap. Had I known . . . Just kidding."

Ah, but many a truth is spoken in jest. The reality is that this week
dueling loyalties on the question of Sox vs. Yanks will open fault lines

right down the middle of many an otherwise harmonious relationship. For better and for worse, OK—but for the American League pennant? Fuhged daboud it. At least for the duration of the series, erstwhile happy couples could find themselves living in the house that wroth built.

"We're in a very loving relationship, but when the Yankees and Sox are playing, we sit in different rooms," admits Alyssa Toro, 33, a Yankees fan in Brookline whose husband, Matt, is a Red Sox fan. "We have to. It just gets too intense."

You want to talk about intensity? When Red Sox fan Julie Rockett exchanged vows with Yankees fan Patrick Paulick, her family told her she was "marrying outside the faith." Rockett will allow Paulick to watch the games with her in their South End apartment, but only on the condition that he not overtly cheer for the Yankees and that he never, not once, ask her what the score is. "I have so many weird voodoo rules," says Rockett. "I am so filled with rage, and he is not."

Eighty-five years of World Series futility will do that to you. That grim history was brought up all summer long by Ron Czik of Sharon whenever the three Red Sox fans in his household—wife Wendy, daughter Shoshana, 15, and son Joshua, 12—got too excited about Boston's chances against New York. Czik would simply say three things: "Bol-shevik Revolution, 26, and Bill Buckner," referring to the fact that the Soviet Union has come and gone since the Sox last won a World Series, that the Yankees have won the series 26 times since 1918 (when the Sox last won it), and that Buckner . . . well, you know.

"His obnoxiousness about the Yankees is becoming . . . more obnox-ious," says an exasperated Wendy Czik. So last night, as the family gath-ered around the TV set, Dad was not to be allowed on the couch—he was slated for banishment to a spot near the kitchen—and his wife was plan-ning to wear a T-shirt sporting an oft-heard anti-Yankees slogan.

The Czik family feud is a good-natured one, as seems to be the case with most of the two dozen fans interviewed by the *Globe*. "It's all in good fun," insists Jessica Morris, 28, of Shrewsbury, a Yankees fan whose hus-band, Michael, is a Red Sox partisan. "It's certainly a rivalry that gets the best of both of our emotions, but it's certainly not something that would end a relationship."

That doesn't mean emotions won't be running high as the Sox and Yanks battle it out at Yankee Stadium and Fenway Park in the days to come while those battles are echoed verbally in family rooms all over New England and beyond.

Nor will those battles be as one-sided as might be supposed here in the heart of Red Sox Nation, where a surprising number pledge allegiance to the Yankees. Transplanted New Yorkers or New Jerseyites, many of whom came to Boston to attend college and stayed to pursue careers and start families, have swollen the population of Yankees fans. Consequently, the ancient rivalry is woven into the fabric of many a young marriage—one couple reports that they placed Derek Jeter and Nomar Garciaparra bobblehead dolls on a table at their August wedding reception—and such unions are now facing a test stiff enough to tax the ingenuity of the savviest marriage counselor.

Before Amy and Danny Kramer of Charlestown exchanged vows a year ago, they had the traditional pre-wedding confab with the priest who was to marry them. Amy's family members were longtime Red Sox season ticket holders, and one of her proudest possessions was a baseball that former Sox slugger Jim Rice had fouled right into her lap. Danny, by contrast, had only recently moved here from Staten Island, N.Y. When the priest asked whether either of them had any reservations about entering into the holy state of matrimony, Danny somberly replied, "Yes, I do have one concern." Amy was stricken. Then her groom-to-be spelled it out: "She's a Red Sox fan, and I'm a Yankees fan." The priest, a New York native himself, sympathized but assured Danny, "You'll eventually convert."

It hasn't happened yet, and Danny says it never will. In fact, the Kramers will probably watch the pennant showdown in separate rooms. During Sox-Yankees jousts over the summer, Amy, 30, had to put up with the sound of her husband heckling the Red Sox. "The '1918' thing is coming from the other room," she sighs. Says her 31-year-old husband: "It's the answer to everything."

For relationships still in their early stages, this pennant series could prove to be the defining moment. Sarah Stiglmeier, 25, of Brighton, has loved the Yankees since she was a toddler in Albany rooting for "Reggie

Jacks." She has retained a loyalty to the Yankees in the seven years since she moved here to attend Boston College and has even gone so far as to wear her Jeter T-shirt or Yankees hat to Sox games. But she has been dating a Red Sox fan for two years and admits, "I'm a little bit nervous about this upcoming series." They were not planning to watch last night's game together.

"We get feisty. We make comments back and forth," Stiglmeier says. "It's all in good fun, but you take it a little bit to heart."

When children enter this charged equation, the Sox-Yanks rivalry sometimes intensifies in unpredictable ways. As a young child in New Jersey, Suzie Byers of Lexington believed that her father actually played for the Yankees because he used to talk to the players on the TV set as if he knew them. Later, in high school, she was in Latin class with the son of Yankees outfielder Lou Piniella. Even after she married Red Sox fan Carl Byers, who did his best to, in his words, "get her to come over from the dark side," she kept rooting for the Yankees. But her pinstripes fervor began to fade after their 5-year-old son, Jake, began rooting for the Sox.

"I cannot be a full-fledged Yankees fan anymore, because my son adores the Red Sox so much," she says. "But every time the Yankees win, I'm happy for my father. I'm secretly on the fence."

In the Breslin household in Milton, 9-year-old Nate has staked out a position as a Yankees fan even though father Mark, mother Bonnie Sosis, and big brother Zack are all Red Sox fans. "I like [Alfonso] Soriano and Roger Clemens and Derek Jeter," says Nate. "And all my friends like them. Well, some of them."

In deference to his son's feelings, Mark Breslin has waived his usual rule against the wearing of Yankees hats or shirts in the house. In a few weeks, Nate has an even bigger costume adventure in mind: "I'm being Alfonso Soriano for Halloween," he confides.

But then parenthood is full of surprises. Take the Croughs, out in Boulder awaiting the birth of their first child at the end of the month. Kerry, the Yankees fan, recently told her husband that if the baby is a boy, she might not mind if they named him Trot or Grady (his Sox loyalties notwithstanding, he nixed both). As for Alyssa and Matt Toro, whose baby is due in two weeks, they are taking no chances. Matt went out and bought a Red Sox onesie for the little one—and Alyssa promptly countered by buying a Yankees onesie.

"We might make her wear them both until she's old enough to decide," she says.

FAMILY FEUDS

"On the field it's going to be no holds barred. And then after we'll go out to dinner and rag on each other." —Jeremy Giambi on what he expected it to be like to play for the Red Sox against his brother Jason's Yankees

"I come from a mixed marriage: Dad . . . was a Red Sox fan. Mom . . . is a Yankees fan, as was her dad . . . Religious and ethnic differences were ignored but my grandfather never got over his daughter marrying a Red Sox fan." —From a fan's letter to *USA Today*

"He was ecstatic [that I was called back up to the majors]. . . . But it's not going to change the fact that he's a Red Sox fan." —Recently promoted Yankee pitcher Tanyon Sturtze on why on his father might not be rooting him as strenuously as in the past

"We have banned baseball from our conversations until the season is over. It's best for all involved." —A Red Sox fan on her relationship with a Yankee fan, in an e-mail to Boston.com

"I love my cousins but they think I am 'evil' and don't talk to me for six months of the year." —From a letter to *USA Today* written by a fan whose family is divided between New England and New York

"I can't be involved in any family that's not a Red Sox family." —Overrated actor and Red Sox fan Ben Affleck on the future sporting allegiance of any children he might have with overrated singer and Yankee fan Jennifer Lopez. The couple solved the problem by splitting up before procreating.

When the Yankees and Red Sox battled on the field during a routine game in 1998, passions were even more heated in the Yankee Stadium stands.

"MAD CATHEDRAL"

from *Esquire* (October 1998)
by Thomas Kelly

BASEBALL IS ONE THING. YANKEE STADIUM IS ANOTHER.

I SIT IN THE Yankee Tavern with Spank and wait for Chickie and Mickey to show up with tickets. It's late afternoon, and the place is going from church-service quiet to shore-leave boisterous. The few courthouse employees gnawing on corned-beef sandwiches and a handful of old drunks curling themselves thoughtfully around cheap whiskeys are being squeezed by hordes of Yankee fans priming themselves for game time. The Tavern sits one block west of Bronx County Courthouse and one block east of the endangered cathedral of baseball, Yankee Stadium. This puts it beyond the pale for casual fans spooked by Steinbrenner's defamation of the Bronx, so most patrons are either from the borough or once were. They've been serving cold beer here since Lou Gehrig was a rookie.

I was born in one of the most magnificent of Yankee Octobers, 1961, and remember being five years old and coming here after seeing Mantle, all busted knees and burnt promise, smack a pitch into the bleachers. I remember my long-gone father, who as a teenager used to lug trays of bottled beer up and down the stadium stairs, screaming "beah heah," rubbing my head and saying with pride, "Now that was Mickey Mantle." Not much has changed at the Tavern since. The walls are plastered with photographs of Yankee greats and cheesy murals of players in action. The jukebox still kicks out Tony and Frank, the bathroom still reeks of antiseptic, and I'll lay seven to one that the old snaggletooth quaffing Early Times next to me has been sitting on that stool longer than Derek Jeter has been alive.

The man waves at all the memorabilia adorning the walls. "They always talk about the good old days," he says. "Well, these are the good old days." Indeed. Like good Yankee fans, we gloat and fret in equal measure. This team is being compared not only to the mighty Bronx Bombers of 1927 and 1961 but to teams that were playing hardball when the Spanish-American War was a fresh memory. It's a team that lost a total of six home games before the All-Star break. But all is not well in the Bronx. We cannot escape the ominous braying of a mayor and an owner, two cocker spaniels who conspire to turn this place into a mausoleum. It hangs over this glorious season like a terminal prognosis. They howl on, a chorus of two, comparing attendance records with those of Starbucks stadiums in third-tier cities. Who cares? More people are paying to see these Yankees than paid to see Ruth and Gehrig, more than DiMaggio, more than Maris and Mantle, more than Mr. October or Donnie Baseball. The Whiskey Pete next to me says, "Sounds like two clowns who don't get enough of the old slap and tickle."

A friend of Chickie's friend is supposed to have tickets lined up for us. It's always like that with Chickie. He's friends with a lot of people who have friends and is so adept at procuring difficult ducats that he is the only guy I know whose nickname has a nickname. On days like today, we call him Chicketron. Spank nudges me, and I turn to see our savior shouldering his way through the scrum. He slaps the tickets on the wood and says, "Read 'em and weep."

The Red Sox are in town, and blackmarket vendors up and down River Avenue are offering their latest lines of BOSTON SUCKS attire.

These were the only remotely bad words I was able to mutter openly in my youth. Any others, I got slapped. Damn, slap. Hell, double slap. Shit, triple slap. The f-word, yeah right. But Boston Sucks, a pat on the head. It's a chant that has reverberated through so many Bronx days and nights that it qualifies as the official Bronx cheer. The Red Sox need not be around or even in contention for it to be the mantra. During the '96 Series against Atlanta: Boston Sucks. Opening day 1998 against Oakland: Boston Sucks.

The number 4 train rumbles overhead, and along the shadow of the el a number of souvenir shops and bars that are wired directly into the fortunes of the stadium are open for business. The smell of roasting pig parts hangs heavy in the air. The crazy energy that is the Bronx on game night is firing up. The bleacher creatures are waiting for the scramble to the general-admission seats: seven bucks for the theater of the absurd and the mad. They lean against the stadium wall striking harmless poses, trying not to offer any reason for preemptive ejections. A man wanders around with a large sign that says MIKE PIAZZA IS UGLY. Fans are signing petitions to put a stadium referendum on the November ballot that will keep the Yankees where they belong. Fathers and mothers, as they have for three quarters of a century, tow wide-eyed kids through the gathering crowd.

Scalpers chum the waters. Some are Bronx street kids trying to make a living that does not involve cheeseburgers or crack. Others are more professional: They skitter about, wearing beepers and flipping cell phones, affecting the manner of media moguls. They wear slick, expensive watches or at least rip-offs. "My man, my man, whatcha need?" It is easy to picture them standing in front of the last titty bar in Times Square with leaflets or booking sex tours to Asia. In a scripted ritual, the cops will pop a couple for the record. Need a ticket? Wait till the Star-Spangled Shuffle, when the prices drop like a prom queen's dress after a pint of Wild Turkey. Except for sellouts, you're in the door for a sawbuck or less.

THE BIG HOUSE

We take our seats in the stadium that David Cone describes as "the most extreme home-field advantage in all of sports." Our tickets tonight are in the loge, halfway between first and home, the balcony in the Bronx. Beautiful. Vendors squawk. A guy two rows down balks at the five and a quarter for a tepid beer. None of that phony service-sector obsequiousness in Yankeeland: The beer man responds, "You got a problem with that? Head over to Jerome Avenue and buy yourself a six-pack. See if they let you back in the joint."

Mickey waits for the man to move on and then cracks open a couple cans of frosty Bud from his private supply. "I'd pay the five and a quarter, but . . ." He pours a round into official Yankee soda cups: Mickey knows people, too. We settle in—cold beer, a warm summer breeze, shadows lengthening across the field on which perhaps the best team of the century is playing ball.

Jeter boots a grounder, and Spank is all over him. "You piece of shit! They should trade your Mariah Carey-loving ass!" If New York fans are notoriously fickle, Yankee fans are downright bipolar. I'll admit it. We just figure it's tough love. A guy in front of us turns alarmed, his mouth a concerned little o. "How can you say that? He's a good player."

Spank and I look at each other. Huh?

"Where the hell are you from?"

"Boulder, Colorado."

"Ahhh. Yeah, well, JonBenet, this is the Bronx. We got higher standards."

I hit the head, and when I get back, Spank is regaling Chickie and Mickey with his adventures in center field. Back in the Mattingly era, Spank knew a guy who worked at the stadium, and one hot July night when the Yanks were on the road, he popped by with a date. A wink and a nod, and in they went. (Ah, the good old days.) What started out as a surreptitious tour turned into a passionate tumble on the very spot where Bernie Williams is now awaiting the crack of the bat. It's Spank's proudest moment. He starts to supply too much detail, and the sextet of sorority girls next to us begins blanching. "You should have seen the goose bumps on this chick. Up and down her arms, bro. She was into it."

His reverie is interrupted by an argument between the cotton-candy guy and a fan who has accidentally careened into him. It doesn't last long. The cotton-candy man lays down his pink, fluffy load and, wham, hits him with the sharpest right hand thrown here since Marciano decked Ezzard Charles. The fan does half a pirouette and collapses in his seat. You can almost see the tweety birds circling his head. Just when we are starting to feel for the guy he manages to get up, take off his shirt, flex, and say, "Oh yeah? You want me?" He's sporting a gold nipple ring, and this enrages the crowd. Cries of "Hit him again!" rip through the night. Luckily, security intervenes and tosses the bum out. The victor hoists his tray and barks, "Cotton candy heah!" You figure a few more shots like that and he's a lock to be bumped up to Cracker Jacks.

Posh Seats

Down below, as usual, the Yankees are toying with their opponents. I decide to take a closer look. I borrow JonBenet's binoculars and do a little reconnoitering. I note a weakness in the security, and I plan to exploit it. I time my move with the precision and daring of a commando raid. I make my way down behind the Yankee dugout. The usher turns his back to ogle a female, and I pounce. I saunter down the aisle till I am a half dozen rows behind the Yankee bench. I plop down in the seat like I've endowed it. Cheerio. I'm now a corporate fat cat in repose.

The first thing I notice is that the vendors address me as sir and that there is waiter service. Menus! Fruit salad delivered to your seat! My head swims. The beer guys pronounce the r's. I can feel my father rotating counterclockwise in his grave. I notice other things, too: blond people and cell phones—lots of cell phones. I nod and wave to my new buddies. That's right, old man, buy low, sell high. Two rows ahead of me, a man refers to Irabu as "that Chinese fellow." Another exhorts the pitcher not to worry, because "you have eleven men behind you." Is he counting the umps? I realize with an icy jolt that this is the future: luxury boxes, spoiled brats, and fairweather fans. Seats paid for in advance by some guy in accounting. They'll outlaw dirty-water dogs and stomp the fanaticism out of random for the sake of guaranteed revenue streams. It's harrowing.

I stand and scream when O'Neill scorches a double. "Fucking A, Paulie!" Golf claps all around me. "Down in front." The usher eyes me suspiciously. I sit down. On my hands. A few boxes over, a large woman wearing a canary-yellow visor seems to have a Chuck Knoblauch fetish. She screams when he is at the plate; she hollers any time he makes a play. He hits a ground ball, and she comes out of her seat like a catcher trying to gun down a base stealer. "Run, Chuckle, run!" She outweighs him by a refrigerator. The people in her box look embarrassed, flustered, put upon. They lean away from her as if she were in the throes of delirium tremens. I want to dash over and give her a big, sloppy kiss. I imagine her being secreted off in the night for shock therapy.

But the proximity, oh, the proximity. You can smell the grass from these seats, hear Joe Torre's cough. Please let me stay. I'll behave. No profanity. I swear. I'll practice my golf clap every chance I get, work on my r's. Soon enough, I feel the shadow of reproach fall across my little fiesta. The bastards are on to me. I look up. Two guys and their dates, sleek and glorious in their summer suits, glare as if they have just come upon me grappling with a blowup doll on their porch swing.

The usher merely says, "Yep."

I stand and pat my pockets as if to say, Oh, good heavens, how could this have happened? I nod and smile and mutter.

The usher repeats, "Yep," as if my kind is not worthy of any more syllables.

As I backpedal up the aisle to catch a last glimpse of the zit on Jeter's chin, I hear one of the women say, "Wow, I've never been to a game before."

Now I finally understand the French Revolution.

THE BLEACHERS

I need an antidote, a little balm for my Yankee soul. I need the mosh pit. This will require leaving the stadium and going to the bleachers with a separate ticket. They don't let the creatures mingle with the rest of the house. It's best for everyone.

The right-field bleachers are the only place in America where you can enjoy not only a ball game but improv theater and paramilitary tactics. A security honcho tells me, "I take a look at the beer line. That tells you how much trouble you're gonna have."

Woe to the uninitiated. In the bleachers, attire is destiny. A befuddled fellow is wearing a Cowboys hat. The chant starts with "Cow-boys suck," rolls into "Dal-las convicts," and runs right into "Hey hey, you killed JFK." A young woman is sporting a crisp new Red Sox cap. Ouch. I can't even get into it. Let's just say the hat came off Quickly. Wearing a tie?

"Lose that tie" rolls into: "Yup-pie scum," which sashays into the ubiqui-tous "Asssss-hooole." Women? Well, this is a crowd that notices women. Young or old: "Show your tits." Of course, by the end of the night, the chant is reduced to a beery snarl: "Tits! Tits! Tits!" This being the bleachers, the invitation is occasionally obliged.

Opposing outfielders dread playing here. It's the closest an American athlete can come to understanding the plight of the Christians in the Colosseum. Most will say only things like "Oh, they sure are fans up there in New York. Really know their baseball." They don't want to provide any more motivation for abuse than their lack of pinstripes. Canseco was rou-tinely pelted with debris in right field. Griffey would rather play center field in hell. It turns really ugly only when you are playing well. Make a game-blowing error and the creatures will keep you like an ogre keeps a fair-haired squire as a pet. Hammer the ball or get theatrical with your defense, well, whaddya expect? This ain't Camden Yards, pal. In the Bronx, the acid rain falls encased in batteries.

Yet most of the strife is internecine. Fans against fans, fans against the security forces, class war between the creatures and the folks in the adja-cent box seats, who are separated by a gulf just wide enough to discourage personal kamikaze attacks. Some creatures spend the entire night chanting, "Box seats suck!" only to be answered with "Wel-fare seats, get a job." I watch two fat guys in Flashdance sweatshirts and a gross of tat-toos between them start smacking each other over who is better, the Giants or the Jets. This brings the heat.

Steroidal goons sweep in and perform extractions like screws pulling people out of a cell-block riot. To be sure, there are atrocities on both sides. This year's chief enforcer bears an unfortunate resemblance to the current mayor, both physically and in jackbooted exuberance. Every time he enters the area, the chant "Rooo-deee, Rooo-deee" bounces off the walls. Since the bleachers operate under a permanent state of martial law, you don't expect justice. Habeas corpus, your ass. Ejections can be arbitrary, capri-cious, warranted, undeserved, or overdue. Most are accompanied by a hail-storm of warm beer, half-eaten pretzels, and Cracker Jacks. A young lout beside me belches and confesses to having been tossed out of one game four times. "It was excellent."

For all the rowdiness, bloodletting is rare. It's a kind of contained chaos. Still, it is best to mind your bleacher p's and q's, or you can quickly become Piggy in Lord of the Flies. Assss-hooole. Oh yeah, rule number one: Never, ever try to keep a home-run ball hit by the other team. Proper procedure is to sneer and throw it back onto the field. Promptly. Unless, of course, you are trying to beat Dr. Kevorkian out of his fee.

Row X

When I am looking to get away from it all, I head for the upper tier and start climbing. You can go up and up and sit high above it all in the last row in the house, row X. The view is superb. You can see the top of the Manhattan skyline and look down on all but the loftiest of home runs. You can drop a plumb line 14 feet straight down to the ground. Fifty rows below, some clown is trying to get the wave going. Hey, chief, this ain't L.A. Where's that cotton-candy guy when you need him?

Here, I must confess I am not a baseball fan. I am a Yankee fan—or, more to the point, a fan of this place. So much has transpired here. Not just the championships and the gridiron heroics and the title bouts and two popes. More important are the hundreds of little moments that take place on muggy afternoons or crisp nights between fathers and sons and daughters and brothers and pals.

When I want to visit my father, I forgo the cemetery and sit here. It is easy to imagine him on hot Bronx days decades ago, lugging bottles of Ballantine up to the working stiffs in these cheap seats and pausing with his quick smile to trace the arc of a blast off DiMaggio's bat. It is stunning to sit here and contemplate this silence becoming eternal or, worse, the wrecking ball tearing through these walls.

The Yankees have won again, and Sinatra croaks "New York, New York" over the stadium speakers. I sit and watch the crowd spill toward the exits. This place is New York. They build the new joint on the Hudson and it might as well be in Minneapolis. If the Yankees leave the Bronx, they are going without me. Ditto Chickie, Mickey, and Spank.

With major league ballplayers returning to the field barely a week after the tragedies of September 11, 2001, Roger Angell of the *New Yorker* took a look back at the Red Sox latest late-season collapse.

"LEGENDS OF THE FENS"

from the *New Yorker* (September 24, 2001)
by Roger Angell

MAKE MINE BOSTON, JUST for a while again, after all baseball news went glimmering last Tuesday morning. This was before, back when we could still take pleasure in our games.

The Red Sox, as I was saying, have blown another season, this time falling on their faces with a thirteen-out-of-fourteen-game string of losses. They've lost a manager, the quirkily oblique Jimy Williams, who perhaps found his fungo bat the most enjoyable attribute of the job, and once, responding to a query about the team's lack of speed on the base paths, offered the Zenlike "You can't get a ticket riding a bicycle on a freeway, can you?" The bleacher fans chant "Yankees suck!" on a day when the team is playing the Atlanta Braves. (I was there and can swear to this.) The Sox's everyday catcher, Scott Hatteberg, has thrown out ten of a hundred and nine enemy base stealers, the worst such average in memory. On the other hand, he is the only man ever to bat into a triple play (on August 6th, against the Texas Rangers) and then smack a grand-slam home run in his very next at-bat. Boston loyalists can spray the Yankees' incomparable thirty-nine-year-old Roger Clemens with unspeakable invective when he warms up in the bullpen just in front of the Fenway Park bleachers but more or less applaud him when he goes on to beat them, 3–1, as he did on August 31st, striking out ten batters and lifting his won-lost totals to 18–1 for the season—this because they take bitter pleasure in the knowledge that their mistrusted general manager, Dan Duquette, let Roger depart the Sox in 1996, declaring him to be in the "twilight of his career." The Red Sox are also the only team whose favorite slugger, the gently ferocious d.h. Manny Ramirez, wears the outsized uniform pants of the fattest player on the squad, reliever Rich (El Guapo) Garces, for style's sake. And the Red Sox are the only team with a curse.

I confess that I've made light of the "Curse of the Bambino"—a neat tagline and title used by the *Globe* columnist Dan Shaughnessy, when he wrote a book about the home team's extensive and eloquent failures to nail down another world championship after they last did it, in 1918, and stuck needles into the club's owner, Harry Frazee, for his decision, a year later, to sell Babe Ruth, then a star pitcher for the Bostons, to the Yankees because, it was said, he needed cash as a backer of a Broadway musical. Kitschy kid stuff to me—right up to the moment at the end of May this year when the Red Sox' double-incumbent Cy Young Award starter, Pedro Martinez, mouthing off a bit after beating the Yanks by 3–0, laughingly offered, "I don't believe in damn curses. Wake up the damn Bambino and have me face him. Maybe I'll drill him in the ass." As every grandmother, tavern keeper, and six-year-old in New England knows by now, Pedro has not won a game since. Struck down almost on the instant by a shoulder ailment, he sat out two months, then pitched valiantly on his return but without picking up another win. Now doctors have found that he is suffering from a slight tear in the rotator cuff, and he may be through for the season. Only in Boston.

Writers waiting to gain postgame admission to the Red Sox manager's office at Fenway Park line up outside the clubhouse, separated by a metal rail from the jammed-together, slowly departing right-field-side patrons, who are headed home in the opposite direction. If the Sox have won, the crowd is noisy and uninteresting, but when they have lost again, as they do by habit in late summer, this year and every year, the tableau becomes weighty and shadowed, with more irony and history and atmosphere to take in than any mere game can account for. It's dark brown here under the stands, for one thing, and the shuffling, oppressed humanity, the dingy lighting, the food smells, the bunched strands of wires and cables running haphazard overhead, and the damp, oddly tilting stone floor cast a spell of F Deck aboard the *Titanic*. Fenway Park floods a visitor with more images than a dozen other ballparks put together, every image apt. The joint opened on August 20, 1912, less than a week after John Jacob Astor and Leonardo DiCaprio gallantly left the lifeboats to the ladies. The Sox beat the New York Highlanders (the pre-Yanks), 7–6, that first Fenway afternoon, beginning a season that would feature Smokey Joe Wood's 34–5 pitching record for the Bostons, and a World Championship over John McGraw's Giants.

Not many of the faces facing me now, on a more recent date, appear comforted by the memory. Many of the men have thick upper bodies, partly concealed behind loose shirts or sweats, but with boyish-looking shorts and big sneakers below. Here comes a large, dignified-looking gent with well-tended white hair, a bankerish demeanor, and a white T-shirt emblazoned with, yes, "YANKEES SUCK," in blue block letters. There are more kids than you see at Yankee Stadium; fewer Latinos but perhaps more families. Some of the nine- and ten- and eleven-year-old boys, with their big mitts and Red Sox wristbands and summer buzz cuts, carry an unmistakable Fenian bloom—look that is confirmed in the faces of their dads. I know what they know, and it comes to me once again—forget the *Titanic*—that these lads could be from Armagh or Roscommon instead of Melrose or Walpole or West Newton, and their heads already full of the Battle of the Boyne and the Easter uprising and Cuchulainn the Hound of Ulster. These local heirs have been handed a similar burden of oppression and unfairness from their earliest breakfast memories, which have the old man groaning over still another bleeding headline in the *Globe* sports pages ("BOGGS SLAPPED WITH PALIMONY SUIT," "SOX POST-SEASON LOSS SKEIN AT 13," "PEDRO FALLS TO BOMBERS"), and you can almost envision the kids exchanging miserable glances as they try to fit the fresh stuff in with the troubles they were born into and the long tales imparted during their first trips to Mass at the Fens. There's 1975 to remember, and Why Did We Take Out Willoughby? and Bucky Dent's dying screen shot on a haunted October afternoon in '78, and black Billy Buckner slowly straightening up behind first base at Shea Stadium in '86, with the easy ground ball skittering off behind him, and farther away, Pesky holding on to the ball in St. Louis while the Cardinals' World Series–winning run comes in: throw the ball, Johnny, for the love of God. There's Pudge leaving us, and Roger and Mo as well.

We haven't won since before Grandpa's time, Timmy my boy, when we let Babe Ruth go—yes, he was ours, a thug of a lefty pitcher then, and he got away. It doesn't mean anything this Curse of the Bambino, but some day, maybe in your lifetime . . . Don't you go worrying about it.

While I stood in line outside manager Joe Kerrigan's office, moments after the Sox had lost to the Yankees in familiar but heartbreaking fashion, to run their losing streak to six, a teen-age boy, mournful under his backward-facing Sox cap, was nudged closer to me by the outflowing crowd. Spotting the credential hung around my neck and my clutched tape recorder and notebook, he leaned close, tilted his head, and murmured, "Ask him what's going on."

Good question. This year's promising Red Sox saw their vibrant shortstop Nomar Garciaparra, a two-time defending batting champion, go down early with wrist surgery, and in June lost Pedro, the best pitcher in baseball, to that aching shoulder. Against all expectations, the Sox hung in, mounting an offense around the electrifying Ramirez, a free-agent slugger who fired a home run into the left-field screen off his first Fenway pitch. They also sent a succession of tough elder non-Pedros to the mound—the knuckleballer Tim Wakefield, the thirty-eight-year-old ex-Yankee David Cone, and the erstwhile Dodger (and Met and Brewer and Tiger) strikeout machine Hideo Nomo, who threw a no-hitter against the Orioles in the second game of the year. The Sox grabbed first place in their division, at times leading the pack by as much as four games, and then, yielding to the inevitable, fell behind the Yankees in early July, but hung close to as they waited for their missing icons to get better—Nomar by

August; Pedro, with luck, in September—and help win a shot at the wild-card opening the playoffs.

But rosiness never lingers long around the Red Sox. Despite the team's success, a cranky dislike festered between some of the regulars and their semi-silent manager, Jimy Williams, who rarely visited the clubhouse, posted late and mystifying lineups, and responded to press queries with a gnomic and infuriating "Manager's decision." Irritability became a clubhouse refrain. Why am I sitting out again? Why the hell am I coming out of the bullpen so often in no-win games? Manny Ramirez smiled through it all, with CD earphones clapped on to blank out the sounds of bickering. Somewhere in my notes is a reminder about the flaplet that began when Trot Nixon let drop that the ailing Carl Everett might be "waiting around and not rehabbing or anything" and attempted to take it back the next day with "I am not trying to piss off Carl by any means because that is not my job."

The clubhouse hostility was benign, a heat rash, compared with relations between Williams and his boss, the executive vice-president and general manager, Dan Duquette; the two parted so vividly a year ago (perhaps when Duquette refused to back the manager in a dispute with the ill-tempered and scary Everett) that it was not expected that Williams would be back this spring. Duquette, stiff and cautious by temperament, is not above tossing the occasional player or manager to the writers, in the manner of a fox loin to the hounds. Asked on the Red Sox radio show why Pedro Martinez had been removed after the sixth inning of a strong effort against the Yankees in June (the Yanks rallied against the Boston relievers and won the game), he said, "I think Jimy needs to talk to the fans about his thinking on that, because it caused a lot of controversy in the market here throughout New England." Martinez, it turned out, was already suffering from the shoulder inflammation that would put him on the disabled list, but neither the manager nor the G.M. could find a way to be straight with the media about the news.

It all came apart on August 16th, when the consonantally challenged Jimy was axed, after the team, in slow decline, had slipped behind the onrushing Oakland Athletics on the wild-card sideline. Managers always get canned during bad news, and the Sox' hopes had long since turned sour. Jason Varitek, an essential catcher and pitch-caller, broke his elbow making a diving catch in foul territory; Everett sat out too many games with a sore knee and swung at too many up pitches when he did play; Manny fell into a depressing slump; and, worse, Garciaparra's return to action was cut short when his wrist blew up again, finishing him for the year. The emotional high-water mark at the Fens, it turned out, had come with a 4–3 win over the White Sox on July 29th, Nomar's first day back, when he tied the game with a homer in the sixth and won it with a single in his next at-bat.

The burdened inheritor of these woes was Joe Kerrigan, the lean and furrowed pitching coach, who was named manager only when Duquette, by his own unhelpful admission, failed to persuade Felipe Alou, the revered ex-Montreal skipper, to accept the post. Kerrigan, a computer apostolic, was widely credited for the Sox' astounding conversion from their long tradition of Wall-bashing into a pitching-and-defense club, with the lowest earned-run average in the league over the previous two years. He also served as advance scout, scouring game tapes, from around the league and disseminating them in daily printouts of pitcher proclivities and situational batting scenarios. Hardworking and intellectual, he was handicapped—in the minds of his players, if not his own—by having never previously managed a game, at any level.

Quickly it became clear that Kerrigan lacked another essential managerial attribute: luck. The departed Jimy, for all his veterans' injuries and whinings, had put a respectable, fiercely contending lineup on the field every day that could coax out wins under unlikely circumstances, but on Saturday night, August 25th, ten days into the Kerrigan regime, the Bostons ran into an abutment in Texas: a ghastly eighteen-inning, six-hour-and-thirty-five-minute standoff against the Rangers, played in soaking ninety-degree weather, which was lot, 8–7, at two-forty in the morning. Only a bit earlier, the schedule had twice forced the Sox to play a game a continent away from one completed the previous day (this happened within a span of ten days, in fact), and the psychic toll of those post-dawn arrivals and screwed-up body clocks, taken with the nine pitchers wasted in Texas, finished the club just as it was about to enter the critical stretch of the season—thirteen successive games against the Indians and the Yankees, away and at home and away again. Every player and fan sportswriter had stuck a Post-it on these couple of weeks in his mind and looked forward to them since spring training. Too late. The Sox, down to the Yankees by four games after the eighteen-inning debacle, were six behind by the time the two met at last, at Fenway Park, less than a week later, and in the toils of the free-fall streak that would push their season into nullity and despond.

The Yankee games, it turned out, were high entertainment, stuffed with old-fashioned low-score baseball and great pitching, and played out in front of a gallant, beaten-down audience that half expected loss and irrelevance and could handle irony with the flair of a Nomar plucking up a low line drive behind second. Baseball news was piling up elsewhere, to be sure—Barry Bonds in avid pursuit of Mark McGwire's home-run record; the embarrassments of the Atlanta Braves; the inexorable successes of the Mariners and their skinny new star, Ichiro; and the recent moment, undreamed of in "Fields of Dreams" or "Casey at the Bat," when Omar Vizquel, the Indians' shortstop, complained to an ump about the distracting earrings sported by Seattle reliever Arthur Rhodes, and won an on-the-spot disjewelment—but these bonbons would have to wait.

The outsized Clemens, riding the wave of his fourth or fifth or fiftieth career reinvention, filled the Friday-night game with himself, throwing ninety-two-mile-an-hour splitters that had the Sox batters waving at his stuff in the dirt (Dante Bichette even reached first after fanning on a wild pitch), coughing up doubles off the wall, shouting at himself for a mistake or another great pitch, and drawing sustenance from the low, baiting cries of "Ro-ger! Rohhhhh-ger!" rolling in from the bleacher wolfpack. The Rocket will pick up his sixth Cy Young Award this winter, and he has pitched so well for so long—eighteen years now, with active-career leading marks in wins, innings pitched, complete games, and strikeouts—that seeing him work is like watching Monet at his easel or F.D.R. lighting a Camel. Almost every game he gets into produces another hysterical voice-over. His strikeout of Chris Stynes to close the Boston seventh became his ninety-eighth outing with ten or more K's, and moved him (we were told) past Sandy Koufax and into third place in the annals in this category. It was an effort to notice that Clemens was actually trailing in the game, 1–0, at this juncture, having been clearly outpitched by the Boston starter, the veteran Frank Castillo, whose exquisite in-and-out, fast-and-slow stuff had the Yankee batters swaying at the plate like cobras to a flageolet.

The fans had noticed, though, and their cries of disbelief when a different pitcher, the deeply fallible Derek Lowe, came out in Castillo's place to start the eighth were followed by noises of shock and outrage when the infield misplayed a grounder, putting the lead-off Yankee batter on base, and Jorge Posada swiftly deposited another Lowe offering into the center-field stands—the game-winning poke, as it turned out. Boston baseball had once again proved confirmatory: Roger can't lose this year, and the abiding tradition in this traditional rivalry is a Yanks win.

Kerrigan, in his office, was rational. This had been only Castillo's fourth effort since a stint in rehab, he pointed out, and Lowe was well rested—the kind of humane considerations that most September managers of contending teams keep safely stuffed away with their New Year's resolutions. Cruelly, I preferred Lowe's summation, which he delivered from beneath his clubhouse sun visor: "Every little bad thing has turned into a big bad thing for me lately. The booing has been going on for months. We've had a good year and now it seems like we've faded in the last couple of weeks. I'd boo, too."

Saturday morning put the Kerrigan decision into perspective; it was madness. Up in the press box, Dan Shaughnessy, the amiable, pink-haired *Globe* master, said, "It's a legend every day around here. The whole scene of Kerrigan taking out Castillo after two hits and fourteen straight outs—why, it's a fable already. It'll never be forgotten."

"It's like the other manager getting the can with his team only four games out of first place," said a New York columnist. "The story of Jimy is improving every day. It's just a matter of time before he's beloved."

Pleasure in bad news is an old reporters' game, but one perhaps played best here in Boston. I'd heard the raw anger of the fans the night before, and the resident writers told me that general wrath over the Sox' recent failings was deeper than it had ever been. The other local obsessions, the

Bruins and the Celtics, have fallen from the heights of late, and in May and June expectations about the Sox were almost off the charts. Manny Ramirez, leading the league in batting and home runs, was living at the Ritz for a thousand dollars a day. Eddie Andelman, the veteran sports announcer on Boston's WEEI, announced a "Yankee Elimination" party on his show, and the call-ins went wild. The Sox had spent a hundred and ten million dollars in salaries this time around, the second-highest total in baseball. The Sox had Nomar and Pedro. The Sox had to win.

Why, amid such blighted memories, do I find Fenway such a benign baseball setting, and baseball happiness closer at hand here than anywhere else? It can't just be the postcard setting: that dinky red peanut-and-cashew wagon plunk in the middle of Yawkey Way, or the patio street signs for sale inside the souvenir shop across the street (a Palazzo of Memorabilia) that say "Hideo Nomo Drive" (forty smackers), or the stunning not-for-sale poster in there depicting a skinny young Yaz in those pinkish striped stockings, just finishing his swing. Inside the doomed park, an older souvenir stand by the front gate bears a "Red Sox Apparel" sign, and outdoors again, down by the players' parking lot, on Van Ness Street, the kid autograph hunters lie face down on the pavement, peering under the canvased-off chain-link fence, where they can pick up no more than inch or two of the shoes of their arriving heroes or the make of the tires on their swollen S.U.V.s. "Mr. Ramirez!" the kids cry out, shoving pens and baseball cards and pennants under the barrier. "Mr. Everett, Mr. Everett!" Fenway Park will be torn down before long—as soon as the sale of the club to one or another of the six current bidding consortiums is completed, in the next few months, and the new management gets its acts and its political connections (and its new general manager) together and finds a spot to put up a nice modern five-hundred-million-dollar park with luxury suites and limo parking. One fan I know has begun a last-minute "muttering campaign," to persuade Jack Welch, the retired G.E. genius, to snap up the club. "Self-made Salem boy, fanatic fan, practitioner of tough love," his e-mail runs. "God knows they need something."

I don't care that much. I will sign no petitions to save Fenway (I've been asked), and I don't believe that it's simply habit and an old-green-walled brick ball yard and my faded memories of Yaz and the Kid and El Tiante that make Fenway work. I think it's pain and anger, and all the gruesome, farcical losses as well. Yankee Stadium sells you winning and nothing much else, but Fenway offers the full range—rage and sweetness and ridiculous remembering—and makes games here matter, however you groan or curse.

The Saturday disappointment differed only in the barest details from its predecessors. There was bright and blowy September weather this time, and a quicker insufficient lead for home side: a solo homer by Trot Nixon, the first Boston batter of the day. You could almost hear the "uh-ohs" as the ball went out. Pedro Martinez and Orlando Hernandez held it right there for the next hour or so, while a nice little flow of K's and mannerisms and accumulated in the sunshine. In the fifth, El Duque shouted "I got it!" while fielding a mini-pop by Mike Lansing—a magical tipoff, on the order of Patty Duke at the water pump, that he is bilingual at last.

The convalescent Pedro took his leave after six, and the Sox unravelment built itself around a modest eighth-inning fly ball that was lost in the sun glare or the gusting breeze in short right field, good for the tying run in time, and Bernie Williams's ninth-inning homer, which reached the first row of seats in center. In two games, the starters had nothing to show for their thirteen goose-egg innings, and the Sox trailed by eight in the East instead of a coulda-been four. Over.

Sunday promised little more than a spicy pitchers' pairing—David Cone versus his Yankee replacement, Mike Mussina, who had signed on with the Bombers for $88.5 million over six years—but the quality of the game quickly put secondary distractions to one side. Mussina had pitched so well this year that a little more run support could have found him at Clemens's level, instead of his entering 13–11. Cone, for his part, had rediscovered himself at the Fens, bouncing back from his horrific, injury-marred 4–14 record and that 6.91 earned-run blot last year. Adopting a mini-windup fashioned by Kerrigan, and waiting out a two-months' sidelining with a shoulder inflammation, he found better results even while working within pitch limitations on his thirty-eight-year-old arm. He stood at 8–3 on this day, with the Boston rooters and interloper Yankee fans perhaps finding equal pleasure from the Sox' run of a dozen consecutive wins in starts of his this summer. As Cone said last year when things were going the other way for him, "Sometimes it's not how you pitch but which games you pitch that matter."

This game—which would end up 1–0, Yankees, with the losing pitcher more or less in triumph and the winner in near-despair—will go straight into the Boston family storybook. Indeed, you can already savor the bitter, flushed-face joy of future Back Bay grandpas and barflies when they come to the good part—the ninth-inning pinch-hit, two-out, two-strike single sailed into left center by Carl Everett for the first and only Sox hit of the evening, and the ruination of Mussina's masterpiece. "Sure, the Yankees won it, lad—what did you expect—but oh, my!"

Mussina and Cone pitch with intensity and with the same leaning stillness while they take in the catcher's sign and begin their little back step. Mussina had such stuff and command this time that he rarely threw the knuckle curve that has been his signature. Nor, of course, did we see the deep courtier's bow of his that inaugurates a pitch with base runners aboard. He was brooding and hunched—a man who wanted no news at all this day and almost got that wish. Nine of his eventual thirteen strike-outs went into the books in the first five inings—he struck out the side in the second—with most of the victims standing immobile as the dismissing ninety-plus fastball or the downflared two-seamer flicked by.

Cone's work provided greater amusement, but mostly he avoided the high counts, bases on balls, or crisis innings that we have come to know so well. He throws more curves than sliders these days, and as always on a good Cone day you enjoyed his thinking almost more than the speed or slant of a given pitch—the wisdom of his four pitches just out of the strike zone to Tino Martinez in the fourth, say, before he fanned Posada to end the inning. The game was going by in a rush, with the accruing edginess of the Mussina no-hitter and possible perfecto matched now by anxiety about Cone's pitch count and potential removal by attrition. Still no score. The Yankees, in fact, brought in no runs at all in the first seven of any game of their three-game sweep—another first, for any pair of teams, in the annals.

Cone, visibly less by now, worked through an eighth inning of lowering troubles, with the quick Soriano on first after a lead-off single. Knoblauch went down with a fly ball and Jeter on a strikeout; Derek said later that his tottering wave at Cone's side-armer was the worst swing of his professional career. With Soriano on second now, Bernie Williams stroked a high drive that was pulled in by Nixon a step in front of the center-field wall. The end—the first ending, that is—arrived predictably enough in the Yankee ninth, when the fill-in Boston second baseman, Lou Merloni, botched a hard-hit double-play grounder that would have closed the inning. Enrique Wilson's double brought in the run at last, and finished Coney for the day. At least he got the shot, having talked his manager into letting him go back out there and take what came: death by the bullet, not the bullpen.

The building, no-hit, nobody-on melodrama by Mussina had been buzzed about and gabbed over in the stands all evening, because it was Cone, of course, who had last turned the trick, two years ago past this July, when he shut down the Montreal Expos on Yogi Berra Day at the Stadium, for the sixteenth such marvel on record. The coincidence added a flair of moral drama to the proceedings, and now in the ninth Everett's two-out, 1-and-2-count single, struck off a third successive high fastball, was greeted by pathetically exulting Fenwayian cries. Mussina had got within two outs of a perfect game four years ago in Baltimore, but he had to come up here to be inaugurated into the Hall of Pain.

No gleam of light has showed itself for the Red Sox since that day, and their season has trailed off into scandal and bottomless loss. A pitching coach (Kerrigan's successor) was fired moments after a losing game, more or less in full sight of the media, causing Garciaparra to mutter, "That's why nobody wants to fucking play here." The whine was delivered to a teammate but overheard and disclosed by a hovering writer, as has happened before in the players' slummy little tenement. Pedro has continued to pitch, despite his subpar shoulder; he was taken out of his start in New York ten days ago, down by 3–2, after fifty-four pitches. No one in baseball—well, no one outside of the Boston management—can understand how a franchise arm could have been put at such risk.

After winning a game at last, against Cleveland, the Red Sox dropped four more—"AGAIN, A CRUSHING DEFEAT FOR REGION" was the headline over a prior Shaughnessy column in the *Globe*—and trailed the Yankees by thirteen games before the Trade Center tragedy intervened,

David Cone lost to Mussina once again, with the teams in New York, in a suspense-free 6–2 renewal. Coming off the field in the sixth after throwing a second home run of the day to Martinez (Tino drove in five runs, all told), David received a handsome, non-ironic standing O from the fans. He was gracious in the clubhouse: "It was very very appreciated. I can't remember the last time I tipped my hat after giving up five runs." But his season of hopes of pitching in Fenway in the post-season had gone south, along with everyone else's, and it came out in time that he'd gone wild in the clubhouse after the accolade, throwing chairs and food around—a "snappage," in his lexicon.

Cone will be back next year—his great game up in Boston assures it— but I don't think it will be with the Red Sox. Losing him will be sad for the Fenwayites, but it fits nicely within the legend. He is bitterly disappointed about the collapse of the Red Sox, but loss, of course, is something these pros encounter almost every day. When Cone learned that the dour and inward Mike Mussina was still feeling the shock of Everett's killer single, he arranged to met him at the Stadium, where he comforted him with a longer view. "It's not so bad to talk about a game like that after it's over," he explained to me. "You don't want to turn a masterpiece into a negative. It feels pretty good to be told that you were part of the best game played this year."

"I don't think there's anything as good in sports history as the Yankees and the Red Sox."

—Yankees first baseman Jason Giambi

THEY SAID IT...

Some Red Sox fans until recently saw nothing but suffering and loss in their team's history. Ned Gulley had a different viewpoint.

"WHAT BEING THE FATHER OF AN AUTISTIC SON TAUGHT ME ABOUT BEING A RED SOX FAN (AND VICE VERSA)"

from the Paracelsus Weblog (www.starchamber.com)
[first posted on October 20, 2003]
by Ned Gulley

WHICH RED SOX FAN do you choose to be? The embittered one that mumbles about curses and looks forward to defeat with perverse relief, or the one who is pained but pleased with an excellent season and some extraordinary post-season play? What I really want to know is: why is it so damned easy to be the first one? Why are there so many people eager to say "I told you so" or "See . . . they always let you down"? But really I do understand this urge. I understand living with chronic disappointment because my son is autistic. The connection to baseball may not seem so obvious, but bear with me for a few minutes while I explain.

Some years ago I was flying out of Miami after a hectic family vacation.

We were running late getting to the airport, and since we couldn't find a gas station to fill up the rental car, we had to shell out $5 a gallon at the car return. I was already fuming about that, and then the rental guy found a dent in the car we'd have to pay to fix. A few minutes later I was angrily shoving a tottering heap of rolling luggage through the stifling heat outside the airport, and I remember thinking "Oh, wouldn't it be JUST GREAT if all this luggage fell over?" And because the sentence was so clearly formed in my mind, I suddenly realized it was literally true. Some part of me thought it actually would be great if the luggage all fell over. Why? Lots of reasons. It would justify my shitty mood. I would have something to kick. I could curse and shout and do a little stomping dance. But my realization calmed me down. I was able to say to myself "I don't want this luggage to fall over." I wheeled it carefully through the airport and the day improved dramatically from that point on.

My son Jay was a year old then (he took his first steps in Miami). He is now four years old and completely unable to talk. He shows little interest in his parents or anyone else. He is a struggle to deal with every day. Working with him is, as a general rule, tedious and unrewarding. When he does something new or successful, it is a small victory—he pulls his socks off on command, or maybe he pedals a tricycle ten feet before losing all interest in the exercise. I am always tempted to measure these small victories against his larger dysfunction. I am tempted to say "Great, but he's still hopelessly retarded." Because I don't want him to make me hope, I have nursed hopes, coaxed dreams along superstitiously and been crushed again and again. At this point it is very unlikely that Jay will "recover." A manageable status quo is what I hope for now. I recede into bitterness. Damn you for making me hope! Keep up your predictable failings and my heart can take it. But if I keep hoping it will kill me.

I have only lived in Boston for 12 years, and to tell the truth, I've never really been that much of a baseball fan. But I'm amazed at how this history just seeps into you, as if I've had season tickets at Fenway since Babe Ruth's last season here. It's hard work to be a Red Sox fan, but you get drawn into it anyway. On the other hand it couldn't be easier to be a Yankees fan. Just put your car in cruise control and watch the championships pile up. Yogi Berra has a championship ring for each of his ten fat fingers.

Ted Williams went into his icebox without a single one. Former Boston ace Roger Clemens finally got his—he moved to New York. Similarly, it's so easy to have a normal son. I see them at the playground, these fathers and sons, kicking the ball back and forth, laughing at each other's jokes. They can speak to each other! Then I look at my son running around in circles making squealing noises, lost in his own world. And I lose myself in a whirlwind of anger and jealousy.

It's so easy to be a Yankees fan.

Only recently have I managed to enjoy my son's small successes by celebrating them as successes. A good day is a good day. Let it be a good day. A good day is not an instrument of torture designed to ratchet up the agony of your ultimate and inevitable anguish. When you start to fear good days, you have gone down a dangerous path. A good day can lead to hope, and hope can later be extinguished, but a good day is a good day, and you have to find a way to weave that into your life.

The day you think of a post-season victory by the Red Sox as an act of cruelty aimed at your heart, you have become less human. A post-season victory is a good day. Happiness is not an end state, but a fleeting moment. When it catches you (it never seems to work the other way around) gather it like a thirsty, shipwrecked sailor gathers rain. Honor it. There were some beautiful moments this season before that crushing Yankee home run in the eleventh inning that pulled down the curtain on it all. Does that home run have the power to turn all those gemstones into daggers? No . . . a beautiful moment is a beautiful moment. I hate the Yankees. And I don't give a good goddamn about building character by losing. I wish my son's brain wasn't so cruelly ravaged by this hateful malady. I am not well adjusted. I am angry and unreformed. Every day I ache. But a beautiful moment must not be denied. If I can see my son smiling and that makes me smile, that's a good moment. And for all the Sox did this season, well, I challenge you to take away from them what they did for you. They gave you something wonderful and you took it. That's as happy as happy gets. They were not taunting you. They were not setting you up. They were playing their hearts out. As I say to Jay when bitterness wells up in my throat and my teeth clench in frustration, "It's not my fault. It's not your fault." No one can make you hope. You have to take responsibility for it yourself when you do hope. You cannot make happiness conditional, because there is no end to conditions. Make up your mind now: either let victories be victories when they happen or live forever in the dark shadow of defeat. Some days grind you into bitterness. But a good day is a good day.

As the cruel Red Sox losses accumulate, the lore deepens and the story only gets richer. It's so painful! But how can you not fall more tragically and completely under their spell? As for me, after a long day of dealing with Jay, dealing with scratching and screeching, I want you to see him on my lap with his sippy cup, smiling and looking into my eyes. Do I dare fall more deeply and tragically in love with him? Yes.

In the end, José Contreras would win just 15 games for the Yankees. In the end, everyone would agree that the big-money free-agent signing had been a failure. But in the beginning, back in late 2002, Contreras was the pitcher both the Red Sox and the Yankees wanted. Boston thought the big Cuban could pitch them past New York after five straight second-place finishes. New York thought Contreras' right arm was just the weapon they needed to return to championship form after two straight years of postseason defeats. Officially it was baseball's off-season. These days, the rivalry never sleeps.

LANDING CONTRERAS

from *Chasing Steinbrenner* [2004]
by Rob Bradford

THERE WAS NO FACE affixed to his name, just a title: The Missing Piece to the Eighty-Five-Year-Old, Seemingly Unsolvable World Championship Puzzle.

This was how the fans of the Boston Red Sox viewed José Contreras. If the Sox got Contreras, they had started to believe, all of their problems would be solved. But who was Contreras? Talk-show caller Joe from Quincy could pick out the New England Patriots' special teams coach before he might identify his favorite baseball team's savior. It was blind faith, and Red Sox fans had become really good at it.

The general population of Red Sox Nation did know this much: Contreras was from Cuba, the scouts liked him, and so did the Yankees. To the fans, just that limited bit of information was the hot stove league equivalent of watching the pitcher strike out twenty-seven hitters in a row before 35,000 sets of eyes at Fenway Park.

Perhaps the innocence was a good thing. If the people of Boston knew the full story behind Contreras, then they might just start telling visitors that the "Freedom Trail" wasn't a Revolutionary War landmark, but rather the path for all Cuban pitchers with ninety-seven-mile-per-hour heat and a pinch-me-when-it-has-landed forkball who want to make the Fens their home.

But there were some Bostonians who realized why there was such promise in putting Contreras in between Pedro Martinez and Derek Lowe in the team's rotation, and most of them resided in the offices at 4 Yawkey Way. The Red Sox front office, like the rest of Major League Baseball, knew just about everything there was to know about Contreras, thanks to the brief glimpses Cuban president Field Castro would give the world of his nation's premier athlete in international competition. It's not easy to see too far into the Communist shadow cast over the Cuban players, but in Contreras's case some numbers gave enough of an introduction.

The thirty-one-year-old had pitched in the 1999 Pan-American Games, the 2000 Olympics, and 2001 World Cup, finishing the three tournaments with a 7–0 record, a 0.59 ERA, and sixty-six strikeouts in sixty-one innings. In the Pan-Am Games against the United States, Contreras had struck out thirteen American batters in eight innings pitching on one day's rest en route to a 5–1 Cuban victory. And just for good measure, the performance came on the same day as that which marked the beginning of Castro's revolution forty-six years before. For this sort of drama, the nation's ace ultimately got what might have been an oppressed citizen's ultimate prize—a blue Peugeot 400C sedan automobile.

Castro nicknamed Contreras "El Titan de Bronce" (The Titan of Bronze) after the most famous general in Cuba's war of independence against Spain, Antonio Maceo. There was no doubting that, among athletes, Fidel had a short list of his most beloved, and José was at the top of the list.

On the first day of October 2002, it was Major League Baseball's turn to play favorites.

Perhaps if it weren't for Castro's admiration of Contreras, teams like the Red Sox would still be viewing the pitcher as the unattainable supermodel Joe Everyman dreams about but knows he will never have. The first proof of this came when José's prized car broke down.

The repairs to the vehicle were going to cost $453, an exorbitant amount of money for virtually any Cuban without the first name of Fidel and the last name of Castro. Contreras, who was making $275 a year, turned to the Cuban Sports Federation for help, but there was none forthcoming. The wheels then started turning, not on the Peugeot, but in José's head. This was the final straw.

Contreras's frustration spilled over to the mechanic who was charging him to fix the car. He told the man he wasn't coming back. As vague as the statement might have seemed, in the world of always looking over your shoulder, it might have been too much. The next day, José was fighting back tears while saying good-bye to his wife of fifteen years, Myriam, and their two daughters. As far as they knew, he was simply taking off from José Marti Airport for another baseball tournament. He knew otherwise.

The Cuban national team headed to Santillo, Mexico, to play in the America Series Tournament. The morning after a relatively easy 6–0 win over the Dominican Republic, Contreras told his coaches that he would prefer to stay behind at the Hotel Camino Real because of a pain in his hip. The request was accepted for two reasons. First, Cuba was playing a weak Guatemala team, so he wouldn't be needed, but he was also Castro's poster child for the virtues of Cuban baseball—a superstar of the world who had repeatedly said he had already turned down an offer of $50 million to defect.

Except that this time, Contreras actually was going to switch sides.

He called Jaime Torres, an agent who had told Contreras years back that if defection was ever an option, José should contact him and arrangements would be set. The words were, *"Lo voy a hacer!,"* the Spanish version of "I am going to do it!," and never meant more to the world of professional baseball. So a car arrived, José jumped in, and he was quickly driven to the airport. There he met up with Torres, who had a surprise guest with him, longtime Cuban coach Miguel Valdes and his nineteen-year-old son, Miguel Jr.

Contreras's first reaction was that he might have been set up, since Valdes's affiliation with the Cuban team had stretched more than thirty years and included thirteen world championships and two Olympic Gold Medals. Contreras had entered the world of defection just ten years after giving up his dream of becoming a veterinarian, not long enough to be fully classified as a lifelong Castro loyalist. Valdes, on the other hand, was an institution within Cuban baseball circles, one who surely wouldn't partake in the ultimate risk of defection.

But like Contreras, Valdes had also been pushed too far.

The four men successfully boarded the plane for Tijuana, where a car took them for the short ride to the United States border. If they had been discovered before reaching the gateway to California, the Cubans would have been detained by the Mexican authorities and returned to Cuba under the countries' repatriation agreement. Forget pitching for the pride of an entire country. Forget getting calls in the dugout after every inning of a 2000 Olympic game from Castro. Pressure for José Contreras suddenly had a new definition.

When the border was reached, United States customs agents immediately took the three Cubans into custody. This was a mere formality, as was evidenced the next morning when the group was released into Torres's custody. They had run the gauntlet without getting caught. On one hand, the accomplishment elicited a feeling of overriding elation, while in other respects it generated a slap-in-the-face reality. Contreras still hadn't told Myriam, the couple's children, his sixty-six-year-old mother, Modesta, and most frightening, the family's eighty-one-year-old patriarch, Florentino, a man who had sung the praises of Castro's revolution. This wasn't exactly on par with getting home after curfew, as José's reluctance to call his parents' hometown of Las Martinas might suggest.

Nine days into his new life in the United States, José finally worked up the courage to call Myriam, a smooth-skinned beauty who had married her husband at age fifteen. It would be the first of a stream of calls from Contreras, whose only connection to his family now hinged on the Nokia cell phone residing in the family's two-bedroom apartment in the Cuban city of Pinar del Rio. The posters of the pitcher may have been stripped from the streets and meeting places of his former nation, but his face still littered the walls surrounding Myriam and her two daughters.

Contreras finally called his father, although the communication would have to be placed through a neighbor across the field from his parents' home (they did not have a phone). Florentino knew baseball, having played on a team sponsored by the sugar mills, and he knew his son. Perhaps that is why the man who had raised José was surprisingly understanding upon receiving the call. Jose was still José, and that would never change.

What would be altered was Contreras's everyday existence. And the Red Sox were hoping that at least a portion of that metamorphosis could take place inside the gates of Fenway Park.

"Do not hire a man who does your work for money, but him who does it for love of it." —Henry David Thoreau

Like Florentino Contreras, Luis Eljaua knew baseball, and he thought he knew José.

Eljaua, a man with a football fullback's low-to-the-ground build and straight-ahead approach, grew up playing baseball in high school and then college in Miami. He was a middle infielder who was good enough to join future major leaguers Alex Fernandez, Jorge Fabregas, and Ricky Gutierrez in playing a key role in bringing Monsignor Pace High School to two straight Florida high school championship games. But he didn't run well, and lacked the power to make up for his limited legs. The scouts stayed away, leaving Eljaua without a minor league contract and with an uncertain future.

So the son of Cuban immigrants made the logical decision: If you can't beat them, join them.

Al Avila, Eljaua's former college coach at St. Thomas University, had gotten a job with the Florida Marlins and recommended his former player for a position as a bilingual scout in South Florida. Luis spoke Spanish before he uttered a word of English, and he knew the territory's playing fields intimately, so the fit was natural. A career had begun.

By the time Marlins owner John Henry officially joined a group in paying $700 million to own the Boston Red Sox in February 2002, Eljaua had ascended to the position of director of Latin American scouting. But Henry was raiding the Marlins' cupboard, and one of the pieces he was going to take with him was Eljaua, who would be Boston's man in charge of all of the team's international scouting. It was an honor, but also a transition considering the entire world was now under his umbrella. He had been to Japan just once, helping the Marlins seal the sale of pitcher Hector Almonte, but he never knew the feeling of working in an unfamiliar language and culture.

Chasing down Contreras, however, was anything but foreign to Eljaua.

Like most other major league representatives, Luis wasn't able to get close to Contreras during his outings with the Cuban National Team, but with José, seeing has always been believing. Eljaua's first eyeful of Castro's Titan of Bronze came at an international tournament in Millington, Tennessee, in 1995. "Wow" was the operative word that day, and would be for the twelve more times the then-Marlins scout viewed Contreras until his defection day.

The world may have been introduced to Contreras in his eight shutout innings against the Baltimore Orioles in an exhibition game at Havana's 45,000-seat El Stadio, but that was simply a footnote for Eljaua, whose familiarity with José couldn't be thwarted by the ninety-seven miles separating Cuba from Key West. And now, with nothing dividing Luis from Contreras except his agent, the Red Sox representative was going to try and get to know this figure he had been chasing. They were going to be friends, and just maybe they could be coworkers.

The first step came just weeks after the journey from Tijuana, with Eljaua meeting up with Team Contreras in Miami's La Carreta Restaurant. The evening didn't include negotiations, since that still wasn't allowed while Major League Baseball decided how to classify Contreras's free agent status. There was just talk of Luis's and José's common interests—baseball and Cuban-born parents. The strangers quickly became like brothers, making the three-hour meal feel like the most informal of fast-food experiences. The first step had been made, and a relationship was being built.

Contreras was humble and personable in his meeting with Eljaua, easily rattling off knowledge of the big leagues with the aplomb of a teenage baseball card nut. It was a familiarity aided by knowing some of Cuba's previous sixty or so defectors, a group that began with Rene Arocha in 1991 and had peaked in 1999 with the $14.5 million contract signed by the country's third-best pitcher—behind Contreras and Pedro Luis Lazo—Danys Baez. If Contreras was nervous about his fate in the majors, he didn't show it, either in his workouts on the fields of Miami or at any of the subsequent dinner meetings with Eljaua.

The comfort level between the two was high, which was the first necessity. If the Red Sox were going to be throwing the amount of money at Contreras that they thought they might be, it was Eljaua's job to find out exactly what they would be getting in return. He needed to find out what made Cuba's greatest pitcher tick.

Boston's next step came in early November, when Eljaua brought Contreras, Torres, Valdes, and his son, along with former Red Sox great and fellow Cuban Luis Tiant, to John Henry's home in Boca Raton. Most Cubans couldn't have imagined such a palatial estate such as the one Contreras was being introduced to courtesy of the Red Sox owner. But there is one, and perhaps only one, place on the island nation that could compare, and José had been there—Fidel Castro's palace. When the Cuban teams would win international tournaments, the players wouldn't even get the chance to go home. It was straight to Castro's palace, just for a taste of what could never be anybody's but Fidel's.

Henry's place was different, just as big, but perhaps even more modern. It was the hosts, however, who really separated the two experiences for Contreras—Castro, the fear-inducing dictator who oozed bravado, and Henry, as soft-spoken and gentle a man as one could find in the world of big business.

For two hours Henry did his best to make José feel welcome, while trying to get a read on this man into whom he was potentially pouring millions of dollars. The two were alike in the sense that both erred on the side of modesty and a quiet nature. The only obstacle standing in the way of a fast friendship was the inability to speak one another's language. But thanks to Eljaua and Torres, bridges were built, and a rapport was born.

Eljaua knew that familiarity was the Red Sox's ally when it came to Contreras, and further dinner meetings were paving the road to the desired familiarity. Even employees not yet hired by Boston were contributing to the general food-on-the-table, good-feelings-in-the-air cause. The plan seemed to be coming together for the Red Sox, thanks in part to the Pittsburgh Pirates' Latin American pitching coordinator.

Marta Rojas is a great cook. Fantastic cook. It was just that the fifteen or so people she and her husband, Euclides, were expecting for dinner in their Miami home on the November night were a bit much to prepare for.

So a Cuban restaurant was enlisted to cater their affair. Cuban food isn't hard to find on the edge of the Everglades.

The Rojas family knew most of their guests—Rene Arocha, Danys Baez, Orlando Hernandez, and a room full of other Cuban baseball-playing refugees. There was one visitor, however, that Euky had met just in passing in his days of pitching for the Cuban national team—José Contreras.

The theme for the get-together was "Welcome to Freedom," and nobody embodied the slogan better than Contreras. José knew many of his fellow dinner visitors, especially the man they call "El Duque," but it was Euky whom he truly wanted to get to know better. It was, after all, Rojas's story and hospitality that exemplified the story of all of the dinner guests. In Contreras's eyes, he was being hosted by a hero.

Rojas was a savior for his team, for his friends, and for his family. While playing for Havana in the Cuban League, he had saved more than ninety games, including setting a league record in 1994. He was a guy who could pitch all day, every day, sometimes going the final four innings to close out a game. But, then again, when you're playing in Cuba, choices such as when and where you pitch aren't usually a luxury.

Rojas's good-natured, selfless demeanor wasn't lost on his teammates, either. After Arocha became the first baseball-playing defector in July 1991, it was only Euky who chose not to ignore the nation's new embarrassment, collecting his friend's bags from the floor of the airport terminal to give to Arocha's family. Three rounds of questioning by the Cuban authorities later, and Rojas was officially in the authorities' crosshairs.

Rojas's worries concerning who he might find looking over his shoulder escalated when it was learned that an investigation was forthcoming regarding his involvement in Democratic Solidarity, an anti-Castro organization. That's when the player who had been part of the Cuban national team's bullpen since 1987 decided that floating on four empty fifty-five-gallon drums might not be such a bad thing. So at 11 P.M. on August 17, 1994, Euky, his wife, and their two-and-a-half-year-old son joined thirteen other dreamers in plunging a fifteen-foot raft into Havana's More Castle for a five-day ride that would take them sixty-seven miles out to sea.

The first night was the toughest—there was a big surf, and even bigger anxiety. Just 40 percent of the Cubans who attempt to make the voyage to freedom make it, and trying to accomplish the feat with a wife and a son suffering from a respiratory disorder surely dropped those odds substantially. But Rojas knew what the past and present had delivered for them in Cuba, and the uncertainty of a future outside of that oppression seemed far more appetizing.

Then Euky saw those numbers—721—and he knew the decision to weather the waves, the wind and Castro's wrath was justified. The sight of the digits on the side of a United States Coast Guard vessel was destiny's way of giving Rojas a big pat on the back.

It wouldn't be until six months of internment in the squalor of the base at United States-controlled Guantánamo Bay (and an emergency appendectomy) that Euky tasted the fruits of his convictions. Nine years later, Rojas was living the life he had dreamed of, a life in professional baseball and a life without fears. Like the other Cubans partaking in the November feast, Rojas had made it. It was time to celebrate the freedom Contreras had only just begun to comprehend.

What Contreras didn't realize was that one of his chief suitors, the Red Sox, were interested in having Rojas tackle their bullpen coaching position. The influx of Marlins people within the Boston organization knew the even-keeled, knowledgeable approach Euky possessed and saw him as a good fit. The fact that Contreras looked up to him didn't hurt, either.

When the job offer came, Rojas was skeptical. He didn't want advancement simply because of his association with Contreras, a fact made clear when meeting with Sox manager Grady Little and pitching coach Tony Cloninger in a get-to-know-you dinner in North Carolina. His fears were placated. Sure, Boston looked at Euky's relationship with the object of their desire as a plus, but the biggest drawing card was the entire package Rojas maintained. He was the coach they wanted in the Fenway Park bullpen.

By the time early December rolled in, Boston had pieced together its battle plan regarding Contreras and was in position to execute it. Eljaua laid the groundwork, Henry analyzed the investment, Rojas was established as an all-important support system, and now it was simply time to spring into action.

"There are no secrets better kept
than the secrets that everybody guesses."
—George Bernard Shaw

All the Red Sox were left waiting for was the decision by Major League Baseball regarding what to do with Conteras's free agent status. In order not to be subjected to the June amateur draft, the pitcher had to take up residency in a country other than the United States. First, Torres suggested Mexico for his client's new home. "No way," responded the higher-ups at MLB, who deemed the neighboring country just too convenient.

So where was it going to be? Panama? The Dominican Republic? The word finally came down—"Gentlemen, get your plane tickets for Nicaragua."

In the meantime, Epstein, Eljaua, and the rest of Team Red Sox were doing everything short of laying out the dollars and cents in front of Contreras. While at the Grand Ole Opry Hotel in Nashville, the Red Sox contingent took time off from the courtship of other free-agent possibilities (Jeff Kent, Edgardo Alfonzo) to meet with the agent. The underlying theme of the get-together wasn't anything fancy, just simply "We will see you in Managua"—Nicaragua's capital.

They wouldn't be alone.

By the time Contreras was officially declared a free agent by the commissioner's office on December 18, Eljaua had been in Managua for three full days. He still wasn't able to talk money with Torres or Contreras, but that didn't deter him from trying to build on Boston's already well-constructed plan.

Eljaua arrived at the Hotel Campo Real, a less-than-extravagant lodging near the Managua airport, knowing Contreras was staying at the same address. Luis proceeded to discover that his room, No. 3, was conveniently next to Torres's room, No. 2, and near Contreras's room, No. 1.

There were only about fifteen rooms in the ranch-style, yellow-and-green-dominated hotel, so the placement wasn't cosmically accidental by any means. But the rooms' locale did give Eljaua an idea that would undoubtedly aid Boston's master plan.

The morning after touching down in Managua, Eljaua went to Georgina Lacayo, the hotel manager, and asked if any other teams had been represented yet in the complex. The answer was no, not yet. Luis knew the Yankees were coming any day now, along with at least a smattering of other organizations, and trying to maneuver through the halls of a crowded hotel might be a distraction.

"How many rooms do you have available?" Eljaua asked Lacayo. "Eleven," was the answer. "I'll take them all," the determined Red Sox employee responded.

For less than $1,000, Boston not only earned the right to exclusively call Contreras a neighbor throughout the precious few days, but the maneuver also allowed the Red Sox to know who was coming, who was going, and when they were doing it. Everyone realized the bidding for the pitcher was going to be a horse race, so getting out of the gate fastest was the highest priority.

As the days passed, with Contreras continuing to work out with the San Fernando team in Masaya, a town thirty kilometers west of Managua, Eljaua slowly got company. Especially notable was the presence of Seattle general manager Pat Gillick and Yankees' scouting director Gordon Blakely. New York general manager Brian Cashman had left the Contreras affair in the hands of Blakely and his scouts, a move that might have been all the more trusting considering what was at stake.

Cashman is a likable sort, partly because of his matter-of-fact, down-to-earth demeanor, and also due to the perception of what he has to endure while working under the thumb of the infamously spontaneous George Steinbrenner. Cashman had reached the position of general manager at just thirty years of age in 1998, capping a rise through the organization that had started with an internship in 1989.

Cash's first contract as GM had been for just one year, and was sealed with a handshake. Nearly five years later, he was wearing three world championship rings.

When Theo Epstein first got his general manager job, the genial, thirty-five-year-old Cashman called to congratulate his colleague and offer the only piece of advice that he thought worthy of giving: Don't forget to use the power of "no comment" when it comes to dealing with the people with the notepads. Former New York GM Gene Michael had passed the warning on to Cashman and now, AL East rival or not, it was going to be passed along to Epstein.

The cordiality of the relationship between Cash and Theo remained, but a competitive dynamic kicked up in a hurry. It started forming at the winter meetings, when the two bumped into one another, when Contreras was just starting to consume each general manager's attention.

"You know George isn't going to let you get Contreras," said Cashman, half-joking, but fully understanding that nothing could be more based in reality.

"I guess it's going to get pretty expensive then," retorted Epstein, fighting back the same competitive fire that had consumed him from the days in Brookline, except the opponent had now changed: Playing the rival role of twin brother Paul Epstein was George Steinbrenner.

Another curve in the road to Contreras came in the days leading up to the December 22 starting point for negotiations for the Cuban pitcher. The Atlanta Braves made an offer to the Yankees and Red Sox—would they be interested in pitcher Kevin Millwood? It was as if the baseball gods had decided to test both Epstein and Cashman's resolve.

Millwood was any big league starting rotation's dream—a pitcher who had pitched more than 200 innings in three of the last four seasons while maintaining a career ERA under 4.00. The problem was that he was most likely going to make almost $10 million in 2003.

For both teams, it was going to have to be either Millwood or Contreras.

All it was going to take for Boston to put one of the best pitchers in the National League in between the far-from-ordinary talents of Pedro Martinez and Derek Lowe was to send a left-handed pitcher named Casey Fossum to Atlanta.

Fossum represented a part of the Red Sox's future, as well as the unexplained physics of baseball. The left-hander was a slight six feet tall, and his frame elicited constant tugs at the league's thinnest of waistbands. As one baseball executive said when watching him pitch, "It looks like he had liposuction and forgot to say when." But whatever numbers were lacking on the scale were more than made up for on the radar guns. Fossum threw hard, and the Braves wanted that heat to come south.

The overtures relayed by Atlanta, however, couldn't sway Epstein. Fossum was too good, young, and cheap to let go and by all accounts, Contreras was going to be even better than Millwood. Besides, the Cuban said he wanted to be a Red Sox, so why stray from the path to what was supposed to be mankind's best 1-2-3 starting combination?

The problem was that the Yankees were politely declining Atlanta's offer for much the same reason as Boston was. Cashman's scouts told him that Contreras wanted to be a Yankee, so the decision was made that a Yankee he would be.

Unless he mistakenly thought he could play for both teams, Contreras had plunged into the world of capitalism headfirst by partaking in baseball agents' favorite game—playing the Red Sox and Yankees against one another to drive up the price.

Two days after being rebuffed by both the Red Sox and Yankees, Atlanta made its trade, shipping Millwood to Philadelphia for minor league catcher Johnny Estrada. Epstein then got another phone call, but this time it was from Eljaua.

Luis was starting to see interest pick up around Contreras, and there were rumors that Cashman was on his way, raising the stakes exponentially. Torres also made it clear that a decision was going to be made quickly, in part because the agent's kids were expecting his presence in the family's Florida home on Christmas morning. Eljaua believed Epstein was needed in Managua.

Theo had no qualms about making the trip, knowing it might well be a necessity. What he hadn't planned for was having to update his passport on a Saturday, a task that cropped up as soon as he started to pack his bags. The Red Sox had prepared for every eventuality . . . except this one.

Improvisation was now on deck.

A plan was hatched where Boston's traveling secretary would arrange a flight to Miami that went through Washington, D.C. Once in the nation's capital, Epstein would use his two-hour layover to use a connection of team president Larry Lucchino for a rare weekend passport renewal. A quick trip to Miami, followed by two and a half hours in the air to Managua, and Epstein's excellent adventure was set. As a result, in a month full of days like nothing he had ever seen, Epstein would put December 21 at the top of his head-shakers. It was, as he later said, like a movie . . . from a damn good script.

Epstein had never been to Nicaragua before, although he imagined it couldn't be much different than some of those small Mexican towns he had ventured into while working in San Diego. The surroundings did look similar, and the weather upon landing was a welcome seventy-eight degrees, but when that first chicken ran through the hotel lobby, Theo knew this was more than a slightly different world.

Thoughts of the surroundings, however, didn't have much room in Epstein's head. Neither did reflection that he had been on the job less than a month, and he was a week shy of his twenty-ninth birthday. After all, it had been twenty-four years before to the day that a group of NASA engineers with the average age of twenty-six years old had guided the Apollo 8 space-craft around the moon. So, certainly in Epstein's eyes, guiding a Cuban pitcher around the Yankees and into Boston shouldn't be too daunting.

At midnight on the morning leading into December 22, just a few hours after Epstein had arrived, the Red Sox made their initial offer to Contreras. They felt good about it, although the feelings were tempered somewhat just knowing the Yankees were waiting around the corner with a checkbook that was prepared to yield up to $8 million per season.

Later that day, Epstein ran into Gillick. The Seattle general manager was leaving town without his Cuban pitcher. Theo wasn't surprised to see the man who had built two world championship teams in Toronto. He always tended to be where the action was. But this time the action was just a bit too rich for his organization's blood. The Mariners weren't a poor team, carrying an $82 million payroll, but trying to keep up with the Yankees in Managua had suddenly become much less viable.

The word came down that Contreras was going to make his decision that night. Most of the meetings had been solely with Toronto, but now, in the final stages, the pitcher joined the discussions. Boston had already gone over its planned offer, but for this pitcher, the subject of an elaborate two-month chase, that was OK in the eyes of Sox ownership. At $27 million over four years, Contreras appeared to be a wise investment. As Epstein and Eljaua sat out on the hotel's patio restaurant, just thirty yards from where Torres was about to engage with Yankees' officials for the last time, Contreras walked by. "It looks good," was the message a smiling José passed on to the Boston duo. Look good! Both Theo and Luis had learned of ninth-inning heartbreak, but when the object of your attention comes over and says, "Looks good," then the feeling becomes the same as if an All-Star closer was coming out of the bullpen to protect a three-run lead.

Two hours later, the Yankees completed their comeback.

Cashman never did make the trip, relying solely on his scouts while staying back in New York. When he heard Epstein had boarded a plane for Managua, he almost went, but he remained true to his own conviction that his people were steering the Yankees in the right direction. So while the Boston representatives sat an easy field goal's distance away from the negotiations, Cashman stayed close via phone calls placed every half hour or so.

So by the time Torres made the walk from Room No. 2 to Epstein and Eljaua's table at 12:30 in the morning of December 23, Cashman was sitting comfortably in his home having already been informed of the result regarding the bidding war. The Yankees had won with a bid of $32 million over four years. Contreras may have truly wanted to be a Red Sox, but not for $5 million less than what his other favorite team was offering. To rub salt in the wound, just days before New York had laid out a three-year, $21 million deal for Japanese outfielder Hideki Matsui.

Every time the Yankees' $150 million-plus payroll rose, the hearts of the Red Sox sunk just a little bit more. The realities of competing in the American League East reality had gotten that much more intractable.

The next morning, Eljaua got a knock on his door. It was Contreras. The pitcher was a huge man, and his face reflected both the size of his stature and of his inner struggle. To see the tears falling down his face upon saying good-bye to the man he befriended two months before just didn't quite seem natural. Neither did the fact that he was going to be finally pitching in *las liguas majores* for a team other than the Red Sox.

The plane ride back to the States flat-out sucked for Epstein.

Contreras's second defection, this time to a Yankees organization

Larry Lucchino had deemed the "Evil Empire" in the post-Nicaragua backbiting, was like the biggest lump of Christmas coal that anyone could imagine. Epstein's return voyage on Christmas Eve was filled with questions of where it had all gone wrong. It was going to take more than just a couple of hours in a window seat to find the answers.

In the days to come, Epstein heard it all: Contreras was offended by the Red Sox's purchase of all the hotel rooms (it was a freedom thing); former Yankee Orlando "El Duque" Hernandez had gotten to his friend, singing the praises of living the big league life in pinstripes. But, when it was all said and done, the Boston general manager would accept only one explanation—Contreras was smarter than both sides involved. He had played one team against the other and come up with a deal above and beyond what anybody thought would be struck in Managua. The fledgling capitalist had immersed himself into a new way of life and emerged smelling like million-dollar roses.

The psychological corner from the setback in Managua turned slowly, but it did turn. On December 29, five days after leaving the scene of what the Red Sox classified as another Steinbrenner-bankroll-induced crime, Epstein started receiving some solace. It was his and Paul's twenty-ninth birthdays, a notable occasion if for nothing else than it got Theo closer to thirty and farther away from the repetitive boy-meets-general-managing-job references in the media. The daylight hours also presented another gift for the GM—the Red Sox officially signed a player away from the Yankees.

The free agent defection of relief pitcher Ramiro Mendoza from New York to Boston might not have left a ripple on Steinbrenner's usually furrowed brow, but for the Red Sox it was a step toward steering their off-season journey back on the right path. It is one of the beauties of baseball—there is no time to stew. If a hitter goes 0-for-4, there is usually another four at-bats waiting the next day. If a pitcher surrenders a confidence-crippling home run, vindication is only a five-day waiting period (at the most) away. If a team loses out on a one-of-a-kind Cuban flamethrower to its archrival, there's always another player, or two, or three just around the free agency corner. Boston might have struck out down south, but the Far East was waiting, and so was a man named Kevin Miller.

"The rivalry is something
we think about every day."

—Red Sox assistant general manager
Josh Barnes

THEY SAID IT...

Few Yankee fans knew Larry Lucchino's name before December 2002. Lucchino was the president and CEO of the Boston Red Sox, but unlike team owners and general managers, team presidents don't often get much publicity. Lucchino changed all that with two words. When he called the Yankees the "Evil Empire," he wrote his name into rivalry lore.

"STRIKING BACK AT THE EMPIRE"

from the *New York Daily News* (March 29, 2004)
by Sam Borden

FORT MYERS, FLA. THE Devil wears Paul Stuart, preferably bought on sale. He also favors khakis, French blue button-down shirts and, if nobody's looking, a smile composed of equal parts mischief and goodwill with the requisite smidgen of big-shot BS.

The Devil is from Pittsburgh, educated at Princeton and Yale and polished in Washington. He is handsome, charismatic and Catholic, which may be why, unless you're looking at him through pinstriped-colored glasses, it's difficult to see the blood-red, "B"-shaped horns that curl up next to his ears.

A lingering glance from Yankeeland, however, brings the horns into focus and turns the gospel into heresy: Salary cap? Luxury tax? Evil Empire, for heaven's sake? Who in the name of Murderers' Row is this creature?

His earthly name is Larry Lucchino, though some use a variety of other words to describe the 58-year-old president and CEO of the Boston Red Sox. His friends just call him Luke.

Lucchino's rivalry with the Yankees and George Steinbrenner has roots in the 1980s, dating back to his time with the Baltimore Orioles and continuing with the San Diego Padres. But it wasn't until last winter—when Lucchino started a verbal war after the Sox lost out on prized Cuban pitcher José Contreras—that he became a public pariah around 161st St. and River Ave.

He laughs about it now, saying his description of the Yankees as the "Evil Empire" following the Contreras battle was a "semi-serious, semi-jocular reference to *Star Wars*. We saw ourselves as the good guys, the Jedi knights, not the dark side." But Steinbrenner wasn't laughing.

"I'm the president of the Boston Red Sox," Lucchino says with only a hint of exasperation. "The mighty, mighty Red Sox. If I can't have fun with this job, it's a sin and a crime."

He claims it's always been that way. At a league meeting in the early '90s, Lucchino was one of numerous executives who hatched a plan to show up dressed in white turtlenecks and blue blazers—Steinbrenner's sartorial standard.

"I don't think George even got it," Lucchino says through a rolling chuckle. "We all got the joke—I mean, three-quarters of the room was dressed the way he was. I don't think he even noticed. But that's just George."

Lucchino is measuring his words, trying carefully to avoid saying anything inflammatory about Steinbrenner. The flames are still smoldering in Boston over the Yankees' trade for Alex Rodriguez, something the Sox had tried and failed to do weeks earlier. In the aftermath, Steinbrenner and Boston owner John Henry traded zingers before Commissioner Bud Selig ordered everyone to pipe down.

Lucchino does not want to whip up another tempest, so while he fidgets in a padded office chair and Henry stands by the window watching the Sox play the Devil Rays, the two men throw occasional darts at the Yankees that are cellophane-wrapped in humor.

Take, for example, the reaction when it is suggested that perhaps

Lucchino and Steinbrenner, who declined to comment for this article, have some similarities. Lucchino pretends to take offense, saying, "That's it, this interview is over!"

Henry, who once worked with Steinbrenner, bursts into uproarious laughter—literally pounding his chest to recover normal breathing—and then demands incredulously, "Name one!"

Well, Lucchino's mentor, legendary attorney and former Orioles owner Edward Bennett Williams, championed a militaristic lifestyle he called "contest living," which Lucchino says means reveling in life's constant competitions. With constant measuring of successes and failures, it's easy to determine if someone is a winner or a loser.

Doesn't that sound a little like Steinbrenner's "winning is second to breathing" mantra?

"Yeah, right, and I watch *Patton* every night and break furniture," Lucchino deadpans.

Then, seriously, he adds, "I suspect our differences are greater than our similarities. I'd like to think that, at least—for obvious reasons."

As the Red Sox bat outside the window, the hilarity continues inside the office. There is an air of celebrity about Lucchino and it's well-founded—he roomed with Bill Bradley at Princeton, worked on the Watergate impeachment committee with Hillary Rodham Clinton and even dated Maria Shriver before she became Mrs. Arnold Schwarzenegger.

But who would play Lucchino in a big-screen version of *The Empire vs. The Nation*? Who would play Henry? And what about Steinbrenner?

Lucchino is suddenly struck by this concept, and launches into a voice-over tone, mimicking the "A long time ago, in a galaxy far, far away" text that opens the *Star Wars* trilogy.

"Hope struggling, fighting for its independence," he whispers, "taking on the gigantic Empire that is controlling all of civilization!"

Satisfied with that prologue, he spends a few moments rubbing his hands and pondering a potential cast. "This is really interesting," he says, admitting that Sox chairman Tom Werner—who counts *The Cosby Show* and *Roseanne* among his producing credits—would probably have better ideas.

Suddenly, he slaps his hands together and spews out a few thoughts.

"Well, Andy Garcia should play Tom, right?" he says, nodding to himself. "And a young Peter O'Toole could play John. But what about George?

"I know who he'd like to play him—George C. Scott!" But the *Patton* star died in 1999, so he won't be available.

Lucchino hesitates to cast himself, but Werner—reached by phone at his California office—has no such troubles. After expressing gratitude that Lucchino tabbed Garcia to play him, Werner graciously suggests Paul Newman—specifically, Newman in *Butch Cassidy and the Sundance Kid*—to play Lucchino.

It's not too hard to imagine Newman, as Cassidy, playing Lucchino saying, "Boy, I got vision, but those guys in the Bronx wear bifocals."

Werner has slightly more trouble when it comes time to cast Steinbrenner, and asks for a reprieve to chew on the query a little longer. Two hours later, he calls back and announces the "perfect idea."

"James Gandolfini!" he crows. "Can't you see it? James Gandolfini, with dyed hair of course, as George! Perfect!"

The game is moving into the middle innings, which means Lucchino has popped out of his chair and peered out the window at least 20 times by now. If he's not doing that, he's balancing the chair on two legs or twisting his torso to look around the room. He is drawn to movement like a moth to a light, his eyes constantly finding something else to stare at, lest he miss anything.

When the conversation turns toward Selig, Lucchino actually sits still for a moment before falling into a give-and-take with Henry that would make Abbott and Costello blush. Whereas the Red Sox often criticize the Yankees' "out of this orbit" payroll, as Lucchino describes it, the Bombers have frequently targeted Boston ownership's chummy connection with the commissioner.

On various occasions, the Yankees have, either publicly or privately, questioned whether Selig has given the Sox preferential treatment. Most recently, the Yankees were upset that Selig approved Boston's trade for Scott Williamson last July despite the fact that more than the maximum $1 million in cash changed hands. A day later, Selig vetoed the Yankees' proposed deal for Aaron Boone and Gabe White, which included about $1.4 million in cash, forcing the Yanks to split the transaction into two separate deals to complete it.

There were also Yankee murmurings this winter about how long Selig allowed the Sox to negotiate with A-Rod when the Rangers were trying to deal him to Boston, as well as some grumbling when the Sox landed Cliff Floyd from the MLB-owned Expos in 2002.

But the biggest shot at the perceived coziness was the widespread speculation that Selig—who calls Lucchino "an asset to the game and a personal friend"—steered the former Sox ownership to sell the team to the Lucchino/Henry/Werner group in 2001, even though their bid for the team was reportedly lower than the top offer.

"Let me call Bud and see what he says about this," Henry cracks, rushing to Lucchino's desk and pretending to hit the top button on the speed dial. "Yes, let's get the 'red phone' working, will you?" Lucchino fires back.

Lucchino seems to take pride in making light of the rivalry, and points out several times that the Yankees may be taking things too seriously. He mentions a day last season when Yankees president Randy Levine, upon hearing that Lucchino was holding on his phone line, answered the call with, "Hello, Evil Empire," and wonders why that sort of thing doesn't happen more often.

After a moment, however, he answers his own question. His history with Steinbrenner goes all the way back to when Lucchino was general counsel for Williams' Orioles in 1979, continues through his involvement on a committee that scrutinized (and eventually increased) how much revenue Steinbrenner had to share with other teams after signing a mammoth cable deal in 1988 and snakes on through the Yanks-Padres World Series 10 years after that, and to the present day on opposite sides of the biggest rivalry in sports.

"As a practicing Catholic, we're not supposed to believe in curses," Lucchino says. "But I think there's a track record that needs to be changed."

He leans back then, stretches his arms behind his head and offers a cool, toothy smile that can only be described as . . . well, devilish.

When *Sports Illustrated* writer Steve Rushin moved from Manhattan to New England in 2003 he found himself in a strange and confusing land.

"RESIDENT ALIEN IN RED SOX NATION"

from *Sports Illustrated* (May 26, 2003)
by Steve Rushin

NORTH OF NEW HAVEN but south of Hartford, running the breadth of central Connecticut, is the border that separates Yankees and Red Sox fans. It's a baseball Mason-Dixon Line—a kind of Munson-Nixon Line, below which you love Thurman, above which you love Trot. Just last week I moved north of that line, from Manhattan to New England, which share a currency but not a clam chowder. Nor much of anything else.

And so, like all relocated sports fans, I'm now forced to learn a new set of secret handshakes: The in-jokes, the back stories, the cultural touchstones my neighbors have been accruing since birth. Like the subtle difference between NESN and Nissen. The former, I know now, is a cable carrier for the Red Sox, while the latter is a brand of bread endorsed for countless years by Ted Williams. In manifold local TV commercials,

Williams could be seen fishing with Maine sportswriter Bud Leavitt, when talk would turn, as it naturally does between two grizzled men in a boat, to the orgiastic pleasures of J. J. Nissen's Buttertop Wheat.

This is not to be confused with Big Yaz Special Fitness White Bread, whose Carl Yastrzemski–adorned wrapper enlivened supermarket shelves in the 1960s. If Ted Williams was the best thing since sliced bread, this was the best sliced bread since Ted Williams.

Or so I'm now learning. But absorbing all of this is rather like learning a foreign language. Indeed, it is a foreign language when you consider that tuna in Boston is a stereo component, while tuner in Boston is former Pats coach Bill Parcells.

And thus I'm literally illiterate in parts of New England. An enormous billboard that hangs in left-centerfield at Fenway communicates entirely in Morse code. But any Fenway fan can tell you what it says: Red Sox Nation.

A resident alien in Red Sox Nation, I have much remedial research remaining. It isn't easy to commit to memory every beer-sponsor jingle in the history of New England sports. But I must try, if I'm to hold my own at parties. The Sox have pushed both Carling ("Hey Mabel, Black Label!") and Narragansett ("Hi, Neighbor! Have a Gansett!"), and the Pats once plied fans with Schaefer, whose slogan—"The One Beer to Have When You're Having More Than One"—was a bold invitation to binge drinking.

Indeed, I was having more than one last Friday night, inside the venerable Cask 'n' Flagon, the bar behind the Green Monster at Fenway, imbibing beers near a man whose T-shirt bore the phrase, libelously inaccurate, JETER'S GAY.

"There's a whole range of hatred T-shirts for sale out there," Sox season-ticket holder Kathy Gilmour, 31, explained to me at the Cask. "That one makes YANKEES SUCK look classy." She appeared mournful for a moment and then added, apologetically, "Yay, Boston!"

John Burkett moved to Boston two seasons ago. That's when the 38-year-old Red Sox righthander—who has bowled 10 perfect games in his lifetime—learned that the lanes in New England are largely devoted to candlepin bowling. "Smaller ball, smaller pins, they leave the deadwood on the lanes," sighs Burkett. "I tried it once, two years ago, and haven't done it since. But I'd like to go again this summer."

Give him Tommy Points for perseverance. Tommy Points, awarded to hustling Celtics players by color analyst Tommy Heinsohn, are now bestowed, throughout New England, by ordinary citizens—as, say, when a friend agrees to take your shift at the Steak Loft.

The Steak Loft, in Mystic, Conn., is distinct from The Movie Loft, the late, late show airing after Red Sox games on Channel 38 in Boston. If you've never heard of that, you're doubtless ignorant of Brass Bonanza, the fight song of the Hartford Whalers, whose presence is still felt, like the phantom leg of an amputee, six years after the franchise fled for North Carolina. So you can still consult devotional Whalers websites with names like The Blowhole. And you can still hear radio reports, like this one from Hartford last week, which identified white-hot Anaheim goaltender Jean-Sebastien Giguere as "Whalers draft pick J. S. Giguere."

But then this is New England, where Whalers are heroes and heroes are grinders, which it helps to know when buying a sandwich. Indeed, all of this is vital information for anyone hoping to hold even the simplest conversation. So if you're asked to meet at the Red Seat, beyond the Pesky Pole, beneath the Jimmy Fund sign, will you know that it's in rightfield at Fenway, in the bleacher seat, painted scarlet in a sea of green, where Williams deposited the longest homer in park history, beneath a sign for the ubiquitous New England charity that honors a 12-year-old cancer patient from 1948 whose name was not Jimmy but . . . Einar?

It's all very confusing, and I often mistake the Chowder Pot (a seafood joint on I-91) with the Beanpot (a college hockey tournament in Boston). But there's so much more that confounds me. The Big Dig. Wicked pissah. Make Mine Moxie. And the grin some grownups get when they think of George Scott, late of the Red Sox, examining his bats to see which ones had taters in 'em.

A PSYCHIATRIST
WEIGHS IN ON THE RIVALRY

In a touching show of concern for the mental well-being of the baseball fans of the Northeast, the *Miami Herald* recently asked a psychiatrist to examine the Yankee–Red Sox rivalry. With tongue at least partially lodged in cheek, she offered the following diagnoses:

Yankee fans: "The narcissistic personality style is very preoccupied with their own sense of self-importance. They tend to think they are the most special. They are preoccupied with their own sense of greatness and grandeur. 'It's all about me.' Fans that like to root for the Yankees feel like *they* are winning, and can adopt the team's prestige. There is a merger of identity. The fan is no longer a postal worker; he is an exalted Yankee fan, and therefore a winner."

Red Sox fans: "So much of their life has been built around suffering and enduring hardship, but with the hope that at some point they will be rewarded. Masochistic people have a lot of sadness and deep, unconscious guilt feelings. 'Why is this happening?' They feel cursed, through no fault of their own. For masochists, situations that happen in childhood tend to repeat themselves in adulthood, which for Red Sox fans has been their life."

"I guess I hate the Yankees now."

—Pitcher Curt Schilling,
shortly after he was traded to the Red Sox.
Only weeks earlier, Schilling had told his previous
team that he would accept a trade to Boston . . .
or the Yanks.

THEY SAID IT . . .

In 1995, Major League Baseball added the wild card rule. The best team in each league that didn't win a division now would join the division winners in the playoffs. For the rivalry, the implications were obvious: The Yankees and Red Sox could meet in the post-season. That's exactly what happened in 1999, with the Yankees taking the series four games to one. When New York and Boston faced off in the playoffs again, in 2003, the series was a classic, reaching extra innings in the seventh game.

FROM "GONE SOUTH"

from the *New Yorker* (November 24, 2003)
by Roger Angell

AT TWO-THIRTY-SEVEN in the morning, Steve Wulf, a Red Sox fan who is also the executive editor of ESPN: *The Magazine,* was alone in the living room of his house in Larchmont watching on television the first game of the Sox-Athletics American League divisional playoff from Oakland. The A's had loaded the bases in the bottom of the twelfth inning when catcher Ramon Hernandez dropped down a killer bunt, to bring home the winning run. "Fuck," Wulf said to himself, turning off the set—and heard the same summarizing blurt softly repeated from above by his wife, Bambi, who had long since gone to bed, and still more faintly, by their seventeen-year-old son, Bo, on the top floor. Here was a harbinger, the first leaf of another hard Bosox autumn ahead—eleven more games of breathless and mindless, heroic and incomprehensible ball, ending in a fresh seismic shock to the Red Sox Nation, by consensus the worst one of all. I was at

Fenway Park for most of the action, but cannot offer a reliable summary —certainly not of the divisional third game, which featured a collective six errors and several baserunning grotesqueries by the visitors.

Scrolling ahead, we alight in Game III, Scene 4 of the next series, the A.L.C.S., at Fenway Park, just as Pedro Martinez lets fly that fastball aimed behind Yankee batter Karim Garcia, grazing him high on the left shoulder as he flinches away. Vintage Pedro or something, but there's no doubt about his intention. Handed a two-run, first-inning lead against Roger Clemens, Martinez has given back a run in the second, then a solo homer to Jeter, and, just now, a walk and a single and an R.B.I. double to Hideki Matsui. The Yankees lead, and will hold on to win, despite chaotic distractions. When play resumes, Garcia bangs irritably into second baseman Todd Walker at the front of a double play, and in the ensuing pushing and grabbing, Martinez glares at Jorge Posada in the Yankee dugout and aims a finger at his own forehead: you're next! After the teams change sides Manny Ramirez comes out at Clemens, bat upraised, in response to an eye-level pitch that was actually over the plate. ("If I'd wanted it near him he'd have known it," Clemens said later.) Benches and bullpens empty, old Zimmer swings at Martinez and goes down—what was that?—and will be taken away tenderly as the players at last dispense and the umps confer. Later, there's a minifracas in the Yankee bullpen, where reliever Jeff Nelson and right fielder Garcia (vaulting the fence to get there) get into a street scuffle with a Red Sox employee. This game had been billed as a classic between the best pitcher of his day and the best of his era, but turned into low farce.

The next day, a rainy Sunday, Zimmer wept and apologized, fines were assessed (fifty thousand to Martinez on down to five thousand for Zimmer), and the Red Sox management, defying a team-silence edict from the commissioner's office, staged an embarrassing press conference while attempting to put a Sox spin on the debacle. "This is a band of brothers," explained chief executive officer Larry Lucchino: Fra Pedro, whose team record had just gone to 9–15 in games he'd started against the Yankees, dismissed Zimmer's apology but offered none of his own. "It's not a good feeling to have to apologize," he said. "I don't know if you realize this." With a 14–4 record and a 3.22 E.R.A. this year, Martinez is not exactly in decline, but after this weekend you had the sense that even in the stoniest New England precincts he will no longer be defined by his numbers. In his *Globe* column, Dan Shaughnessy wrote, "Pedro was an embarrassment and a disgrace to baseball Saturday. . . . And the Sox front office enables him, just as they do Manny Ramirez. Just as they did with Roger when was here and Yaz when he was here and Ted when he was here."

Don Zimmer, who has retired, deserves at least a footnote, here at the end of one of those "Glory of Their Times" baseball careers. His fifty-five years in the game included a marriage (it's still going) at home plate at Elmira when he was a young infielder in the Eastern League; a dozen years in the majors, with five different teams; and a manager's post with four more, including the Red Sox. Just this past season, he turned up in a dazzling new baseball trivia question, in good company. Q. Name four guys who were ejected from major-league games in six different decades. A. Casey Stengel. Leo Durocher. Frank Robinson. Zimm.

It comes to a seventh game—could anyone have doubted it? This will be the twenty-sixth time the Red Sox and Yankees have faced off this year—a record for any two teams in the annals—and while there have been stretches when the latest renewal held all the drama of a couple of cellmates laying out a hand of rummy, this is another killer denouement. For all we know, it's up there with the 1978 Bucky Dent playoff and the DiMaggio late return of 1949. There's a wired, non-stop holiday din at the Stadium, which dies away only with the first intensely watched pitches. Everything matters now. Clemens is back and so is Pedro—but this Roger appears frail and thought-burdened. The No. 2 Boston batter, Todd Walker, raps a safe knock after a ten-pitch at-bat, and Nomar Garciaparra lines out hard to right. An inning later, Kevin Millar singles, and Trot Nixon, from his flat-flooded left-handed stance, delivers a businesslike homer into the stands in right—his third two-run job in the post-season. With two out, the bearded, dadlike Jason Varitek doubles into the right-field corner. Johnny Damon's grounder looks like the last out but— geez!—third baseman Enrique Wilson mishandles the ball and his throw pulls first baseman Nick Johnson off the base, as Varitek turns the corner and scores. It's 3–0, and when the teams change sides the Stadium has gone anxious and pissed-off conversational: fans up and down the stuffed tiers complaining to their seatmates or sending the bad news home on their cells, with gestures: . . . plus Wilson is in for defense, right? . . . Our only chance was stay close to goddamn Pedro.

Martinez, for his part, survives some first-inning wobbles and is soon in rhythm: the stare-in from behind his red glove, the velvety rock and turn, and the strikes arriving in clusters. After each out, he gloves the returning ball backhand, and gazes about with lidded hauteur. No one else in the world has eyes so far apart. The Yanks go down quickly again, and we're at the top of the fourth—and the startling sound, it's like a tree coming apart, of Kevin Millar's solo shot up into the upper-deck leftfield stands. Clemens, down 4–0 and almost helpless, gives up a walk and a hit-and-run single to Mueller and departs, maybe for the last time ever. A ten-year-old Yankee fan I know named Noah had by this time gone down on his knees on the concrete in front of his seat near first base, hiding his head.

There were Sox fans here, too, of course—you could see them in red-splashed knots and small parties around the Stadium, and pick up their cries. The Boston offense had been a constant for them all year, including the sixteen-hit outburst in the series-tying 9–6 win the night before. This year, the Sox set major-league records for extra bases, total bases, and slugging percentage. The Boston front office, headed by the twenty-nine-year-old G.M., Theo Epstein, had traded vigorously to build a batting order with no soft sectors or easy outs in it. Mueller, the double-grand-slam switch-hitter, was batting eighth today. For me, Kevin Millar, a free agent acquired for cash from the Marlins last winter, was the genius pick. On April 1st, the second day of the season, he contributed a sixteenth-inning game-winning home run in Tampa, and in June pinch-hit a grand slam that helped pull off a seven-run turnabout against the Brewers. With his blackened cheekbones and raunchy grin, he became the model for the Sox' newfound grunginess—dirt-stained uniforms and pine-smudged helmets, and an early-October outburst of shaved heads that transformed sluggers and pitchers and old coaches into plebes or pledges. His "Let's cowboy up!" rallying cry from the dugout and the on-deck circle caught on with DJs and schoolkids and Green Line subway riders, inundating Greater Boston in "Cowboy Up!" caps and T-shirts and fan towels and diapers and souvenir glassware. Somebody found a clip of eighteen-year-old Kevin mouthing the lyrics to Bruce Springsteen's "Born in the U.S.A." in a Beaumont, Texas, karaoke solo, which became a staple on the Fenway message board. The unimaginable had happened: the Sox were loose.

Mike Mussina, called into the crisis with Boston runners at first and third, and no outs—Clemens has just gone—went into his ceremonial low-bowing stretch and struck out Varitek, the first batter, on three pitches. Three more brought a handy 6-6-3 double play at Damon's expense. "MOOOOSE!" the bleacherites cried. It was Mussina's first relief appearance after four hundred lifetime starts, but he understood the work. Jason Giambi, struggling at .190 in the series, hit a homer barely into the centerfield seats, for a first dent in Pedro, and liking the range, did it again to the same sector in the seventh, bringing us to 4–2, with the old house roaring and rocking. The press box floor thrummed under my feet, as I had felt it do on an autumn late night or two before. Young Noah had lifted himself off the deck by this time and stood by his seat, yelling.

I had been looking about the familiar Stadium surround in valedictory fashion—the motel-landscape bullpens, the UTZ Potato Chip sign over in right—but from here to the end sat transfixed by the cascade of events, scarcely able to draw a full breath. No other sport does this, and even as we stare and cry "Can you believe this?" we forget how often it comes along, how it's built into baseball.

Joe Torre, patching in relievers after Mussina's three-inning stint, produced David Wells, whose first pitch was sailed deep into the bleachers by Sox d.h. David Ortiz. 5–2 now. Checking the video monitor, I saw Wells's top teeth hit his bottom lip with expletive. But Pedro had been long at his tasks, and when Jeter doubled to the right-field corner in the eighth and was singled home by Bernie Williams, the margin narrowed again to two, and here came manager Grady Little, out to hook his ace and pat him on the rump as he left. Little likes to stand below a pitcher, on the downslope of the mound, and here again, looking up at Pedro like a tourist at the Parthenon steps, he said a few words and walked away. This could not be. Martinez had thrown a hundred and fifteen pitches, and given up ringing hits to five of the last seven batters. A Sox-fan friend of mine, Ben, watching in his apartment on West Forty-fifth Street, had gone on his hands and knees, screaming. But Pedro stayed on: a ground-rule double by Matsui, then the dying bloopy double by Posada that landed untouched out beyond second base, for two runs and the tie.

"There's a lot of grass out there," Posada explained later. Grady Little, in his own brief post-game, said, "Pedro Martinez has been our man all year long, and in situations like that he's the one we want on the mound," which was understandable but untrue. This had been only the fifth game in thirty-one starts in which Martinez was allowed to pitch into the eighth.

It was Mariano Rivera time—the waiting Boston bad dream—and Mo, defending the tie, poised and threw, poised and threw, whisking through the ninth. There was a scary double to left by Ortiz with two gone in the tenth, but Rivera, sighing, delivered the cutter to Millar, who lined gently to Jeter. Midnight had come and gone, but the Yankees could do no better against Embree and then Timlin, the tough Sox relievers Grady Little had slighted in extremis (the two surrendered no runs at all in this series, in sixteen-plus combined innings). The top of the eleventh went away, to noisy, exhausted accompaniments; the latest Boston pitcher was Tim Wakefield, the tall knuckleballer who had embarrassed the Yankees with his spinless stuff, twice beating Mussina in close, low-scoring games. Mo was done: the balance had swung the other way. I looked at my score-card to confirm the next Yankee batter—Aaron Boone, who had come into the game as a pinch-runner in the eighth—looked back, and saw the ball and the ballgame fly away in his low, long first-pitch home run into the released and exulting and rebelieving Yankee crowds. I yelled, too, but thought, Poor Boston. My God.

News and reviews of this game poured in even while the World Series was cranking up. A woman I know, riding a late taxi downtown that night with a friend, was stopped at a light at Twenty-third Street and Seventh Avenue when she heard the earphoned, Urdu-speaking driver suddenly shouting "Aaron Boone! Aaron Boone!" A man in the Abbey Tavern, around the corner from the Piazza Navona in Rome, turned to say something consoling to a new Sox-fan acquaintance after the Boone homer—it was six-fifteen in the morning—and found the seat empty. In Gramercy Square, light from his home TV screen illuminated the patrician visage of eighty-six-year-old Gardner Botsford, a retired editor and writer who was wearing the first messaged garment of his life, a classic white cotton T-shirt, with "Yankees Suck" in 75-point blue capitals. Botsford is no Red Sox fan, but his shirt, the gift of a friend just back from Fenway Park, summed up his convictions: Voltaire could not have put it better. When Boone had done his deed, Botsford took off the shirt and went upstairs. "Didn't work," he said to the silent form across the bed. Eighteen-year-old Pat Sviokla had asked a bunch of friends and classmates over to watch the game at his house in Newton, outside Boston, but when Boone's shot went out the party disappeared. "Nobody said a word," Pat's mother, Eileen, said later. "Six or seven of them going out the door, single file. They looked like P.O.W.s." Bill Buckner letting the ground ball go through his legs at Shea Stadium had happened in 1986, when these young men were one-year-olds. Bucky Fucking Dent, Joe Morgan, Jim Willoughby taken out, and Throw the ball in, Johnny, was stuff their fathers and grandfathers talked about. Now they belonged.

Much of the buzz collected around Grady Little. "Grady *Sutton* is a better manager than Grady Little" was the gist and entire content of a note I had from an unknown correspondent who'd somehow realized that I would recognize Grady Sutton as the moonfaced ninny in the old W. C. Fields flicks. "Grady Little is the George Bush of managers," a friend across the hall from me in my office came by to announce. "Letting Pedro stay in is like George Bush staring into Putin's soul."

Grady Little has been let go, and the Red Sox have offered waivers on Manny Ramirez, hoping to trade him and his twenty-million-dollar-a-year-contract for new pitching. If you want to tap into the Sox fans' psyche now, you have to consult a new Web site, www.redsoxhaiku.com, where it comes in eloquent triplets:

> *Bright leaves falling. Clear*
> *Blue sky. Frost at dawn. Autumn.*
> *Red Sox lose again.*
> *Or:*
> *Buckner or Little*
> *It doesn't really matter*
> *Someone will fuck up*

And:
Hey, wait till next year:
Every eighty-six years
Like clockwork. Go Sox.

Joe Torre, who called the Red Sox the best team his Yankees had faced during his eight-year tenure as manager, was short a haiku by a beat or two in the interview room just before that seventh game, but also on target: "This really is fun, but you don't know it's fun until it's over."

"We didn't want to be the team
that let the Red Sox go to the World Series"

—Yankee shortstop Derek Jeter,
shortly after Aaron Boone's home run downed Boston
in game seven of the 2003 American League Championship Series

THEY SAID IT...

Graig Nettles played his last game for the Yankees in 1983. Goose Gossage left the Yankees in 1983 as well, though he returned briefly in 1989. But when Red Sox players Pedro Martinez and Manny Ramirez touched off an on-field fight between New York and Boston during game three of the 2003 American League Championship Series, Nettles and Gossage were Yankees once again.

"GOOSE, NETTLES SEEING RED OVER SHENANIGANS BY SOX"

from the *Bergen County Record* (October 14, 2003)
by Bob Klapisch

BOSTON—IT'S BEEN a quarter-century since Goose Gossage and Graig Nettles fought in the Yankees-Red Sox wars but the years haven't softened their animosity toward the Fenway army. Ask Goose and Puff about Pedro Martinez and Manny Ramirez, and you might as well be talking about Carlton Fisk and Bill Lee.

"I was watching [Game 3] lying in my bed, and when Ramirez starts walking to the mound with a bat in his hand, I jumped up and started screaming at the TV set, 'Kill that [expletive],'" Gossage said before Monday night's 3–2 Red Sox win.

"Manny Ramirez is a [coward]. I hope he reads that. If he pulled that stuff in the old days, he would've gotten back in the box and I guarantee you he would've had the next pitch in his earlobe. The guy is a one-dimensional player. He can hit—a little. But he can't even hit when it counts."

Nettles went even further in his indictment of the Sox' slugger, flatly calling him "a dog . . . who does nothing but loaf. Ramirez loafs on the bases, in the field, he loafs all the time. For all the money he makes, he should buy a book about how the game is played.

"To be honest, I hope the Yankees kill the Red Sox, embarrass them, 18–0. I hope I never have to watch Ramirez play again. That's what a dog he is."

Nettles, speaking from his home in Knoxville, Tenn., and Gossage, speaking by cellphone while driving to his house in Colorado Springs, obviously have no problem conjuring up the old hate toward the Red Sox. To them, Martinez and Ramirez are Fisk and Lee: different faces, different names, but still the enemy.

Yet, Goose and Nettles both say the Yankees-Sox war is different today—softer, with less score-settling. Even after watching Martinez throw at Karim Garcia's head, and after Ramirez challenged Roger Clemens over a relatively benign fastball, the elder Yankees say this is Rivalry-Lite.

The incidents did, indeed, make for compelling TV drama, but the benches-clearing episode—during which Martinez flung Don Zimmer to the ground—would been handled differently in the seventies.

"I can't believe no one in the bullpen went after Martinez," Gossage said. "If it was me, I would've gone right for him. We would've finished it right there. That skinny little [expletive]. There's no question he threw right at Garcia's head. That's totally gutless. It's too bad he doesn't have to hit, because I guarantee you he wouldn't be throwing at hitters like that."

Gossage was so worked up that five minutes after hanging up, he called back. He wasn't finished.

"Those guys think they can intimidate the Yankees? [Bleep] them. No one does that," Goose said. "All they did was wake the Yankees up."

"We would've chased Pedro right into the stands," Nettles said in agreement. "There's no way we would've been milling around like that. Garcia should've been the first one to go after Pedro. That's how you know the game has changed today. There's no way you let a 72-year-old man do your dirty work for you."

Goose has a particular dislike for Ramirez, he said, not just because he works for the Red Sox, but because he represents all that's wrong with today's insolent hitter.

Goose believes Ramirez is spoiled and pampered by umpires, over-protective of the inside corner, and ready to fight at the slightest imagined provocation, and that the Sox slugger would've been pummeled by the 1970s Yankees had he approached any of their pitchers with a bat.

"You want to bring a bat to the mound? Let him try," Gossage said. "Ramirez might've gotten one of us, but he wouldn't have gotten all 10. You wouldn't have seen him the rest of the series, I promise you, because we would've put him in the hospital.

"I saw what he did [in Game 5 of the ALDS against Oakland], pointing into the dugout after he hit a home run. Someone should've put him right on his butt for that. That made me sick. He hardly ever hits when it counts, and he has the [guts] to do that? Give me a break."

To be fair, Gossage does admire a few of the Red Sox' players. He cited Jason Varitek as an example of "a real hard-nosed ballplayer, someone who could've played on our teams, for sure."

And Nettles was surprisingly benevolent toward Martinez, whom he said "had no other choice" but to force Zimmer to the ground as the coach charged him.

"I really don't blame Pedro for that," Nettles said. "It was like, 'Get away from me.' But once [the Yankees] saw Zim on the ground, one of them or 20 of them should've gone right after Pedro."

But that's as far as either Yankee goes in the pursuit of objectivity. Gossage said Ramirez still hasn't paid for his crime—"He should've been thrown out of the game right on the spot"—and that punishing the slugger would send a message throughout baseball.

But Goose doubts it's going to happen.

"Nah, the game has changed too much for that," the former closer said. "All the hitters today want fastballs down the middle. They don't know the difference between a fastball up and in and one that's meant for their head.

"They want it all their way, and they're getting it because it's the pitchers who are afraid. They're all the same: Ramirez, [Sammy] Sosa, they're all [cowards]."

As for Red Sox-Yankee battle, Gossage has no doubt the Yankees will prevail. Nettles agrees, saying Boston's destiny was decided a quarter-century ago.

"[Bill] Lee said [in 1975] that the Yankees fought like a bunch of Times Square hookers, that we used our purses and long fingernails," Nettles said. "We got him the next year" in a bench-clearing brawl that started when Lou Piniella collided with Fisk at home.

"Lee ended up with a broken shoulder and two black eyes," Nettles said with a laugh. "He must've run into some pretty tough hookers."

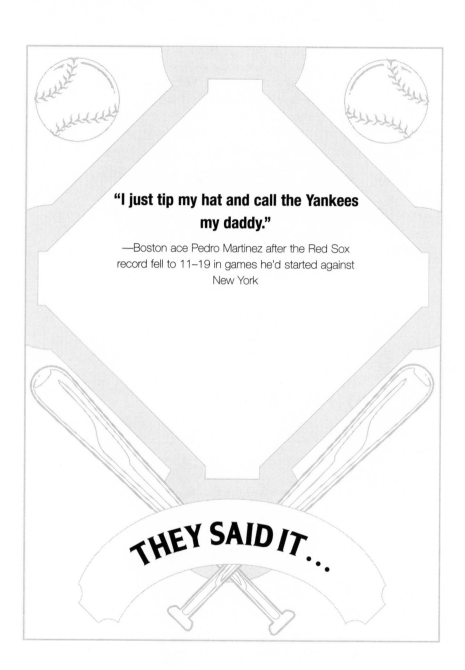

"I just tip my hat and call the Yankees my daddy."

—Boston ace Pedro Martinez after the Red Sox record fell to 11–19 in games he'd started against New York

THEY SAID IT...

The Yankees led the 2003 American League Championship Series three games to two heading into game six. All New York had to do was take one of the remaining two games in Yankee Stadium and they would earn a ticket to the World Series. But Boston rallied to even the ALCS at three games apiece, and led late in game seven as well. What happened next is told in this parody of the famous nineteenth-century baseball poem "Casey at the Bat."

"GROUND HOG DAY, 2003"

[November 26, 2003]
by Paul Thomas Hunt

The outlook wasn't brilliant when the Red Sox went to work;
the Yankees led three games to two, with the last games in New York.
We faced Pettitte and Roger Clemens, on his last tour around the circuit,
and before we could pitch Pedro we had to send out Johnny Burkett.

The newcomers to Red Sox Nation were amazed at our deep despair.
"This team is different from the past, there's a new feeling in the air."
But the faithful know that with the Sox there's never another way,
The names and faces may be new but in the end it's Ground Hog Day.

Game Six started as expected, though Torre showed Pettitte the door,
Burkett was gone, the crowd was loud, and the Sox trailed 6-4.
But Nomar had surprised us by snapping out of his postseason woe,

and he scored a fifth run for the Sox on a triple and a wild throw.
Manny preceded Ortiz and the Sox finally "moved the line,"
And when Trot's homer reached the upper deck, the Sox took it 6–9.
It was the highlight of the season, we would later learn,
But at that moment all of us to Game 7 had to turn.

Upon followers of the team did a curious feeling fall;
a win would finally Reverse the Curse, but a loss would be the worst of all.
There was still time to suspend belief, not watch or other things,
That protected us for all these years when the Sox didn't get their rings.

But Trot crushed an early homer, to the wonderment of all.
And Millar, who to date had not done much, put a charge into a Clemens ball.
Pedro silenced the hecklers by twirling inning after inning,
And much to the surprise of Yankee fans, the Sox indeed were winning.

The game continued with just a blip or two when Giambi hit a couple late,
But Pedro glared, struck Soriano out, and we headed to inning eight.
When Ortiz blasted a homer to begin that fateful frame,
Even those of us who expect the worst began to believe this was the game.

Though this was happening in New York, where even safer games have gone awry,
One look along the Yankee bench showed they knew their end was nigh.
A three-run lead into the eighth should prove to be sufficient,
For weeks Timlin and Williamson had proved more than just efficient.

Across beautiful New England, from hill to sea, eyes watched the screen,
Here we were, on all new ground, which none of our fathers had ever seen.
Six outs to go with a 3-run lead, we thought, is good enough for me,
They'll have 26 rings to polish but we'll savor this one memory.

Then after some commercials that we nervously waited through,
a sight which will live in infamy appeared for us to view,

A mistake, we knew, without a doubt, a sure path to a loss,
It was clear to even casual viewers, all but the Red Sox boss.

They'll blow it now, they surely will, though it seemed the past was behind us,
But that voice we hear inside our heads returned then to remind us.
It pounded through our heads, and we recoiled from the sound;
for Pedro, stubborn Pedro, was advancing to the mound.

The rest of the game belonged to the Yankees for to win is their destiny,
Much of what happened after that had to be relayed to me.
I watched until Jeter crushed a ball, surely that would be it for our proud starter,
But Grady never moved a muscle and my heart just beat harder and harder.

I missed the late innings, or most of them, just like in '86,
I paced around in the next room wondering why it always comes to this.
It's just a game, players come and go, it's a bat and a ball and a glove,
But why, oh why, do the Red Sox have to break the hearts of the ones who love?

I guess there are New York fans who'll remember every play as thrilling,
But Stephen King, in all his books, never wrote a script so chilling.
Sure, somewhere in this favored land the sun is shining bright.
The band is playing somewhere, and somewhere hearts are light.
And somewhere men are laughing, and little children shout, but there is no joy in Boston:
Grady didn't take Pedro out.

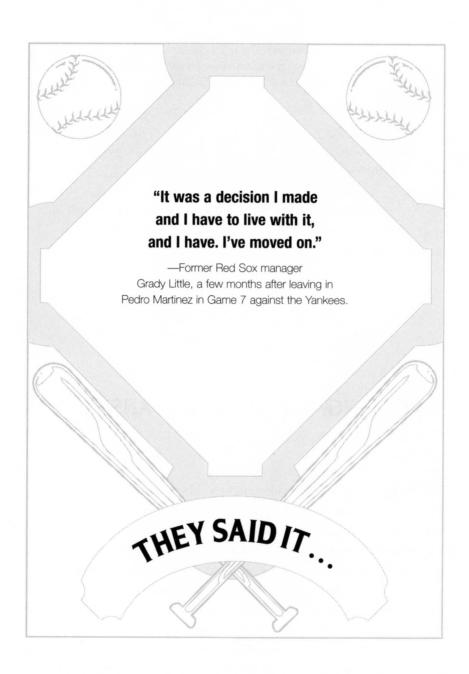

"It was a decision I made
and I have to live with it,
and I have. I've moved on."

—Former Red Sox manager
Grady Little, a few months after leaving in
Pedro Martinez in Game 7 against the Yankees.

THEY SAID IT...

Boston's dramatic loss to the Yankees in game seven of the American League Championship Series taught a new generation of Red Sox fans that pulling for New England's team isn't always easy.

"DROOPING? NOT TRUE SOX FANS"

from the *Deseret Morning News*
by Tad Walch

PROVO—MY 11-YEAR-old daughter sat on my lap for an hour Thursday night and wept after Aaron Boone broke her heart.

I hope no man ever does this to her again.

She's too young for unrequited love, but that's what the Boston Red Sox have given her at this tender age. She's fallen for them, and they won't return her devotion. Boone's sudden, crushing home run in extra innings sent the New York Yankees—yawn—back to the World Series and sent my sweet child to bed with tear-stained cheeks.

At 11, we still believe the world was made for us, that maybe it even revolves around us and will provide everything we need. Anything is possible and even probable.

It's also the age, however, of those first painful realizations that maybe it's not so, that maybe the world is a cruel place where faith and love of family and friends is all that can be relied upon and that anguish stalks us every day.

That dark thought comes with membership in Red Sox Nation. Boone's awful blow baptized my daughter, provided the sorrow necessary for a rite of passage of a real Sox fan. The scarlet B is now burned into her bosom.

There has been much talk of the Curse of the Bambino in our home the past fortnight, about how the sale of Babe Ruth to the Yankees—after he hit and pitched the Sox to a World Series championship in 1918— placed a whammy on the Olde Towne Team.

The 85-year hex quickly gained credence in the minds of our children, a fact I didn't fully realize until the Sox took a 4–0 lead in Game 7. As his dad and older sister jumped about the living room celebrating Kevin Millar's home run, 7-year-old Cooper smiled and declared, "The curse has been lifted!"

We plan lessons over dinner on how not to tempt the ghosts of Ruth, Gehrig, Mantle and DiMaggio.

But for a moment, I believed the boy. Somehow, the Curse had been lifted. I would be relieved of the burden of my own unrequited love, which was born eight months after I was, when my dad sat me on his lap to watch Game 7 of the 1967 World Series and see the Curse end after a short 49 years.

Hah.

The Curse marched relentlessly on, through my own 11-year-old tears when Yankees shortstop Bucky Dent hit his pop fly home run to beat the Sox in the epic one-game playoff in 1978. Through the unthinkable collapse in the 1986 World Series when the ball dribbled through Billy Buckner's wobbly knees. And through the 17 years since, during which I married a woman who bravely endures my obsession.

Our four children would be born to baseball famine, the second child a girl named Boston.

We didn't name her for the Red Sox. Don't even go there. It was my deep love for my childhood in the Boston area that prompted the idea.

Boston loves her name, and fully understands its origins, but I'm afraid it has also imbued her with a need to love all things Bostonian, maybe especially the Sox. Last night, with seeming randomness (and the Red Sox still ahead), she said, "Babe Ruth wore my name on his uniform!" An hour or two later, the Greek tragedy having repeated itself once more, she cried. I had tried to prepare her for this. I had locked up my own heart until the Sox won Game 1 in Yankee Stadium. They made me believe once again, and again they dumped me, this time with my daughter.

It doesn't matter. The Red Sox will always be No. 1 in the hearts of Boston—the city and the girl. We sat on her bed last night and determined next season could indeed be the year. Then I told her she could stay up and read but, satisfied, she sighed and said she would go to sleep.

This morning, Boston woke up with puffy eyes, but her bright smile had been restored.

My own broken heart immediately began to heal.

THE CLERGY WEIGHS IN ON AARON BOONE'S HOMER

Aaron Boone homered in the 11th inning of the seventh game of the 2003 American League Championship to sent the Red Sox home disappointed once again. Religious leaders in the Northeast weren't buying the talk of a Red Sox curse, but they did have a few things to say on the matter . . .

"As a Jew, being a Red Sox fan makes perfect sense. You don't expect the world to be redeemed in your lifetime."
—Rabbi Jeffrey Sirkman, Larchmont, New York

"It's an Old Testament lesson about Job. [God] is teaching us about patience . . . [But as for the Yankees] God would want them to share."
—Reverend Chris Mickey, St. William's Church, Dorchester, Massachusetts.

—as reported in the *Boston Globe*

There's always a goat. Sometimes it's the pitcher who gives up the key hit, sometimes it's the fielder who makes the big error. When a team loses an important game in dramatic fashion, one man always shoulders more than his share of the blame. In game seven of the 2003 American League Championship Series, that man was the manager. The Red Sox had the lead in the eighth inning of that decisive game, but Boston manager Grady Little stayed with starter Pedro Martinez a little too long, and New York scored the tying run. The Yankees won it in the 11th on Aaron Boone's home run. Little was fired not long after the game.

"GRADY LITTLE IS RELIEVED"

from *GQ* (April 2004)
by Peter Richmond

GRADY LITTLE HAS ALREADY made up his mind. Watch the videotape: Jogging toward the pitcher's mound in Yankee Stadium, hands jammed in his jacket pockets, he moves purposefully, almost impatiently, as if he's about to take care of a minor chore.

At the mound is Pedro Martinez, the best player Little has ever managed. Martinez is five outs from taking the Boston Red Sox to the World Series. But he has thrown a lot of pitches, and the Yankees have started to hit him hard. There's one Yankee runner on and one out. It's the bottom of the eighth inning, and though the Red Sox still lead by two runs, the sense of an impending Boston derailment has enlivened the crowd in the Bronx.

Pedro thinks Grady has come to take him out. You can see it on the tape: A moment after Little appears on the mound, Martinez's eyes narrow, shoot a glare at his manager: Don't even think about it.

Little's already thought about it.

"Can you get this done?" Little asks, already knowing the answer.

"Yeah," Martinez answers. "Let's do it."

The manager slaps his pitcher on the shoulder and turns and trots back to the dugout. It all takes ten seconds. It's 11:01 P.M. on October 16, 2003.

You remember what happens next.

QUESTION, DEMOCRATIC PRESIDENTIAL DEBATE, BOSTON, 2003: You're the manager of the Boston Red Sox. Do you make an executive decision and take him out? Or do you listen to your star and let him . . . finish that job?

JOHN KERRY: *[laughs]* Like most of you here, I was throwing things at the television set, screaming at Grady Little, "Get him out of there! Get him out of there!" And regrettably, he didn't.

Grady little gets letters.

"I don't open some of them," he says.

That's wise. What with anthrax and all.

"The stuff I get is worse than anthrax," Little says, and he smiles. His drawl is Texan and slow, as if there were a couple of pebbles stuck beneath his lower lip where the chewing tobacco should be, and where the chewing tobacco usually is. His white-gray hair is newly trimmed into an emperor's cut. His round, 53-year-old face is burnished from decades of working outdoors.

"The best letter was one with no return address," he says. "I opened it, and there were World Series tickets for the games we didn't get to play, and a note. It wasn't signed or anything. It just said, 'Thanks, Grady.'"

Little laughs. Three months have passed since the Decision, the one that cost him his Red Sox job and etched his name into baseball history, for none of the reasons he'd hoped for. He is driving through the streets of Pinehurst, North Carolina, at the wheel of a Cadillac CTS, extolling the virtues of his adopted hometown. Little loves Pinehurst. He explains that the town was settled a century ago by some New Englanders driving south to Florida, fleeing the winters, only they never got farther than Pinehurst, because Pinehurst was everything they were looking for in a place to escape New England. Little let his observation come and go, without irony. He had other things on his mind. Today he is wondering whether to take a position with the Chicago Cubs. It is not the ideal job, but it will keep him in the game.

We are en route to Grady's golf club. Little loves golf, and is known to be a bit of a prankster on the course. He likes to do things like scatter marshmallows to confuse opponents searching for their golf balls. One time he pulled a .22 pistol and shot his brother's ball. When we play, Little pulls out a gag twelve-inch tee, and tells some Michael Jackson jokes.

I figure our round of golf is not the time to ask him what I've come to ask him. I've driven 700 miles to find out how the Decision has affected Grady Little.

I wait until we're in the parking lot.

"Do I look like I'm affected?" Little says, hefting his bag into the back of the car.

No, I admit, he doesn't.

Then he says, "Do I sound like I'm affected?"

No, I admit, he doesn't.

"That must be because I'm not," he says. Then he laughs and says again, "That must be because I'm not."

Fate is funny. If a flare over second base had landed in a glove, Grady Little would still be the manager of the Red Sox. Of course, he'd still be farming cotton in Texas if the sudden storm back in '77 hadn't blown the blossoms off a good part of his crop and doomed his season.

The storm steered Little back to baseball. His playing career as a catcher had topped out at Double A, but he figured he could be a manager. His dad, Bill, had been a catcher who made it as high as Triple A in Indianapolis before breaking his ankle. When Grady was a kid, his dad would play both ends of semipro doubleheaders.

Grady liked managing in the minors as much as he liked farming. In both, you were pretty much your own man. Over the course of sixteen years, Grady's teams won in Kinston, North Carolina, where none of his starting pitchers spoke English; Hagerstown, Maryland, where the team bus once tipped onto its side during a road trip; Greenville, South Carolina, where Little's team put together the first hundred-victory season in the hundred-year history of the Southern League; and Durham, North Carolina, where Ron Shelton hired him to be the baseball adviser for the movie *Bull Durham*. Little's name is in the credits.

In 1997, Grady's friend Jimy Williams was hired to manage the Red Sox and brought in Little as a bench coach. Three years later, Little went to Cleveland to sit on Charlie Manuel's bench, but in 2002 the Red Sox were sold, and during spring training that year, the new owners fired manager Joe Kerrigan and hired Little to his first big-league managing job. He was 52.

In Boston, Little inherited two things: a talented team and a curse, which is really nothing but the city's pathological obsession with its ongoing baseball misfortune. Little didn't believe in curses, and in his first year, his Red Sox won ninety-three games. Still, they did not make the playoffs, and the new ownership recast the team's front office. They hired Theo Epstein, a 28-year-old Yale grad and an acolyte of Oakland's Billy Beane, the guru of quantum baseball—the school that holds that statistics, not instincts, should determine personnel moves. Boston also brought aboard Bill James, a famous statistician who'd never spent a day inside the game.

Epstein and James's approach to baseball did not mesh with Little's reliance on hunches—"educated hunches," he calls them. Unlike his bosses, Little did not think about how his left-handed pinch hitter fared in day games on turf.

At times during the season, Little was presented statistical research to disseminate among his staff prior to series against certain teams. On occasion it wasn't disseminated. Little apparently didn't think highly enough of these front-office strategies to employ them in games. When the subject of Bill James came up, Grady couldn't remember his name.

In particular, Little disagreed with Epstein and James's idea that a team's best reliever should be used when he is most needed, not necessarily in the ninth inning. Teams have typically relied on a single reliever to close out games for nearly two decades now. But no one among the roster of relievers Grady was presented with emerged, and almost from its inception, the "bullpen by committee" was a disaster. No pitcher was more affected by this than Martinez, who'd repeatedly leave a game with a lead only to watch a win evaporate.

"It got to be so much of a joke," Little recalls. "I can remember asking [coach] Jerry Narron on one flight after a game—it was June and Pedro's record was, like, 4 and 1 because he had so many no-decisions—'You think anyone's ever won the Cy Young with a record of 7 and 3?' Because that's the way a lot of those games were going. He'd pitch his heart out for a length of time, then we had to get him out, then the lead would disappear."

Little says he finally confronted Epstein about the bullpen situation in June.

"One night we came into that clubhouse, and I said, 'Theo, Kim'—Byung-Hyun Kim, the former Diamondback closer who'd been acquired to start for Boston—'is not going to start for us anymore. He's gonna be our closer.' What are they gonna say? I didn't have a contract for the following year. If they come in and say, 'We'll pick up both your options for the next two years,' then it's a different story. I'll do whatever they want me to do. That's simple. That's arithmetic there. If they had wanted to extend me, they would have done it in spring training. So I've got this in the back of my mind all year long. But I don't let it bother me. I didn't care."

The absence of any backing from his employers only further fueled Little's determination to run the team his own way. His educated hunches coaxed fourteen wins out of Martinez. He stood up to his gifted, if petulant, left fielder, Manny Ramirez, benching him after a game in which Ramirez refused to pinch-hit—sparking a September full of comeback victories and an inspiring five-game triumph over Oakland in the first round of the playoffs, setting up a showdown with the Yankees.

When you first walk into Grady Little's house, there's no sign of baseball. The television is tuned to the Country Music Television network, and the artwork depicts fox hunts. You have to walk down a hallway to a room in back to see all his baseball stuff. There, on one wall, is a framed scorecard from a one-hitter Pedro Martinez pitched against the Yankees in 1999. "One of the greatest games I ever saw pitched," Little says. On another wall is an autographed photo of Martinez. Says Little: "I can't imagine any pitcher being more prepared, a better competitor or having as much talent as he has."

But it only took a few seconds for Pedro Martinez to unravel Grady Little's life. After Little left the mound that October night, Hideki Matsui lined a ground-rule double down the right-field line, and Bernie Williams stopped at third. Martinez worked the count to two balls and two strikes to Jorge Posada, then threw a 96 mph fastball down and in. Posada fisted it, inside out. The ball flared toward center field, dying even as it left the bat, but fell in the Bermuda-grass triangle in short center field. Two runs scored, game tied.

Little finally pulled Martinez, but everyone in Boston knew the doom that awaited. Three innings later, the Yankees won the game, 6-5, on an Aaron Boone home run off Tim Wakefield.

Little drove to North Carolina before the Red Sox could fire him in person, so they did it by phone. Back in Boston, principal owner John Henry said the decision to terminate Little wasn't based on the Decision. Nobody believed him.

"That one decision that I made there on that pitcher in the seventh game of the ALCS this year?" Grady says. We are sitting in a Pinehurst coffee shop. A girl in a college sweatshirt is filling our coffee cups.

"Time after time after time this year, when this kid got into a jam in an inning where it's getting close to the end of his outing, he's the one we left in there to get out of the jam that inning. Then we'd take him out of the game. We'd done it through the year, over and over and over. We got a bad result this time. Most of the time, we got good results. And he'd have gotten it done. What beat him was the bloop hit by Posada."

But if you'd brought in a reliever after Williams's single—

"And take Pedro Martinez out of the game?"—he jumps in—"who

threw the highest-velocity pitch he threw the whole game on the last pitch he threw?"

Grady looks disgusted for the first and only time all day.

"Nobody knows any better than the manager in the dugout," he says. "Nobody knows. Nobody else can see what's going on in that dugout or that clubhouse but you. Everybody's got his opinions. Opinions are great. You don't have to be accountable for them. If someone has no responsibility for the outcome of anything, inevitably he's going to have all the answers. But it's always afterward."

Little still didn't believe in curses. But he admits that during the Yankees series, some Sox players confessed that during the games, they were worrying about making mistakes, lest the hysteria brand them for posterity.

"I had players come and tell me that when they're on the field they're thinking about those ghosts," Little says. "They think about Bill Buckner—and not wanting to be a Bill Buckner. And if I got a couple of players come tell me that face-to-face, then I know in my heart I got twenty thinking that. It's just a couple of them got the balls enough to say it out loud."

Grady suspected that no player was going to get the blame for this one: not Martinez, not Tim Wakefield.

"I knew that if we didn't win the World Series this year," he says, "somebody was gonna be the goat."

The new Red Sox manager is Terry Francona, whose major league managing experience is limited to four years in Philadelphia with the Phillies, where his winning percentage was .440, the worst four-year managing record in Philadelphia since the late 1930s. In four years managing in the minors, Francona finished first once. But last year he was a bench coach in Oakland, where he worked for Billy Beane.

"I think they want someone they can control," says Grady's ex-coach Mike Cubbage. "I think there's going to be an NFL-type game plan for each and every game the Red Sox play from here on out. I think they're going to have the manager manage on a nightly basis to execute the game plan."

Francona will face more hurdles than Little did. This winter the Red Sox tried to acquire Alex Rodriguez, the best player in baseball, and unload perennial stud Nomar Garciaparra—and failed on both counts. Then the Yankees snatched Rodriguez for themselves, giving them the most intimidating batting lineup the game has seen in three-quarters of a century. Meantime, Boston first baseman Kevin Millar said he'd rather play with Rodriguez, which was taken as a rip of Nomar. It was the kind of controversy the team never faced under Grady, and Nomar immediately phoned Grady for advice, even though he was no longer the manager.

Grady wouldn't tell me what he told Nomar. Even now, he takes the high road when discussing the 2004 Red Sox.

"If Boston plays 170 or better games next year, then maybe the result of their decision was the right one," he says, referring to the number of games his team played, regular season and playoffs combined. "But they better not forget they have to play those games with some human bodies. And they have to play 170 or better. And that's a lot of games."

Grady wishes Francona the best.

"I just hope," he says, "he knows what he's getting into."

A few days later, it is officially announced that Grady has been hired to assist the general manager of the Chicago Cubs, where he'll wear a blazer in a Wrigley Field skybox. The arrangement allows him to accept another managing job should one come up later in the season. Every time the phone rings, Little will be hoping it's someone offering him a second chance.

He knows he'll have to get back there, to another October night, and possibly beyond. Only a World Series will exorcise the demons he inherited in Boston and put an end to questions about the Decision.

Over the past few months, Little tells me, he's thought a lot about something his dad used to say not just about baseball but about life in general:

No one ever knows who finished in second place.

"This experience I've had has about halfway proven my dad to be a liar," Grady Little says. "Sometimes people do remember who comes in second."

"So what if it's the Yankees?
Who are they anyway?"

—Boston pitcher Tim Wakefield in May 1998.
New York would finish that season with a record of 114–48,
a full 22 games ahead of second-place Boston.
Five years later, Wakefield would surrender the home run to Aaron Boone
that sent the Yankees to the World Series and sent the Red Sox home
for the winter.

THEY SAID IT…

The Red Sox came up one run short of toppling the Yanks in the 2003 American League Championship Series. To put them over the top, they set their sights on acquiring Alex Rodriguez, the reigning American League MVP. But somehow A-Rod wound up in New York instead.

"HELLO, NEW YORK"

from *Sports Illustrated* (February 23, 2004)
by Tom Verducci

BY AGREEING TO MOVE to third base, Alex Rodriguez got out of Texas and into pinstripes as the Yankees pulled off another blockbuster

Once upon a time, Mrs. O'Leary left a lantern too close to her cow, five burglars broke into a Watergate office, and Aaron Boone decided to play a little pickup basketball. History, Voltaire observed, is little else than a picture of human crimes and misfortunes. Over the coming years the exact details are to be revealed as to how the misfortune of Boone, the New York Yankees third baseman who blew out his left knee in a Jan. 16 hoops dalliance, will alter baseball history, especially the raging neo-Peloponnesian War between the Yankees and the Boston Red Sox. But altered it shall be.

When Boone went down, the Yankees needed a third baseman, and when the Yankees needed a third baseman, Texas Rangers shortstop Alex Rodriguez reconsidered his objection to playing third base. And when

Rodriguez reconsidered, the Yankees succeeded in less than 72 hours where the Red Sox had failed for five constipated weeks earlier this winter, swinging an unprecedented trade over the weekend for a reigning MVP who also is the game's best all-around player.

Boone, mind you, is the same chap who four months ago hit the 11th-inning home run that ended Game 7 of the American League Championship Series and Boston's season. Now this A-Rod business. In the annals of New England oral history he will forever be referred to as Aaron Bleeping Boone. "I only wish to God," one Red Sox official bemoaned after the trade, "that Aaron Boone never picked up a basketball."

With Rodriguez, the Yankees become the Beatles of baseball, such is their talent and global star power. They open camp this week with 17 All-Stars, including seven regulars who have won an MVP award or finished among the top seven in the voting, and four of the eight players in baseball history who signed a contract worth more than $100 million (Rodriguez, Derek Jeter, Jason Giambi and Kevin Brown). The teams chasing this club can only hope that the mass of New York's stars is so great that it collapses inward like a black hole.

How, for instance, will Rodriguez, 28, and Jeter, 29, coexist? Both are signed through 2009 with no-trade clauses; the superior defender of the two, Rodriguez, will play out of position; and their friendship has been strained since A-Rod's critical comments about Jeter in an '01 magazine interview. "Everybody knows their best lineup would be A-Rod at short and Jeter at second," one American League manager says, "but it won't happen because it's Jeter's team."

As of Sunday night Rodriguez had not spoken to Jeter about the trade, but as for deferring to the Yankees shortstop and moving to third base, A-Rod says, "I don't see it as a big deal at all. I look at it as a new challenge. I won two Gold Gloves and an MVP at shortstop. I thought I achieved just about everything personally at shortstop. Now it's time to win. I've always thought of myself as a team player. Playing third base is the ultimate team move."

Never before have George Steinbrenner's Yankees been more befitting of Fitzgerald's take on the very rich: "They are different from you and me." With the Rodriguez trade the other 29 franchises look on New York with further contempt not only because it makes the Yankees richer, but also because they were lucky. A-Rod fell into their lap less than a week before spring training started, and they were able to negotiate such a relatively small financial obligation to Rodriguez ($16 million annual average) that they will pay him less than Jeter and Giambi, less than what the Red Sox will pay Manny Ramirez and Pedro Martinez, and less than what the Houston Astros pay 35-year-old first baseman Jeff Bagwell.

What's more, Rodriguez will add only $2.4 million to New York's 2004 payroll as it stood before Boone played basketball. While the Yankees will pay Rodriguez $15 million this year, they got off the hook for the combined $12.6 million they would have owed Boone ($5 million, assuming he gets only termination pay for violating his contract's no-basketball clause); failed third base prospect Drew Henson ($2.2 million), who quit to pursue an NFL career; and second baseman Alfonso Soriano ($5.4 million), who was sent to Texas with a minor leaguer to be named in the Rodriguez deal. The Rangers are to choose from a list of five prospects before March 31.

Texas agreed to pay $67 million of the $179 million (over seven years) left on Rodriguez's original record-busting $252 million, 10-year contract. The trade still lightened the Rangers' long-term obligations by about $120 million (including interest), freeing them to save or spend the savings as they rebuild what has been a last-place team for four years running. For instance, Texas immediately worked to finalize a five-year extension for third baseman Hank Blalock, a commitment that one team source said would not have been possible without the A-Rod deal.

The Rangers' $67 million sweetener did, however, give some pause to commissioner Bud Selig, who, according to one major league source, heard complaints from owners such as the Baltimore Orioles' Peter Angelos. Selig had pushed hard to accommodate Rodriguez's trade to Boston so the game's best player could get to a competitive, high-visibility franchise. He fretted more about Rodriguez as a Yankee, one source in the commissioner's office said, because New York's payroll of about $190 million figures to be about $70 million ahead of the rest of the field, led by Boston. Selig, though, approved the trade on Monday after almost three days of study.

Boston could have had Rodriguez in December for Ramirez, but after trying to restructure A-Rod's contract, it killed the deal because of a $15 million difference between what it was willing to pay Rodriguez and what the union would allow in the devaluation of A-Rod's contract. When the Red Sox heard late last week that New York was engaged in talks with Texas about Rodriguez, they made a futile attempt to get back in the hunt, according to two sources involved in the negotiations. "Too little, too late," one source said.

With the trade Texas owner Tom Hicks made the figurative admission that his business plan to build a winning team around Rodriguez was a colossal failure. A-Rod missed only one game over three years in Texas while hitting .305 with 156 home runs and 395 RBIs, but other investments, such as $65 million over five years for pitcher Chan Ho Park, bombed, and Hicks could not afford to continue pumping money into the payroll. Talk about a costly divorce: By 2025, when the last of his deferred payments is due, Hicks will have paid Rodriguez $140 million for three years of service.

After the Boston talks died, Hicks had given Rodriguez a let's-make-up bouquet: On Jan. 25 he named A-Rod captain and promised a long-term relationship. It lasted three weeks. On Feb. 8 Scott Boras, Rodriguez's agent, called Yankees general manager Brian Cashman about another client, free-agent first baseman Travis Lee. Cashman mentioned how much trouble he was having trying to replace Boone. He had failed to get Adrian Beltre from the Los Angeles Dodgers, for instance. Then it hit Boras: Why not Rodriguez? A Mets fan growing up, Rodriguez had always wanted to play in New York. Boras made a joke about it to Cashman to plant the seed of an idea, then immediately called Rodriguez.

"You'd have to decide what the [shortstop] position means to you," Boras told him, "and understand what you'd be giving up for a chance to win. Think about it."

Rodriguez called Boras back the next day and said, "Let's do it."

Said Boras on Sunday, "I knew for the last three years how hard it's been on Alex to be on a losing team and to have to hear that it's because of his contract. I also knew the business plan the Rangers were talking was not what was presented to him three years ago. The situation was possibly going to get worse."

On Feb. 10 the Rangers conducted an internal conference call with Rodriguez, Boras, Hicks, G.M. John Hart and manager Buck Showalter regarding the direction of the club. Boras just happened to mention that Rodriguez might reconsider a trade to the Yankees. Hicks scoffed at the idea. "Alex isn't going to play third base," the owner said. "He's always said that."

"Alex," Boras said, "what do you think about third base?"

"I wouldn't rule it out," Rodriguez said.

Silence fell over the line. Said Boras on Sunday, "Frankly, Tom Hicks was stunned."

The next day Hart and Cashman were negotiating the framework of the deal. By Sunday, Rodriguez had his Yankees uniform number picked out: 13, his high school football number. His usual baseball number, 3, was retired by the Yankees in homage to another young slugger who slipped through Boston's fingers to New York: Babe Ruth.

"Once Scott brought it to my attention, it made perfect sense," Rodriguez says about moving to third base to be a Yankee. "I began to think about the pinstripes. I felt the allure of the tradition and the opportunity to win and asked myself, Why not do it?

"You know the best part? Getting there while I'm still young and knowing I have seven years to play with Derek and set my legacy as far as being a part of Yankees history. Getting there at 37 and playing two years wouldn't be the same."

His Yankees history, born of misfortune, already has begun.

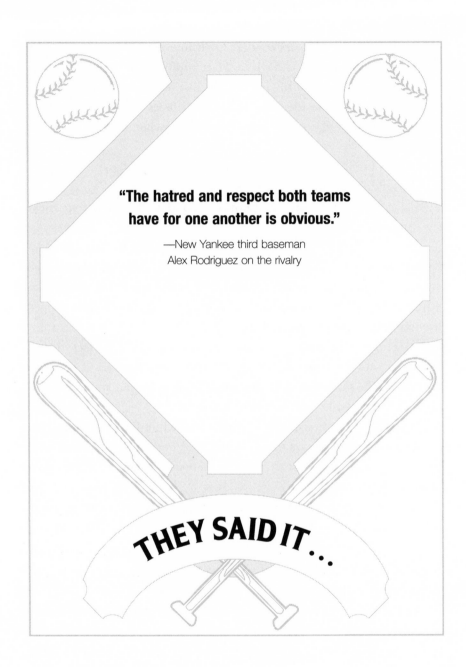

"The hatred and respect both teams have for one another is obvious."

—New Yankee third baseman
Alex Rodriguez on the rivalry

THEY SAID IT...

The New York Yankees' seemingly limitless budget makes it all but impossible for most other teams to compete. And what, asks Joel Stein, is wrong with that?

"IN DEFENSE OF DOMINATION"

from *Time magazine* (February 23, 2004)
by Joel Stein

YOU YANKEE-HATERS, YOU don't understand America. You've been deluded by the likes of Rocky, the Miracle on Ice and Clay Aiken into believing this myth that we are some sort of scrappy, underdog nation that needs to fight against the privileged bullies. Not me. I've never rooted for underdogs, or, as I like to call them, losers. I loved the preening arrogance of those great Dallas Cowboys teams. I wish Shaq were a little bit bigger. For me, every Halliburton contract is a tiny victory.

And after a century of watching the Yankees club America's small-market teams like baby seals and tigers and red sox, you have to suffer during the off-season too. In the biggest moral affront yet to your sense of fairness, last week the Yankees—already the richest, best team in baseball—traded for Alex Rodriguez (A-Rod)—the richest, best player in baseball. The Yankees now have a slightly better lineup than the

National League All-Star team, one of whose members will undoubtedly be the Yankees' second baseman by the playoffs.

The worst part for you is that the rich Yankees got A-Rod at a subsidized price just by being smart. Baseball's most expensive, egregious contract was given to Rodriguez three years ago by the Texas Rangers: $252 million over 10 years, much of which they will still have to pay to unload him. Imagine how much more they would have given him if President Bush were still the Rangers' owner. That guy loves giving rich people more money.

Consider the A-Rod deal a Dr. Phil-esque opportunity for national self-realization. Americans haven't been underdogs since 1812. We like to remember the Alamo because we fought long odds and had to give up an entire building; the Mexicans remember Texas. If ever a country's character demanded that it root against the underdog, it's ours. We are the country of crushing, monolithic corporations—of McDonald's, Wal-Mart and companies such as Aramark, Cendant and Sysco that are so powerful we don't even know what they do. We crush foreign dictators for looking at us funny. We are geniuses at supersizing the good stuff and McRibbing the losers. Underdogs are for Canadians.

The other 29 teams in Major League Baseball are around just to spur New York to further greatness, but when the Diamondbacks, Angels and Marlins do accidentally win, it's all the more exciting for them because they felled the rich, advantaged Yankees. I know it seems unfair that New York's vast television revenue gives the Yankees a permanent advantage. If all the cities had the same amount of money, every year might be as exciting in a roll-of-the-dice way, but there would be no truth in it. America is a nation of vast economic, educational and ethnic disparities. The Yankees are the real America. Where else can whites, blacks, Asians and Hispanics play happily together except on a team worth $180 million? If I were an Inuit second baseman with a good on-base percentage, I'd get my résumé to the Bronx as soon as possible.

People come to America for the same reason that A-Rod wanted to join the Yankees: both are well-run organizations with long histories of success. "I felt the allure of the tradition and the opportunity to win," said Rodriguez. People confuse pity with morality, but, as America has been arguing explicitly for several decades, there is nothing amoral about strength if it is used properly. The Yankees have good players, and the Romans made awesome aqueducts. Do you really think it makes you a better person to wish success upon a team with bad management, poor decision making and lesser talent? Then maybe you should hire Michael Eisner for his next job.

Every team has its creation myth: the Cubs teach the value of loyalty through suffering; the Red Sox, that every day is a new opportunity; the Expos, that for Canada, World's Fairs are as exciting as it gets. The Yankees are the only team that teaches the true story of our country—that might mixed with class, talent and hard work often breeds success. Also, that pinstripes have a slimming effect. Except on David Wells.

You want to teach your kids that the Yankees are evil, that the true way lies in the struggles of the sickly Brewers and Devil Rays? Go ahead and tell them bedtime stories for losers. But don't go on pretending that there is something righteous in it. Sure, your child might grow up to be Eliot Spitzer, but wouldn't you rather he became Bill Gates? Or better, Alex Rodriguez. That guy is going to be a lot happier in New York.

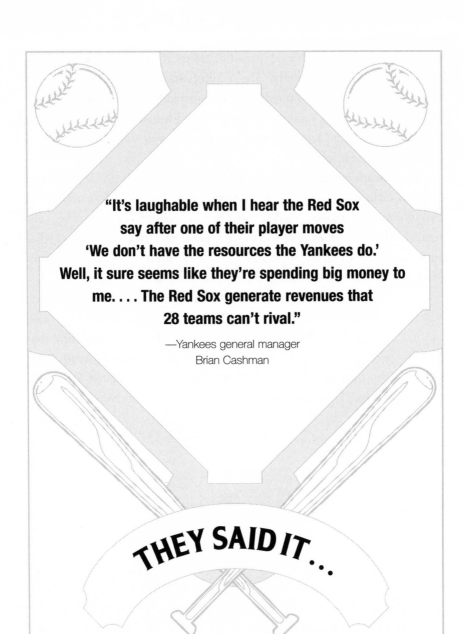

"It's laughable when I hear the Red Sox
say after one of their player moves
'We don't have the resources the Yankees do.'
Well, it sure seems like they're spending big money to
me. . . . The Red Sox generate revenues that
28 teams can't rival."

—Yankees general manager
Brian Cashman

THEY SAID IT . . .

Is it possible to root for both the Yankees and the Red Sox? Pulitzer Prize—winning author David Halberstam says it is. Who are we to argue?

"A FAN DIVIDED:
HE GETS TO FOLLOW TWO TEAMS"
by David Halberstam

I GREW UP WITH my soul divided. For I am both a man of New York and of New England. Things as critical as this, the selection of a favored base-ball team, are not, as some suspect, a matter of choice; one does not choose a team as one does not select his own genes. They are confirmed upon you, more than we know an act of heredity. By an odd blend of fates and geog-raphy, I am somewhat schizophrenic in my baseball loyalties; I think of baseball, and I think American League, and then New York and Boston. The National League has always been a distant shadowy place. I was born in New York in the very borough where the Yankees play; my father, a small-town boy with a small-town obsession about baseball, took me to the Stadium in 1939 when I was 5, having in the previous two years talked almost exclusively about the great DiMaggio. So I began not just with loyalty to a locale, but to a mythic figure, a man worthy of his myth and who did not disappoint. He was to the little boy sitting there that day, pleasure of pleasures excused early from school, every bit as dazzling and graceful as my father had claimed he would be. The Stadium seemed not so much a sports coliseum as a cathedral; never had grass seemed so green, never had any group of men caught my attention; this, unlike the world of elementary school I had just left behind, was real. I departed that day a confirmed Yankee fan. Soon the war came, my father went back in the service, and we moved to Winsted, in northwest Connecticut, which serves as the selected site of my otherwise dislocated childhood. Winsted then was the classic New England mill town of about 8,000, a serious baseball town, its own loyalties somewhat divided between Boston and New York. But it is about 20 miles nearer New York and the magnetic pull of the Yankees was somewhat more powerful then, in large part I suspect because the reception for the Yankee games, WINS-1010 on your dial, Ballantine Blasts and White Owl Wallops with Mel Allen, was stronger than that of the Red Sox.

But we were a divided family; my mother's family had grown up in Boston, and my Uncle Harry, her oldest brother, had become successful in the wholesale paint business. He occasionally visited us in Winsted and was intrigued by the idea of a young nephew whose knowledge of batting averages was so encyclopedic, and who could repeat so faithfully the wisdom of that era's sports casters. He also had, it turned out, season tickets to the Red Sox games. That seemed almost beyond comprehension to me; it was not that we were so poor, but we were, in those immediate post-Depression years, most assuredly frugal. We lived on a World War II officer's allowance, and something like going to a baseball game was at best a pleasure permitted once a season. Uncle Harry was said within family circles to be something of a dandy; that is, he not only made a lot of money but he was quite willing to spend it. That he could go to all 77 home games, and sit in the very same seats, seemed both miraculous and quite possibly frivolous. We simply did not know people who did grand things like this. It seemed to mark him not so much as a relative, but as someone from another family who had mistakenly wandered into our lives. His seats, he said, were right behind the first base dugout, and he loved them because he could see the ballplayers' faces up close. They were

such clean-looking young men, he said. Could this really be true? Did he have seats this good? If it were, then it struck me that Uncle Harry, if not actually on speaking terms with these distant and vaunted celebrities, was at least on seeing terms with them. He seemed to know a great deal about them—Pesky, Doerr, York, the mighty Williams. Pesky's name, he confided, was not really Pesky. It was Paveskovich. Mel Allen, to my knowledge, had never mentioned this. Could I doubt Uncle Harry and his inside knowledge anymore? But it was true; in time the war was over and we were allowed to travel again and we visited Boston and Uncle Harry made good his pledge. He *did* have wonderful seats and I could see on the players' faces up close the disappointment after they had grounded out, and turned back toward the dugout. They seemed quite wonderful, so large and powerful, and on that day, against Detroit, with Hal Newhouser (Ron Guidry before Guidry) pitching, I found myself rooting for them.

So it was that my childhood concluded with two conflicting loyalties. The first was one to the Yankees, and most of all DiMaggio. When I think of DiMaggio, I see him, not so much at bat, though the stance was classic, but of him going back on a fly ball, or of running the bases, particularly going around second on his way to third; I have never seen a tall man run with more grace. He was the first of my heroes; my true (and pure) loyalty to the Yankees ends with his retirement. Never in the age of Mantle was I able to summon the commitment and obligation innocence that I had brought to the age of DiMaggio. I was growing older. By the time DiMaggio retired in 1951, I was 17, and it was time to go on to other things.

But even as a young man, the vision and the loyalty were clouded. For there was the other vision, that of the Red Sox, and most of all, of Williams. As DiMaggio seemed so natural in the field, so Williams seemed equally natural at the plate, first seemingly loose, and gangly, and then suddenly bound tightly and perfectly together, the swing at once so smooth and yet so powerful, all of it so completely focused—as if he was destined to do this one thing, hit a baseball and nothing else. Of his talents, there was no lack of admiration among Yankee fans: When I was a boy, there was a constant schoolboy debate not just about the respective merits of DiMaggio or Williams, but of what would happen if each had played in the other's park, DiMaggio with the Green Monster, Williams with the short Stadium right-field porch. It was the ultimate tribute to Williams that had the trade been made, it would have been accepted without complaint by most Yankee fans.

In the summer of 1946, my father had come back from the war, and he had taken my brother and me to the Stadium to see a Yankee–Red Sox game. That was a glorious year for the Red Sox, all their players had come back from the war, and the Red Sox players more than those of the Yankees were making a comfortable readjustment to baseball. Their pitchers were healthy, and by mid-season they held an immense lead over the Yankees. On that day, Aug. 10, 1946 (you could look it up, as Casey Stengel said), Williams hit two home runs, the first of them a truly massive three-run shot off Tiny Bonham that went into the upper deck. The memory of that drive, the hardest-hit ball I have ever seen, remains with me today; I still see the force of it, the unwavering majestic trajectory, the ball climbing as it hit the seats, the silence of the fans, stunned not just that the Red Sox had scored three runs, but that a ball had been hit that hard. Williams seemed that day to a young boy a glorious figure, a hero who did what heroes are supposed to do.

I went on to college in Boston a few years later. There I was, like most visitors to the city, puzzled by the harshness with which the Boston press treated him. He was clearly the greatest hitter of his generation in baseball, he had just returned from his second tour of duty as a combat pilot, he was, it seemed, defying baseball's actuarial tables, and it was a pleasure to go out early to Fenway and watch him taking batting practice, a game within a game. I did not know as much about the media then as I do now, but I knew that the Boston papers were by and large bad (in fact, they were probably worse than that in the early fifties), that he was personally victimized by the most primitive kind of circulation wars, and that he, proud, idiosyncratic and unbending, was red meat for newspapers which were desperately trying to survive in a world which no longer needed them. What they did to him seems in retrospect to border on cruelty. It is probably true that he played into their hands, and was his own worst enemy, though his behavior, so much criticized then, seems by the modern Richter scale of athletic behavior mild enough. I did not share that view of the

Boston writers that the problem with the Red Sox was Williams. (I suspect that this was why John Updike's piece "Hub Fans Bid Kid Adieu," has itself taken on such singular importance. It is as if after hundreds of lower courts had ruled unfairly against Williams for all those years, Updike, a writer of skill and knowledge, taking time off from the chronicling of suburban infidelity, became in effect the Supreme Court ruling in favor of him, overturning the lesser judgments of lesser courts.) It was not the fault of Williams at all. Quite the reverse: It struck me that the late forties was a time of marvelous matchups between two almost perfectly equal teams, that the advantage that the Yankees held was one of pitching and depth— the ability to trade for a particular player. For example, in 1946 the Yankees traded additional bench strength for Eddie Lopat. That gave the Yankees a pitching staff of Reynolds, Raschi and Lopat, the core of the strongest pitching staff in the league for the next six years.

The memory of Williams and that special grace lingers. I now think often of him; we live in a nation which seeks heroes and cites as its heroes the kings of celluloid like John Wayne and Sylvester Stallone, each of whom managed to stay out of his generation's war. I am wary of heroes in general, but as I grow older, I have become more and more intrigued by Williams, the man apart. Perhaps it is that wonderfully leathery face, for Ted Williams even looked like what he was and what he did with that William Holden cragginess. Perhaps it is the deeds, that prolonged exquisite career, the willingness to go for it on the last day of the .400 season. But finally it is as well the ability to stand apart, crusty, independent, outspoken, true to himself, living to his own specifications and rules, the frontier man of the modern age. I have a sense of a life lived without regret and I hope that that is true. Grown now, I can still close my eyes and I can see DiMaggio going back on a ball, or kicking the dirt at second base after Gionfriddo had caught the ball in the 1947 World Series; I can as clearly still see these 40 years later Williams swinging, the ball heading for the third tier.

As I grew older, my loyalties softened, and my priorities changed. I went to school in Boston, and I soon was overseas as a foreign correspondent. Other issues clouded the purity of my baseball loyalties. I would root for certain teams based on their special character or my feeling about their cities (I root as a matter of course against all Texas and California teams, and I was deeply disappointed when Houston knocked off the Lakers this year, thus depriving the Celtics of the chance to do it.) The real world began to interfere with the fantasy world of baseball; my pull to the Yankees weakened and to that of the Red Sox began to grow, for I liked the Red Sox teams of the late sixties, Yastrzemski-Smith-Conigliaro-Petrocelli. In 1964, just back from two years in Vietnam, I went to Opening Day at the Stadium with my editor and a few other writers, and I remember two things, Ann Mudge, the girlfriend of Philip Roth, refusing to stand for the National Anthem as an antiwar protest, the first I had ever seen, and the sweet swing of a young rookie named Tony Conigliaro. In 1967 I went to an early-season game at Yankee Stadium. On that day a Red Sox rookie pitcher named Billy Rohr was pitching. About the sixth innning, it was obvious that he had a no-hitter going. The fascination grew, the crowd inevitably rooting not so much for a team, but for the event. The seventh and eighth innings passed. Still a no-hitter. In the ninth inning, with one out, Tom Tresh hit a shot to left field. Yastrzemski was playing shallow, if memory serves, and went back, and dove just at the right moment, his body tumbling into a complete somersault as he made the catch. It ranks with the Gionfriddo catch as the greatest I have ever seen, made more remarkable by the fact that it saved a no-hitter. The next batter, Elston Howard, lined a hit into right-center. I thought, as I had of Conigliaro, that Rohr had a great career ahead of him. He was to win two more games in his major league career.

That summer and fall, I was back in Vietnam; it was a bad time for me. The American mission was optimistic (this was just before Tet) and I was pessimistic, convinced that 500,000 men had managed only to stalemate the other side. I hated the futile violence of the war. It was not a face of America I was comfortable with, and the combination of the flawed commitment—so many men and so much hardware to a job which could not be done, and the self-deception which accompanied it had put me in a grim mood. That was also the season of Yastrzemski; that summer and fall when I was not out in the field, I would go over to the AP office. Saigon was 12 hours different from Boston and so the results of the night games would tend to come in about 11 A.M. There was also a man who hung around the AP office, for the same reason: Doc, as he was known. Doc was Dr. Tom Durant, a Boston doctor helping the Vietnamese with their medical training (he is now assistant director of Mass. General), and each morning I would meet him there, bonded by this need to escape, and this common passion, and we would follow the results of a wonderful pennant race and perhaps the greatest one-man pennant drive in modern baseball history by standing over the AP ticker. I felt very close to him; we never agreed in advance to meet at the office but indeed we always did. We would sit there in that small airless room, and we could almost see Yaz as he was in Fenway, the exaggerated stance; it was all oddly exhilarating. Each day the heroics seemed even more remarkable, the box score would come clicking over the printer—Yaz, 2 for 4 with two RBIs—and then, more often than not, the mention of some extraordinary catch as well. In what was for me a bad season, his was a marvelous season and it reminded me of the America I loved, and which otherwise seemed quite distant. I have felt fondly of him ever since, and my affection has weathered even the current hokey hot dog commercials.

That next year I became a citizen of New England again, buying a home in Nantucket, connecting myself once again to Boston sports coverage, which now in modern times seemed to make the Red Sox players larger than life (Williams had played 25 years too soon, I suspected; he should have played in an era of semi-monopoly journalism) and returning to Fenway once again. I had remembered it as a small shabby park, an embarrassment after the grandeur of the Stadium, but now I saw it differently; in an age of antiseptic ballparks, gimmicky electronic scoreboards, fans who cheered every pop fly, it was a real ballpark. Going there was like going back in time, stepping into a Hopper painting. It must have been like this, I thought, when Smoky Joe Wood was ready to pitch. I had rooted for the 1975 team, a glorious and exciting team in a wonderful Series, wondering what might have happened if there had been two Luis Tiants instead of one. Then in 1978, for the last time, I faced the question of divided loyalties, the human heart in conflict with itself, to use Faulkner's phrase. I was no longer an automatic Yankee fan, but that was a good and gritty Yankee team, Munson-Nettles-Chambliss-Piniella-Jackson-Hunter, a Gabe Paul rather than a Steinbrenner team, not yet contaminated by the worst of all baseball owners. I like the chase as much as anything else, and that summer I found myself cheering the late-season New York surge. It was also a very good Red Sox team as well, Rice-Lynn-Yastrzemski-Evans-Fisk, weaker as usual in pitching. The season was as good as any I have ever seen, the early, seemingly insurmountable Boston lead, the feral, almost ruthless late Yankee surge to reclaim part of first place. One hundred sixty-two games played and both teams dead even—that was not a flawed season, that was an almost perfect season. Of that in the bitterness of postmortem charges and countercharges, there was much talk about a Red Sox collapse. I never believed it. The Yankees, as usual, had a demonstrably better pitching staff. Perhaps, I thought, the key moment took place six years earlier when the Red Sox made one of the worst trades of modern times, swapping Sparky Lyle for Danny Cater. Lyle was then young, a proven lefthanded reliever, 53 saves in his last three seasons; Cater was a good, albeit limited, pinch hitter. Lyle was the perfect relief pitcher for the Stadium and he gave an improving Yankees team exactly what it needed, a kind of instant late-inning legitimacy. In seven years as a Yankee, he had 141 saves, and in that year, 1978, when his star was already in descent in New York (Goose Gossage had arrived and Lyle went, said Nettles, from Cy Young to Sayonara in one season), he nonetheless had nine saves and a 9-3 record. In a season where two teams end up with the same record, that was all the difference the Yankees needed.

That team is gone: Piniella as manager and Randolph and Guidry are the only survivors. In the age of narcissus, Steinbrenner is the perfect modern baseball owner now, the bully as owner (if Tom Yawkey was flawed because he loved his players too much, Steinbrenner is flawed because he envies them their talent and youth and fame too much). He has won the tabloids, and lost the team. The 1978 team struck me as one which was bonded together by a mutual dislike of him; now, eight years later, his act has played too long, he is the national bore, and contempt has replaced dislike. It's not easy, in an age of free agency, to screw up owning a baseball team in the media capital of the world, but he has done it. The team is a wonderful extension of him, overpaid, surly, disconnected; the quintessential Steinbrenner player is Rickey Henderson. I do not doubt his talent, indeed his brilliance, but he seems, whenever I watch, in a perpetual sulk, entirely within himself, and watching him is almost as much fun as watching Carl Lewis during the 1984 Olympics. In this year I wish the Red Sox well, I did not think it was a good race, there was too much stumbling around. In a personal sense, if I am pleased for anyone, it is Don Baylor; trashed by Steinbrenner, he gained the sweetest kind of revenge, hitting against righthanders. His trade subtracted character from the Yankees and added it to the Red Sox. And I rooted as well for Tom Seaver, carried in this season as much by a feral instinct to compete as by natural skill, awesome if not in talent anymore then in toughness of mind.

If the Red Sox stumble through, however imperfectly, then I am pleased, for there have been enough very good Boston teams which, playing far better baseball, had their pennants denied. If they win, so be it: The gods owe them one.

On October 17, 2004, the New York Yankees were three outs away from sweeping the Boston Red Sox in the American League Championship Series. The Red Sox fielded a strong team, but once again it appeared they wouldn't be strong enough to get past New York. The Sox rallied to win that game in extra innings, but up three games to one, New York still seemed certain to claim the pennant. Then Boston won game five in extra innings, and hobbled ace Curt Schilling pitched Boston to victory in game six. The American League pennant would be decided by a game seven between New York and Boston, just as it had been the year before. If the Red Sox won, they would become the first team in major league history to take a best-of-seven postseason series after trailing three games to none. If they lost, Boston would crush their fans' hopes one more time.

"YANKEES MEET RUTHLESS END"

from the *Daily News* [October 18, 2004]
by Anthony McCarron

IS IT FINALLY OVER, after all the years, the stinging heartbreak, the jokes? Did the Red Sox shatter the Curse of the Bambino last night? Maybe they have to win the World Series to accomplish that, but, for all of New England, this will do for now.

Even if the Yankee-Red Sox rivalry reverts to being a painful experience for Boston, the city, the region and the Sox will always have this, their stunning victory over the Yanks in the AL Championship Series, the greatest comeback in the history of sports.

The Red Sox completed it last night with a dominating 10–3 victory at the Stadium, thanks to two homers—one a grand slam—by Johnny Damon, one by the big Yankee-killer David Ortiz and another by Mark

Bellhorn. The Red Sox will play in the World Series for the 10th time—the first since 1986—beginning Saturday at Fenway.

In the most spectacular fashion, the Red Sox may have exorcised the demons that have routinely wrecked Octobers since 1918, becoming the first team in baseball history to win a best-of-seven series after losing the first three games. They also may have changed the dynamic of the greatest rivalry in sports.

"This is for those teams that couldn't beat the Yankees," Sox GM Theo Epstein said. "That's behind us now. We never have to think about that again."

The Sox won at the stadium where they experienced such lows in the past, including last year when Aaron Boone and the Yankees stole a pennant in a very different Game 7. The Sox even got to celebrate their first pennant in 18 years on the Yankees' home field.

The Yankees, meanwhile, face what could be a bleak winter after blowing a 3–0 lead in the series. George Steinbrenner's team pulled maybe the worst choke job ever and certainly suffered the most embarrassing loss in franchise history. Making it worse, two of their headline acquisitions for the rotation last offseason, Kevin Brown and Javier Vazquez, were awful last night.

"We have no excuses," said Alex Rodriguez, who was 0-for-4. "They beat our asses, that's it. It's frustrating, because we felt coming into tonight that the winner of this game was going to win the World Series. "I'm embarrassed right now," Rodriguez added. "Watching them celebrate, being up 3-0 and not being able to deliver the knockout punch."

Boston starter Derek Lowe, who allowed one run and one hit in six innings on two days' rest, called it a "historic event. I really know they are going to appreciate it and I know how the city appreciates how hard this was because this was the best team in baseball for a lot of years.

"We just kept winning and we wanted to try to get to the next day and we kept doing that."

The Yankees could have avoided all of it had they closed out the spirited Sox in either Game 4 or Game 5. They were three outs away from a sweep in Game 4 with closer Mariano Rivera on the mound, but he botched a one-run lead and they lost in 12 innings. In Game 5, they were ahead, 4–2, in the eighth and Tom Gordon and Rivera lost the lead and the Sox won in the 14th. Joe Torre called them both "positions we'd take any day of the week."

"We had a couple of games where we had situations the way we wanted it, leads late in the game and we just could not close the deal," Torre said.

The Red Sox could, despite a strange misstep in the seventh inning when manager Terry Francona brought in Pedro Martinez. It fired up the crowd, which teased Martinez with chants of "Who's your dad-dee, who's your dad-dee?" while the Yankee lineup came alive for the only time all night. Martinez allowed two runs and three hits in one inning.

But Pedro couldn't spoil the Sox party.

Damon had had a dreadful series entering last night, with only three hits in 29 at-bats (.103). No one will remember that stretch now, not after he hit the second grand slam in the Sox's postseason history and drove in six runs. Ortiz was voted the ALCS MVP—last night's homer was his third of the series and he hit .387 with 11 RBI.

Brown left in the second inning with one out and the bases loaded. Vazquez came on in relief and gave up a grand slam to Damon on his first pitch. Damon later hit a two-run homer off him, too, also on the first pitch.

Both pitchers were booed when they departed. Brown allowed five runs in 1⅓ innings and Vazquez gave up three in two innings. Rodriguez was booed, too, after making outs in the sixth and eighth innings.

The Yankees had tried to revive the old days before the game, bringing back Bucky Dent to throw out the first pitch. His catcher was Yogi Berra. Dent got a huge cheer from the crowd of 56,129, but the gesture smacked of desperation by a team desperate not to be on the wrong side of postseason lore.

Late in the game, several executives could be seen sitting forlornly in an office behind the press box, staring into space.

There will be a similar look among Yankee fans this morning—the

Red Sox are going to the World Series and they beat history and the Yankees to get there.

"They played better than us, that's the bottom line," Jeter said. "You have to be able to finish them. We didn't do the job.

"I'm not going to forget it. This is going to be there."

A week later Boston completed a four-game sweep of the St. Louis Cardinals to claim the club's first World Championship since 1918.

YANKEE–RED SOX SCOREBOARD

	BOSTON RED SOX	NEW YORK YANKEES
World Championships	6	26
Postseason appearances	16	44
Times unfairly deprived of a postseason appearance	1 (No postseason in 1904)	1 (No postseason in 1994)
Head-to-head regular season wins	865	1,055
Seasons finishing second behind rival	14	3
MVP Awards	10	20
Cy Young Awards	6	5
Rookie of the Year Awards	5	8
Hall of Famers	28	33
Payroll (opening day, 2004)	$127 million	$184 million
Annual revenues (*Business Week* estimate, 2004)	$230 million	$320–$340 million
Franchise value (*Forbes* 2004 estimate)	$533 million	$832 million
Average ticket price (2004)	$40.77	$24.86
Stadium capacity	33,871	57,546
Percent of neutral territory (Connecticut) controlled (based on 2004 Quinnipiac University poll of which team Connecticut baseball fans support)	33%	43%

Note: All stats through 2004 season

A YANKEES-RED SOX
RIVALRY TIMELINE

JANUARY 28, 1901   American League president Ban Johnson announces that Boston will have a team in the A.L. for the inaugural 1901 season. The surprise decision comes as a blow to baseball fans in the Empire State, since the last-minute addition of Boston requires the last-minute eviction of another franchise—the one promised to Buffalo, New York.

APRIL 26, 1901   The Boston Americans—the team that would come to be known as the Red Sox—play their first game, losing to Baltimore 10–6. In 1903, that Baltimore franchise would be moved to New York and become—eventually—the Yankees.

APRIL 22, 1903   The New York Highlanders, the team that would later be known as the Yankees, play their first game, losing to Washington 3–1.

MAY 7, 1903   New York and Boston face each other for the first time in American League history. Boston wins the game, 6–2. New York would rebound to beat Boston 6-1 the following day.

OCTOBER 13, 1903   Boston wins the first modern World Series, five games to three over Pittsburgh. Boston's Bill Dinneen throws a 3–0 shutout in the clincher.

DECEMBER 20, 1903   In the first trade between New York and Boston, the Highlanders obtain pitcher Tom Hughes in exchange for pitcher Jesse Tannehill. Boston fans are outraged, believing their team has been pressured into surrendering Hughes, a 20-game winner in 1903, simply to strengthen New York. (It was thought that the young American League couldn't prosper without a competitive club in the New York market.) But the trade would turn out well for Boston. Tannehill would rebound from his mediocre 1903 season to win 21 games for Boston in 1904, then another 22 in 1905. Hughes would post a record of 9–24 in 1904 and never again win 20 games in a season.

October 10, 1904   New York and Boston go head-to-head on the final day of the regular season with the American League pennant on the line. Boston wins the big game 3-2 and captures its second straight AL flag when New York ace Jack Chesbro wild-pitches the winning ran home in the ninth. Chesbro's 41 wins in 1904 still stand as the modern single-season record, but thanks to the wild pitch, he will always be remembered as a goat.

June 30, 1908   New York is no-hit by the oldest pitcher in the majors, Boston's 41-year-old Cy Young. Young allows just one base runner, a walk to second baseman Harry Niles. The 8-0 win is the last of Young's three career no-hitters.

April 20, 1912   Boston wins the first regular-season game played at Fenway Park, securing a 7-6 victory over New York when Tris Speaker delivers an RBI single in the bottom of the 11th inning. Boston would win 19 of 21 meetings with New York in 1912 and claim its first pennant since 1904.

May 6, 1915   Red Sox pitcher Babe Ruth hits his first career home run. The landmark clout occurs in New York, during a 4-3 Boston loss to the Yankees. Ruth would go on to hit 49 career home runs for the Red Sox . . . then another 659 for the Yanks.

November 1, 1915   New Yorker Harry Frazee purchases the Boston Red Sox.

June 21, 1916   Sox pitcher George Foster no-hits New York, 2-0, thanks in part to Boston's superb outfield defense.

September 30, 1916   The Red Sox win three of four from the Yankees in the final week of the season. Thanks to the victories, Boston takes the pennant by two games over Chicago.

April 24, 1917   New York pitcher George Mogridge holds the World Champion Red Sox squad without a hit through eight innings. But Boston's pitcher, Dutch Leonard, is nearly as good, allowing just one hit into the seventh. When the Red Sox score a run in the seventh on a error, two walks (one intentional), and a sacrifice fly, the game is tied 1-1. New York scores a second run in the top of the ninth, thanks in part to shoddy Boston defense, and Mogridge shuts the Sox down in the ninth to earn his no-hitter.

SEPTEMBER 10, 1918   Boston Red Sox and Chicago Cubs players threaten to strike before game five of the 1918 World Series. The players are concerned that low Series attendance will shrink their post-season bonuses, but they back down and the game is played after a short delay. One day later, Boston wins its third World Series in four years. The team has captured the AL pennant six times in the past 16 years, and won every one of the five World Series it has played. New York has yet to win an American League pennant. But neither the Cubs nor the Red Sox won a World Series during the remaining years of the 20th century, leading some superstitious baseball fans to speculate that threatening to strike during a World Series might be behind the Cub and Red Sox "curses."

DECEMBER 18, 1918   Boston trades popular outfielder Duffy Lewis to the Yankees, along with pitchers Ernie Shore and Dutch Leonard. In return the Red Sox receive pitcher Ray Caldwell, three lesser players, and cash. None of the players involved in the trade would have a significant impact on their new teams' fortunes—the best among them were past their prime. But the deal would signal a turning point in Red Sox history, marking the end of Boston's run as a buyer of talent, and the beginning of a long stretch of player sales—mainly to the Yankees—that would push the Red Sox out of contention for close to two decades.

JULY 29, 1919   Boston trades star pitcher Carl Mays to New York for pitchers Allan Russell and Bob McGraw, and cash. The enigmatic, unpopular Mays had refused to pitch another game for Boston. Mays would go 9-3 down the stretch for New York in 1919, then win 53 more games for the Yanks during the following two seasons. Russell wouldn't win more than 10 games in any season for Boston. McGraw never won the Sox a single game.

JANUARY 3, 1920   The Yankees purchase Babe Ruth from the Red Sox for $125,000, plus a loan of $300,000. Ruth, already a star, would soon become the most popular and arguably the greatest baseball player of all time.

DECEMBER 15, 1920   The Yankees obtain pitcher Waite Hoyt and three additional players from the Red Sox in exchange for second baseman Del Pratt and three lesser talents. Pratt would have two fine seasons for Boston. Hoyt would spend close to a decade with the Yanks on his way to a Hall of Fame career.

OCTOBER 2, 1921 The Yankees end the regular season with a 7-6 victory over the Boston Red Sox and celebrate the team's first pennant. New York's biggest stars in 1921 include outfielder Babe Ruth, and pitchers Carl Mays and Waite Hoyt, all former Red Sox.

DECEMBER 20, 1921 New York acquires shortstop Everett Scott and pitchers Joe Bush and Sam Jones from Boston. Jones and Bush had been Boston's best pitchers in 1921, and between them would win 79 games for the Yankees over the next two years. The best of the four players Boston receives in return is shortstop Roger Peckinpaugh—whom the Sox quickly deal to Washington for Joe Dugan and Frank O'Rourke. O'Rourke is a backup infielder who plays just one season in Boston. Dugan spends even less time with the Sox, as Boston trades the talented third basemen to the Yankees in July 1922, receiving little besides cash in return.

SEPTEMBER 30, 1922 With a 3-1 win over Boston on the next-to-last day of the season, New York eliminates the St. Louis Browns and locks up the Yanks' second straight pennant. Former Red Sox pitcher Waite Hoyt earns the win for the Yankees. Boston had taken the first two games of the three-game set against New York to keep the pennant in doubt. The Red Sox finish the season in last place for the first time since 1906.

JANUARY 30, 1923 The Yankees acquire pitcher Herb Pennock from Boston in exchange for three prospects. Pennock would have a Hall of Fame career with the Yankees. None of the prospects Boston receives ever make much of an impact.

APRIL 18, 1923 The New York Yankees beat the Red Sox 4–1 in the first game ever played in Yankee Stadium. The largest crowd in major league history sees Babe Ruth hit a three-run homer off his former club in the third.

SEPTEMBER 27, 1923 Future Yankee Hall of Famer Lou Gehrig hits his first major league homer. The hit helps the Yankees top the Red Sox 8-3 in Fenway Park.

OCTOBER 7, 1923   New York finishes first in the American League, Boston last for the second straight year. (This pattern would recur four more times in the coming decade: 1926, 1927, 1928, and 1932.) New York goes on to win the team's first World Championship. Of the 24 players on New York's World Series roster, 11 are former Red Sox, including four of eight starters and all but one of the pitchers used by New York in the Series.

SEPTEMBER 16, 1925   The musical *No, No Nanette* opens at the Globe Theater on Broadway. The play runs for 321 performances, plus 861 more in a 1971 revival. Its signature song, "Tea for Two," remains well known. Red Sox lore later would hold that the play's backer, Red Sox owner Harry Frazee, sold Babe Ruth to raise money for its production, though this appears not to have been the case.

MAY 6, 1930   Boston trades faltering pitcher Red Ruffing to New York for spare outfielder Cedric Durst and cash. Ruffing had compiled a career record of 39-96 with Boston. He would put together a record of 234–129 in New York and make the Hall of Fame. Durst would hit .245 with Boston in 1930, then disappear from the majors.

MAY 29, 1932   An AP report rumors that New York might send an the aging Babe Ruth back to Boston, where he would serve as an outfielder, manager, and part owner of the team. "Ruth is Perfect Tonic for Panic in Red Sox Camp," reads the headline in the *Chicago Daily Tribune*. "Babe Can and May Save Club—as Owner." Ruth downplays his ownership prospects. "Right now I haven't the dough," he explains. Ruth would remain in New York for another three seasons before joining Boston's other team, the Braves.

OCTOBER 1, 1933   Babe Ruth appears as a pitcher for the final time in his major league career. Though it's only his second trip to the mound since 1921, Ruth beats his former club, the Red Sox, 6–5. Ruth has pitched in five games in his years with the Yankees and won all five.

SUMMER 1936   Yankee scout Bill Essick attempts to sign 17-year-old phenom Ted Williams. Williams' mother, May, refuses to agree to the deal, so the outfielder joins the Pacific Coast

League and later is sold to the Red Sox. Many years later, a rumor would circulate that Boston nearly swapped Williams to New York for Joe DiMaggio.

MAY 30, 1938   The largest crowd in Yankee Stadium history sees Joe Cronin of the Red Sox and Jake Powell of the Yankees engage in an extended on-field fight after Powell is hit by a pitch thrown by Boston's Archie McKain. Both combatants are ejected and removed from the field, but they meet under the stands and continue to throw punches.

OCTOBER 2, 1938   After two decades of poor play, Boston returns to respectability with a second-place finish in the American League. The Yankees finish first, nine-and-a-half games ahead. Meanwhile, Boston's Jimmie Foxx wins the 1938 MVP award, while New York's Bill Dickey is second in the voting. Boston would finish second behind New York again in 1939, 1941, and 1942, before finally toppling the Yanks and winning a pennant in 1946.

APRIL 20, 1939   Ted Williams collects his first major league hit, a double, in his first major league game. It's served up by Yankee star— and former Red Sox—Red Ruffing.

NOVEMBER 11, 1941   Joe DiMaggio of the Yankees wins the MVP over Ted Williams of the Red Sox despite the fact that Williams has hit over .400 for the season. DiMaggio's 56-game hitting streak is apparently considered the greater accomplishment, though Williams had a higher batting average than DiMaggio even during the 56-game run. Ted Williams would finish second in the MVP voting four times in his career. Each time the man who finished first was a Yankee. (Williams also won two MVPs; on one of those occasions a Yankee was second in the voting.)

SEPTEMBER 27, 1942   Boston beats New York 7-6 on the final day of the regular season. Second-place Boston still finishes nine games back of the pennant-winning Yanks, but the win means that the Sox have won 12 of 22 meeting between the two clubs in 1942. It's only the third time in the past eight seasons that any club has had a winning record against New York—the others are Detroit in 1940, and the Red Sox in 1939.

SEPTEMBER 29, 1946   Boston finishes the regular season in first, 17 games ahead of third-place New York. It's Boston's first pennant since 1918—not to mention the first time the Sox have finished ahead of the Yankees in the standings since 1918. Boston would lose the World Series to the Cardinals in seven games.

OCTOBER 2, 1948   The Red Sox knock the Yankees out of the pennant race on the next-to-last day of the season. Boston would beat New York again the following day to force a one-game playoff with Cleveland for the American League title. The Red Sox would lose that game, 8–3.

OCTOBER 2, 1949   New York holds on to win the final game of the regular season 5–3 when Boston catcher Birdie Tebbetts pops up with a man on to end a ninth-inning Red Sox rally. The Red Sox also lost to New York the day before, by one run. Had Boston won either of these games, they would have claimed the pennant. Instead, the Yankees are American League champs.

SEPTEMBER 23, 1950   Boston arrives in New York just two games behind the first-place Yankees with barely a week left in the regular season. The Red Sox get blown out, 8-0, then fall again the following day. They end the season in third, four games off the pace.

SEPTEMBER 28, 1951   Yankee pitcher Allie Reynolds no-hits the Red Sox, 8–0 in the midst of a tight pennant race between New York and Cleveland. Reynolds gets the legendary Ted Williams to hit a foul pop-up with two outs in the ninth, but Yankee catcher Yogi Berra drops the ball. Unfazed, Reynolds gets Williams to pop to Berra once again. This time Berra holds onto the ball to complete the no-hitter. New York goes on to win the pennant.

MAY 24, 1952   Boston rookie outfielder Jimmy Piersall and Yankee second baseman Billy Martin fight in a tunnel under the stands at Fenway Park.

AUGUST 22, 1954   Boston completes a three-game sweep of the Yankees in Fenway Park that *Sports Illustrated* refers to as "The Boston Massacre." Though not as well known as the 1978 "Boston

Massacre," in which the Yankees trounce the Red Sox, this series drops New York from two-and-a-half games back of first-place Cleveland to five-and-a-half back, virtually ending New York's hopes of winning the 1954 pennant.

SEPTEMBER 18, 1955   New York completes a three-game sweep of the Red Sox with a 3–2 win. When the series began, New York was in second place, one back of Cleveland, with less than two weeks to go in the season. When it ended, the Yankees were two games in front. New York would win five of their remaining seven to take the pennant by three games.

OCTOBER 1, 1961   Yankee outfielder Roger Maris topples one of the most celebrated records in American sports when he hits his 61st home run of the 1961 season. The record-breaking homer is served up by Red Sox pitcher Tracy Stallard and accounts for all the scoring in a 1–0 New York win.

SEPTEMBER 27, 1966   Boston beats the White Sox 2–1 in their final game of the year. Thanks to the otherwise meaningless Red Sox victory, the New York Yankees finish the season in last place for the first time since 1908.

APRIL 14, 1967   Boston pitcher Billy Rohr comes within one pitch of no-hitting the Yankees in New York's home opener. The game is Rohr's first appearance in the major leagues. The no-hit bid fails when Elston Howard singles on a 3–2 pitch with two down in the ninth. Many observers believe Rohr's 1–2 pitch should have been called a strike. The Red Sox win the game and go on to claim the American League pennant. The Yankees finish the season in ninth place. Howard finishes the season as a Red Sox.

MARCH 22, 1972   New York acquires relief pitcher Sparky Lyle from the Red Sox in exchange for first baseman Danny Cater. Lyle would win a Cy Young Award and be named to three All-Star teams in New York. Cater would play a grand total of 211 games for Boston.

AUGUST 1, 1973   Yankee batter Gene Michael fails to make contact on an attempted suicide squeeze bunt in the bottom of the ninth inning, ensuring that Thurman Munson will be tagged out. Munson barrels into Boston catcher Carlton Fisk, and the two fight at home plate in Yankee Stadium. The bench-clearing brawl that follows would later be credited with reinvigorating the rivalry. Three years later Michael would sign with Boston, but be released before getting into a single game, ending his playing career. Michael would claim that his release was triggered by Red Sox teammates who didn't like having a "Yankee" around.

SEPTEMBER 10, 1974   Yankee first baseman Chris Chambliss is hit in the arm by a dart thrown from the grandstand in Fenway Park. New York trails 1–0 in the ninth when Chambliss, who has remained in the game, doubles in the tying run. New York wins the game in the 12th.

SEPTEMBER 24, 1974   Boston sweeps a doubleheader from New York in Yankee Stadium. Though New York wins five of its remaining six games, red-hot Baltimore wins 13 of its final 14 to take the AL East by two games over the Yanks. The lost double-header against Boston has cost the Yankees a shot at their first postseason in a decade.

MAY 20, 1976   The Yankees and Red Sox brawl in the Bronx when New York outfielder Lou Piniella steamrolls Sox catcher Carlton Fisk in an unsuccessful attempt to score. In the course of the fight, Yankee third baseman Graig Nettles drops Boston's Bill Lee on his pitching shoulder. By many accounts, Lee's arm never completely recovers. Lee had previously compared the Yankees to Nazi Brown Shirts.

SEPTEMBER 10, 1978   New York completes a four-game sweep in Fenway that comes to be known as "The Boston Massacre." New York outscores Boston 42-9 in the four games and moves into a tie for first place. Boston had held a 14-game lead in late July.

OCTOBER 2, 1978   Bucky Dent's seventh-inning "pop fly" off Boston's Mike Torrez clears Fenway's Green Monster for a home-run. The three-run homer stakes New York to a lead it won't relinquish in the one-game playoff for the 1978 AL East title. With two on, two down, and the Red Sox trailing by one in the bottom of the ninth, Boston's future Hall of Fame outfielder Carl Yastrzemski pops out to third to end the game.

MAY 18, 1979   Bucky Dent faces Mike Torrez for the first time since hitting his famous home run. He taps weakly back to the mound.

JULY 4, 1983   Yankee pitcher Dave Righetti no-hits the Boston Red Sox. Future Yankee Wade Boggs strikes out to end the game. "If I did get a hit that day," Boggs would later say, "I wouldn't have gotten out of New York alive."

OCTOBER 5, 1986   Wade Boggs doesn't play in any of the Sox' final four games, thereby protecting his slim lead in the AL batting race over Yankee Don Mattingly. The Yankees beat Boston in all four Boggs-less games to finish second, five-and-a-half games behind the Red Sox. It's the first time New York has finished second behind Boston since 1904. The Red Sox reach the World Series, but lose in dramatic fashion to another team from New York.

JUNE 6, 1990   Red Sox nemesis Bucky Dent is fired as New York's manager the day after Boston beats his last-place Yanks. Dent receives the news while the Yankees are in Boston, the site of his greatest baseball accomplishment. "I'm still a Yankee," says Dent, "but now I'm a fired Yankee."

SEPTEMBER 15, 1991   Red Sox pitcher Roger Clemens hits Yankee catcher Matt Nokes with a pitch after previously telling reporters "Nokes is going down." Nokes catches the ball between his arm and body and fires it back at Clemens. "How many times do you catch it?" Nokes said later. "I figured I'd never get the chance to throw it back like that again." Boston wins the game 5-4.

SEPTEMBER 22, 1991   The Red Sox are one out away from a 5–4 victory over the Yankees that will pull Boston into a tie with Toronto atop the AL East. But Yankee outfielder Roberto Kelly homers with two down in the ninth, and New York scores twice in the tenth for the win. Boston, which had won 17 of its previous 21 games, loses 11 of its final 14 to finish seven back of Toronto.

DECEMBER 15, 1992   The Yankees sign free agent third baseman Wade Boggs, formerly of the Red Sox. Boggs had hit just .259 for Boston in 1992, convincing some in the organization that his best days are behind him. Boggs would rebound to hit over .300 for four straight years in New York.

SEPTEMBER 18, 1993 With two down in the bottom of the ninth and New York trailing 3–2, Yankee pinch hitter Mike Stanley's fly ball to left is caught by Sox outfielder Mike Greenwell, giving Boston an apparent victory. But a pair of fans had rushed onto the Yankee Stadium field moments before the fly out, and—unbeknownst to the players—third base umpire Tim Welke had called time prior to the pitch. Given a new life, Stanley singles and New York rallies for a 4–3 win that keeps New York within three games of the first-place Blue Jays. "They don't want to run on the field [during the next day's game]," says infuriated Boston pitcher Roger Clemens afterwards. "Because if security drags them [out] through our dugout, it's going to get ugly."

MARCH 8, 1995 Though it's spring training and the regular major leaguers are on strike, 4,287 fans show up to watch the replacement Red Sox beat the replacement Yankees 1–0. "A game between the Yankees and Red Sox," writes the Associated Press, "will draw even when it's Randy Brown vs. Jeff Yurtin instead of Don Mattingly vs. Mo Vaughn."

NOVEMBER 23, 1998 Free agent center fielder Bernie Williams, a career Yankee, meets with Red Sox general manager Dan Duquette for the second time. Faced with the prospect of losing their All-Star outfielder to Boston, the Yankees reportedly decide to pursue another All-Star outfielder—Albert Belle. Williams later would accept an 11th-hour offer to return to New York. Williams hits .342 for the Yankees in 1999; Boston's center fielder Darren Lewis hits .240. New York finishes first that year, just four games ahead of Boston. A bad hip soon ends Belle's career.

FEBRUARY 18, 1999 New York trades for future Hall of Fame pitcher Roger Clemens. The trade is made with the Toronto Blue Jays, but the impact is felt in Boston, which had allowed Clemens to leave as a free agent following the 1996 season.

OCTOBER 13, 1999 Thanks to the wild card rule, the Yankees and Red Sox meet in the American League Championship Series. Boston appears on the verge of claiming the lead in the tenth inning of game one when Chuck Knoblauch drops a throw at second base, but umpire Rick Reed rules that Knoblauch held the ball long enough for the out, killing the Red Sox rally. Bernie Williams wins game one with a walk-off homer in the bottom of the tenth. Reed would later admit that he missed the call on the Knoblauch play. Boston would roll to a 13–1 victory over Roger Clemens in game three, but lose the series four games to one.

JUNE 19, 2000
New York beats Boston 22–1. It's the worst home loss in Sox history. The win moves the Yankees past Boston and into first place in the division. "It was embarrassing for everyone," said Sox catcher Jason Varitek, "the players, the coaches, the trainers . . ." The Sox lose nine of their next 12 games and finish second in the division, two-and-a-half games behind New York.

MAY 31, 2001
Red Sox ace Pedro Martinez responds to a question about the so-called Curse of the Bambino by saying "Wake up the Bambino . . . I'll face him and maybe I'll drill him in the ass." Martinez soon experiences shoulder trouble and doesn't win another game all year. The Red Sox lose all seven of their remaining meetings with the Yankees in 2001.

SEPTEMBER 2, 2001
Yankee pitcher Mike Mussina is one strike away from a perfect game when Boston pinch hitter Carl Everett lines a single to left. "I'm going to think about that pitch until I retire," says Mussina after the game.

DECEMBER 24, 2002
The New York Yankees outbid the Boston Red Sox for coveted free agent pitcher José Contreras. In response, Sox president Larry Lucchino refers to the Yankees as "The Evil Empire." Contreras remains with New York for less than two seasons before he's traded away.

MAY 21, 2003
Bucky Dent, now manager of the Yankees' AAA affiliate, attends a Yankee/Red Sox game at Fenway Park. He sits in the new "Monster Seats" just a short distance from where his famed home run landed in 1978.

MAY 26, 2003
Roger Clemens fails to earn his 300th win against his former club, as the Red Sox beat New York 8–4 on Memorial Day in Yankee Stadium.

JULY 7, 2003
Boston ace Pedro Martinez sends both of New York's All-Star middle infielders to the hospital when he hits Alfonso

Soriano and Derek Jeter with pitches *in the first inning*. The Yankees win 2–1 despite playing the rest of the game with a makeshift lineup that includes third baseman Robin Ventura at second base. "[Martinez] has been doing it his whole career," says Jeter later. "It's nothing new."

AUGUST 31, 2003   Roger Clemens pitches the Yankees to an 8–4 win over the Red Sox in what then seems likely to be his final career appearance in Boston. The Fenway crowd, long hostile toward Clemens, gives the future Hall of Famer a standing ovation as he leaves the game in the seventh.

OCTOBER 11, 2003   The Red Sox and Yankees brawl during game three of the American League Championship Series. In the course of the fight, 72-year-old Yankee coach Don Zimmer charges Boston pitcher Pedro Martinez and is thrown to the ground. Later in the game two Yankees players get in a fight with a Fenway groundskeeper. The Yankees win the game and take a 2–1 lead in the series.

OCTOBER 16, 2003   The Red Sox are just five outs from the World Series—until the Yankees rally for three runs in the bottom of the eighth inning to tie the seventh game of the ALCS at five. Boston fans fault Sox manager Grady Little for not removing tiring starter Pedro Martinez from the game sooner. Aaron Boone wins the game with a walk-off homer off Tim Wakefield in the 11th. The Yankees go on to lose the World Series.

FEBRUARY 16, 2004   The New York Yankees trade second baseman Alfonso Soriano for reigning American League MVP Alex Rodriguez. Earlier that off-season, the Red Sox believed *they* had acquired Rodriguez, but the players' union ruled the terms of that deal unacceptable.

MARCH 7, 2004   Tickets for a spring training exhibition game between the Yankees and Red Sox reportedly sell for more than $300. The Yankees win the meaningless affair 11–7.

JULY 24, 2004   Boston catcher Jason Varitek precipitates an on-field brawl by shoving his catcher's mitt in the face of New York's Alex Rodriguez. Rodriguez had been voicing his displeasure at being hit by a pitch thrown by Bronson Arroyo. The Red

Sox win that game and 33 of their next 44 to cut into New York's lead in the AL East.

AUGUST 31, 2004   A foul ball off the bat of Boston outfielder Manny Ramirez knocks out the two front teeth of 16-year-old Red Sox fan Lee Gavin. Gavin resides in the Sudbury, Massachusetts, farmhouse once owned by Babe Ruth, so some Red Sox fans see the injury as a sign that the so-called "Curse of the Bambino" has been broken.

OCTOBER 16, 2004   The New York Yankees, winners of the American League East, bash their way to a 19–8 win over the Boston Red Sox, winners of the American League wild card, in game three of the American League Championship Series. The victory gives New York a seemingly insurmountable three-games-to-none lead in the series.

OCTOBER 20, 2004   The Boston Red Sox beat the Yankees 10–3 in the seventh game of the 2004 American League Championship Series. With the victory, Boston becomes the first team in baseball history to win a seven-game postseason series after trailing three games to none. Adding to the drama, Boston's wins in games four and five occur in extra innings, and the Sox win game six behind the strong pitching of ace Curt Schilling, who has a dislocated ankle tendon that only days before seemed likely to end his season. Boston goes on to win their first World Series since 1918.

PERMISSIONS

BIBLIOGRAPHY

Anderson, Dave. *Pennant Races.* New York: Bantam Dell, 1995.

Angell, Roger. "Gone South." First appeared in *The New Yorker,* November 24, 2003.

————. "Legends of the Fens." First appeared in *The New Yorker,* September 24, 2001.

Aucoin, Don. "Irreconcilable Differences." First appeared in the *Boston Globe,* October 9, 2003.

Borden, Sam. "Striking Back at the Empire." First appeared in the *Daily News,* March 29, 2004.

Boswell, Thomas. "Baseball's Finest Hours." First appeared in the *Washington Post,* April 1, 1979.

Bradford, Rob. *Chasing Steinbrenner: Pursuing the Pennant in Boston and Toronto.* Dulles, Va: Brassey's, 2004.

Bradley, Mark. "Ted Williams." First appeared in the *Atlanta Journal-Constitution,* July 10, 2002.

Cantwell, Mary. "Hating Doris." Edited by Ron Fimrite. *Birth of a Fan.* New York: Macmillan, 1993.

Caple, Jim. "In Boston, the Yankees Always Suck." First appeared on ESPN.com, March 8, 2004.

Chapman, Con. *The Year of the Gerbil: How the Yankees Won (and the Red Sox Lost) the Greatest Pennant Race Ever.* Danbury, Conn.: Rutledge Books, 1998.

Creamer, Robert. *Babe: The Legend Comes to Life.* New York: Simon & Schuster, 1974.

Crehan, Herbert, and Ryan, James. *Lightning in a Bottle: The Sox of '67.* Boston: Branden Books, 1992.

Doyle, Paul. "Lee vs. Nettles: Time Hasn't Healed Sore Feelings." First appeared in the *Hartford Courant,* May 20, 2001.

Engelberg, Stephen. "The Home Team." First appeared in the *New York Times Magazine,* July 4, 1999.

Fimrite, Ron. "Yankees Go Home." First appeared in *Sports Illustrated,* September 26, 1988.

Frazee, Spencer. "Still Frazee after All These Years." First appeared in *Yankee Magazine,* June 2000.

Gammons, Peter. "The Boston Massacre." First appeared in *Sports Illustrated,* September 18, 1978.

———. "Fisk vs. Munson: A True War." First appeared on ESPN.com, July 23, 2003.

Giamatti, A. Bartlett. *A Great and Glorious Game.* Chapel Hill, N.C.: Algonquin Books of Chapel Hill, 1998.

Gulley, Ned. "What Being the Father of an Autistic Son Taught Me about Being a Red Sox Fan." First appeared on Paracelsus Weblog, October 20, 2003.

Halberstam, David. "A Fan Divided." First appeared in the *Boston Globe,* 1986.

Hunt, Paul Thomas. "Ground Hog Day." First appeared on Redsox-haiku.com, October 2003.

Jacobson, Steve. *The Best Team Money Could Buy: The Turmoil and Triumph of the 1977 New York Yankees.* New York: Simon & Schuster, 1978.

Keene, Kerry. *The Babe in Red Stockings.* Champaign, Ill.: Sports Publishing LLC, 1997.

Kelly, Thomas. "Mad Cathedral." First appeared in *Esquire,* November 1998.

Klapisch, Bob. "Goose, Nettles Seeing Red." First appeared in the *Record,* October 14, 2003.

Lee, Bill. *The Little Red (Sox) Book.* Chicago: Triumph Books, 2003.

Linn, Ed. *The Great Rivalry.* New York: Houghton Mifflin, 1991.

Marshall, Bob. *Diary of a Yankee-Hater.* New York: Franklin Watts, 1981.

McCarron, Anthony. "Yankees Meet Ruthless End Suffer History-Making Loss to Accursed Red Sox." First appeared in the *Daily News,* October 21, 2004.

Richmond, Peter. "Grady Little Is Relieved." First appeared in *GQ,* April 2004.

Rushin, Steve. "Resident Alien in Red Sox Nation." First appeared in *Sports Illustrated,* May 26, 2003.

Ryan, Bob. "Bad Blood Infusion." First appeared in the *Boston Globe,* April 2, 2004.

Schwartz, Jonathan. "A Day of Light and Shadows." First appeared in *Sports Illustrated,* February 26, 1979.

Smith, Red. *On Baseball.* Chicago: Ivan R. Dee, 2000.

Stein, Joel. "In Defense of Domination." First appeared in *Time,* February 23, 2004.

Verducci, Tom. "Hello, New York." First appeared in Sports *Illustrated,* January 23, 2004.

Walch, Tad. "Drooping? Not Red Sox Fans." First appeared in the *Deseret Morning News,* October 18, 2003.

Wood, Allan James. *Babe Ruth and the 1918 Red Sox.* New York: Writer's Club Press, 2001.